223.2 07 T728 1991
Tournay, Raymond Jacques.
Seeing and hearing God with the
 Psalms : the prophetic liturgy
 of the second temple in

D1706616

COLUMBIA BIBLE COLLEGE

4444 00042 9506

JOURNAL FOR THE STUDY OF THE OLD TESTAMENT
SUPPLEMENT SERIES
118

Editors
David J.A. Clines
Philip R. Davies

JSOT Press
Sheffield

Seeing and Hearing God with the Psalms

The Prophetic Liturgy
of the Second Temple
in Jerusalem

Raymond Jacques Tournay

translated by
J. Edward Crowley

Journal for the Study of the Old Testament
Supplement Series 118

Copyright © 1991 Sheffield Academic Press

Published by JSOT Press
JSOT Press is an imprint of
Sheffield Academic Press Ltd
The University of Sheffield
343 Fulwood Road
Sheffield S10 3BP
England

Typeset by Sheffield Academic Press
and
Printed on acid-free paper in Great Britain
by Billing & Sons Ltd
Worcester

British Library Cataloguing in Publication Data

Tournay, Raymond Jacques
    Seeing and hearing God with the Psalms: the prophetic
    liturgy of the second temple in Jerusalem.
    —(JSOT supplement. ISSN 0309-0787: v. 118)
    I. Title II. Voir et entendre Dieu avec les Psaumes ou
    la liturgie prophetique du second temple à Jerusalem.
    III. Series
    223.207

    ISBN 1-85075-313-X

CONTENTS

The title of this work may surprise the reader. The purpose of the book is both to bring out the value and to give an interpretation of the prophetic dimension of Israelite psalmody as this has been transmitted to us, starting from the description of the process given in the books of Chronicles about 300 BCE. King David and the Levitical cult personnel of the Second Temple are presented there as inspired by the Spirit of YHWH. The latter acted as real cultic prophets in a period when prophetic activity had come to an end, having given way little by little to the apocalyptic movement.

From such a perspective, it is reasonable to suppose that the Levitical singers took upon themselves the mission of making up for the silence of the divine word by multiplying in their lyrical and liturgical works theophanic and oracular passages. To do this, they revived the themes, motifs and expressions of the ancient prophets in order to celebrate in the worship of the Second Temple the name and the glory of YHWH, God of the covenant and of the messianic promises.

In recent commentaries on the psalter, a great deal of attention has been given to the study of genres and literary structures, as well as to sources and borrowings. Too often there has been a neglect of the prophetic dimension of Israelite psalmody as a whole. This dimension was clearly perceived by the first Christian generation as can be seen in the discourse of Peter (Acts 2.25ff.) and in the prayer of the Apostles (Acts 4.25): God has spoken by the Holy Spirit and by the mouth of David, God's servant and model of the poor of YHWH.

Today, just as twenty centuries ago, it is a prophetic reading of the psalms which allows us, with them, to see and hear God.

Raymond Jacques Tournay, OP
Ecole Biblique et Archéologique Française de Jérusalem

TRANSLATOR'S NOTE

All references to biblical texts use the verse numberings of the Masoretic text. This is to be noted especially in the case of the psalms where considerable variation in verse numbering occurs, often depending on whether or not the superscription is included in the verse numbering.

As in the French edition, the Hebrew personal name of God is transliterated by the consonants YHWH. The reader may substitute each time the traditional translation 'the Lord'.

Transliterated Hebrew words are sometimes included so that the reader who does not know Hebrew may appreciate the sound and shape of significant words and phrases. This especially helps in the recognition of assonances, alliteration and paronomasia, as well as allusions important in interpretation. However, the translation is always indicated in such cases. The system of transliteration is that given in 'Instructions for Contributors' in *Journal of Biblical Literature* 95 (1976), p. 334 and *The Catholic Biblical Quarterly* 38 (1976), nn. 23-25.

In the translation of the psalms I followed Père Tournay's rendering of the Hebrew text, while trying to keep in mind the sensitivities and expectations of today's readers. The unaccustomed wording is the price that must be paid on the way to non-sexist language. The translation of the psalms as well as the rest of the book was done in consultation with Père Tournay and any changes were approved or in some cases requested by him.

I wish to thank Père Tournay for agreeing to this translation and for his promptness in answering my letters and questions as I progressed through the translation. I wish to thank too my wife, Dr Pamela Milne, for her technical and other help in preparing the translation.

J. Edward Crowley

ABBREVIATIONS

AB	Anchor Bible
AbrN	*Abr Nahrain*
AfO	*Archiv für Orientforschung*
AnBib	Analecta biblica
ANET	*Ancient Near Eastern Texts*
AnOr	Analecta Orientalia
AOAT	Alter Orient und Altes Testament
AOS	American Oriental Series
ARW	*Archiv für Religionswissenschaft*
ATANT	Abhandlungen zur Theologie des Alten und Neuen Testaments
ATD	Das Alte Testament Deutsch
BBB	Bonner biblische Beiträge
BdJ	*La Bible de Jérusalem*
BeO	*Bibbia e oriente*
BETL	Bibliotheca ephemeridum theologicarum lovaniensium
BHS	*Biblia Hebraica Stuttgartensia*
Bib	*Biblica*
BibOr	Biblica et orientalia
BK	*Bibel und Kirche*
BKAT	Biblischer Kommentar: Altes Testament
BN	*Biblische Notizen*
BTS	*Bible et terre sainte*
BWANT	Beiträge zur Wissenschaft vom Alten und Neuen Testament
BZ	*Biblische Zeitschrift*
BZAW	Beihefte zur *ZAW*
CAD	*The Assyrian Dictionary of the Oriental Institute of the University of Chicago*
CAT	Commentaire de l'Ancien Testament
CBQ	*Catholic Biblical Quarterly*
CBQMS	*Catholic Biblical Quarterly* Monograph Series
ConBOT	Coniectanea biblica, Old Testament
CTA	A. Herdner *et al.*, *Corpus des tablettes en cunéiformes alphabétiques*
DBS	*Dictionnaire de la Bible, Supplément*
EBib	Etudes bibliques
EstBíb	*Estudios Bíblicos*

ETL	*Ephemerides theologicae lovanienses*
EvT	*Evangelische Theologie*
FRLANT	Forschungen zur Religion und Literatur des Alten und Neuen Testaments
HALAT	*Hebräisches und aramäisches Lexikon zum Alten Testament*
HAT	Handbuch zum Alten Testament
HSM	Harvard Semitic Monographs
HSS	Harvard Semitic Series
HTR	*Harvard Theological Review*
HUCA	*Hebrew Union College Annual*
IEJ	*Israel Exploration Journal*
Int	*Interpretation*
JANES(CU)	*Journal of the Ancient Near Eastern Society (of Columbia University)*
JAOS	*Journal of the American Oriental Society*
JB	Jerusalem Bible
JBL	*Journal of Biblical Literature*
JBLMS	Journal of Biblical Literature Monograph Series
JJS	*Journal of Jewish Studies*
JNES	*Journal of Near Eastern Studies*
JQR	*The Jewish Quarterly Review*
JSOT	*Journal for the Study of the Old Testament*
JSOTSup	Journal for the Study of the Old Testament Supplement Series
JSS	*Journal of Semitic Studies*
JTS	*Journal of Theological Studies*
KTU	*Keilalphabetische Texte aus Ugarit,* ed. M. Dietrich, O. Loretz and J. Sanmartin
LAPO	Littératures anciennes de Proche-Orient
LavTP	*Laval théologique et philosophique*
LD	Lectio divina
LXX	Septuagint
MT	Masoretic Text
MTZ	*Münchener theologische Zeitschrift*
NedTTs	*Nederlands theologisch tijdschrift*
NICOT	New International Commentary on the Old Testament
NRT	*La nouvelle revue théologique*
OBO	Orbis biblicus et orientalis
OTL	Old Testament Library
OTS	*Oudtestamentische Studiën*
PEFQS	*Palestine Exploration Fund, Quarterly Statement*
PG	*Patrologia graeca,* ed. J.P. Migne (1886–88)
PL	*Patrolojia Ratina,* ed. J.P. Migne
PUF	Presses Universitaires de France
RB	*Revue biblique*

RechBib	Recherches bibliques
RevQ	*Revue de Qumran*
RevScRel	*Revue des sciences religieuses*
RHPR	*Revue d'histoire et de philosophie religieuses*
RHR	*Revue de l'histoire des religions*
RivB	*Rivista biblica*
RQ	*Römische Quartalschrift für christliche Altertumskunde und Kirchengeschichte*
RSR	*Recherches de science religieuse*
RTL	*Revue théologique de Louvain*
RTh	*Revue Thomiste*
Sem	*Semitica*
SBB	Stuttgarter biblische Beiträge
SBFLA	*Studii biblici franciscani liber annuus*
SBLDS	Society of Biblical Literature Dissertation Series
SBLMS	Society of Biblical Literature Monograph Series
SBS	Stuttgarter Bibelstudien
SEÅ	*Svensk exegetisk årsbok*
SIDIC	*Service internationale de documentation judéo-chrétienne*
SJT	*Scottish Journal of Theology*
TBü	Theologische Bücherei
TDNT	*Theological Dictionary of the New Testament*
THAT	*Theologisches Handwörterbuch zum Alten Testament*
ThZ	*Theologische Zeitschrift*
TLZ	*Theologischer Literaturzeitung*
TOB	*Traduction oecuménique de la Bible*
TRu	*Theologische Rundschau*
ThWAT	*Theologisches Wörterbuch zum Alten Testament*
TWNT	*Theologisches Wörterbuch zum Neuen Testament*
TynBul	*Tyndale Bulletin*
TZ	*Theologische Zeitschrift*
UF	*Ugarit-Forschungen*
VS	Verbum salutis
VSpir	*Vie Spirituelle*
VT	*Vetus Testamentun*
VTSup	Vetus Testamentum, Supplements
WMANT	Wissenschaftliche Monographien zum Alten und Neuen Testament
ZAW	*Zeitschrift für die alttestamentliche Wissenschaft*
ZTK	*Zeitschrift für Theologie und Kirche*

GENERAL INTRODUCTION

1. Recent Research on the Psalms

There are countless works on the structure and origin of the psalms. It would be tedious to list them, even if we limited ourselves to recent years. It will suffice to refer to the recent commentaries of L. Jacquet (1975–1979, in French) and of G. Ravasi (1981–1984, in Italian) (each of these commentaries consists of three huge volumes); the bibliographical summary of K. Seybold (1981); the annual Elenchus of *Biblica* (Rome); the Swedish bibliographies of Leif Holmström Nilssen (1985–1986); and the extensive catalogue of the *Ecole Biblique et Archéologique Française de Jérusalem*.

In spite of the enormous amount of material that has been accumulated in this area, many problems remain unresolved, and many hypotheses follow one after the other without any real consensus developing among contemporary exegetes. As J. van der Ploeg wrote in 1969, one gets the impression of still being in a period of groping and uncertainty. Nevertheless, there has been some progress, as B.S. Childs emphasizes (1976: 377-88), especially in the greater interest shown in post-exilic psalmody and in the rereadings and adaptations carried out by the psalmists as required for the needs of the Jewish community.

The discovery of many fragments of psalters in the caves of Qumran, especially in Caves 4 and 11, has made it possible to determine to what extent the traditional Masoretic text reflects the text current at the beginning of the Christian era. The works of J.A. Sanders (1967), J. Ouellette (1969), P. Skehan (1979), G.H. Wilson (1983), and others, make clear to what extent the received text is a faithful witness to the long manuscript tradition. Was not the phrase *sēper hattĕhillîm*, 'the book of psalms', found in a fragment from Cave 4 (Baillet 1982: 41, n. 17, line 4)? There is less and less inclination to correct the Masorah, although this does not lessen the importance of textual criticism or the need to consider the various versions. The divergences that may be observed, as well as some of the obscurities in the text, could be explained as the effect of more or less intentional alterations whose origins it is important to discover.

The study of *literary forms* has made considerable progress and should be kept in mind. The research of W. Richter (1971; cf. F. Langlamet 1972: 275-88) should be mentioned here. As is known, Richter concentrates on the analysis of the structural form and on the description of units discernible in the narrative prose. The study of ornamental details (imagery, sonority, rhythmic and strophic elements, etc.) in the text at the level of phonemes and syllables is only possible in a limited way. As a matter of fact, although the consonantal system of the Hebrew can be described, it is a different matter for the vowel system which must have undergone change in the course of centuries.

Poetry

When it comes to poetical texts like the psalms, rhythmic analysis immediately encounters the difficulty that we are ignorant of the exact pronunciation at the time when these poems were composed. Many uncertainties remain in this phonetic area. This is why several recent attempts to recover fixed rhythms or set metrical patterns are doomed to failure as D.W. Goodwin (1969) and D. Broadribb (1972: 66-87) have clearly shown. The same can be stated in regard to the isosyllabic system advocated for a long time by F.M. Cross and D.N. Freedman (1975; cf. Tournay 1976d: 625), as well as their disciples, such as P.D. Hanson (1975; cf. Tournay 1976c: 151) or F.I. Andersen (1980; cf. Tournay 1981c: 612). D.K. Stuart has dealt with this system in a lengthy study (1976). The same criticisms can be made in regard to the dipodic or alternating system of prosodic type, with one of the variants being based, as D.L. Christensen thinks (1984–1985), on the morae (mora refers to the amount of time required to pronounce the simplest syllable) and the length of the vowels. A long discussion on this subject would not suit our purpose here (see Alonso Schökel 1988).

Most contemporary exegetes have, as a matter of fact, good reasons for maintaining the validity of the *rhythm* of the stressed syllables in Hebrew poetry, as is the case in other ancient Semitic poetry (Assyro-Babylonian, Ugaritic, Aramaic), as well as in Egyptian poetry. The same is true in many modern languages. Here again we will not deal with this at length (the reader is directed to consult grammars of biblical Hebrew). It will suffice to refer to the recent discussion between C.B. Houk and R.E. Bee (1978: 41-57) on the subject of rhythm (whether it is based on syllable count or stress count) in Psalm 132. The excellent presentation by Bee seems preferable to the critique of T. Longman (1982) which concentrated on a text in oratorical prose, Jeremiah 12, instead of a poetical text (see Landy, Watson, P.D. Miller, Kugel: all in *JSOT* 28, 1984: 61-117).

The masoretic stress did not necessarily correspond to the primitive metrical stress. Every monosyllable or assimilated syllable (as in words of the segholate type) can lose its stress, or be made proclitic, or be followed by a *maqqeph*, which is used in a very haphazard way. In long words, there is occasionally a secondary stress, separated from the main stress by at least a full syllable. That secondary stress is often indicated by a *metheg*. The oxytone stress of the word (on the final syllable) can move back to the penultimate syllable and become paroxytonic to avoid contact with the accented syllable that immediately follows (rule of the *nesiga*). If two stresses are contiguous, this means that there is a pause or caesura between them, sometimes indicated by a disjunctive accent. There can be up to three successive unaccented syllables, but rarely four. A secondary accent would then be inserted, indicated by a *metheg*.

The primary form of the verse, doubtless the oldest too, would be a verse with 2 + 2 accented words (subject and predicate, in a nominal sentence). This binary rhythm is very common in Egyptian and Assyro-Babylonian poetry. It occurs in the song of Deborah (Judg. 5), and in the elegy of David over Jonathan (2 Sam. 1.19ff.). It is the rhythm of marching and of the beating of the heart. This rapid rhythm is also found in pieces of rhythmical oratorical prose, such as the oracle of Nathan, or the oracle about Emmanuel, etc. (Tournay 1986: 306). Such a verse may be expanded to 4 + 4 stresses; it then becomes epic verse, corresponding to the alexandrine in French. An example of this would be Exodus 15.

If the first colon is longer than the second, we have an asymmetrical verse; this is the form of the verse in the *qînâ* (3 + 2 stresses; cf. Garr 1983: 54; Ruppert 1983: 111). This broken cadence ends with a sigh, a pause. Such impassioned and lyrical verse is found in Lamentations, Song of Songs, the Psalms of Ascents (120–134, except 132). The

verses of the *qînâ* have many variations: 2 + 3 stresses (enjambment
with emphasis), 4 + 3 (long elegiac verse), 4 + 2 (a verse that can be
binary), 3 + 2 + 2 (elegiac verse of 3 lines), or 4 + 3 + 2, or 3 + 3 + 2
stresses. Extended verses in *qînâ* meter are found in Psalms 9, 10,
140, 141, etc.

A verse of 3 + 3 stresses is the most usual: this *māšāl* verse is found
in the didactic books (Proverbs, Job) and in many psalms and
canticles. It appears already in the poem on Heshbon (Num. 21), the
Blessings of Jacob (Gen. 49) and Moses (Deut. 33), the Song of Moses
(Deut. 32), and the Balaam oracles. This ternary rhythm is the rhythm
of breathing (inhaling, exhaling, pause); it has some variations: 2 + 2
+ 2 (double caesura), 3 + 3 + 3 (tristich). This ternary rhythm seems
to be the most common in Ugaritic. It may be compared to Latin
hexameter.

Due to the rule of parallelism in Semitic poetry, colons tend to be
perceptibly equal in length, with a correspondence between pairs of
synonyms and antonyms. The cadences are often mixed and any tendency to correct the text *metri causa* under the pretext of restoring
symmetry must be resisted.

There is some consensus among contemporary exegetes in regard to
strophes. It will suffice to refer here to the important study of O. van
der Lugt (1980). The strophe portrays the logical unity of the poem.
Concentric structures have often been pointed out, especially by P.
Auffret (1977-82).

Important works have been devoted to the various kinds of parallelism (cf. Geller 1979; Kugel 1981; Berlin 1985), a sort of binary way
of speaking with symmetrical or antithetical propositions and some
correspondence between words. Numerous pairs of words have already been pointed out in Ugaritic poetry. Various ways to explain
this law of duality or binary way of speaking have been attempted.
One explanation is that a singer or leader would alternate with a
crowd who would repeat a section of the words, while the singer or
leader would develop a certain theme. This would explain how litanies
and responsorial psalms (such as Pss. 118, 136, and also 145 at
Qumran, according to 11QIs[a]) originated. It has been pointed out too
that the tendency to use synonyms may be due to an emotional factor,
as every emotion looks for a way to linger. Moreover, the Semitic
world was fond of repetitions and cyclical structures, in poetry as well

as in music.[1] This synthetic and sweeping approach to reality is contrasted with the rational analysis of the Greco-Roman world. The Semitic approach is often expressed in poetry through the concentric forms of chiasmus and inclusion. We may mention the studies of M. O'Connor (1980), W.G.E. Watson (1982), J.-N. Aletti and J. Trublet (1983) and M. Girard (1984).

As early as the first edition of the *Psaumes de la Bible de Jérusalem* (1951) by R.J. Tournay and R. Schwab, strophic analysis of the text of the psalms was carried out side by side with the analysis of the rhythm produced by the accented syllables. Since the tonic stress is on the last, and less often on the second-last syllable of the Hebrew word, there was no problem in producing these cadences in French where the stress in the word is also at the end (cf. Tournay 1946: 351-57). It was on the basis of that correspondence that the *Psautier de la Bible de Jérusalem* (1961) was produced in cooperation with Père J. Gelineau. Twenty-five years later, a new French translation came out, the *Psautier de Jérusalem* (1986), which reproduces the essentials of the old psalter; however, its wording has been made more flexible and use has been made of new knowledge in the interpretation of the frequently obscure Hebrew text.

Chronology

As a matter of fact, it is not in the specifically literary or structuralist sphere (Collins 1987: 41) that the main effort to understand and interpret the psalms should be made. To understand clearly their content and precise significance, we must situate them in their proper time period (at least approximately), specify if possible the *Sitz im Leben*,

---

1. In regard to Israelite music, see E. Gerson-Kiwi, 'Musique de la Bible', *DBS*, V (1956), cols. 1411-68; A. Sendrey, *Music in Ancient Israel* (London: Vision Press, 1969); '*zmr*', *ThWAT*, II, pp. 603ff.; C. Schmidt-Colinet, *Die Musikinstrumente in der Kunst des Alten Orients. Archäologisch-philologische Studien* (Bonn: Bouvier-Grundmann, 1981); J.H. Eaton, 'Music's Place in Worship: A Contribution from the Psalms', *OTJ* 23 (1983), pp. 85-107; H. Seidel, *Musik im Altisrael. Untersuchungen zur Musikgeschichte und Musikpraxis Altisraels anhang biblischer und ausserbiblischer Texte* (Bern: Peter Lang, 1986); E. Werner, *The Sacred Bridge*, II (New York: Ktav, 1984); M. Duchesne-Guillemin, *A Hurrian Score from Ugarit: The Discovery of Mesopotamian Music* (Sources Ancient Near East 2/2; Malibu: Undena Publications, 1984); *Le Monde de la Bible* 37 (Jan.-Feb. 1985).

and rediscover the biblical and extra-biblical sources of inspiration. On this matter of extra-biblical influence, much recent research has already been carried out, especially through comparisons with Mesopotamian psalmody—as R.G. Castellino did as early as 1940—or with Egyptian prayers—as A. Barucq did in 1962. A comprehensive summary of these links is presented, for example, in F. Crüsemann's book (1969: 135-50), with regard to hymns and thanksgiving psalms in Israel. Numerous Ugaritic parallels have also been pointed out. But the most important problem is that of knowing in what milieu Israelite psalmody developed as it was handed down to us by tradition. What needs of the community did it meet? How did the psalms fit into the religious life of the people of Israel? These questions have already given rise to many different hypotheses. The opinions of contemporary exegetes are widely divergent here. In 1961, C. Hauret concluded his study on the chronology of the psalms by stating that such a problem was perhaps insoluble.

According to E. Lipiński (1965), Psalms 93 and 99 should be dated to the time of Solomon, just like Psalms 68 and 78; Psalms 97 and 149 come from the Maccabean period. For many exegetes, however, (A. Feuillet, J.D.W. Watts, P.E. Dion, J. Coppens, *et al.*) the group of Reign of YHWH psalms (95 to 100) depend for style and themes on the second part of the book of Isaiah (Isa. 52.7: 'Your God reigns!') and not the other way round. To give another example, according to E. Lipiński (1967), Psalm 89.2-5 and 20-38 date from the second half of the 10th century BCE. That opinion has been refuted, particularly by T. Veijola (1982); it is agreed that Psalm 89 in its entirety should be placed in the exilic period, no matter what its antecedents (see p. 201).

Great efforts have been expended to discover allusions to the history of Israel in the psalms. After A. Lauha and J. Kühlwein, E. Haglund (1984) has resumed this investigation. According to him, Psalm 81 comes from the north of Israel; Psalm 83 dates from the Assyrian period. Psalm 78, a didactic composition, dates from the reign of Hezekiah; it is the only psalm containing allusions to traditions relating to the Exodus and the conquest of Canaan and to David. With regard to this, it could be said in reply that all these traditions are referred to all through the psalter. Psalm 105 is the only psalm that mentions the three Patriarchs (vv. 6-10); but it is certainly from the post-exilic period. Along with a number of other exegetes, E.

Haglund appeals to linguistic, morphological and syntactical criteria. Such criteria, so difficult to handle, are never really decisive, for it can be a matter of archaizing and not archaic compositions. Too many authors, it seems, do not take this possibility into consideration and accept dates much too early for these poems, which they consider very ancient. Does the antiquity of a poem make it more interesting or more important? This is a false conception of the development of religious ideas in Israel and, among believers, of the content of revelation which goes on deepening itself and enriching itself in the midst of human existence and human suffering. These preconceived theories are often enough put forward, especially following the publications of F.M. Cross and D.N. Freedman. Accordingly, for D.A. Robertson (1972), the Song of Miriam (Exod. 15) goes back to the 12th century; the Song of Moses (Deut. 32), the Psalm of David (2 Sam. 22 = Ps. 18), the Prayer of Habakkuk (Hab. 3) and even the poetic section of the book of Job must be placed in the 10th or the beginning of the 9th century. A similar chronology is proposed by W.G.E. Watson (1984a: 40). These authors, however, make no secret of the fact that such a chronology remains highly conjectural.

On the contrary, S. Pratt had concluded in 1913, after a very thorough analysis of vocabulary, that the bulk of the psalter had been formed in the post-exilic period. This opinion was strongly challenged, especially by M. Tsevat (1955). But the recent studies of A. Hurvitz (1968, 1972, 1985) indicate that, for a certain number of psalms, we should assume their composition to have been in the Persian and Hellenistic periods. It is true that the presence of Aramaisms (M. Wagner 1966)[1] cannot by itself provide a criterion for a late dating, unless there are many in the same poem. These Aramaisms may be met in every epoch of Hebrew literature, although they normally should be more numerous in the post-exilic period.

Ugaritisms
Ugaritisms are not infallible indicators of great antiquity, no matter what may be claimed. Many researchers, following the example of the late M. Dahood, have tried to clarify the meaning of words and phrases, in the psalms and elsewhere, through recourse to the texts of Ras Shamra. It must be admitted that frequently they have been suc-

---

1. On Aramaic poetry, cf. J. Greenfield 1979: 45-50.

cessful, as has been pointed out by A.S. Kapelrud (1975a), E. Jacob and H. Cazelles (1979), M.P. O'Connor (1983: 205), *et al.* Ugaritic prosody has become the subject of careful studies, such as that of B. Margalit (1980: 219), while lengthy lexicographical works have gathered together material that helps in the comparison of the poetical vocabulary of Ugarit and that of the Bible, particularly in the area of parallelism and merismus (cf. Krašovec 1977). It is not a matter of belittling these finds and these comparisons, but we must be wary of historical conclusions which some claim can be extracted in order to date this or that poem, this or that psalm. In recent years, a very strong reaction has set in against what is called 'Pan-Ugaritism'.[1]

No one would think of denying the profound influence, although indirect and diffuse most of the time, that Canaanite culture and literature exercised on Israel right from the beginning of its existence. Commentators mention Ugaritic parallels in such ancient poems as the Song of Deborah, and the 'Blessings' of Isaac, Jacob and Moses. Canaanite practices and beliefs would inevitably penetrate into Israel, in every period, because of the linguistic relationship (even though Ugaritic represents a special branch of the Semitic languages, somewhat more closely related to Arabic), as well as commercial and political contacts, especially in the North, particularly in the time of Hiram of Tyre. But the Israelite religion based on a covenant with YHWH could not accommodate itself to the religion of ba'alism and polytheism as these are known, for example, in the time of Solomon. Opposition to ba'alism developed rapidly; the prophet Elijah was the one who first took up the challenge and became the victorious conqueror in the struggle; Amos and Hosea carried it forward in their denunciation of the worship of idols.

The fall of the monarchies of Samaria and Judah created an entirely new situation. The nobles and dignitaries of Israel and Judah were deported to Mesopotamia, especially in 597 BCE (2 Kgs 24.12-16) when the prophet Ezekiel and the disciples who had gathered round him were deported. We know incidentally that the populations of Phoenicia and Chaldea had intermingled on the banks of the Tigris

---

1. Cf. R. de Vaux: 1966: 465; H. Donner 1967: 322; R. Tournay 1969: 450; 1970: 620; 1971d: 292; B.G. Sauer 1974: 401; J.C. de Moor and P. van der Lugt 1974; R. Tournay 1974b: 463; 1975: 281; S. Kreuzer 1983: 347; O. Loretz 1984; S. Talmon 1986: 279.

and Euphrates for a long time. The contacts which had always existed between Phoenicia and Babylon did not stop developing in the Neo-Babylonian period. The Chaldean armies were encamped for a long time in Phoenicia. Priests, soothsayers, scribes could have associated with their Phoenician counterparts. When Tyre surrendered in 574 BCE after a protracted siege of 13 years, it was not destroyed (cf. Ezek. 29.18). It was from Babylon that they brought the son of Itho-Ba'al III, Mer-Ba'al, to make him king of Tyre (558-554). After his death, it was the turn of his brother Hiram who had also been raised at the royal court of Babylon and then reigned at Tyre for twenty years (Josephus, *Against Apion*, I, 158). In lower Mesopotamia there was a place called Bit-Surayya (*Ṣûr* is the Semitic name from which Tyre is derived; cf. RLA2, 1938: col. 52). As a result of all this, the Jews in exile were living in cosmopolitan surroundings; the people from Jerusalem then could easily associate with Phoenicians.[1]

They already had available to them a vast documentation on Canaanite religion and the mythology of Ugarit thanks to the works of Sankhuniaton. O. Eissfeldt (1963: 127-29) places the literary activity of Sankhuniaton in the second half of the first millenium. W.F. Albright saw no problem in situating this activity as early as the 7th century (see Attridge and Oden 1981). Sankhuniaton had gathered together old writings and ancient mythological traditions, in this way making available to the learned a fund of information. While exiled in Babylon, Ezekiel could have heard people speaking of the wise man Danel (Ezek. 14.14; 28.3) as well as the god Melqart, patron of Tyre and called the 'philosopher'. Ezek. 28.14 speaks of 'stones of fire' which would be an allusion to the funeral-pyre of Melqart and his *egersis* or Spring-awakening (Tournay 1964: 102). The *cherub* motif (Ezek. 1.10; 28.14, 16) is Syro-Mesopotamian.

Assyriologists believe that the kings of the Neo-Babylonian dynasty, especially Nabonidus, wanted very much to discover foundation depositories of temples and step towers (Ziggurats) in order to restore these ruined edifices and in that way be connected with their ancient predecessors of the second millenium, and even with the Sumerians. The scribes took pleasure in using archaic cuneiform writing in order to bring themselves near the ancient script. In Egypt too it has been

---

1. Cf. Tournay 1956: 177; 1957b: 127; 1963b: 592; 1966b: 422; Zimmerli 1983: 24.

discovered that the sculptors of the Saite dynasty imitated works from the Amarna age. In Israel it was a time when they were fond of recalling ancient times, the period of the Patriarchs (Isa. 41.8; 51.2; 63.16; Ezek. 33.24; Gen. 14; Ps. 105.6ff.; etc.). The learned took over the ancient myths which were no longer offensive and had become merely literary motifs.

That is why in the 8th century Amos (9.3) speaks simply of the 'serpent' in referring to the fabulous great dragon (Day 1985). After the exile the hagiographers were not afraid to give him the name *Ltn* which he had had at Ugarit, Leviathan, the 'twisting one [root *lwh*] of seven heads' (Pss. 74.14; 104.26; Job 3.8; 7.12; 26.13; 40.25; Isa. 27.1). The taunt-song of Isaiah 14 on the death of the Mesopotamian tyrant refers in v. 12 to *hêlēl ben šahar*, 'the brilliant star [Vulgate: Lucifer], son of the dawn'.[1] In v. 13, the poet speaks of 'the Mountain of the North', which becomes the theme of Ps. 48.2 and indirectly of Ezek. 40.2. This mythical mountain, compared to Mount Cassius, the Phoenician Olympus north of Ras Shamra, was considered to be the place of assembly of the 70 sons of the great god El, head of the Canaanite pantheon (Tournay 1949a: 40; Clifford 1972; Attridge and Oden 1981).

The Song of Moses (Deut. 32.8) alludes to these 'sons of El': 'God set the limits of the people according to the number of the sons of El' (LXX; MT: Israel). Many exegetes place this song in the period of the exile.[2] The theme of the sons of El appears in other texts, either before the exile (Gen. 6.2; Exod. 15.11), or more explicitly after the exile (Pss. 29.1; 82.1,6; 89.7; Job 1.6; 38.7; Dan. 3.25). This theme has been dealt with at length by J.L. Cunchillos (1976b).

The first son of El, Mot, god of fertility and fruitfulness, is supplanted and killed by the god Ba'al, god of thunder and conqueror of the sea; Ba'al is dangerous and beneficent at the same time. Mot then becomes 'Death', the antithesis of Ba'al, as all vegetation withers and dies under the scorching sun of summer. In Israel, Ba'al is supplanted by YHWH to whom they transferred the attributes of the god of the thunderstorm, the master of watery chaos, the 'mighty waters', so that YHWH dwells on the celestial ocean. That is why YHWH is referred to

1. Verse 12 has been compared to the Greek myth of Phaethon.
2. Tournay, 1960c: 120; 1973: 441; von Rad 1964: 143; Crüsemann 1964: 42; Carrillo Alday 1970; Labuschagne 1971: 92; 1974: 97.

as 'rider of the clouds', *rkb 'rpt*, in Ps. 68.5 (see pp. 83 and 135); Deut. 33.26; Isa. 19.1 ; Jer. 4.13; Isa. 66.15; Ezek. 1 and 10. The theme of the divine chariot (Vanel 1965: 121; Weinfeld 1973: 421) is found completely demythologized in the Old Testament. The same thing is true in regard to the title *'Elyon*, used so often in the Psalms (see p. 110) and connected with the divine name *'ly* in the legend of *Krt* at Ugarit (*Keret* II III, 6), in which the rain of Ba'al is called the rain of *'ly*, that is, of the Most High (see Rendtorff 1966: 280; *ThWAT*, VI: 134).

The process of demythologizing is complete by the post-exilic period, while at the same time the tendency to archaize increases among the hagiographers, as may be seen in the books of Job, Jonah, etc. Therefore, the greatest prudence is necessary in comparing biblical psalms and songs on the one hand and Ugaritic texts on the other. The latter are to be dated to approximately the 14th century BCE; their cultural and religious milieu is altogether different. The semantic evolution of the language during such a long period of time should be taken into consideration too. It should be mentioned besides that a genuine psalm has not yet been found at Ugarit. Despite the numerous Ugaritisms brought to light in Psalm 29, it has not been possible to come up with its Canaanite prototype. A detailed exegesis, like that of O. Loretz (1984b), leads to the conclusion that this psalm should be situated in the post-exilic period (see p. 134).

Here is the only prayer found in the Ugaritic texts: it is a prayer of the people of Ugarit in time of danger (*KTU* 1.119; cf. Watson 1984b: 361).

26   If a powerful (enemy) attacks your gate, a gallant one
27   your walls, you will raise your eyes to Ba'al.
28   'O Ba'al, may you drive off the powerful one from our gate,
29   the gallant one from our walls. A bull, O
30   Ba'al, we will consecrate (to you); the vow (to) Ba'al
31   we will fulfil: a [ma]le (bovid) (to) Ba'al we will conse[cra]te;
32   a slaughtered sacrifice (for) Ba'al we will fulfil; the meal for Ba'al [we
33   will of]fer; to the sanctuary of Ba'[al] we will go up, (on) the paths to
        the temple [of Ba'al]
34   we will travel.' Then [Ba]'a[l] will listen to [your] prayer,
35   he will drive the powerful one from your gate,
36   [the gallant one] from your walls[.[1]

---

1.   This is a translation of the version in Caquot *et al.*, *Textes ougaritiques*. II. *Les Rituels* (LAPO, 14; Paris: Cerf, 1988), pp. 210-11.

It will be noted that the bull is the only offering made to Ba'al here; it is as a matter of fact the animal which depicts Ba'al. In nourishing oneself from it, one is nourishing oneself from the power of the god, in order to face enemies. Despite certain formulas which reappear in the biblical psalms, this Canaanite prayer on the whole provides only a rather remote parallel.

2. *A New Approach*

If extra-biblical comparisons fail to account for the origin and the appropriate role of the psalms in the religious life of Israel, then it is necessary to analyse them for their own sake, in the light of the writings of the whole Old Testament.

In connection with that the study of literary genres is essential. This was the predominant preoccupation of H. Gunkel and his school. Most recent commentators still follow this route, but have introduced considerable modifications or developments. As G.W. Ahlström (1959: 9) has noted, radical revisions of Gunkel's work have had to be carried out. To be convinced of this, one need only compare the classifications proposed by P. Drijvers (1965), A. Descamps (1962), L. Sabourin (1964; 1969), L. Jacquet (1975), E. Lipiński and E. Beauchamp (1979: 1). *La Bible oecuménique* (TOB, 1975: 1260-66) distinguishes three main classes of psalms: (1) praises, hymns, kingdom songs, songs of Zion, royal psalms; (2) prayers calling for help, psalms of confidence, thanksgiving psalms; (3) instructional psalms, historical psalms, liturgical psalms, prophetic exhortations, wisdom psalms.

This last category has drawn the attention of all those who are struck by the didactic aspect of the psalter, following the lead of M.H. Ludin and A. Robert (1939: 5-20; 1953: 224). The latter laid stress on the use by the psalmists of an anthological style, but did not give the underlying reason for this, as we will see later on. Robert had a tendency to minimize the specifically cultic and liturgical aspects of the psalms. The study of the sapiential dimension of the psalter has given rise to important works, whose authors must be mentioned here: J.K. Kuntz (1974), L. Perdue (1977), F. De Meyer (1981b), J. Reindl (1981), F. Stolz (1983). It is clear that many of the psalms point out to the faithful the moral conduct demanded by the covenant and in this way played an important didactic role, especially among the young who had to be instructed about their duties to God and to their brothers and sisters. But this aspect, of course, did not exhaust the rationale for the composition of the psalms.

Literary Genres

C. Westermann (1954; 1965; 1978) has shown that genres in a pure state do not exist in the psalter. There is good reason to reject over-rigid and preconceived plans which fail to recognize the flexibility and spontaneity of poetic inspiration. Westermann distinguishes two main categories: (1) praises and hymns of thanksgiving (the latter do not constitute a distinct literary genre); (2) prayers, petitions, complaints, lamentations. What we have here are two fundamental attitudes of human beings before God, and these two 'poles' are far from exclud-ing one another; they are complementary. R. Murphy (1959) recog-nized the justification for this classification which corresponds to what St Augustine wrote[1] 'Now we are praising God, but we are begging him. Our praise allows for joy; our supplication, wailing.' Such complexity is not surprising. The same is true of the prayers of ancient Egypt, as A. Barucq (1962: 39) shows in several examples: 'The association of praise with entreaty (Ps. 77), of confidence with complaint (Ps. 12), of entreaty with thanksgiving (Ps. 85) is quite natural'. The unity of composition does not necessarily require the continuity of themes, for 'the heart has reasons that the mind does not know'. As we will see later on, divine intervention in the form of theophanies and oracles reassures the supplicant and leads to thanksgiving (see Kim 1984).

Going beyond the traditional classifications, S. Mowinckel tried to regroup almost a third of the psalter around the liturgical life as it de-veloped in the Jerusalem Temple for the principal feasts: Passover, Pentecost and especially the Autumn celebrations (New Year, Day of Atonement, Eight-Day Festival of Tabernacles or Booths). He pro-posed that the Feast of the New Year should be considered the feast of the enthronement of YHWH as ruler of Israel, like the Mesopotamian rituals of the *akitu* (New Year). This hypothesis has been favourably received and has led to important developments from the Scandinavian School of Uppsala (*Myth and Rituals*, cf. Merrill and Spencer 1984: 13-26). An attempt has been made to restore the ritual patterns which

---

1. *Enarrationes. in Ps. 148* [Series Latina. Corpus Christianorum 40, 1956], col. 2165)

would have provided the basis for the annual ceremonies of the Temple of Jerusalem, especially during the month of Tishri (September–October). A great number of studies on this subject have appeared.

These studies, prompted by comparisons with Mesopotamian rituals at Uruk, Babylon, etc., have given rise to much discussion; these have found only a feeble echo in France (Hauret 1959–60). We may refer here to the studies of H. Cazelles (1960, cols. 620-45), K.H. Bernhardt (1961: 182-261), J. van der Ploeg (1966: 272). Many exegetes consider the role given to the royal ideology in these theories (cf. Eaton 1986) to be overstated; such a royal ideology would allow for the placing of a good number of psalms in the period of the monarchy, despite the scarcity of the indications put forward. Kingship in Israel would differ from the pagan kingships in Babylon, Syria and Egypt. Despite certain similarities, the king in Israel had to follow the precepts of the Davidic covenant and was obliged to practise a strict monotheism (Gonçalves 1986: 480), although there would be weaknesses and deviations. YHWH was the real ruler (Allman 1984: 142-99. See p. 83).

The treatment of Jewish festivals in these theories, however, is illuminating. The festival of Booths (*Sukkoth*, from 15th to 22nd Tishri) which preceded the New Year Festival (*Ro'š ha-Šana*) and the great Day of Atonement (*Yom Kippur*), became more and more important in Israel. The theme of YHWH as ruler was at the centre of this annual liturgy. There is every indication that a great many psalms should be connected to this festival, as S. Springer (1979), for example, has shown. There are a number of liturgical instructions which support this conclusion. One example is what we read in the Septuagint and Talmud for Psalm 29: 'For the last day of Booths' (Lev. 23.36). According to the Targum of the Psalms, Psalm 81 was recited on the first day of Tishri, for the New Year festival (Lev. 23.24; Num. 29.1); the same thing is indicated for Psalm 47. It is true that these indications are late, as are the annual cycles for the recitation of the psalms (Arens 1961); but they may be echoing ancient traditions.

Following A. Weiser, M. Mannati (1966: 33) had proposed covenant (*běrît*) as the central theme of the psalter. Even though a covenant feast properly so called did not exist in the liturgical calendar of Israel, it must be acknowledged that the theme of covenant is not out of place in connection with any feast. Even though the word *běrît* appears only 19 times in the psalter[1] (Sakenfeld 1978; Kellenberger 1984), it is indirectly suggested by the word *hesed* (a possible equivalent of Arabic *hašada*) which occurs in the psalter more than 120 times. *Hesed* is the moral behaviour demanded of those who have entered into a covenant: fidelity, devotedness, benevolence, mutual willingness to help, reciprocal love. If it is a matter of divine *hesed*, there is added an essential nuance of mercy, in other words, of grace and love. This is what is expressed by the frequently used antiphon:[2] 'Give thanks to the Lord who is good and whose love [*hasdô*] is eternal'. This attitude is fundamental and often called to mind. The prophets Hosea and Jeremiah were the first to be its advocates. This is not, however, a truly specific and central feature of the psalter.

If we wish to discover in the psalter a dominant theme over and above the great variety of literary genres or discern a possible liturgical setting, we must restore the psalms to their place in the religious life of the Jewish people. The books of Ezra, Nehemiah and Chronicles provide valuable information for us here, even though they are too often neglected by commentators on the psalter. As a matter of fact, we learn that in the period of the Second Temple, during the rule of the Persians, Greeks and Romans, the singing of psalms and sacred music had a privileged place among all the liturgical celebrations, sacrifices, fasts, vigils, pilgrimages, etc., in Jerusalem. We may recall that the chronicler in 1 Chronicles 16 quotes three excerpts from the Psalms (105.1-15; 96.1-13 and 106.1,47-49; cf. Hill 1983: 159), and in 2 Chron. 6.41-42, he quotes Psalm 132.8-10. It was in this period that the collection of the psalter was completed, doubtless with the diptych formed by Psalms 1 and 2. These represent in fact an introduction to the five 'collections' of psalms which imitate the plan of the Pentateuch. Psalm 1 extols the Torah and Psalm 2, the king-messiah of Zion: these are the two key components of Judaism, the first referring to the Mosaic past and the second to the much hoped-for messianic future.

It must be noted right from the beginning, however, that the Torah

1. Pss. 25.14; 44.18; 50.5, 16; 74.20; 78.10, 37; 83.6; 89.4, 29, 35, 40; 103.18; 105.8, 10; 106.45; 111.5, 9; 132.12.
2. Jer. 33.11; 1 Chron. 16.34, 41; 2 Chron. 5.13; 7.3; 20.21; Ezra 3.11; Pss. 100.5; 106.1; 107.1; 118.1-4; 136; Jdt. (Vg) 13.21; 1 Macc. 4: 24.

itself is mentioned rarely enough by the psalmists. Besides those psalms which, with Psalm 1, speak in praise of the Torah (19.8ff.; 78.1, 5, 10; 119.1ff.: 25 times), it is mentioned in just five other psalms (37.31; 40.9; 89.31; 94.12; 105.45). It is true that the Targum on the psalms frequently mentions or alludes to the Torah, just as the other Targums do, in accordance with the predominant place that the Torah had from that time on in later Judaism (see pp. 53-54). But this is not yet the case in the psalter; A. Deissler (1955) places the long Psalm 119 at the beginning of the Hellenistic period; it is a typical example of a piece written in a strongly anthological style; according to S. Bergler (1979: 286), it could already have been in existence in the time of Nehemiah (Neh. 8).

Prophetic Dimension
It is the second component, the prophetic-messianic, which is predominant throughout the rest of the psalter. Commentators, in fact, agree in emphasizing the countless contacts in style and motifs between the prophetic writings and the psalms. The rest of this work, I hope, will present the evidence to show this. We will limit ourselves for now to a few examples. The theme of the *'ănāwîm*, the 'poor of YHWH', which is present in many prophetic texts, is also a favourite theme of the psalmists.[1] The Trisagion of Isaiah 6 is echoed in Ps. 99.3, 5, 9. Psalm 51 has long been compared to the book of Ezekiel (Tournay 1985b: 417-24). The metaphor of the loincloth with which YHWH is girded (Ps. 76.11b) could be derived from the oracle of Jer. 13.11. The theme of the day of YHWH, the day of anger, is common to both the prophetic writings and the psalms.

For that reason, in the third edition of the Psalms (*BdJ*, 1964: 76-77) there were listed under the heading 'prophetic and eschatological psalms' a significant number of psalms where the following themes were met: cup, fire, crucible, salvation, rock, light and darkness, morning and night, sleep and awakening, kingdom of YHWH, universalism, cosmic disorders, songs of Zion with its vivifying waters, end of wars, return of exiles, messianism. Two headings were reserved for oracles and theophanies. Several monographs have dealt with this

1. Gelin 1953; van der Berghe 1962: 273; Dupont 1969: 11; Delekat 1964: 35; Croft 1984; Lohfink 1984a: 100, and 1986: 153; *THAT*, 1976: 341; *ThWAT*, VI: 271.

subject, such as that of P. Bonnard, *Le psautier selon Jérémie* (1960) and the recent work of W.H. Bellinger, *Psalmody and Prophecy* (1984). But these authors see in these 'oracles' and 'theophanies' merely literary devices and examples of anthological style (cf. Robert 1935: 348) and nothing more.

Already in 1883, F. Delitzsch had noted that the psalms of Asaph are distinguishable from the psalms of Korah through their prophetic-juridical content. After him, H. Gunkel (1928–1933: 329-381) established a special category for those psalms called 'prophetic, eschatological, messianic'. For him, the vast majority of these psalms should be dated to the post-exilic period. They would be dependent on prophetic oracles; what was original in the prophets became imitation (*Nachahmung*) in the psalms, as can be seen, for example, in the songs of the enthronement of YHWH (cf. Pss. 95–100). These psalms expressed the motifs of hope which animated the Jewish community in the period of the Second Temple: YHWH's coming and the universal reign of peace and justice, the nearness of the Day of Judgment, the joy associated with the restoration of Jerusalem and the chosen people, the salvation for Zion where God dwells forever, the disappearance of idolatry, the submission or chastisement of the pagan peoples.

The position of Gunkel was criticized by S. Mowinckel: he proposed, on the contrary, that priority be given to the liturgical texts which must have accompanied the ceremonies in Solomon's Temple during the period of the monarchy. He acknowledged the existence of cultic prophets such as, according to him, Nahum, Jeremiah and Habakkuk. He stressed the prophetic tone of Ps. 45.1 and 49.4 and drew attention to the many 'oracles' through which YHWH was supposed to have responded to the faithful. He especially mentioned the oracles relating to the king of Israel.[1] The inspired psalmist pronounced promises of victory and blessing (Pss. 12.6; 91.14-16) and of the restoration of the people (Pss. 75 and 82); there might be a request for a sign (Ps. 86.17) and a hope expressed for salvation to come (Ps. 50.23), together with an exhortation to the faithful to be docile (Ps. 95.8). Mowinckel pointed out as well that a number of texts in Chronicles (1 Chron. 15.22ff.; 25.1ff.; 2 Chron. 20.19) spoke of the inspiration of the Levitical singers; these would receive a portion of

---

1. Pss. 2.7-9; 18.51; 20; 21; 28.8 (?); 45; 61.7-8; 63.12; 84.10 (?); 85.9ff. (?); 89.20ff.; 101; 110; 132.

the inspiration of the ancient prophets. This is an all-important point whose importance Mowinckel did not understand; it will be the subject matter of the next chapter.

As a matter of fact, Mowinckel improperly extrapolated the information provided by the books of Chronicles and conjectured that it could be applied to a situation that existed three centuries or more earlier. As will be mentioned later on, the existence of 'cultic prophets' in the time of the monarchy is sharply debated and remains very problematic. We should bear in mind also that the two fundamental institutions in the period of the monarchy in Israel, monarchy itself and prophetism, were closely linked, just as elsewhere throughout the ancient Near East; this was, for example, the case at Mari on the Euphrates in the 18th century BCE. The definitive disappearance of the king in Israel was accompanied by the progressive extinction of the institution of prophecy. After the catastrophe of 587 BCE, it was the Levitical singers who took over this role in their own way and conducted themselves as cultic prophets, fully aware of being inspired by the Spirit of YHWH. These Levites claimed David as their model, in so far as he was a prophet (2 Sam. 23.1; see pp. 42-43). They fulfilled a role that was genuinely prophetic. This explains why they so frequently take up again, thanks to the anthological method, the phrases and motifs of the ancient oracles and the descriptions of theophanies. The psalmody of the Second Temple in this way acquired a prophetic dimension. As D.L. Petersen writes (1977: 87), liturgical singing then became a prophetic performance. This is the view of various other authors as well (Booij 1978; Wilson 1980: 292).

Mowinckel admitted that at a relatively late date a new element was added to the traditional themes in the psalms: the idea of the re-establishment of Israel and of definitive salvation for the poor of YHWH— in other words, an eschatological element pertaining to an indefinite future. He thought that Psalms 75 and 82 could have been reused in the liturgy at a later period. Such rereadings are in fact likely, especially in view of the increasing importance given to the Davidic origin of the psalms, which were considered to have been composed by the royal musician himself. But these rereadings do not prejudge the question of the period in which the psalms originated. J. Jeremias (1970: 127) also admits that Levites after the exile composed psalms which speak of divine judgment, the day of YHWH and the coming of the Kingdom of God.

Keeping everything in perspective, we could say much the same thing of wisdom writings composed in the period of the Second Temple, such as Psalm 119 and the book of Job. As A. Vanel (1986: 39) writes, 'the transposition of prophetic ideas (especially those from the books of Isaiah, Jeremiah and Deuteronomy) into a language which tends to confer on them a universal significance appeared only from the 5th century onward when prophecy had ceased; the reflection on divine wisdom and human wisdom is at that time revived and renewed in a way that activated the religious memory of Israel'. From a similar perspective it seems possible to give an account of the origins of the texts themselves, as they have been handed down to us. As we will show later, the Levitical singers of the Second Temple wanted to make up for the stilling of prophecy, the silence of the hidden God (Isa. 45.15). Infidels and pagans ironically ask: 'Where is their God?' (see p. 46). The response was as follows: Zion has become the new Sinai; it is there, and there alone, that the word continues to be manifest. It is in the official liturgy of the Temple that this mystical meeting between YHWH and the faithful takes place. It is there that God listens to prayers and praises, appears to the people and speaks to them in cultic oracles. For God's name dwells there forever and it is there that God's glory resides.

Such a *prophetic* dimension to the canonical psalter, too often neglected by present-day commentators, was recognized by Judaeo-Christian tradition. The psalter is the book most often quoted in the New Testament, with the same status as the prophets. David is given there the role of a prophet (Acts 2.30; 4.25). For their part, the rabbinical writings recognize the prophetic inspiration of David and the psalmists. This is clear from the Targum on the psalms: Ps. 14.1, 'To praise, in the spirit of prophecy, through the intervention of David'; Ps. 103.1, 'Through the intervention of David, a prophetic word'; Ps. 45.1, 'In praise of the members of the Sanhedrin of Moses, as was said prophetically through the intercession of the sons of Korah'; Ps. 46.1, 'To praise, through the intercession of the sons of Korah, in the spirit of prophecy at the time their father had hidden them; they were delivered and spoke the canticle'; Ps. 72.1, 'By the intercession of Solomon, it was said prophetically'; Ps. 78.1, 'Instruction of the Holy Spirit by the intercession of Asaph'; Ps. 98.1, 'Prophetic psalm' (Diez Merino 1982b: *passim*).

The *Midrash Tehillim* on Psalm 44 may also be quoted: 'Why do they say: We have heard with our ears; our fathers said to us? Because they prophesied concerning the present generations' (W.G. Braude 1959: 446). This prophetic aspect is emphasized again in Ps. 45.2: 'My heart overflows with prophecy. For the sons of Korah predicted the future' (*ibid*.: 452-53). The Midrash has its own explanation for the difference between the two titles, 'Psalm of David' and 'To David. A Psalm': 'When David implored the Holy Spirit to remain upon him, he appealed in these words, "Psalm of David". But when the Holy Spirit came to him on his own, he said, "To David. A Psalm"' (Braude 1959: 336).

If we wish to place the psalms as a whole in their real *Sitz im Leben* (cf. Buss 1978: 157-70), we must go beyond the examination of structures and literary genres, liturgical calendars, and comparisons with documents of the ancient Near East. Following the Judaeo-Christian tradition, we must rediscover and develop the prophetic dimension of the psalter. At the same time, these ancient psalms will be for us in the twentieth century a momentous present reality. The greatest evil people can suffer is loneliness.

But God has taken the initiative in overcoming this: thanks to the psalms, we can directly see and hear God.

PART I

LEVITICAL SINGERS, CULTIC PROPHETS

Oracle of David:
'The Spirit of YHWH spoke through me;
God's word is on my tongue' (2 Sam. 23.1-2).

Chapter 1

THE LEVITICAL SINGERS
IN THE SECOND TEMPLE PERIOD

The books of Chronicles (Jenni 1980: 97-108; Japhet 1985: 83-107) have rightly been called a 'prophetic' history (Robert 1949: 19). It is striking how very many prophets are mentioned, some of whom are otherwise unknown (Willi 1972a: 216; D.L. Petersen 1977: 88). Here is a list of them: Samuel (1 Chron. 11.3; 2 Chron. 35.18); Nathan (1 Chron. 17); Gad (1 Chron. 21.9); Gad and Nathan (2 Chron. 29.25) ; Ahijah of Shiloh (2 Chron. 10.15); Shemaiah (2 Chron. 11.2; 12.5); Iddo the seer (2 Chron. 12.15; 13.22); Azariah, son of Oded (2 Chron. 15.1); Hanani the seer (2 Chron. 16.7); Micaiah, son of Imlah (2 Chron. 18.7); Jehu, son of Hanani the seer (2 Chron. 19.2); Jahaziel, son of Zechariah (2 Chron. 20.14); Eliezer, son of Dodavahu of Mareshah (2 Chron. 20.37); the prophet Elijah (2 Chron. 21.12); prophets (2 Chron. 24.19); the priest Zechariah, possessed of the Spirit of God (2 Chron. 24.20); a man of God (2 Chron. 25.7); a prophet (2 Chron. 25.15); Isaiah, son of Amoz (2 Chron. 26.22; 32.20, 32); Oded (2 Chron. 28.9); Hozai (2 Chron. 33.19; LXX 'the seers'); Huldah the prophetess (2 Chron. 34.22); Jeduthun, the king's seer (2 Chron. 35.15); Jeremiah (2 Chron. 35.25); messengers and prophets (2 Chron. 36.15-16).

According to 1 Chron. 29.29, the deeds of King David were written from beginning to end in the chronicles of Samuel the seer, the chronicles of Nathan the prophet and the chronicles of Gad the seer. The chronicler seems to assimilate already the books of Samuel and Kings to the 'Former Prophets', which was to become the traditional designation in the Hebrew Bible. We may recall too how, in 1 Chron. 12.19, the Spirit of God inspired one of David's chiefs, Amasai, chief of the Thirty, and made him speak an oracle which asserts the favour of YHWH with respect to David: 'It is your God who aids you'. The rule of David over all Israel is in conformity with the plan of YHWH; it is kingship in the pattern of prophecy, for David has received the Spirit of God (1 Sam. 16.13) which possessed him (verb *ṣālaḥ*: Puech 1971: 5-19; Cazelles 1978: 71), as it possessed Samson.

As Y. Amit wrote (1983: 206), there is really a kind of prophetic inflation in Chronicles. But he rightly adds that all these 'prophets' are quite stereotyped and possess scarcely any individuality; they follow one after the other as if outside time and are only artificially connected to this or that king. They no longer perform signs and are content to interpret history in line with traditional Deuteronomistic historiography. If the chronicler makes use of earlier prophetic writings, it is to make his own authority secure and give a prophetic force to his writings.

This purpose clearly appears in the 'Levitical Sermons' which have been the object of careful and converging studies (von Rad 1966b: 267ff.; Newsome 1975: 201ff.). These sermons would appear to be a kind of literary game on the part of the chronicler. We find there an echo of the ancient oracles. For example, 2 Chron. 20.20 quotes Isa. 7.9 where there occurs the famous play on words: 'Stand firm in YHWH your God, and you will be firm. Stand firm in God's prophets and secure success.' These Levitical sermons begin with a didactic exordium that has a distinctive Deuteronomistic tone: 'Listen to me, my brethren and my people' (1 Chron. 28.2); 'Listen to me, Asa and all Judah and Benjamin' (2 Chron. 15.2); 'Listen, all of Judah and inhabitants of Jerusalem' (2 Chron. 20.15, 20). Next come exhortations and encouragement: 'Be strong' (1 Chron. 28.10); 'Take heart' (2 Chron. 15.7); 'Do not be afraid, YHWH is with us' (2 Chron. 20.17; cf. 1 Chron. 22.16-17); 'Be strong and take heart' (2 Chron. 32.7; cf. 1 Chron. 22.13). All these phrases turn up again in the psalms; we find in both the same terminology, the same style. Besides, the Levitical sermons are written in a rhythmical, oratorical prose which would be worth studying for its own sake.

1 Chronicles 15

This indicates that prophecy plays an essential role in the life of the Judaean community described by the chronicler. It is a different matter in the books of Ezra and Nehemiah. These do not contain sermons, but psalmic prayers (Ezra 9.6ff.; Neh. 1.5ff.; 9.5ff.). The Hebrew of these two books reflects an earlier stage of the language than that of the chronicler, and their theological thought is quite different too (Japhet 1968: 330ff.; 1986; Williamson 1977: 107).

It is in this prophetic context that the chronicler speaks of Levitical singers to whom he assigns a very important place among the officials of the Second Temple. He presents them in several texts (and not only in 1 Chron. 25.1-3) as inspired seers and prophets. The first text, 1 Chron. 15.16ff., refers to the preparations for transferring the Ark to Jerusalem. David at that time gathers together the priests and Levites who were to carry out this solemn transfer to the sound of music and singing. The three leaders of the guilds of singers, Heman, Asaph and Ethan, were to sound cymbals of bronze (v. 19). We may recall that Ethan appears in the title of Psalm 89, while Heman appears in the title of the preceding Psalm 88.

These three leaders are named elsewhere in a different order and the name of Ethan is replaced by that of Jeduthun (von Rad 1930: 107; D.L. Petersen 1977: 61). Therefore, we find Asaph, Heman, Jeduthun in 2 Chron. 5.12; 29.13-14; 35.15 and Asaph, Jeduthun, Heman in 1 Chron. 25.2-6. The Asaphites had possessed the primacy at first. Ezra 2.41 names them alone at the time of the resumption of worship in 520 BCE; they numbered 128, singers and Levites (cf. Ezra 3.10). Rivalries must have afterwards arisen among the classes of singers (D.L. Petersen 1977: 87). The sons of Korah wanted to be equal to the singers (*BdJ*, 1973: 452); it was Heman who later took the first place, as is indicated by 1 Chron. 6.18ff. and the revisions made to the text of Neh. 12.46. The Masoretic reading is as follows: 'For from ancient times, the days of David and Asaph, there were leaders of singers, canticles of praise and thanksgiving to God'. However, one Hebrew manuscript, and the Greek and other versions, omit the *waw*, 'and', before Asaph; the *kĕtîb* and the Greek also have 'leader' in the singular. This original reading speaking of Asaph as leader is confirmed by Neh. 11.17: 'Asaph, leader of praise [LXX; MT, 'from the beginning', arises from a confusion of *he* and *ḥeth*], intoned the thanksgiving at prayer'.

These rivalries among the Levitical singers will have to be studied at greater length. It will suffice for now to bring out the prophetic role of all the Levites. We find the first allusion to this prophetic role in 1 Chron. 15.22. However, there are difficulties in the text: 'Chenaniah, leader of the Levites, was in charge of the transfer [*maśśā'*]; he directed [*yāśar* from *yśr*] the transfer, for he was skilled in it'. We read in v. 27: 'the Levites carrying the Ark, the singers and Chenaniah, the leader [*śar*] of the transfer [of singers].' This last word is thought to be a dittography; but this doublet suggests that we give the meaning 'raising the voice' to the word *maśśā'* here; the verb *nāśā'* followed by *qôl* ('the voice') means in fact 'raise (the voice)'. This is what was understood by LXX which translated in v. 22, *archōn tōn ǫdōn hoti sunetos ēn*: 'the leader of songs, for he was skilled at it'. The Vulgate translates in the same way: *prophetiae praeerat ad precinendam melodiam*, 'he presided over the prophecy, to give out the tune'. In v. 27, LXX has *ho archōn tōn ǫdōn tōn ạdontōn*: 'the leader of the songs of the singers'. And the Vulgate has *princeps prophetiae inter cantores*, 'the ruler of the prophecy among the singers'. However, in 1 Chron. 26.29, the same Chenaniah and his sons are put in charge of tasks extraneous to the Temple, namely as scribes and judges. In ch. 15, it seems that there was a desire to give *maśśā'* an ambivalent meaning, as is the case in Jer. 23.33-40 where this word means at the same time 'burden' and 'oracle'. Such polysemy allows for an emphasis on the prophetic inspiration of the 'leader of the Levites'. At least this is the opinion of a number of commentators (Cazelles 1961: 84; Tournay 1976a: 386; 1982a: 117; D.L. Petersen 1977: 63; McKane 1980: 35); S. Mowinckel had already emphasized the ambiguity of the word *maśśā'* in 1 Chron. 15.22.

It would be well to compare here the episode presented in Numbers 11. Moses complains to YHWH that he is not able 'to carry' all the people, for this 'burden' is too heavy for him. God replies by asking him to gather 70 of the elders of Israel: 'I will come down to speak with you, but I will take some of the Spirit which is upon you and put it upon them. So they will bear the burden of this people and you will no longer bear it alone' (v. 17). YHWH descends in the cloud and takes some of the Spirit which rested on Moses to put it upon the 70 elders. 'When the Spirit rested on them, they prophesied, but they did not continue to do so' (v. 25). Two men had remained in the camp, Eldad and Medad; the Spirit came down on them and they began to prophesy in the camp. Moses did not wish to stop them and wished that 'all the people of YHWH were prophets and that YHWH would give them the Spirit' (v. 29). In the Persian period, the book of Joel (3.1-2) again returned to this theme of collective inspiration, a theme with a renewed popularity today. We may retain for now the fact that this theme is linked in Numbers 11 with that of the burden (*maśśā'*) of directing the people, attributable to divine inspiration (Michaeli 1967: 90-91; Ramlot 1971: 962).

1 Chronicles 25

In 1 Chron. 25.7, the total number of singers, sons of Asaph, Jeduthun and Heman, was 288, that is 4 × 72. Is it a coincidence that in adding Eldad and Medad to the 70 elders we get the number of inspired persons to 72?

In ch. 25 which deals with the status of singers, the chronicler speaks explicitly of the 'prophetic' role of the sons of Asaph, Heman and Jeduthun, 'the prophets who accompanied themselves with lyres and harps and cymbals' (v. 1). Verse 2 gives the list of the 'sons of Asaph who were under the guidance of their father who *prophesied* [the Targum adds: 'by the Holy Spirit'] under the direction of the king [David]'. Verse 3 gives the list of the sons of Jeduthun: 'There were six of them under the direction of their father Jeduthun who *prophesied* to the sound of lyres to the honour and praise of YHWH'. The threefold repetition of the verb *nb'* (*hithpael* and *niphal*), 'prophesy', is certainly intentional, as has often been noted. A number of exegetes, however, give this verb a watered-down meaning; they say that it merely refers to musical and poetical inspiration, not genuine prophecy. But everywhere else the verb *nb'* is directly concerned with prophetic and ecstatic activity in the strict sense (cf. 1 Sam. 16.14-16; 19.20-24; etc.). The noun *nābî'*, 'prophet', is explained as a passive participle of the first form of the verb *nb'* (the *qal* form), like the nouns *nāśî'*, *nāgîd*, *nādîb*, *māśîaḥ*, etc.; it means 'someone called (by God)'. The Targum accepts this interpretation and further strengthens the aspect of divine inspiration. It paraphrases v. 5 in this way: 'Heman, the king's prophet, who had to sound the shofar to accompany the prophetic words from God' (Le Déaut and Robert 1971: 94).

1 Chron. 25.4-6 (Myers 1965: 171; Michaeli 1967: 125; D.L. Petersen 1977: 64) tries to magnify the authority of the Korahite group of Heman, called a seer of the king, at the expense of the groups of Asaph and Jeduthun. The title of seer (*ḥōzeh*) is elsewhere applied to Gad, the seer of David (1 Chron. 21.9; 2 Chron. 29.25; cf. 2 Sam. 24.11) as well as to Asaph the seer (2 Chron. 29.30). 2 Chron. 33.18 mentions seers who spoke to Manasseh in the name of YHWH.

Iddo is a seer (2 Chron. 9.29; 12.15; 13.22), and likewise Hanani (2 Chron. 19.2). In 2 Chron. 35.15, the primitive text has been retouched to give the pre-eminence to Jeduthun: 'The singers, sons of Asaph, were in their place, by command of David and Asaph and Heman and Jeduthun, the seer [Targum: prophet] of the king'. Two Hebrew manuscripts and the versions (LXX, Syriac) have the plural, 'the seers', which refers to Asaph and Heman as well.

It has long been noted that the last nine names of the sons of Heman, omitted by the Syriac version, have been added in 1 Chron. 25.4 to obtain the number 24 in 25.31. The 24 classes of singers were to correspond to the 24 classes of priests (ch. 24) and of Levites (ch. 23). We may recall that the section 1 Chron. 23.3–27.34 forms, according to many exegetes (but not Williamson 1979: 255), a long addition, a sort of priestly revision or reply; 1 Chron. 28.2 would continue 23.1 (23.2 is obviously an editorial addition).

These last nine names of the sons of Heman form a fragment of a psalm (Haupt 1914: 142; Torczyner 1949: 247). Here is its translation: 'Have mercy on me, YHWH, have mercy on me; you are[1] my God, I have glorified and magnified [your] support; still afflicted,[2] I spoke. Grant many visions.' The last two names of v. 4 (literally: 'increase the visions') suggest that these two sons of Heman were 'seers' too. This peculiar poem in this way emphasizes the Levite singers' claim to prophetic status. Verse 5 confirms this interpretation: 'All these were sons of Heman, the king's seer, who passed on to him the words of God to exalt his horn' (that is, his power).[3] And the text adds: 'God gave Heman fourteen sons and three daughters.[4] Under the direction of their father, they all sang in the Temple of YHWH, to the sound of cymbals, harps and lyres, for the service of the Temple of God, under the orders of the king.' This whole passage indicates the importance that the editor attributed to the prophetic role of the Levitical singers (Gese 1963: 222).

---

1. The translation 'come', based on 2 Chron. 35.21 (versions) and Deut. 33.2, 21, has been proposed.

2. Dividing the noun into two words: *yōšēb qāšeh* (cf. TOB *in loco*). This avoids correcting MT.

3. Cf. Deut. 33.17; 1 Sam. 2.10; Lam. 2.17; Zech. 2.4; 1 Kgs 22.11; Pss. 18.3; 75.5; 89.18, 25; 92.11; 112.9; 132.17; 148.14.

4. As in the Targum of Job 42.13.

This is the context in which 1 Chron. 16.4ff. should be interpreted;
it describes the service of Levites before the Ark, 'to celebrate, glorify and praise YHWH, God of Israel: Asaph, the leader, and his assis-
tant, Zechariah...Jeiel had harps and lyres, and Asaph was to sound
the cymbals...That same day David for the first time charged Asaph
and his associates to praise YHWH' (v. 7). There follows the long,
complicated psalm which repeats with some variants Pss. 105.1-15;
96; 106.1.47-48. A.E. Hill has shown (1983: 159) that this collection
possesses a special structure with repetitions, chiasms and deliberate
alterations. It might be asked why there is a break in the text of Psalm
105 at v. 15: 'Do not touch my anointed ones [= messiahs], do no
harm to my prophets'. This would be an allusion to the two groups
who served in the Second Temple: the priests anointed with oil (Exod.
30.30, etc.), and the Levites who assisted them through their prophetic
ministry.

2 Chronicles 20

The prophetic role of the Levites, Asaphites and Korahites is clearly
indicated in 2 Chronicles 20 during the 'holy' war waged by Jehoshaphat in the south of Judah (D.L. Petersen 1977: 68). After the prayer
offered by Jehoshaphat, the spirit of YHWH (Targum of Chronicles:
the spirit of prophecy coming from YHWH) came upon Jahaziel, a descendant of Asaph. He addressed the people of Judah like a real
prophet, such as Micah (3.8) or Ezekiel (1.5): 'Listen, all of you,
people of Judah and citizens of Jerusalem, and you, King Jehoshaphat!
YHWH says this to you: Do not fear, do not dread this great multitude,
for this battle is not yours, but God's' (2 Chron. 20.15). In his discourse, Jahaziel draws his inspiration from the ancient oracles (Exod.
14.13-14; Josh. 8.1; 10.8; 1 Sam. 17.47; etc.). He echoes Isaiah when
he cries out in v. 17: 'YHWH will be with you' (Isa. 7.14; 8.10). In 2
Chron. 15.2, the prophet Azariah too says: 'YHWH is with you when
you are with him'. In the same way King Hezekiah states: 'With us is
YHWH our God' (2 Chron. 32.8). You would think that you were listening to the psalms (refrain of Pss. 46; 73.22-23, 25; 91.15; etc.).
After Jahaziel finished speaking, all bowed down before YHWH; the
Levites, descendants of Kehath and Korah, began to praise YHWH, the
God of Israel, in a very loud voice (2 Chron. 20.19). King
Jehoshaphat cried out as they were about to depart: 'Listen to me,

Judah and citizens of Jerusalem! Stand firm in YHWH your God and you will be firm'. He is repeating Isa. 7.9 here and continues: 'Stand firm in God's prophets and you will be successful'. He then placed in front of the army the singers of YHWH who praised God in sacred vestments (a phrase from Ps. 29.2) and said: 'Give thanks to YHWH whose love is everlasting'. This traditional psalmic refrain here replaces the war cry or *tĕrûʿâ* (a word derived from *rʿ*, with a rumbling guttural sound: *resh* and *ʿayin*).

After the victory, they all return to the Jerusalem Temple with harps, lyres and trumpets. This great liturgical procession reminds us of the one at the transfer of the Ark, described in 1 Chron. 15.16ff., and makes us think too of Ps. 68.25ff.: 'They view your solemn procession, O God...' Throughout the account, the Levites have the main role beside King Jehoshaphat, and they all speak 'prophetic' words in the Deuteronomistic style. The prayer of Jehoshaphat has been compared to several psalms (Pss. 44, 60, 74, 79, 80, 89, 123). The words of Jahaziel form a regular oracle of salvation and victory which corresponds to the prayer of Jehoshaphat (Begrich 1934, 82; Booij 1978: 261).

2 Chronicles 29

At the time of the celebration of the Passover under King Hezekiah, the Levites again carry out a prophetic kind of activity (D.L. Petersen 1977: 77). In 2 Chron. 29.25, it is said that Hezekiah 'stationed the Levites in the Temple of YHWH with cymbals, harps and lyres, according to the order of David, of Gad the seer [Targum: 'the prophet'] and of Nathan the prophet, for this order came from YHWH [MT is unclear; *bdwd hyh*, 'it came from David', has been suggested] through his prophets'. We should note that David is placed here on the same level as the prophets. The Levites took their place with the instruments made by David, and the priests with the trumpets (which according to Num. 10.1-10 were reserved to them).

We should note that the priests are mentioned here after the Levites. The king was already seen in v. 5 addressing the Levites exclusively. Verses 12-14 list the names and genealogies of the Levites who came to purify the Temple of YHWH according to the king's orders and according to the words of YHWH. It is then that the priests enter to purify the Temple too. In v. 30 Hezekiah and his officers ask the

Levites, once the holocaust has been offered, to praise God in the words of David and of Asaph the seer. The Levites praise with joyful hearts, falling to their knees and prostrating themselves (as in Ps. 95.6). Finally, in v. 34, the Levites help the priests, who are too few in number, to cut up the holocausts. The chronicler adds that 'the Levites were better disposed [literally, 'more upright of heart'] than the priests to sanctify themselves'. This passage intentionally enhances the office of Levites, setting them in a prophetic context. We should note that Hezekiah asks the Levites to offer incense (v. 11), a prerogative reserved in principle to the Aaronid priests (Num. 17.5).[1] This last text follows the narrative of the punishment of Korah and his followers (Num. 16). It appears that the author of 2 Chron. 29 supports the claims of the Korahites to which the priestly editor is opposed (D.L. Petersen 1977: 81). It seems incidentally that the Korahites who joined David (1 Chron. 12.7) originated in the Hebron region (Tournay 1983c: 604); the Asaphites on the other hand seem to be dependent upon Ephraimite traditions (Nasuti 1983).

When King Josiah assembles all the people to read the words of the book of the covenant, 2 Kgs 23.2 mentions priests and prophets, whereas in the parallel text in 2 Chron. 34.30 priests and Levites are named. This change is revealing, as D.L. Petersen has emphasized (1977: 85). The twofold reference 'priests and Levites' comes up again in 2 Chron. 35.18.

David a Prophet

Throughout the books of Chronicles, David is presented as a prophet. It is under his direction that the Levites prophesy (1 Chron. 25.2). David is mentioned just before the three leaders of the Levitical singers in 2 Chron. 35.15. In 1 Chron. 22.8ff., he receives directly from YHWH the command not to build the Temple, but to defer the project to his son Solomon. The Targum of Chronicles speaks here of a 'prophetic word' coming from YHWH. In 1 Chron. 21.26, David imitates the prophet Elijah (1 Kgs 18.24, 37-38) when the latter invoked God to send down fire from heaven upon the altar of holocausts. Like Moses, he is 'drawn from the waters' (the same verb

---

1. Incense, a symbol of psalmic prayer (Ps. 141.2), recalls the Cloud of the Exodus. The chronicler speaks of it often.

māšâ in Exod. 2.10 and Ps. 18.17). They are compared again in 2 Chron. 8.13-14. In 2 Chron. 8.14, it is stated that Solomon established, according to the ordinance of David, his father, the classes of priests in their service, and the Levites in their duties of praise and ministry alongside the priests according to the daily ritual, for such had been the command of David, 'man of God'. The Targum here paraphrases: 'For such was the command of David, the prophet of YHWH'. David is again called 'man of God' in Neh. 12.24. The same thing is said of Moses (Deut. 33.1; Josh. 14.6; Ezra 3.2; 1 Chron. 23.14; 2 Chron. 30.16; Ps. 90.1), who too is often called a 'prophet'[1] (O'Rourke 1963: 44; Fitzmyer 1972: 32; D.L. Petersen 1981: 41).

David had received the Spirit with the royal anointing (1 Sam. 16.13; 1 Chron. 11.3); he is the ancestor of the king-messiah who will be filled with the gifts of the Spirit (Isa. 11.2). It is in the 'last words' attributed to him (2 Sam. 23.2-3) that he is presented as a charismatic personage, a genuine prophet:

1.   Oracle of David, son of Jesse,
     oracle of the man established on high,
     the anointed of the God of Jacob,
     the singer of the songs of Israel.

2.   The Spirit of YHWH has spoken through me
     and that word is on my tongue;
3.   the God of Jacob has spoken,
     to me the Rock of Israel said. . .

There follows the divine oracle (v. 5) whose wording brings to mind the oracle of Nathan. David contrasts the destiny of his house with the detestable lot of the people of Belial (vv. 6-7). It is agreed that 2 Samuel 22–23 forms a literary unit later inserted into the Second Book of Samuel; 24.1 is directly connected to 21.14. The present arrangement has been patterned on the final section of Deuteronomy, with a hymn and a 'testament'. The beginning of 2 Samuel 23 has often been compared to the Balaam oracles (Rouillard 1985: 352); it is possible that both series of texts were composed by the same school, at the beginning of the Second Temple period. In 2 Samuel this 'testament' of David comes after Psalm 18 (= 2 Sam. 22) which mentions the 'king' and the 'messiah' of YHWH, David and his dy-

---

1. Cf. Exod. 4.12; Num. 12.7-8; Deut. 18.15,18; 34.10; Hos. 12.14; Jer. 15.1; Ps. 99.6; Sir. 45.5; Jn 1.17 (cf. Renaud 1987: 510).

nasty, forever destined to receive divine favours. Recently, 2 Sam. 23.1-7 has been closely analysed (Tournay 1981a: 481; del Olmo Lete 1984: 414). What should be kept in mind here is that, for the hagiographers, David, at the end of his life, is seen to be above all a prophet (Robert 1937: 201). Confirmation of this is provided in the commentary following 2 Samuel 23 in the large scroll of psalms discovered at Qumran (11QPs^a). Ten lines of rhythmic prose praise David the prophet:

> David, son of Jesse, was a wise man, a light like the light of the sun. . .
> YHWH gave him an intelligent and enlightened spirit. He wrote 3600
> psalms. All this he expressed under prophetic inspiration which was given
> to him on the part of the Most High.

The word *něbû'â*, 'prophetic inspiration', already appears in 2 Chron. 9.29 in regard to the prophet Ahijah of Shilo, and in 2 Chron. 15.8 in regard to the prophet Azariah. We should note in the Qumran text the comparison made between 'wisdom' and 'prophetic inspiration'; it is the same in Sir. 24.33: the wise person will pour out instruction (*leqah*) like prophecy (Larcher 1984: 510).

If David is a prophet, it is natural that psalms containing theophanies and oracles should be attributed to him by tradition. Psalm 18 contains a magnificent theophany (vv. 8-16). Other 'Davidic' psalms contain oracles (12.6; 32.8-9; 35.3; 60.8-10; 68.23-34; 110.1ff.). The heading 'of David' takes on a new meaning then. The father of Israelite psalmody according to tradition, David has a role as an initiator in as much as he is a prophet at the head of the Levitical singers who too are inspired by the same Spirit. This is the way he is presented in Chronicles, in the Targum, and later on in the Acts of the Apostles (2.30; 4.25), as well as in Josephus (*Ant.* 6.166): after being anointed, David 'began to prophesy'.

A further step will be taken by the hagiographers who will strive to multiply in the psalms the allusions to the life of King David through links in words and themes with the books of Samuel, sometimes at the cost of slight alterations. In addition to Ps. 30.1, thirteen historical references concerning the life of David clearly indicate this at the beginnings of Psalms 3, 7, 18, 34, 51, 52, 54, 56, 57, 59, 60, 64, 142 (Tournay and Schwab 1964: 17; Mays 1986: 143). These Davidic rereadings (Vesco 1987: 5) will then be able to be extended to the whole psalter which becomes the 'psalter of David'.

This process without doubt reached its peak in the period of the editing of the books of Chronicles, at the beginning of the Hellenistic period. The Septuagint adds 'by David'[1] fourteen additional times, even at the beginning of Psalm 136 (MT 137). At the beginning of Psalm 95 (MT 96) it adds: 'When the House was built after the captivity. Canticle. By David'. As is well known, Chronicles present David and his son Solomon as examples of virtue and piety (cf. 1 Chron. 29.17-19); they pass over in silence the adultery of David (2 Sam. 11; cf. Ps. 51.1) and the shadows over the reign of Solomon (1 Kgs 11). David, father of the psalms, in this way becomes the father of Jewish piety, the model of righteousness for believers and the 'poor of YHWH'. In this way we may account for certain groupings of psalms, such as the 'Davidic' collections of the psalter. L.C. Allen (1986: 544) takes as an example the second part of Psalm 19 (vv. 8-15) which reminds us by its vocabulary and content of Ps. 18.21-31 where 'David' appears as the perfect keeper of the Torah and the divine precepts.

We may note that the Koran mentions the Davidic origin of the psalms in Surah 4.163 and 17.55. Islamic tradition extols in David the singer and the musician (Stehly 1979: 357).

---

1. Pss. 32 (MT 33), 42 (MT 43), 66 (Mss; MT 67), 70 (MT 71), 90 (MT 91), 92 (MT 93) to 98 (MT 99), 103 (MT 104), 136 (MT 137).

Chapter 2

THE GRADUAL DISAPPEARANCE OF CLASSICAL PROPHECY

According to numerous texts, classical prophecy gradually disappeared, beginning in the exilic period. Already in Amos 8.11-12 we read: 'They shall seek everywhere for the word of Yahweh, but they shall not find it'. The same thing is found in Ezek. 7.26: 'They shall pester the prophet for a vision', and in the second Lamentation (v. 9): 'Her prophets themselves no longer receive a vision from YHWH'. For their part, the psalmists explicitly speak of the interruption of prophecy. The Asaphite Levites come back to this on several occasions: Ps. 74.9, 'No signs appear for us; there is no longer any prophet; and no one knows for how long'; Ps. 77: 9-10, 'Has YHWH's love vanished forever? Is the word finished for all generations? Has God forgotten to have mercy or in anger withheld compassion?' Psalm 83 begins with an earnest appeal to God who remains silent and aloof; in vv. 14-18 there is a demand for a divine intervention, a theophany, in the style of the ancient prophets. Ps. 79.10 refers to the sneering words of the pagans who insistently demand of Israel: 'Where is your God?'[1] This sarcastic and blasphemous question comes up again in several psalms (42.4, 11; 115.2; cf. 3.3; 14.1) and in post-exilic texts (Joel 2.17; Mic. 7.10; cf. Exod. 32.12). We may quote as well the last verse of Psalm 86 where David is made to say, 'Show me a sign of your goodness.' In Ps. 99.6 and 8, it is recalled that of old Moses and Aaron among the priests, and Samuel too, called to God and God answered them.

This is no longer the case in the time of the Second Temple, after

---

1. Ps. 79.2-3, when quoted in 1 Macc. 7.16-17, is introduced in this way: 'according to the word which he has written', namely, 'David' (ms 56), 'Asaph' (Eusebius) or 'the prophet' (Lucianic recension of the Septuagint). Cf. Abel and Starcky 1961: 141.

515 BCE, except for the very beginnings of the renewal of worship with the prophets of the return, Haggai and Zechariah (520–515 BCE). Both are mentioned in Ezra 5.1-2, at the time of the building of the Second Temple. They helped Zerubbabel, the Davidic descendant, and the high priest Joshua to rebuild the Temple at Jerusalem. These are without doubt the prophets referred to in Zech. 7.3 and 8.9. They are once more mentioned by name in Ezra 6.14, in an Aramaic document, at the dedication of the new Temple. Then they disappear at the same time as Zerubbabel, the last member of the Davidic line. Ezek. 38.17 already spoke of the ancient prophets through whom God had spoken in olden times. Zechariah speaks of 'prophets of the past' (1.4; 7.7, 12).

According to a widely accepted opinion, the disappearance of classical prophecy coincides with the end of the monarchy with which it was linked. This was the case at Mari, on the Euphrates, in the 18th century BCE (Moran 1969: 15; Heintz 1969: 112; Malamat 1980: 67). In Israel, the prophets from the period of the monarchy conducted themselves to some extent as 'viziers' sent by YHWH to the kings (Ramlot 1972: 896; de Pury 1979: I, 267; Wilson 1980: 262). This is true of the following prophets: Samuel (Saul and David); Nathan and Gad (David and Solomon); Ahijah of Shiloh (Jeroboam I); Jehu, son of Hanani (Baasha); Elijah (Ahab and Ahaziah); Micaiah, son of Imlah (Ahab and Jehoshaphat); Elisha (Jehoram of Israel, Jehu and Jehoahaz); Jonah, son of Amittai (Jeroboam II); Amos (Jeroboam II); Isaiah (Ahaz and Hezekiah); Jeremiah (the last kings of Judah); Uriah, son of Shemaiah (Jehoiakim). Hosea brought accusations against the kings of Samaria (7.3-7; 8.4; 10.3) and predicted the end of the house of Jehu and of the kingdom of the North (1.4). Micah (6.16) denounced the kings of the Omri dynasty and the conduct of the house of Achab.

The whole rabbinic tradition agreed that the end of classical prophecy came at the beginning of the Achemenid period. We read in a baraita (*t. Sot.* 13.2; *t. Sot.* 48b; *t. Yom.* 9b; *t. Sanh.* 11a): 'With the deaths of the last prophets, Haggai, Zechariah, Malachi, the Holy Spirit ceased in Israel'. Josephus writes (*Apion* 1.40) that the succession of prophets continued only until the time of Artaxerxes. The cessation of prophecy, writes Y. Kaufmann (1977) is a historical fact (cf. van Imschoot 1938: 35; Willi 1972b: 110; Chilton 1983: 139). In the Maccabean period, Dan. 3.38 (Greek) echoes Hos. 3.4: 'In our day we have no leader, no prophet, no prince, no burnt offering, no sacrifice, no oblation. . .' The first book of Maccabees speaks of the end of the time of the prophets (9.27) and of the expectation of a trustworthy prophet (4.46; 14.41). It is the same at Qumran where we read in the Rule of the Community (1QS 9.11): 'They shall be ruled by the same statutes. . . until the coming of the prophet and the consecrated ones of Aaron and Israel' (Carmignac and Guilbert 1961: 62; Wernberg-Møller 1957: 35 and 135-36).[1] They, therefore, consulted the Torah (1 Macc. 3.48; 2 Macc. 8.23).

Nehemiah 6

Prophets again get mentioned in Neh. 6.7 at the time of the completion of the walls of Jerusalem, about 445 BCE. But it is merely an isolated oracle uttered with regard to an eventual revolt by the Jews wishing to proclaim Nehemiah king (6.6). Sanballat in a letter accuses the governor, Nehemiah, of seeking to make himself king and writes: 'You have set up prophets in Jerusalem to proclaim in regard to you: Judah has a king! And now these reports are going to be passed on to the king. So come now and we can talk this over together' (Neh. 6.7). Nehemiah denies these reports and goes to the house of Shemaiah, son of Delaiah, son of Mehetabel, who was shut in (or prevented from coming, for reasons we do not know).[2] Shemaiah asked Nehemiah to meet him in the Temple and utters in v. 10 a rhythmic oracle in two elegiac verses (so clearly expressed in *BdJ*, 1956: 480; 1973: 519; and Myers 1965b: 136; see Michaeli 1967: 220). Nehemiah replies that he does not want to run away or enter the Temple in this way, since he is a layman. 'I realized in fact', Nehemiah writes, 'that God had not sent him, but that he had spoken this oracle about me because Tobiah (the Ammonite) as well as Sanballat had paid him. Why had he been paid? In order to frighten me and make me do as he said and commit a sin. Then they would have had the opportunity to give me a bad reputation and call me a blasphemer. Remember, my God, Tobiah and Sanballat for what they have done, and Noadiah the prophetess too, and the other prophets who wanted to frighten me' (Neh. 6.12-14). We learn

---

1. This theme which goes back to Deut. 18.15 comes up again in the New Testament: Mt. 16.14; 17.10; Jn 1.21, 25; 6.14; 7.40; Acts 3: 22; 7.37.

2. 2 Chron. 11.2 and 12.5 mention another prophet Shemaiah in the time of King Rehoboam.

here of the existence of the prophetess Noadiah, bringing to mind Miriam, Deborah and Hulda. However, here false prophets are involved and they intervene precisely in regard to the eventual accession to the throne. We meet again then the linking of kingship and prophecy (Hanson 1971: 46; Baltzer 1968: 544; D.L. Petersen 1977: 6; Becker 1980: 51).

The visions of the false prophets are illusory, as the prophets of YHWH often pointed out.[1] The latter had announced beforehand the termination of the prophetic vision, as in the oracle of Isa. 29.10-11: 'YHWH has poured out on you a spirit of deep sleep and has closed your eyes [the prophets] and covered your heads [the seers]. And every vision has become for you like the words of a sealed book.'

The last part of the booklet against false prophets, Jer. 23.33-40, doubtless from the post-exilic period, plays like 1 Chron 15.22 on the double meaning of *maśśā'*, 'load, burden' and 'oracle', in order to cast, in the name of YHWH, an eternal opprobrium on the false prophets (D.L. Petersen 1977: 27). At the beginning of the Hellenistic period, the same thing is found in Zech. 13.2-6 which brings to mind the massacre of false prophets by Elijah on Mount Carmel (Tournay 1974: 371; Hanson 1975: 18). In this way Judaean circles tended to eliminate from the community those who pretended to be prophets and who now had nothing else to do but disappear, shamed and scorned.

The silence of God in the period of the Second Temple has received various explanations at the hands of the hagiographers. In a large number of texts, it is the anger of God who punishes the unfaithful and unjust people. We may quote for example the priest and prophet Ezekiel: 'Now it is all over for you; I will unleash my anger against you...' (7.3; cf. Zech. 7.12); 'They will pester the prophet for a vision..., the king will go into mourning...' (7.26-27). The divine anger strikes all the guilty, great and small (see pp. 150-52).

The people had listened to the false prophets who were liars and greedy; they had not listened to the word of YHWH conveyed by God's servants, the prophets.[2] 'They would not listen nor pay attention

---

1. Cf. 1 Kgs 22.13ff (Micaiah, son of Imlah); Hos. 4.5; Mic. 3.5; Deut. 18.10ff.; Zeph. 3.4; Jer. 5.31; 6.13; 14.13ff.; 23.9ff.; 26.7ff.; 27.9-10, 16ff.; 28; 29.21-23; Ezek. 12.21ff.; 13; 14.9; 22.28; etc.

2. Cf. 2 Kgs 17.13; Jer. 7.25-28; 26.15; 29.19; 44.4.

to me—oracle of YHWH. Your ancestors, where are they now? And the prophets, are they still alive? But my commands and my decrees, which I had provided to my servants, the prophets, did they not reach your fathers?' (Zech. 1.4-6). It is good to reread the penitential prayers of the Levites (Neh. 9): 'You warned them by your spirit through the ministry of your prophets, but they did not listen...Do not think it is something trifling, all this misery that has happened to us, our kings, our leaders, our priests, our prophets, our ancestors and all your people from the time of the kings of Assyria to the present day' (vv. 30-32). We read the same in 2 Chron 36.15-16: 'YHWH, the God of their ancestors, tirelessly sent them messengers, wishing to spare this people and this house. But they ridiculed the messengers of God, they despised God's words, they laughed at God's prophets, until at last the anger of God against this people rose so high that there was no further remedy.' Dan. 9.6, 10 is similar: 'We have not listened to your servants the prophets who spoke in your name to our kings, our princes, our ancestors, and all the people of the land...and we have not listened to the voice of YHWH our God nor lived according to the laws which had been given to us through God's servants, the prophets'. Bar. 1.15ff. speaks of 'the look of shame which is found on the people of Judah and the citizens of Jerusalem, on our kings and our princes, on our priests and our prophets, on our ancestors..., for we did not listen to the voice of the Lord our God according to all the words of the prophets whom God sent to us' (vv. 15-16, 21).

Unfulfilled Oracles

Yet, if the oracles about evil were fulfilled for Judah and Jerusalem, other oracles remained dead letters. The hagiographers took pleasure in acknowledging that the divine oracles were really fulfilled (Josh. 21.45; 23.14-15; 1 Kgs 8.56; 2 Kgs 10.10; 24.2; Isa. 55.11; etc.). But a certain frustration must have arisen in the community in the face of the non-fulfilment of messianic promises. Ezekiel himself admits that his prophecy on the fall of Tyre (Ezek. 26-28) had not been realized; the city held out for thirteen years (585–572 BCE) against Nebuchadnezzer and the Babylonians (Ezek. 29.17-20: the last oracle of Ezekiel) (Zimmerli 1983: 118). Another more important occurrence was the sudden, premature disappearance of the one whom Haggai and

Zechariah had hailed as the messianic 'Branch', the Davidic Zerubbabel, son of Shealtiel (Hag. 1.1; but son of Pedaiah, son of Shealtiel, according to 1 Chron. 3.19), son of King Jeconiah. According to K.M. Beyze (1972: 49), Zerubbabel died during the first days of April, 515 BCE, while the Second Temple was completed the third of Adar (April 1, 515 BCE), according to Ezra 6.15.[1] In the current text of Zech. 6.11-14, it was Joshua the high priest who received the insignia of power, whereas the primitive text must have contained the name of Zerubbabel (cf. Hag. 2.23; Zech. 3.8). This alteration is significant.

R.P. Carroll (1978) clearly brings out the negative factors in the discredit arising from oracles that are not fulfilled, and in the lack of trust in the most authentic prophecy, not to mention the oracles of false prophets. It is not surprising that Zech. 13.2-6 announced that God was suppressing prophecy, so totally discredited at that time: 'I will rid the country of prophets and the spirit of uncleanness...In those days it will turn out that the prophets shall be ashamed of their visions when they prophesy...' Following him, Sirach (36.15) asks of God that the prophets be proved worthy of belief.

If the hagiographers of the Second Temple period had no difficulty in preserving the oracles of calamity and threats uttered against Israel and Judah, the same was not the case for oracles which announced the salvation of Israel and Jerusalem, the coming of an era of peace and happiness. Events gave the lie to the beautiful promises whose realization they awaited in vain. Exposed to the mockery of unbelievers, a great many must have given in to scepticism. We hear this echoed in the national and individual complaints. Would YHWH be a God who hides (Ps. 10.1; cf. Isa. 45.15) or even sleeps (Ps. 44.24; 1 Kgs 18.27)? Why does God remain invisible (Job 23.8-9), far from people, indifferent to the pleading of the unfortunate (Ps. 22.2-12), while the wicked grow rich and are successful (Pss. 37; 73, etc.)? Could it be that God has forgotten this people, this inheritance and even lost interest in this holy dwelling place on Zion? There is no purpose in serving God; what is the good of keeping God's commands or of going about in mournful attire in awe of YHWH Sabaoth (Mal. 3.14)? Where is the God of Justice now (Mal. 2.17)? God does not see what

---

1. The twenty-third of Adar according to 1 Esdras 7.5 and Josephus (*Ant.* 11.4-7).

our end will be (Jer. 12.4). So many questions, repeated a thousand times and left unanswered, provoked the blasphemies of the wicked: 'There is no God!' (Pss. 10.4; 14.1; Jer. 5.12); 'YHWH has no power for good or for evil' (Zeph. 1.12).

They did their utmost to answer this practical atheism by appealing to the traditional principle of temporal retribution. The success of the ungodly is transitory; the just in the end will receive their reward; it is our own failings which lead to our misfortune. We may take as an example Isa. 59.1-2, 11b: 'No, the hand of YHWH is not too short to save, nor God's ear too dull to hear. But your iniquities have opened up a chasm between you and your God. Because of your sins, God's face is hidden and you are not heard. . . We wait for the judgment and nothing happens! For salvation, and it remains far from us.' Going beyond the usual explanation about retribution, the book of Job sees that there can be no other response but the incomprehensible mystery of divine providence. God is just; we must then have confidence in God, even if we do not know how this justice which infinitely surpasses human understanding is carried out: 'No, God does not sleep nor doze, the guardian of Israel', cries out the psalmist (121.4; cf. M. Weippert 1984: 75).

The ancient prophets had often made an impact on their hearers by proclaiming the nearness of the day of YHWH. This day, it is true, had been presented in that case as terrible and inexorable for sinners (Amos 5.18ff.; 8.9; Isa. 2.6ff.; Zeph. 1.14ff.). What was involved was not just the end of Samaria or Jerusalem, crushed by pagan armies; this day of YHWH was to be accompanied by cosmic signs: earthquakes, eclipses of the sun and deep darkness, etc. This description just kept on being extended after the time of the exile. In the face of the delay brought about by God of the realization of past promises (Isaiah 60–62 could be taken as an example of such promises), the visions of the future, in Israel, no longer concerned a specific epoch, but instead the end of time, a vague, indefinite phrase which still left room for speaking of a certain proximity of the day, since for God a thousand years are like a single day. This is what we find in the book of Malachi (towards 450 BCE), in the book of Joel (about 400 BCE) and later on in the second part of the book of Zechariah (Zech. 9-14) and in the 'apocalypses' of the book of Isaiah (Isa. 24–27; 34–35). It is no longer a matter here of prophetic oracles like those of the 'ancient prophets', but rather of apocalyptic visions which will be developed further in the books of Enoch, Daniel, the Jewish apocryphal books and Christian writings. The cessation of ancient prophecy is in this way directly connected to the birth of apocalyptic literature. Numerous works on this subject have been published in recent years.[1] I recommend these to the reader.

Preponderance of Torah

To this evolution which coincides with the progressive cessation of classical prophecy there is to be added another equally essential development, namely, the growing authority of the Mosaic Law, the Torah. Towards the end of the Judaean monarchy, an important stage had already been reached on the road to the canonization of the written law in the promulgation of Deuteronomy. The 'Law of Holiness' (Lev. 17–26) also strengthens the authority of divinely inspired legislative texts. Ezekiel, a priest and prophet, along with his disciples plays an important role in this process, through the inclusion of what is known as the 'Torah of Ezekiel' (Ezek. 40–48). It is Ezra, a priest and scribe, who officially proclaims the Torah of Moses (Neh. 8), which becomes the law of the Nation (Ezra 7.14ff.) during the reign of the Persian King Artaxerxes, either Artaxerxes I (464-424 BCE) or more likely Artaxerxes II (404–359 BCE). The seventh year of Artaxerxes II (Ezra 7.7; cf. 9.9) would then be 398 BCE, a date accepted by many historians and exegetes.

In any case, the Torah then becomes the indispensable charter of Judaism and through the influence of the priesthood its authority will continue to increase (Chary 1955: 69). This theocratic form of government, becoming more and more legalistic and ritualistic, expresses itself, for example, in the sacrificial code of Leviticus (1–7). The putting into writing of the laws, rites and customs of Israel sounds the death knell of the prophetic word entirely oriented to the future. Zechariah had already put on an equal footing 'the law and the words' which YHWH had spoken by the Spirit through the 'ancient prophets' (7.12). From then on it was the same divine Spirit inspiring the Torah whose teaching is likened to a prophetic word (Schäfer 1972; Blenkinsopp 1983). According to a proverb of the post-exilic period (Prov.

---

1. Frost 1952; Plöger 1954: 291; Steck 1968: 447; R. North 1972: 47; Hanson 1975; Niditch 1983; Knibb 1982; K. Muller 1982: 188; Chilton 1983: 48.

29.18): 'Where there is no vision, people lead dissolute lives; happy are they who keep the Law'. According to this sage, observance of the law would make up for the disappearance of the prophets; this is the most common interpretation of this proverb.

As a matter of fact, the law is identified with wisdom in Sirach and this wisdom is divinely inspired: 'I am going to pour out instruction [*didaskalian*] like prophecy and pass it on to generations to come' (Sir. 24.33). Elihu had already said: 'As a matter of fact, there is a spirit residing in humanity, the breath of Shaddai, that gives them understanding' (Job 32.8). According to Baruch, wisdom is the Book of God's commandments, the law that stands forever (4.1). In this way Torah and wisdom permeate one another and become the prerogative of 'doctors or overseers of the law' (Sir. 15.1). It will be said of the wise man Daniel that he has the spirit of the gods (Dan. 5.11, 14). We read in the book of Wisdom: 'Wisdom is a kindly spirit' (Wis. 1.6; Larcher 1969: 363). The new prophets that wisdom can raise up are associated with the 'friends of God' (Wis. 7.27; Larcher 1984: II, 511). If the Torah is that important, it is necessary to remember it (Mal. 3.22), to murmur it day and night (Ps. 1.3; Josh. 1.8); it is the wisdom of the simple (Ps. 19.8); it is necessary to meditate on it and observe it with all one's heart (Ps. 119).

The Targums and the rabbinical commentaries dwelt continually on the irreplaceable importance of the Torah in the religious life of Israel. The rabbis taught the pre-existence of the Torah, basing this on the creation of wisdom as described in Prov. 8.22 and Sir. 24.8. According to the Targums the revelation of the Torah at Sinai contained the whole revelation given to Israel. The prophets received at Sinai the messages that they should then prophesy to later generations. The prophecy of Malachi was already with him at Sinai, but until the later time he had no authorization to prophesy. It was the same in the case of the prophet Isaiah. All the prophets had received their message at Sinai, just as all the sages discerned their wisdom at Sinai. According to Deut. 5.22, God added nothing to the words addressed to Israel assembled on the mountain. The good news of the Torah reverberated through the prophets and sages. There is no other revelation to be expected. Rabbi Johanan quotes Ps. 29.4 in connection with this: 'YHWH's voice is power, YHWH's voice is splendour', and Ps. 68.12. 'YHWH gave a command and God's messengers are an immense army' (Potin 1971: 251).

The rabbinical writings take up all these themes. According to *Pirqê Aboth* ('Sayings of the Fathers') (1.1), it was the prophets who handed down to the Great Synagogue the Torah received by Moses at Sinai. The *Apocalypse of Baruch* (*2 Baruch*) (44–45) clearly refers to the cessation of prophecy: Baruch is the last prophet and before his death instructs the people to listen to the Torah and obey the sages. Later on (85.1-3), he says that the period of the prophets has passed and now Israel has nothing except God and the Torah. The *Apocalypse of Ezra* is the same: in 12.42 we are told that of all the prophets, Ezra alone is left; in 14.21-22 Ezra speaks to God: 'For your law has been burned ...If then I have found favour before you, send your Holy Spirit to me and I will write everything that has happened in the world from the beginning, the things that were written in your law...'[1] *Seder 'Olam Rabbah* 30[2] speaks of the end of prophecy as well: 'And the hairy he-goat is the king of Greece [Dan. 8.21]—Alexander the Macedonian; until that time the prophets prophesied by the Holy Spirit. But after that prepare your mind and listen to the words of the wise.'

It is true that, in Deut. 18.15-18, Moses was supposed to be announcing the coming of a prophet like himself: 'YHWH, your God, will raise up for you, in the midst of you, from your own people, a prophet like me to whom you will listen'. This text is rarely referred to in rabbinical literature, even though it is an integral part of the Torah (Strack and Billerbeck 1924: II, 479, 626). It seems in fact to be contradicted by Deut. 34.10: 'Since then no prophet has arisen in Israel like Moses, whom YHWH knew face to face'. We may add that Deut. 18.9ff. seems to have undergone several editorial revisions (Garcia Lopez 1984: 289). It should be noted, however, that in Maccabean times they were awaiting the coming of a prophet (1 Macc. 4.44; 14.41). The same thing was true among the Samaritans (they referred to this prophet as Taheb) and the people of Qumran (Dexinger 1985: 97). In the New Testament, Jesus is presented through certain characteristics as a new Moses (Teeple 1951; Brown 1966: 49; de Waard 1971: 537; Boismard 1988), whose coming appeared to awaken in Israel the prophetic spirit.

In any case, classical prophecy had disappeared, even though in

1. B.M. Metzger 1983: 551 and 554.
2. S.K. Mirsky (ed.): 1966, 139-40.

Hellenistic Judaism the continuance of the prophetic charism was still accepted, according to Josephus.[1] The same did not hold true of Palestinian Judaism; there the Torah occupied more and more the central place. But there still remained the liturgical activity in the Temple as well as for the Temple; this was the prerogative of the Levitical singers whenever singing and sacred music were involved. They were aware that they still carried on a certain prophetic activity, in order to make up in their own way for the silence of classical prophecy. This was why they were so much inspired by the ancient oracles, especially by the religious current to which Deuteronomy as well as Jeremiah belonged. They attempted in this way to actualize the presence of YHWH in the midst of the faithful, by means of the theophanies and liturgical oracles incorporated into the entire psalter of the Second Temple.

1. *War* 1.78; 2.159; 3.351-53, 405; *Ant.* 13.299-300.

Chapter 3

THE LEVITICAL SINGERS,
AUTHENTIC CULTIC PROPHETS

The existence of cultic prophets in the Jerusalem Temple is accepted
by some, rejected by others. Many hesitate to express an opinion on a
subject so debated (Rowley 1956: 338; Jeremias 1970; Ramlot 1972:
1121; Blenkinsopp 1983). R. de Vaux (1961: 384ff.) thought it impossible to demonstrate the existence of a class of professional prophets in
the Temple. There is a need, then, for a thorough investigation so as
to be able to assert that the Levitical singers in the Second Temple
possessed a special inspiration which made them authentic cultic
prophets, something which was not the case in the period of the
monarchy.

According to S. Mowinckel and many other exegetes, an institution
of cultic prophecy existed in the period of the Judges. Its personnel
would have been attached to the various sanctuaries of YHWH alongside the priests; they would have continued to function after the Temple was built by Solomon. Johnson (2nd edn, 1962; 2nd edn, 1967;
1979) thinks that these cultic prophets lost their prestige after the destruction of the Temple in 587 BCE. The Zadokite and Aaronide
priests would have reacted against them, reducing them to the rank of
singers and subordinate musicians. A.R. Johnson accepts unquestion-
ingly, of course, the hypothesis of an archaic, pre-monarchical
psalmody created by the cultic prophets; this would have had a profound and continuous influence on the whole religious life of Israel.
The oracles of the classical prophets and the Deuteronomistic and
Priestly writings would have directly depended on this ancient liturgy
whose traditional language would be met again here and there
throughout later biblical literature.

From this theory comes a whole chronology of the Psalms. For example, Psalm 81 would date from the time of Samuel and Saul, and it

would be this psalm which would have inspired the prophet Jeremiah. Verses 12-13 of the psalm, 'My people did not listen to my voice. . . I left them to the stubbornness of their hearts; they followed their own counsels' would be imitated by Jeremiah 7.24: 'They did not listen or pay attention; they walked following their own counsels, in the hardness of their evil hearts'. Jeremiah would have borrowed then one of his favourite words: *šĕrirût*, 'hardness [of heart]'. Besides Ps. 81.13, this word occurs eight times in the book of Jeremiah, but elsewhere just once (in Deut. 29.18). The root *šrr*, however, is derived from Aramaic; in Job 40.16 the hapax legomenon *šārîr* means 'muscle'. In the light of all these facts, is not the psalmist more likely dependent here on Jeremiah than the other way around?

It is true that we should not presume a priori the dependence of the psalms on Jeremiah; it could, in fact, be a case of a common vocabulary in a period close to the time of the exile, when some psalmic liturgy already existed. This is the criticism that can be levelled at the book by P.-E. Bonnard, *Le psautier selon Jérémie* (1960; cf. Coppens 1961: 217). Moreover, the book of Jeremiah has been thoroughly reworked by those responsible for the Deuteronomistic writings which received their definitive form only in the Persian period. It is unlikely that a typically Jeremian expression such as Jer. 7.24 would have derived from a psalm dating from more than three centuries earlier without also appearing in other writings in the intervening centuries; no other prophet uses the word *šĕrirût*.

According to Johnson (following Eissfeldt 1958), Psalm 78 dates from the time of Solomon and the phrase 'Holy One of Israel' (v. 41) would have already been current in Solomonic psalmody. It would have been made current again by Isaiah and his school. It could immediately be objected that outside the book of Isaiah, it is found only in post-exilic texts (2 Kgs 19.22; Jer. 51.5; Pss. 71.22; 78.41; 89.19). It is legitimate then to ask why such a phrase did not occur elsewhere, if generations of priests and the faithful had been using it since the Solomonic era (van Selms 1982: 257).

Eissfeldt and Johnson placed the Song of Moses (Deut. 32) well before the time of Solomon. They believe that it could date from the time of Samuel, more precisely from the time of the disastrous defeat inflicted on Israel by the Philistines at Aphek (1 Sam. 4). This opinion has been strongly challenged (Tournay 1960b: 121; Boston 1968: 198; Carrillo Alday 1970; *et al.*). This hymn in fact contains distinctive

Babylonian elements, as is also the case for the book of Ezekiel; Deuteronomy 32 has close contacts as well with Proverbs 1–9 (post-exilic period), Deuteronomy 1ff. and the book of Job, not to mention Psalm 78. This compendium of the theology of the classical prophets would have been added to Deuteronomy after 587 BCE. Johnson believes that Psalm 51 would have been composed by David at Mahanaim during the revolt of his son Absalom. But the 'historical' title of this psalm, *Miserere*, brings to mind the visit of the prophet Nathan to David, after David's adultery. Like the other 'historical' titles, this one would be a Midrashic rereading of the psalm, in which the king-prophet, model of the poor of YHWH, is supposed to be speaking. This process shows us how Jewish tradition came to this understanding of the psalms, but gives us no objective indicator for assigning a date to them. Psalm 51, as is well known, has clearer affinities with Ezekiel's oracles. How could it happen that Ezekiel would be the only one to be inspired by this psalm? There is every indication that the author of the psalm is a disciple of this great prophet (Tournay 1984: 417). The same may be stated of Psalm 60 which, according to Johnson, refers to the capture of the Ark by the Philistines. There again the 'Davidic' title artificially refers to 2 Sam. 8. However, this oracular psalm seems instead to fit into a well-defined period of Israelite history (see p. 178; Tournay 1989).

We may refer as well to E. Haglund (1984) who has done his utmost to find very ancient historical allusions in the psalter; Psalms 105 and 106 could refer to traditions earlier than those in the Pentateuch, as could Psalm 78. This endeavour, however, is not upheld by a detailed textual analysis of the texts and their parallels, as has already been demonstrated (p. 18).

Priests and Prophets

It is true that certain texts show priests and prophets working together inside the Temple (Jer. 23.11; 26.7ff.). Jer. 35.4 speaks of a chamber of the Temple reserved for the sons of a 'man of God', in other words, a prophet; but this could be an instance of a priest who prophesied. It is also true that a cultic background seems to be apparent in certain oracles of Hosea (6.1ff.; 14.2-9).

R. Vuilleumier (1960) has made a study of the cultic tradition of Israel in the prophecies of Amos and Hosea. A text such as Jer. 3.21ff.

presupposes the existence of penitential liturgies at the time of fasts or expiatory sacrifices (cf. Lipiński 1969). But these multiplied in the post-exilic period, for example, in Jonah (3.4ff.), Joel, the prayers of Neh. 9.5ff., Ezra 9.6ff., Bar. 1.15ff., Dan. 9.4ff. We will see that in these cases it is in actual fact a matter of prayers composed by genuine cultic prophets, the priests and the Levitical singers.

In the time of the monarchy it was the priests who responded to the supplications of the faithful, in their role as technicians of intercession. They gave oracular directives. We have an example of this in the royal liturgy that constituted the diptych formed by Psalms 20 and 21.[1] It was the priests who recalled for the faithful the great events of the history of salvation, the interventions of God in favour of the people (Childs 1962; Schottroff 1964). We know too that, according to Num. 27.21 and Deut. 33.8, the descendants of Levi practised divination through the Urim and Thummim, probably a sort of dice which provided for a response of 'yes' or 'no', as can be seen in 1 Sam. 14.41 (Greek text). This practice is not mentioned after the exile except in Exod. 28.30; Ezra 2.63 ; Neh. 7.65; and Sir. 45.10 (de Pury 1975: I, 243; Auneau 1984: 1224).

In fact, the priesthood is the institution *par excellence* in the monarchical period (Cody 1969; Auneau 1984: 1203). The priests kept a close watch over madmen posing as prophets (Jer. 29.26). Between Gad and Nathan on the one hand, and Isaiah on the other, the texts mention not one prophet in the kingdom of Judah. It is in the northern kingdom, more open to pagan Syro-Canaanite influences, that ecstatics are encountered (cf. Long 1972: 489). M. Gross (1967: 93) and H. Utzschneider (1980) have clearly shown that in the case of the major prophets there is always a personal call, an absolutely unique charismatic experience at the very beginning of their mission. In their case there is no question of a social function, or a hereditary profession, as there is for the priests. Their authority does not come from the king whom they are not afraid to castigate. They lived in their own home and not in the Temple. They were consulted at home (2 Kgs 5.9; 19.2; Jer. 37.3; Ezek. 8.1; Neh. 6.10). They personally attacked abuses on the part of the priests (1 Sam. 2.29; 3.13; Jer. 5.31; 20.1), as well as their ignorance and their contempt for the law (Hos. 4.6; Jer. 2.8;

1. Küchler 1918: 285; Begrich 1934: 81; Tournay 1959a: 161; Ramlot 1972: 1122.

Ezek. 7.26; 22.26). They fought against abuses in the official cult, but not against the cult itself. Hosea heaps invective on the 'calf' of Bethel; and Amos, on that of Dan. They condemn idolatrous and licentious practices. The use of possessives (your pilgrimages, your assemblies, your offerings, your sacrifices [Amos 5.21-22], your new moons, your solemnities [Isa. 1.14]) shows clearly that, as H.W. Hertzberg (1950) emphasizes, it is not the cult itself that is condemned, but the deviations in it.

Three prophets of the 7th century (Nahum, Zephaniah and Habakkuk) have been considered by some to be cultic prophets. The psalm at the beginning of Nahum (1.2-7), an alphabetic composition with a concentric structure (around v. 5), would suggest that the book of Nahum should be considered a liturgy celebrated at Jerusalem in the autumn of 612 BCE, at the time of the feast of the New Year, to celebrate the fall of Nineveh (Humbert 1932; H. Schulz 1973). But this thesis must be rejected, since the text of this initial psalm is written in an anthological style, very similar to the post-exilic Songs of Zion and theophanic passages in other psalms, the works of Levitical singers. The perspective is eschatological (Jeremias 1970: 16).[1] The editors of the prophetic corpus from the period of the monarchy tried to adapt it to the liturgical needs of the Judaic community, beginning in 515 BCE. This produced a number of additions in language similar to that of the psalms; see, for example, Isaiah 12 which concludes the 'Book of Emmanuel', Isaiah 33 which is a prophetic liturgy, the three doxologies of Amos (4.13; 5.8; 9.5-6; cf. Berg, 1974; Crenshaw, 1975; Foresti, 1981), as well as the final verses of Amos 9 (vv. 11-15), Micah 7 (vv. 18-20) and Zephaniah 3 (vv. 14-20, the reviews of Gerleman 1962, and Kapelrud 1975b notwithstanding).

Habakkuk

This question is more complicated in the case of the prophet Habakkuk who is considered by Jörg Jeremias (1970: 85) to be a cultic prophet because of his 'prayer' (Hab. 3). This opinion has been rejected (Jocken 1977: 319), because it should be noted that Habakkuk criticizes the king, something which would have been inconceivable on the

---

1. I now definitively reject the chronological hypothesis I proposed in *RB* 65, 1958: 328-35. The 'psalm' of Nahum is not authentic; it is post-exilic.

part of an official of the Temple (Vermeylen 1971: 265). However, Habakkuk 3 bears the title: 'A prayer of the prophet Habakkuk. Tone as for lamentations', and at the end of the prayer: 'For the choirmaster. On stringed instruments'. The word translated here as 'lamentations' is found in the singular at the beginning of the superscription of Psalm 7: *šiggāyôn*, a word which can be compared to Akkadian *šegû*. According to K. van der Toorn (1985), this term would be first of all an exclamation, a petition for pardon, like 'Mercy!' and afterwards would refer to penitential prayers. The three occurrences of *selâ* (vv. 3, 9, 13) again emphasize the psalmic aspect of the whole piece (Sorg 1969). In the opinion of B. Hemmerdinger (1971: 152), the word *selâ* would be a loan word of Iranian origin. It is certain that the 'prayer' of Habakkuk was used in the liturgy of the Second Temple and probably as *haftārâ* for the feast of Pentecost (Potin 1968). In fact, v. 9b speaks of 'oaths' or 'weeks': *šĕlābu'ôt* here has both these meanings. This double entendre occurs in *Jub.* 4.15. Verse 9b is to be translated: 'The oaths [or the weeks] are the arrows [or the spears] of the word'. Such an enigmatic sentence may perhaps allude to the commemoration of the giving of the law on Sinai, the day of Pentecost, or to the anniversary of the solemn ratification of this law by Israel which swears to observe it. In case of violation of this oath, Israel will incur a divine curse and death (Ezek. 17.16-19; Lev. 26.14ff; 2 Chron. 15.13). The 'oaths' are then similar to the 'spears' which pierce the idolators, as happened of old to Sisera (Judg. 4–5). This legalistic re-reading fitted in perfectly with the Covenant Feast which had become Pentecost or Feast of Weeks (Seeligman 1953: 162; Le Déaut 1963: 126; de Vaux 1961: 494).

The first colon of v. 9 puts us on the right track to a solution: 'You bare your bow'. God gets ready to let fly the arrows, referred to as hailstones elsewhere (Josh. 10.11-14; Isa. 30.30; Deut. 7.1; etc.). God is going to trench the earth with torrents, billows of water will surge on and the deep will give forth its voice; the sun and moon will stay in their dwelling at the gleam of the divine arrows, the flashes of lightning. The poet in this way brings to mind a terrible thunderstorm like that which crushed the Amorites at Gibeon (Josh. 10.11ff.). The name 'Amorite', *'mry* (*'ĕmōrî*), should be read in v. 9b instead of *'mr* (*'ōmer*), 'the word'; all that is needed is to restore a *yod* at the end of the word; this could have been omitted intentionally or through defective writing (Tournay 1959b: 359). The original text would then have been: *šibba'tā* [*HALAT*, 1953: 914a] *maṭṭôt 'emōrî*, 'You overwhelm the Amorites with arrows'. The verb in the second person was read as *šĕlābu'ôt*, 'weeks' or 'oaths'; only the vowels need be changed; however, there were no vowels in earlier times. The great victory of Joshua at Gibeon is recalled in Isa. 28.17-21 and Sir. 46.4-6. In Isa. 17.9, LXX reads 'Amorite' in place of MT *'āmîr* whose meaning is uncertain (cf. also *BHS*, 1972; Deut. 33.27). The Targum had already noted this allusion: 'Just as you showed signs for Joshua in the plain of Gibeon, the sun and moon stayed in their resting place; through your Memra (Word) your people triumphed on the strength of the victory, through your power' (Potin 1971: 168, 177).

If all this is so, this prayer[1] is aptly introduced by Hab. 2.20: 'Be silent in God's presence, all the earth!' This call for silence alerts the hearers to redouble their attention in listening to the theophanic poem to follow. Silence should precede every divine oracle (Zeph. 1.7; Ps. 76.9; Wis. 18.14; Rev. 8.1). Here then is an indication that this 'prayer' should be considered a continuation of the preceding oracle; however, it was adapted to the liturgy of the Second Temple by the Levitical singers. It could have inspired other descriptions of theophanies, for example, Ps. 18.8ff.

Inspired Singers

If it is not possible to speak of the institution of cultic prophecy in the First Temple, the texts still distinguish three classes of spiritual leaders: 'Her rulers (the kings of Judah) render judgment for a jug of wine, her priests give instruction for a profit, her prophets divine for money' (Mic. 3.11); 'Priests and prophets are stupefied from wine... They are confused in their visions, they ramble in their judgments' (Isa. 28.7); 'The priests never ask themselves, "Where is the Lord?" The guardians of the law do not know me; the shepherds [= the kings] revolt against me; the prophets prophesy in the name of Baal and follow those who are good for nothing' (Jer. 2.8; cf. 23.13, 27); ' "Come", they said, "let us hatch a plot against Jeremiah. Then we can always have the law from the priests, counsel from the wise, the word from the prophets" ' (Jer. 18.18); 'They will be seeking a vision from

---

1. See pp. 93-95. I must point out the new study of T. Hiebert, *God of my Victory. The Ancient Hymn in Habakkuk 3* (HSM, 38; Atlanta: Scholars Press, 1986).

the prophet; the law will not be found with the priest, counsel with the elders' (Ezek. 7.26). We may add that in his booklet against the prophets, Jeremiah denounces the prophets of Samaria, and those of Jerusalem, but without ever speaking of their contacts with the Temple (Jer. 23.9-40). The same is true of Ezekiel 13, an oracle directed against false prophets.

S. Mowinckel and his disciples have therefore extrapolated data from the books of Chronicles in regard to Levitical singers (Ramlot 1972: 1125). Only from the time of the Second Temple are we entitled to speak of cultic prophets, and then only in connection with Levitical singers (Ramlot 1975: 1146, 1162; Curtis 1979: 277). Of course, these could claim a connection with the ancient ecstatics mentioned in the books of Samuel and Kings, those 'sons of the prophets' (1 Kgs 20.35; 2 Kgs 2.3ff; Amos 7.14) who used the same musical instruments (1 Sam. 10.5; cf. 2 Sam. 6.5). But those professional ecstatics were suspected of syncretism and were therefore denounced by the classical prophets (Hos. 9.7; Jer. 29.26; etc.). This is why the Levitical singers claimed a connection above all with David, famous as a musician while still young (1 Sam. 16.16), an inventor of musical instruments according to Amos 6.5 (if, 'like David' is really original; Amos 5.23 mentions songs and harps, but not David). While they were continuing ancient musical traditions attested since the time of the Exodus (Exod. 15.20; 32.18), the Levitical singers were aware that they were inaugurating a new epoch under the patronage of David, musician and prophet (1 Chron. 23.5; Neh. 12.24). The chronicler is trying to enhance the prestige and authority of these guilds of which he was probably a member. The priests merely sound the trumpets (1 Chron. 15.24; cf. Num. 10.1-10). The Levites were more conscientious at sanctifying themselves on the occasion of the purification of the Temple under King Hezekiah (2 Chron. 29.34). At the time of the transfer of the Ark to Jerusalem under King David (2 Sam. 6), the Levites had not even been mentioned. This indicates the distance covered in five centuries.

These inspired Levites furthermore had their emulators, authors of post-exilic prophetic liturgies, such as Isaiah 33 (Wildberger 1982: 1322; Vermeylen 1977: 419; Murray 1982, 205). There is nothing to prevent us from considering as cultic prophets also the authors of the books of Joel, of the second part of Zechariah (9–14) and even of the book of Jonah. As a matter of fact, the post-exilic inspired psalmody must be situated in a wider context. The Levitical singers were not the only ones to receive the Spirit. The gift of the Spirit reserved of old to ecstatics, prophets and certain kings (such as Saul, David and Solomon) is from now on granted to the whole community of believers, 'a kingdom of priests and a holy nation' (Exod. 19.6): 'You shall be called priests of YHWH; you shall be named ministers of our God' (Isa. 61.6). The sacred anointing, formerly reserved to kings alone (Elisha is an exception, 1 Kgs 19.16, probably because of the parallelism with the anointing of Jehu), is henceforth bestowed on priests (Exod. 30.30; Ps. 133.2; Sir. 45.15; etc.; Kutsch 1963). In 1 Chron. 29.22, Solomon and Zadok are anointed at the same time (cf. Zech. 4.14), while in 1 Kgs 1.39 it is Zadok who anoints Solomon.

From now on, the anointing, like the Spirit of YHWH, is the prerogative not just of the priests but of the whole community. In the period of the Second Temple, the anointed or messiah could refer then to the whole community of believers, the poor of YHWH, as may perhaps be the case in Hab. 3.13 where 'the salvation of your people' is in parallelism with 'the salvation of your anointed'. In any case, in Ps. 28.8 there is parallelism between 'people' and 'messiah'. The same could be true of Isa. 61.1: 'The Spirit of YHWH is upon me, YHWH has in fact made me a messiah' (Vermeylen 1978: 479).[1] This is a text bearing comparison with Isa. 42.1 where God speaks of putting the Spirit upon the Servant, a figure who, it is increasingly agreed, should be recognized as a personification of the Remnant of Israel, including the prophet himself (Mettinger 1983; Tournay 1984b: 309).

Several important texts speak of a collective pouring out of the divine Spirit upon the whole community in the period of the Second Temple. We read already in Ezekiel: 'I will put a new spirit in them' (36.26-27); 'I will put my breath [= my spirit] in you so that you may live' (37.14); 'I will no longer hide my face from them since I will pour out my spirit on the house of Israel' (39.29). It is the same in Second Isaiah: 'I will pour out my spirit on your posterity, and my blessings on your descendants' (44.3); 'As for me, this is my covenant with them, says YHWH: my spirit which is upon you and my words which I have put in your mouth will not be far from your mouth, nor from the mouth of your descendants, nor from the descendants of your descendants, says YHWH, from now on and forever' (59.21). We

---

1. In regard to Ps. 84.10, see p. 148.

may note that the assertion 'I will put my words in your mouth' (in Isa. 51.16 as well) calls to mind the gift of prophecy, as is the case in many other texts.[1] As a result of this, despite the silence of classical prophecy, the presence of the Spirit of YHWH assures the permanence of the word of God: it will last forever (Isa. 40.8).

Haggai (2.5) also calls to mind the presence of the Spirit of YHWH in 'the holy people': 'My spirit, YHWH says, remains in the midst of you' (cf. Isa. 63.11; Neh. 9.20). Joel especially announces this collective pouring out: 'After that, I will pour out my Spirit on all flesh. Your sons, your daughters shall prophesy, your old men shall dream dreams, your young men shall see visions. Even upon your menservants and maidservants, at that time, I will pour out my Spirit' (3.1-2). This oracle corresponds to the words of Moses in Num. 11.25-30 and can be compared to Zech. 12.10: 'On that day I will pour out on the house of David and those living in Jerusalem a spirit of good will and supplication'. In the same way Isa. 32.15 (which is post-exilic; Vermeylen 1977: 426; Wildberger 1978: 1273) announces a time when 'from on high, the spirit shall be poured out on us'. The leaders of the community, priests, Levites, scribes, shall receive an important portion of the Spirit. The Davidic descendant himself shall receive it in its fulness: the six attributes mentioned in Isa. 11.2ff correspond to those of wisdom personified in Prov. 8.12-14 and are directed toward the exercise of royal power.

In this way, in the period of the Second Temple, the pneumatological and eschatological dimension of the *qāhāl* or liturgical assembly of Israel was prepared, directed by the priests and Levites under the inspiration of the Spirit, while awaiting the day of Pentecost (Acts 2.5ff.; 1 Cor. 12.4ff.; 1 Pet. 4.10-11).

As genuine cultic prophets, the Levitical singers composed for the whole community the formularies for prayers and hymns, in the style of the ancient prophets, to be sung by day and even by night to honour the glory and name of YHWH. As Elihu says (Job 35.10) that God inspires and makes the night ring out with songs (*zĕmirôt*); several psalms make mention of this singing during the night (Pss. 16.7; 17.3; 42.9; 63.7; 92.3; 119.62; 134.1). The Levites carried out their duties by night as well as by day (1 Chron. 9.27-33). Such nocturnal prayer

---

1. Deut. 18.18; 1 Kgs 17.24; Isa. 6.7; Jer. 1.9; 5.14; 15.19; 2 Sam. 23.2; Ezek. 2.8; 3.3; Dan. 10.16.

still continues in Christianity as well as in Islam. Among the psalms, some like Psalm 134 were especially intended for priests and Levites of the Temple.

Prophetic Psalms

Before examining the theophanic and oracular passages in the psalms, we may point out some typical 'prophetic' stylistic features in the psalms of the Second Temple. Such a feature is the frequent use of the first person singular, the 'I' of the psalms. Some exegetes consider this to be a collective 'I' with the psalmist being the spokesperson for the whole community, just like Jeremiah who sometimes identified himself with the people (Polk 1984). Others, such as J.H. Eaton (1976/1986), see here the king himself, a proposal refuted by W.H. Bellinger (1984: 29). D.L. Petersen (1977: 100) has observed that this 'I' is absent in all the deutero-prophetic literature. In the psalms, this 'I' may indicate that the Levitical singers were claiming for themselves a quasi-prophetic authority like that of David, the king-prophet, initiator of the liturgy. This could explain the frequency of the verb *'āmartî*, 'I said' (some twenty times) or of *wa'ănî*, 'and I' (often at the beginning of a strophe and corresponding to *wě'attâ*, 'and you'). The Davidic rereadings of the psalter would suggest then that the very person of King David should be seen in the 'I' of the psalms. He is supposed to be expressing himself in the style of the ancient prophets, often like Jeremiah in his 'confessions'.[1]

Such prophetic style appears too in the solemn exordiums of Psalms 49 and 78, similar to Deut. 32.1-3 and Job 32.6ff. It is found likewise in the 'imprecatory' psalms in which 'those who do evil' are identified with the enemies of YHWH (Ps. 139.21-22). The 'God of vengeance' (Ps. 94.1; *ThWAT*, 1986: 602) will rise up on the day of judgment. As for the faithful, the Hasidim, the poor of YHWH, they should rely on God. Their most efficacious weapon, like a two-edged sword (Tournay 1985c: 349), is their prayers in the psalms (Ps. 149.6), an inspired word. The forces of evil are always at work; the way they must be fought is through these prayers. That is why the Levitical singers lend their 'prophetic' voices to the victims of violence and ungodliness, to those who cannot even speak and call out for justice. It

---

1. Jer. 11.18-20; 15.11-21; 17.14-18; 18.19-23; 20.7-12.

is in their name that the whole community repeats these 'imprecatory' psalms in which no one, it should be noted, is explicitly condemned. These psalms, which run the risk nowadays of offending sensibilities, represent a demand for justice, an act of faith and hope in the omnipotence and justice of God.[1] They wanted this justice to be made manifest during the very lifetimes of the just and the wicked; the reason for this was that before the development among the Jewish people of belief in the resurrection (Dan. 12.2; 2 Macc. 7.9) in the second century BCE, they thought that the dead (except for Enoch and Elijah) all indiscriminately went down to Sheol (Isa. 14.9; Ezek. 32.18; Ps. 6.6; Job 7.9). It may be recalled that the first psalm quoted in the Acts of the Apostles is the great imprecatory litany of Psalm 109 (Acts 1.20), along with Ps. 69.26, in regard to the betrayal by Judas (Costacurta 1983: 538).

The inspired Levites in this way taught their people to rely on God in the midst of trials and persecutions, as the prophet Jeremiah and King David had done in the past. 'According to our readiness to be open to the prophetic dimensions of these psalms, we can judge to what extent we really desire not to water down our Christianity' (Mannati 1966: 59). When, like the Jews, Christians recited the psalms, they were following the example of Christ and presenting to God the great outcry of all those who suffered from human injustice and they left it to God to carry out the judgment: 'Vengeance is mine; it is I who will repay, says the Lord' (Deut. 32.35; Rom. 12.19; Brueggeman 1982: 67). We may recall that in books of Jewish prayers, these imprecatory passages are written in small letters; nothing must be omitted from the word of God. But it is a rule that these texts be pronounced in a low voice.

---

1. Cf. *VSpir* 122/569 (1970), p. 291; Tournay 1988b: 9; Trublet 1986, col. 2523; Ravasi 1981: 172; 1982: 234, 750.

Part II

The Theophanies in the Psalms

Jesus said to Martha: 'Did I not tell you that,
if you believe, you will see the glory of God?' (Jn 11.40).

Chapter 4

ANCIENT THEOPHANY NARRATIVES

In the period of the Second Temple, the priests, the Levites, the scribes and the faithful never gave up reading over and over again the ancient Scriptures which related the manifestations of YHWH to Abraham and his descendants, to the prophets, leaders, judges and rulers of Israel. The sacred writings presented two kinds of theophanic manifestations: those in which God the Almighty repelled the enemies, the oppressors of God's people, and those in which the God of majesty appeared to the servants of God to reveal to them the divine name and the divine glory (Grelot 1962: 366; Janowski 1989: 389).

In his book on theophany (1965), Jörg Jeremias connects the theophany narratives with the victories of YHWH over the forces of chaos and the enemies of the divine sovereignty. God is a 'warrior' (Exod. 15.3) whose weapons are flashes of lightning, hail, thunder, fire, volcanic eruptions, earthquakes. A reaction of nature in turmoil accompanies each theophany (Loewenstamm 1980: 173). The terror that divinity inspires is experienced in Israel as well as in the whole ancient Near East. We read in a letter from el-Amarna (147.13-15): 'My lord ...who utters his war cry in the heavens like the god Hadad, so that the whole earth quakes at his cry'.[1]

There should be no need to restrict unduly the nature of biblical theophany. Is not the apparition or coming of YHWH a real theophany? God becomes visible and audible to an individual or a group. This is what happens, for example, in the accounts of prophetic calls. Although they are not necessarily connected with any commotion in nature, these theophanies do give rise to fear and dread, as in the case of Isaiah (Isa. 6). It is a formidable matter for a mortal

---

1. Cf. 1 Sam. 4.5; 14.15; Amos 8.8; Isa. 14.16; Joel 2.10; Ps. 18.8; etc.

to see and hear the Almighty: *mysterium tremendum*! A human then feels in danger of death; the place where God becomes present (Hultgard 1983: 43) takes on a new significance and becomes a sacred place, the 'house of God', the 'holy land'.[1]

In most accounts of divine apparitions to the patriarchs or prophets or to people in general, visions and words go together. This is what the titles of prophetic books of the Bible or of other passages indicate: the words *dābār*, 'word', *maśśā'* or *n ĕ'um*, 'oracle', are associated with *ḥāzôn*, 'vision' (or *ḥāzâ*, 'have a vision'). We may note by way of example 2 Sam. 7.17: 'According to all these words and according to all these visions Nathan spoke to David'. As we begin the separate consideration of theophanies and oracles in the psalms, we must not forget this existential bond between them. For example, in Pss. 12.6 and 68.2, 8, 33 God rises up and then pronounces an oracle. The most usual occurrence is that which is found in Psalm 50, the first Asaphite psalm; here the theophanic prelude introduces a long oracle. We may refer to Psalm 99 as well: the peoples and the earth tremble before the most holy king; this is the one with whom Moses, Aaron and Samuel entered into dialogue.

Each account of a theophany would call for a separate study. Critical exegesis has done its utmost to distinguish in the various narratives, which are frequently composite, several redactional levels and successive rereadings. We may recall briefly the classical documentary hypothesis: in general four traditions are distinguished: the Yahwist (sigla J), Elohist (sigla E), Deuteronomist (sigla D) and Priestly (exilic and post-exilic, sigla P). These complicated literary problems only indirectly concern us in this study. While we will keep them in mind, the texts will be read here as they were read in the Persian and Hellenistic periods by the Jews and in particular by the Levitical singers who had the duty of actualizing the message of the ancient Scriptures to make clear the lessons of the past. As Second Isaiah says: 'Look to the rock from which you have been hewn and to the quarry from which you were cut; look to Abraham your father, and to Sarah who brought you into the world' (Isa. 51.1-2).

---

1. Cf. Gen. 28.17; Exod. 3.5; 19.12; 40.35; Lev. 16.2; Num. 1.51; Josh. 5.15; Hos. 8.1; 9.15; Jer. 12.7; Zech. 2.16; 9.8; Ps. 114: 2; 2 Macc. 1.7. Often God wants to be reassuring: 'Do not fear!' (cf. Gen. 15.1; 21.17; 26.24; 46.3; Judg. 6.23; Luke 1.30; 2.10). See *THAT*, 1: 771.

Theophanies in Genesis 12–50

We will consider first of all the theophanies with which the patriarchs were favoured (Mölle 1973). It was at Shechem that YHWH appeared to Abram (Gen. 12.7) for the first time; but God had already spoken to him (Gen. 12.1) with the command to leave his homeland to go to an unknown country. It is in a vision (Gen. 15.1; verb *ḥāzâ*) that God promises Abram numerous offspring and a land, by virtue of the covenant concluded between them. During the night, Abram was overcome by a deep sleep (as happened to Adam, Gen. 2.21) as well as by a great terror and deep darkness. A smoking firepot and a flaming torch passed between the pieces of the animals; this covenant ritual would find an echo in Jer. 34.18 and Cant. 2.17 (Tournay 1988a: 85-86.). The same symbol of fire is met again in the vision of the burning bush (Exod. 3.2), in the pillar of fire in the desert (Exod. 13.21), on Mount Sinai (Exod. 19.18), in the sacrifices of Aaron (Lev. 9.24) and Elijah (1 Kgs 18.38), and in the inaugural vision of Ezekiel.

According to the Priestly tradition, YHWH appeared to Abraham to conclude a covenant sealed by circumcision (Gen. 17.1). In the apparition at Mamre (Gen. 18.1), YHWH is accompanied by two 'angels'. YHWH appeared as well to Isaac at Gerar (Gen. 26.2) and at Beersheba during the night (Gen. 26.24).

Like Abraham, who is called a 'prophet' in Gen. 20.7, Jacob too is favoured with several theophanies. In the dream at Bethel (Gen. 28.10; cf. 31.13; 48.3), God stood beside Jacob (Gen. 28.13) who, on awakening, was filled with fear (28.17); he set up as a pillar the stone on which he had rested his head and then poured oil over it, because this stone localizes the divine presence: it is *Bet El*, the 'house of God'. Meanwhile, God visits Laban the Aramean in a night vision (Gen. 31.24). After having struggled with a mysterious personage (an 'angel' according to Hos. 12.5) at the ford of the Jabbok, Jacob declares that he has seen God; he gives the name Peniel ('face of God') to this place, ' "Because", he said, "I have seen God face to face and yet my life has been spared" ' (Gen. 32.31). Peniel is a popular etymology for the place-name Penuel (Judg. 8.8; 1 Kgs 12.25). In the same way, the name Israel which Jacob receives (v. 29) is explained here by the verb *śārâ*, 'to be strong', an etymology repeated by Hos.

12.5 (de Pury 1975: II, 539, 556).[1] Later on (Gen. 33.10), Jacob says to Esau: 'Seeing your face is like seeing the face of God'. God appeared to Jacob one other time after his return from Aram; God blessed him and gave him the name Israel;[2] then 'God went up from him' (Gen. 35.13), a phrase already used in Gen. 17.22 in regard to Abraham. The last theophany Jacob was privileged to receive was the one at Beer-sheba, when God tells him to go down to Egypt (Gen. 46.3). In this last passage, the plural in MT, 'visions', could be explained as resulting from the joining of the two traditions, Yahwist and Elohist.

In Israel as among other Semitic peoples, the dream brings about a certain contact with the divinity. These night visions are sometimes obtained through an incubation ritual; they serve as a setting for a divine message or warning which often needs to be interpreted, as is the case in the dreams of Joseph (Gen. 44.5, 15; cf. Num. 22.8, 20; Job 7.14; 33.15; Dan. 2.1; etc.). Numerous studies have been done on this subject,[3] so we need not spend more time on it.

According to the Elohist tradition, God communicates with humans through the intervention of an angel, the representative, the messenger of God. It is this angel who meets Hagar (Gen. 16.7, 13) and points out a well to her (Gen. 21.19) and who on two occasions (Gen. 22.11-15) in the land of Moriah (identified by 2 Chron. 3.1 with Mount Zion) calls to Abraham from heaven. In Gen. 22.14 (Mölle 1973: 89), 'Abraham names this place "YHWH sees", as it is said to this day: "It is on the mountain that YHWH is seen"' (LXX). In the MT there is the variant reading, 'on the mountain of YHWH, he is seen', a deliberate alteration, since a human cannot see God. It is the angel of God who goes ahead of Abraham's oldest servant (Gen. 24.7), who speaks in a dream to Jacob (Gen. 31.11-13) and appears to Moses (Exod. 3.2). In the desert, God sends an angel before Israel;[4] this angel went from be-

---

1. E. Puech suggests the verb *yāsar*, 'to correct'; 'Israel' would then mean 'God has corrected/struck' (Jacob); he compares this with the title of the Deir 'Alla inscription: 'Admonitions (*yissūrê*) of the book of Balaam, son of Beor, the man who sees the gods' (1986: 40).

2. Gen. 35.9: Priestly tradition (Mölle 1973: 169).

3. Ehrlich 1953; Oppenheim 1956; Lindblom, 1961; Lang 1972; '*ḥālam*', *ThWAT*, II: 986; Conroy 1985.

4. Exod. 23.20; 32.34; 33.2; Num. 20.16; cf. 1 Sam. 29.9; 2 Sam. 14.17ff.; 19.28; Isa. 63.9; Mal. 2.7; 3.1.

fore the people to follow them from behind (Exod. 14.19). Later on, it is still the angel of God who speaks to Balaam (Num. 22.32ff.) and to Joshua (Josh. 5.13), who goes up from Gilgal (Judg. 2.1ff.: a Deuteronomistic text), who sits under the oak at Ophrah in order to appear to Gideon (Judg. 6.11-22; cf. 7.9), and who appears to the wife of Manoah (Judg. 13.3ff.); this angel of God also appears to the prophet Elijah (1 Kgs 19.5-7; 2 Kgs 1.3, 15; cf. Carlson 1969; Macholz 1980). Sometimes an exterminating angel is involved, as in the Exodus (Exod. 12.23), at Jerusalem (2 Sam. 24.16-17), and in the camp of the Assyrians (2 Kgs 19.35; Sir. 48.21). There are many other texts that could be mentioned. The angel of God intervenes frequently in the visions of Zechariah and also comes to the assistance of the just (Pss. 34.8; 35.5; 91.11; Mt. 4.6; etc.). Here then is a personage characteristic of theophanies (Guggisberg 1979; *THAT*, 1: 904; *ThWAT*, IV: 887-904).

Liberation Theophanies

The number of theophanies increases during the Exodus from Egypt and the wandering of the Hebrews in the desert on the way to the Promised Land. The time of the Exodus is a privileged period when the God of Israel manifests the divine name and power and majesty through Moses, God's prophet (Hos. 12.14; cf. Renaud 1986: 510). The first theophany is that of the burning bush (Exod. 3.1ff; 3.16; 4.1, 5; Deut. 33.16; Acts 7.30; cf. Mölle 1973: 56). God has seen, yes, God has seen (to take proper notice of the repetition, cf. 1 Sam. 9.16) the misery of the people and heard their cries. That is why God reveals to Moses the divine name, 'I am'. God is the immutable one, the one existing by the divine essence, who comes down[1] to save and free the people, to make them go up towards the land flowing with milk and honey (Exod. 3.7-8).

According to the Yahwist tradition, YHWH travelled with the Hebrews by day in a pillar of cloud[2] to show them the way and by

---

1. The classical motif of theophanies: Exod. 19.18; 33.9; 34.5; Num. 11.17, 25; 12.5; Mic. 1.3; Ps. 18.10; Isa. 31.4; 34.5; 63.19; Neh. 9.1 3.

2. Cf. Exod. 34.5; 40.36; Num. 10.34; 14.14; Deut. 1.33; 1 Kgs 8.10; Isa. 4.5; Wis. 10.17; 18.3; Mt. 17.5; ' *ānān*', *ThWAT*, VI: 270; ' *ărāpel*', *ThWAT*, *ibid.*: 397.

night in a pillar of fire to give them light (cf. Isa. 60.19-20; Jn 8.12). The pillar of cloud would move behind them to come between the Israelites and the Egyptians (Exod. 14.19), then during the day did not depart from before the people, nor did the pillar of fire at night (Exod. 13.21-22). In this way God's permanent presence in the midst of the people was manifested (Exod. 19.9; 20.21). God 'looked down' from the pillar of fire and pillar of cloud (Exod. 14.24; Holmberg 1983: 31). According to a later text, but still one containing ancient traditions (Lev. 16.2, 13), it is the cloud of incense and perfumes in the temple, which later on symbolizes that divine presence (Haran 1960b: 113; cf. Nielsen 1986). The chronicler is very interested in the incense offerings (1 Chron. 6.34; 23.13; 28.18; 2 Chron. 2.3; 13.11; etc.). The psalmists (18.10; 78.14; 97.2; 105.39; Neh. 9.19) take up again the motif of the cloud. According to Sirach (24.4), the throne of wisdom was on the pillar of cloud (Luzarraga 1973).

Sinai Theophany

When we read the account of the great theophany of Sinai in the received texts, we hear YHWH saying to Moses: 'I am coming to you in a dense cloud' (Exod. 19.9). Nature has its role too: God appears in the setting of some kind of volcanic eruption according to the Yahwist (Exod. 19.18), Deuteronomistic (Deut. 4.11b-12a; 5.23-24; 9.15) and Priestly (Exod. 24.15b-17) traditions. According to J. Koenig (1966: 18; 1973: 89), these Judaean traditions could be evoking the memory of volcanic eruptions and seismic shocks, prevalent in the region of the Red Sea; Koenig recalls the volcanic eruption of 1256 CE at Medina. As for the Elohist tradition, it describes this theophany as a thunderstorm coming from the Mediterranean, as often happens in Palestine (Exod. 19.16, 19); this tradition would originate in the North, in the region of Shechem and Samaria. Reacting to the peals of thunder (literally, 'the voices', *qôlôt*), the lightning, the sound of the trumpet (*šôfār*) and the smoking mountain, all the people 'were frightened' (Exod. 20.18: LXX and Samaritan; MT 'saw', a confusion of the two Hebrew verbs *r'h* and *yr'*). In Exod. 19.16, the people 'tremble' (*ḥrd*), just like the mountain in v. 18; this verb is not found in any other theophany. The people stayed at a distance, while Moses approached the dark cloud where God was present (Exod. 20.21). 'Hidden in the thundercloud, I answered you', we read in Ps. 81.8b.

This theme of the storm will become a stock phrase in many texts (Jer. 23.19 = 30.23-24; Job 38.1; 40.6; Wis 5.21-23).

Such was the first great theophanic event in the history of Israel. It has considerable impact; this imposing manifestation of the divinity in fact accompanies, in the present order of the text of Exodus, the gift of the Torah to Israel. However, it should be noted immediately that the tradition of the 'mountain of God' seems to have developed only in a relatively recent period, well after the tradition of the Exodus from Egypt. Therefore, Jörg Jeremias (1965: 154) thinks that the description of the Sinai theophany does not lie behind the theophanic poems (which we will be studying later on). Originally Sinai was presented as a region, the southern area from which YHWH comes to guide the people toward the land of Canaan. In fact, it is remarkable that, except for Mal. 3.22, the prophets speak of the Exodus from Egypt, Moses, Aaron, Miriam, the sojourn in the desert, the covenant, the waters of Meriba etc., but not of Mount Sinai. Other than the books of Exodus, Leviticus and Numbers, only Neh. 9.13 mentions Sinai as the mountain where the covenant was concluded. According to T. Booij (1984a: 1; cf. Maiberger 1984), the process of 'Sinaitization' began only at the end of the monarchy and developed and became more precise in the writings of the Priestly school and later on in rabbinic circles. The new 'Sinaitic' version would have been inspired by an idea of theophany as described in the epic poems, Judg. 5.4-5; Deut. 33.2-5 (pp. 87-89). We will see later how the hagiographers of the Second Temple transferred the theme of Mount Sinai (the mountain of God, Horeb), to Mount Zion, the permanent dwelling place of YHWH, the new Sinai (cf. p. 85).

Seeing God

It is appropriate to pause here to examine the texts of Exodus which refer to 'seeing God', or 'seeing the face of God'. In Exod. 19.13 we read: 'When the trumpet sounds, they will go up the mountain'. But in v. 21, YHWH says to Moses: 'Go down and warn the people not to break through [or: go beyond the limits] to see YHWH [literally, 'towards YHWH to see'], for many of them would fall and perish'. In fact, Moses alone can converse directly with God: 'Moses spoke and God answered him with peals of thunder' (or with a voice, v. 19).

It is in Exod. 24.10-11 that a whole group sees God. This text combines two presentations of the covenant, one (Yahwist: vv. 9-11) in which the covenant is sealed with a joyful community meal, as in the covenants between Isaac and Abimelech (Gen. 26.26-31) or between Jacob and Laban (Gen. 31.54); and the other (Elohist: vv. 3-8) in which the essential element is the ritual of blood splashed on the altar and sprinkled on the people (Noth 1959: 159). The theophany (vv. 9-11) is described in this way: 'Then Moses and Aaron, Nadab and Abihu and seventy elders of Israel went up; and they saw the God of Israel: under God's feet there was something like a pavement of sapphire [or lazulite, cf. Gradwohl 1963: 32], as clear as the heavens themselves. On these privileged individuals of the Israelites, God did not lay a hand; they gazed upon [*ḥāzâ*] God, they ate and drank'.

In the LXX version of Exod. 24.10-11 we read: 'They saw the place where the God of Israel stood... And of the chosen ones of Israel there was not even one missing, and they appeared in the place of God and they ate and drank.' The Samaritan manuscripts read: 'And they were taken [*aleph* is added at the beginning of the verb *ḥāzâ*] to the place where they gazed...' In the Targum, the phrase 'and they saw the God of Israel' is changed to 'they saw the glory of the God of Israel'. It can be seen that the versions have weakened the text. Here rabbinic exegesis applies the rule attributed to Rabbi Judah ben Ilai (*t. Meg.* 4.41; *t. Qid.* 49a): 'Whoever translates absolutely literally is a perverter; whoever adds something is a blasphemer'. The rabbi gives as an example the phrase 'and they saw the God of Israel'. A literal translation is not possible, for no one can see God; neither can the word 'God' be replaced by 'angels', for that would be blasphemy, substituting a creature for the creator. This rule could go further back than the 2nd century CE (Le Déaut 1966: 43; Potin 1971: I, 153). There may be an application of this rule in Jn 12.41: 'Isaiah said this [Isa. 6.9ff.] because he had [variant: 'when he had'] the vision of his [Christ's] glory...' Jn 8.56 may be compared to this: Abraham saw the 'Day' of Jesus and was glad.

The primitive text of Exod. 24.9ff is an exception to the general principle that one cannot see God without dying.[1] Such an exception had already been made for Jacob at Penuel (Gen. 32.31). But Moses had had to cover his face (Exod. 3.6). The same is true of Elijah (1

---

1. Exod. 19.21; 33.20; Lev. 16.2; Num. 4.20; Judg. 6.22-23; 1 Sam. 6.20; Isa. 6.5.

Kgs 19.13) and even the Seraphim (Isa. 6.2). Every representation of the divinity was absolutely forbidden in Israel.[1] In addition, one could not even hear the voice of God without risking death (Exod. 20.19; Deut. 4.33; 5.26). That is why, in several texts where it is a matter of 'seeing God', the active form of the verb (qal) is corrected by the scribes and replaced with the passive form (niphal) 'to be seen'.[2] The versions often differ from the MT here. For example, the Korahite Levite cries out in Ps. 42.3: 'When shall I go and see the face of God?' Some Hebrew manuscripts as well as the Syriac version and the Targum have 'shall I see', while the MT has 'I shall be seen', that is, 'I shall appear'. Numerous works have been devoted to the theme of the vision of the face of God (Graf-Baudissin 1915; Nötscher 1924; *TWNT*, VI: 769; Reindl 1970; Fritsch 1982). I recommend these to the reader.

The conclusion of ch. 24 of Exodus, vv. 15b-18a, a post-exilic Priestly addition, no longer places YHWH directly in view, but instead God's glory and royal majesty; this marks another stage in the theology of Judaism.

Chapters 32–34 of Exodus combine the Yahwist and Elohist traditions (Moberly 1983: 83). The pericope Exod. 33.7-11 is thought to be pre-Deuteronomic; it would be one of the oldest of the texts which speak of the Tent of Reunion or of Meeting (Noth 1959: 209; Görg 1967: 59; Mann 1977; Haran 1978: 260). This tent served as a provisional sanctuary for the Ark of the Covenant in the desert; according to v. 11, Joshua did not leave the tent. Here is the text: 'Now Moses would take the tent, and pitch it for "him" [or 'it'; God? Moses? the Ark?] outside the camp, at some distance away. He called it "the Tent of Meeting". Whoever wanted to seek [*biqqēš*] YHWH would go out to the Tent of Meeting which was outside the camp... When Moses entered the tent, the pillar of cloud would come down, stand at the entrance of the tent and speak with Moses... YHWH would speak to Moses face to face as one person speaks to another.'

The phrase 'face to face' comes up in other accounts of theophanies (Gen. 32.31: Jacob; Judg. 6.22: Gideon). We read in Deut. 5.4: 'From

---

1. Exod. 20.4, 23; 34.17; Lev. 19.4; 26.1; Deut. 4.15-20; 5.8; 27.15; Hos. 8.6.
2. Exod. 23.15, 17; 34.20, 23-24; 1 Sam. 1.22; Deut. 16.16; 31.11; Isa. 1.12; cf. Pss. 42.3; 84.8; Num. 14.14; Job 33.26. See Mölle 1973; McKane 1974: 53-68. According to Jn 1.18, 'No one has ever seen God'.

the midst of fire YHWH spoke to you face to face on the mountain'. It is true that Jacob's vision took place at night and that Gideon saw only the angel of YHWH. It is in the cloud that Moses sees God face to face. Deut. 34.10 states: 'Never again did there arise in Israel a prophet like Moses, whom YHWH knew face to face'. According to Sir. 45.5, God gave Moses the commandments face to face (LXX); the MT moderates the text: 'God gave the commandments into his hands'.

The continuation of Exodus 33, which includes Deuteronomistic features, such as 'rest' (v. 14) and 'name' (v. 19), restricts the meaning of the phrase 'face to face'. 'If you do not come yourself [literally: 'if it is not your face that comes']', Moses says in v. 15, 'do not make us go up from here'. And Moses continues in v. 18: 'Make me see your glory'. God answers him:

> 'I will make all my beauty pass before you and I will proclaim before you the Name of YHWH. I show favour to whom I show favour, and I have mercy on whom I have mercy. But you cannot see my face, for a human cannot see me and live.' YHWH said, 'Here is a place near me. You will take your place on that rock. Then, when my glory will pass, I will put you in the cleft of the rock, and I will shield you with my hand while I pass by. Then I will take away my hand, and you will see my back, but my face must not be seen.'

The parallelism set up between the glory and the beauty of YHWH has been pointed out; the word *ṭûb*, translated here as 'beauty', is also translated 'my blessings' (TOB); but other texts, especially Ps. 27.13, suggest the idea of beauty; the adjective *ṭôb* is associated with the two meanings, goodness and beauty.[1]

Another text (Num. 12.1ff.), attributed to the Elohist tradition, insists on the intimacy of the contacts between God and Moses. The text may have been retouched by the Priestly school; M. Noth (1966: 83) thinks that the colon 'and he sees the form of God' (v. 8) is an addition; but J.S. Kselman (1976: 500) has shown that vv. 6-8 have a concentric structure. As in Exod. 33.7, the Tent of Meeting is located outside the camp. Moses, Aaron and Miriam go out to it together. Aaron and Miriam complain that God speaks exclusively to Moses. 'Does God not speak through us as well?' Here is how God answers them:

---

1. Cf. Hos. 10.11; Num. 24.5; Isa. 33.17; Zech. 9.17; Sir. 42.14. See Barré 1986: 100.

6   Now listen to my words:
      should there be a prophet among you,
      in a vision I make myself known to him,
      in a dream I speak to him.
7   Not so with my servant Moses;
      he is a man relied on for my whole house.[1]
8   With him I speak mouth to mouth,
      in a vision and not in riddles;
      and he sees the form of YHWH.
      How then do you dare speak
      against my servant Moses?

The word 'form' (*tĕmûnâ*) is quite vague; it is translated 'glory' in the Greek and Syriac versions. The 'form' of YHWH is not the face; it is only a silhouette which one can see from the back (cf. Jer. 18.17), as in the preceding text, Exod. 33.23. The author of Ps. 17.15 makes use of this term again (see p. 121).

The final theophany involving Moses is mentioned near the end of Deuteronomy (31.14-15; Mölle 1973: 131) in a text belonging to the Elohist tradition. Moses is nearing death and God summons him with Joshua to the Tent of Meeting. Moses and Joshua present themselves there and are permitted a vision of YHWH in the tent in a pillar of cloud which comes to rest at the entrance of the tent. This is the only place where the tent is mentioned in Deuteronomy. This tent is like a first rough design of the future Temple; there it was possible to meet God, call God by name and receive the divine commands. For Israel this was the time of the 'engagement' between the people and YHWH, as the prophets Hosea, Jeremiah and Ezekiel recall.

Tent of Meeting

In the Tent of Meeting was the Ark of the Covenant (Maier 1965; Schmitt 1972; Cross 1981) along with the tablets of the law (Exod. 25.16; Deut. 10.5). The Ark disappeared in the burning of the Temple, or perhaps even earlier during the reign of the wicked King Manasseh, in the opinion of M. Haran (1978: 246; Schmitt 1972: 145). The disappearance is recalled in Jer. 3.16 and 2 Macc. 2.4-5. The book of Numbers is the only book in the Pentateuch to portray the Ark as a kind of guide for Israel, like the pillar of cloud. In Num.

---

1. This is a reference to the 'house of YHWH'. Cf. Hos. 8.1; 9.15; Jer. 12.7; Zech. 9.8; Ps. 114.2.

10.33, the Ark goes before the people during a three days' journey, in order to seek out a place where they will be able to camp. The cloud of YHWH was over them during the day when they set out from the camp (v. 34). When the Ark was to set out, Moses would say: 'Rise up, YHWH! May your enemies be scattered, may your foes flee before you!' (v. 35). This sort of antiphon is found at the beginning of Psalm 68; it is found again in the prophetic liturgy of Isa. 33.3. When the Ark halted, Moses would say: 'Return, YHWH...' (v. 36). The text is uncertain (Levine 1976: 122; Tournay 1988: 110, n. 35); LXX places v. 34 after v. 36. In the MT these verses are placed between inverted *nuns*; this seems to indicate a textual difficulty. These verses belong to the Elohist tradition. In the Priestly tradition the Ark remains in the midst of the people and assures them of victory (Num. 14.44).

The period of the Exodus ends with the crossing of the Jordan. Once again the Ark of the Covenant is involved in the beginning of the great theophany which allows Israel to cross the river dry-footed (Jos. 3.9ff.) and then conquer Jericho (Josh. 6; Langlamet 1969a: 104). Simply recalling these texts is enough to show how the Jews of the Persian period were aware of the divine presence in their midst.

The accounts of the 'wars of the Ark' (1 Sam. 4-6) and of the transfer of the Ark to Jerusalem also witness in a remarkable way to this awareness (de Tarragon 1979). This formidable presence of the God of Israel, warrior chieftain, deliverer of the people, leads to the death of Uzzah, son of Abimelech (2 Sam. 6.7; cf. 1 Sam. 6.19). In this text of 2 Sam. 6.7 the word *šal* should be compared to Aramaic *šl'*, 'make a mistake, be guilty of an offence or of carelessness', like Akkadian *šelû*. Uzzah should not have touched the Ark of the might of YHWH as Ps. 132.8 (= 2 Chron. 6.41) calls it, or of God's 'strength' (Ps. 78.61).

Ark and Cherubim

In the case of Samuel, God appears to him in a dream (Gnuse 1984) near the Ark at Shiloh (1 Sam. 3.3ff.) and continues to appear there (v. 21). It is at that time that the phrase 'YHWH Sabaoth who sits upon the cherubim' occurs for the first time (1 Sam. 4.4). Once the Ark is transferred to Shiloh, it becomes the footstool, the step, the base of the throne of YHWH, as Pss. 99.5 and 132.7 state. In the Temple of Solomon, the Ark was placed under the wings of the two cherubim (1 Kgs 8.6), in the *děbîr* (mentioned just once in the psalter: Ps. 28.2). The cherubim were placed side by side, with wings extended so as to touch the two side walls of the *děbîr*. The cherubim measured 10 cubits in height and 10 cubits in breadth (1 Kgs 6.23-24), that is 20 cubits for the two of them which was the width of the Holy of Holies (1 Kgs 6.20). They were carved from wood and covered with gold and silver and set against the back wall. According to Syro-Phoenician iconographic ideas, they were supposed to form the base of the throne on which YHWH was invisibly seated. T.N.D. Mettinger (1982) describes several very significant examples of such iconography. On the sarcophagus of Ahiram at Byblos, a god or a king is seated on a throne supported by two winged sphinxes. On the site of Megiddo in Galilee, a discovery has been made of an ivory plaque of a prince upon a sphinx throne. The same site has yielded an ivory model of a cherubim throne. At Ugarit, one of the ceremonies was the 'exposition' of the divine statues with the king presiding. There was nothing like this at Jerusalem where any representation of the divinity was forbidden. The Ark and the cherubim symbolized, each in its own way, the mysterious presence of God. All forms of worship were celebrated 'before YHWH', a frequently-used phrase, especially in Deuteronomy.[1] Consequently, there existed in the *děbîr* a sort of perpetual theophany of YHWH, present in the midst of the people (Haran 1978; de Vaux 1967b: 231; Schmitt 1972: 145).

After 515 BCE the Ark was replaced in the Second Temple by the *kappōret* or 'propitiatory', perhaps the ancient support of the Ark.[2] It was a large plaque of solid gold with two small golden cherubim projecting out at the two extremities. They faced one another with their faces toward the propitiatory, according to Exod. 25.17-21. But vv. 21-22 wrongly combine the Ark and the propitiatory which was placed over the Ark (Lev. 16.2; Num. 7.89). The text of Exodus 25, belonging to the Priestly tradition, united the two objects in this way (de Tarragon 1981: 5). On *Yom Kippur* (the Day of Atonement, tenth of Tishri), the high priest sprinkled the propitiatory to atone for the sins and impurities of Israel. This ritual, unknown in the time of the

1. Deut. 12.7, 18; 14.23, 26; 15.20; 16.11; 18.7; 2 Kgs 19.15; 1 Chron. 17.16; Ps. 61.8.
2. In *ZAW* 89 (1977), p. 115, M. Görg compares *kappōret* with Egyptian *kp(n) rdwj*, 'sole of the foot (of God)' (cf. Ezek. 43.7).

monarchy, is still unknown in the time of Ezra, since at that time it is only on the twenty-fourth of Tishri that an expiation ceremony took place (Neh. 8-9).

The phrase 'YHWH who is enthroned on the cherubim' (2 Sam. 6.2; 1 Chron. 13.6) reappears in the psalter (Pss. 80.2; 99.1; 2 Kgs 1 9.15 = Isa. 37.16). It is Ezekiel who in a special way makes use of the theme of the cherubim, which he describes as if they had the form of *kāribu*, guardians of Mesopotamian sanctuaries. These hybrid winged creatures become for him divine mounts which personify the storm clouds. In Ezek. 10.18, the throne of the cherubim had no Ark and moved about with the celestial chariot, the *merkābâ* (Halperin 1980; Newton 1985: 48). This imagery, found again in Ps. 18.11, corresponds to that which makes YHWH the 'rider of the clouds' (Deut. 33.26f.; Isa. 19.1; Isa. 66.15; Pss. 65.12; 104.3), a phrase derived from Ugaritic *rkb 'rpt* which referred to the great Phoenician god Ba'al, a god of storm and rain. In Ps. 68.5, the 'rider of the clouds (*'rpt*)' becomes the 'rider of the steppes (*'rbwt*)' of the Sinai desert, by means of a paronomasia.

YHWH Sabaoth

The phrase YHWH Sabaoth, 'YHWH of armies', is applied to YHWH for the first time at Shiloh (1 Sam. 4.4) and is found again 12 times in the book of Samuel (in the story of the Ark). It is found 9 times in Amos, 56 times in the first part of Isaiah (1–39) and 82 times in the MT of Jeremiah. In the latter book, it is probably a matter of post-exilic additions, since in the LXX of Jeremiah there are only 10 references to YHWH Sabaoth (Jansen 1973: 75, 162; Gefter 1977; Mettinger 1982: 12; Cazelles 1984: 1123). These additions should no doubt be associated with the frequency of this phrase in the prophets of the Return: Haggai (14 times), Zechariah (53 times), Malachi (24 times). It occurs 15 times in 8 psalms, especially in the refrains of Psalms 46, 80 and 84.[1] This phrase is not found in the Priestly Code, in Deuteronomy or anywhere else in the Pentateuch, or in Joshua and Judges; nor is it found in Ezekiel (Zimmerli 1983: 558). In any case, it cannot be an indication of the antiquity of this or that psalm; the

---

1. Pss. 24.10; 46.4, 8, 12; 48.9; 59.6; 69.7; 80.5, 8, 15; 84.2, 4, 9, 13; 89.9 (Veijola 1982: 91); cf. 1 Chron. 17.24.

very opposite is true, given its frequency from the beginning of the Second Temple period in 515 BCE, in Haggai and Zechariah 1–8.

It is the captain of the army of YHWH who appears to Joshua (Josh. 5.13-15). Micaiah, son of Imlah, sees YHWH seated on the throne and the whole army of heaven standing nearby, on the right and on the left (1 Kgs 22.19). Isaiah sees in the Temple the Lord seated on a very high throne and hears the Seraphim praising God Sabaoth, three times holy; the prophet declares that he has seen the ruler YHWH Sabaoth (Isa. 6.3, 5). This text, which finds an echo in Isa. 51.15 and especially 52.7 ('Your God reigns'), asserts that YHWH reigns over Israel; the king of Israel is YHWH's vassal (de Vaux 1971: 156-57). The importance of this fundamental theme is obvious and is frequently discussed nowadays (Lipiński 1965; Langlamet 1970: 176). At Ugarit too, the god Ba'al is ruler (Caquot, Sznycer and Herdner 1974: 32-34; Gibson 1978: 45). In Israel, it is after the disappearance of the monarchy that the reign of YHWH will be exultingly celebrated, especially in the psalms. O. Camponovo has insisted recently (1984) on the eschatological interpretation of the psalms which celebrate YHWH as Ruler. While still enthroned in heaven,[1] YHWH establishes an earthly throne on Zion: it is the 'throne of YHWH'.[2] There, heaven and earth meet; there, God has found the 'place for repose'; there, the divine glory which Ezekiel saw returning from Babylon (Ezek. 43.2) and the divine name (1 Kgs 8.29; Deut. 12.11; etc.) reside. From the very beginning of his prophecy, second Isaiah was announcing that all flesh would see the glory of YHWH (Isa. 40.5), whereas at Sinai, Israel alone caught a glimpse of it. While nature then had its own way of reacting through fire, storm, etc., from now on it will rejoice in the way stated in the hymnic sections of second Isaiah (42.10-12; 44.23; 49.13; 55.12). The psalms of the Reign of YHWH (47; 95–100) develop this cosmic and universalist theme.

Theophanic Liturgy

We will see later (pp. 103-105) that the Deuteronomistic writings took advantage of the paronomasias between *šēm*, 'the name'; *šām*,

---

1. Isa 66.1; Pss. 9.8; 11.4; 29.10; 89.15; 93.2; 97.1-2; 102.13; 103.19; Acts 7.49; etc.
2. Jer. 3.17; 14.21; 17.12; Ezek. 43.7; cf. Rev. 11.19; 22.3.

'there'; *šālôm*, 'peace'; *Yĕrûšālēm*, 'Jerusalem' (Tournay 1983b: 329). Another comparison between Sinai and Zion made the latter the new Sinai, a theme revived later on by the Targumists (Le Déaut 1963, 162). The deacon Stephen substituted the Jerusalem Temple, 'this very place', for Horeb (Acts 7.7). This is the place where God would be revealed after Horeb, mainly during the celebrations of Passover, Pentecost and Booths. There God has come (Deut. 33.2), is coming (Hab. 3.3; Zech. 2.14; Ps. 50.2), and will come (Pss. 96.13; 98.9; etc.) to set up a divine reign, to save those who are God's own and to judge men and women (Schnutenhaus 1964: 14; *ThWAT*, I: 562). The whole liturgy of the Jerusalem Temple becomes the setting for cultic theophanies. This is the proper context in which to reread the prologue of Isa. 2.2-5 (Mic. 4.1-3), so close to the oracles of Isa. 60-62. H. Wildberger maintains that this prologue is from the time of the monarchy. But B. Renaud (1977: 150) has shown that this text originates in the post-exilic period; though written in oracular style, it has a cultic perspective. The ancient theme of the mountain of the god El is demythologized and applied to Mount Zion, as in Ezek. 20.40; 40.2; 43.12 and Ps. 48.3 (Loretz 1984: 63). It is there that God will dwell forever, in the midst of the people (Congar 1958: 15; M. Metzger 1970: 139; Clifford 1972; Weinfeld 1981: 505). It is no longer from Sinai, but 'from Zion that the law will go out, and the word of the Lord from Jerusalem'.

Chapter 5

ANCIENT THEOPHANIC POEMS

The marvellous interventions of YHWH on behalf of the Israelite people did not fail to inspire Hebrew poets. The Bible has preserved for us some wonderful examples of this ancient poetry which even now has lost nothing of its lyrical inspiration. It presents us with a celebration of the triumphs of YHWH over enemies who were enemies of the Israelite people as well: Egyptians, Canaanites, Assyrians, Babylonians. God ordinarily displays divine power through storms and providential floods, by opening up the flood-gates of the celestial ocean or those of the great rivers and the sea (Kloos 1986). In this way the Hebrew poet transfers to YHWH the attributes of the Syro-Canaanite Ba'al or his Mesopotamian counterpart, Hadad.[1]

Many studies have been published on these poems. If these ancient works are referred to here again, this is done in order to permit a better comparison with other more recent texts which they inspired. These ancient poems had become the literary patrimony of Israel, as indicated by the existence of such collections as the *Book of the Wars of YHWH* (Num. 21.14) or the *Book of the Just*. In the latter work we find the elegy over Saul and Jonathan (2 Sam. 1.17ff.) and the couplet of Solomon on the Temple (1 Kgs 8.12f.). Some Greek manuscripts place this short poem after 1 Kgs 8.53 and presuppose here the Hebrew *šîr*, 'song', instead of *yāšār*, the 'just' (two letters being interchanged); this may have been the original title of the compilation: 'Book of the Song'. In addition, we find in it the entreaty of Joshua at the time of the combat with the five Amorite kings (Josh. 10.12):

> Sun, stand still over Gibeon,
> and you, moon, over the valley of Aijalon!

---

1. Cf. 1 Sam. 7.10; 12.17-18; Exod. 9.18ff.; Job 38.22ff.; Ps. 29; etc.

God had said to Joshua: 'Do not be afraid, for I have delivered them into your power; not one of them will be able to withstand you' (v. 8). In actual fact, the poet continues:

> The sun stood still, and the moon halted
> till the nation had vengeance on its enemies.

The account continues in rhythmic prose: 'Is this not written in the *Book of the Just*? The sun stood still in the middle of the heavens; it delayed its setting for almost a whole day. Neither before nor since has there been a day like this day when YHWH obeyed a man, for YHWH fought for Israel' (vv. 13-14).

YHWH had hurled huge hailstones from heaven: 'More died from the hailstones than from the sharp edge of Israelite swords' (v. 11). This episode was frequently recalled.[1] Assyrian literature mentions such 'stones' hurled by the god Hadad (Thureau-Dangin 1912; *The Chicago Assyrian Dictionary*, A I, 1964: 60). All these texts are epic poems (de Vaux 1978: 634-35; Woudstra 1981: 174; Sawyer 1972: 139). An editor took literally the couplet with two parallel cola in Joshua's incantation. Actually, a terrible storm could have come up, obscuring the sky for a long time; there might have been a cloudburst, accompanied by huge hailstones.

Song of Deborah

The same literary style is found in the Song of Deborah: 'From high in heaven the stars fought; from their orbits they fought against Sisera. The torrent of Kishon swept them away' (Judg. 5.20-21). This canticle which mentions Seir and Edom seems to be fairly close to the events, the victory of the northern tribes over the Canaanites at Taanach by 'Megiddo's waters' (Judg. 5.19), perhaps about the middle of the 12th century BCE.

After the hymnic prelude (vv. 2-3), the poet calls to mind the theophany in the wilderness (vv. 4-5):

> 4 YHWH, when you set out from Seir,
> when you left the plateau of Edom,

---

1. Hab. 3.9-11; Isa. 28.17, 21; 30.30; Ezek. 13.11; 38.22; Sir. 46.4-6; cf. Rev. 11.19; 16.21.

> the earth trembled, the very heavens poured down,[1]
> yes, the clouds turned into streams of water;
> 5   the mountains melted[2] before the face of YHWH (that is, Sinai),
> before the face of YHWH, the God of Israel.

This strophe is imitated in Ps. 68.8-9 (Elohist collection):

> O God, when you went out at the head of your people,
> when you marched through the desert, the earth trembled,
> the heavens too turned into streams of water before the face of God
>   (that is, Sinai),
> before the face of God, the God of Israel.

The words 'that is, [or: 'that of'] Sinai' have given rise to many hypotheses; some have tried to explain them through recourse to various Semitic dialects (Lipiński 1967b: 185; Globe 1974: 168). It is simpler to assume that someone added a gloss in order to specify the place of this great theophany by referring to Exod. 19.16-19. The Priestly scribes, we may recall, were partial to a process which placed many events of the time of the Exodus on Mount Sinai; this would be one more example of this. We may add that the two extra words interrupt the rhythm of four accents of the epic verse in each of the two strophes.

The theme of the 'going out of God' (Schnutenhaus 1964: 2) is borrowed from military vocabulary. At the time of the plagues in Egypt (Exod. 11.4), God declares: 'I will go forth among the Egyptians'. Ps. 81.6b makes an allusion to this text: 'It is a law for Israel..., a lesson given to Joseph, when God went forth against the land of Egypt'. The versions understood this incorrectly to refer to Joseph going out from Egypt. In 1 Sam. 8.20, the people say to Samuel: 'Our king will judge us, he will go out at our head and fight our battles'. God said to David: 'YHWH will go out before you to attack the army of the Philistines' (2 Sam. 5.24). This theme of the going out of God comes up again in Hab. 3.3 (pp. 93-96) and in many other texts.[3]

---

1.   The Greek reads 'tottered' (Vogt 1965: 207).
2.   The Greek and Isa. 63.19 read 'quaked'.
3.   Pss. 44.10; 60.12; Mic. 1.3; 7.15; Isa. 26.21; Judg. 4.14; Zech. 14.3.

Blessings of Moses

The psalm which forms a framework around the Blessings of Moses
(Deut. 33.1-5, 26-29) likewise celebrates the victorious march of
YHWH at the head of the people (Deut. 1.30) from the region of Sinai
as far as Transjordan, facing the Promised Land. This material could
date to the time of King Jeroboam II (first half of the 8th century;
Tournay 1958a: 182; 1975: 282). I.C. Seeligman (1964: 75) proposes
an earlier date; H. Rouillard (1985: 228) suggests the time of Josiah.
Here are the first two strophes of this psalm:

> 2   YHWH came from Sinai
> and shone upon them from Seir;
> YHWH was resplendent from Mount Paran
> and arrived at Meribah of Kadesh,
> coming from the south as far as the foothills, for them.
> 3   A parent cherishing the ancestors,[1]
> in your hand are all the holy ones;[2]
> but you caused the death of all the adults,[3]
> for they cried out against your commands.

In spite of the poor state of the MT and the variants in the versions,
this prelude describes the coming of God under the form of some
luminous phenomenon, very likely calling to mind the pillar of fire of
the Exodus. Compared to a brilliant star or to the rising sun, God advances and shines forth, a motif taken up in the psalms (50.2; 80.2;
94.1), Isa. 60.1 and Mal. 3.20. The 'foothills'[4] are the slopes of Mount
Pisgah, east of the Jordan. The beginning of Deuteronomy (1.1-2:
post-exilic) mentions the names of Paran, Horeb, Seir and Kadesh-

1. Reading *'āb*, 'parent' (Samaritan Pentateuch), in place of *'ap*, 'yes' (MT). The
bêth has been modified in pronunciation. Moses is considered to be speaking to
YHWH as in vv. 7-11; Israel is the child of YHWH, who is their parent (Exod. 4.22;
Deut. 8.5; Hos. 11.1; Isa. 1.2; Jer. 3.19; Deut. 32.6; Isa. 63.16; Mal. 2.10; etc.).
'YHWH loved your ancestors' (Deut. 4.37).

2. A theme taken up in v. 27. The divine arms support Israel as an eagle does its
young (Exod. 19.4; Deut. 32.11); God carries them as one carries a child (Deut.
1.31). Cf. Ps. 68.20b.

3. Reading *wĕhēmattâ kôl raglî 'yiśĕ'û*...(cf. Num. 11.21; 14.3, 32; etc.). MT
is corrupted: 'At your feet they fell (?); he gathers (?) what comes from your word'.
The primitive text, not to the liking of the community, has been touched up; errors by
scribes are also possible.

4. Cf. Deut. 3.17; 4.49; Josh. 12.3; 13.20. G. Rendsburg (1980: 81) compares
Hebrew *'šdt* to Ugaritic *'išdym* (*UT* 8.9).

barnea. Num. 13.26 (a Priestly text) mentions Paran and Kadesh-barnea; Gen. 14.6-7 refers to Seir, Paran and Kadesh. Meribah is found in the blessing of Levi (Deut. 33.8) and in Deut. 32.51. 'The myriads of holiness' in MT instead of Meribah of Kadesh comes from a rereading, perhaps prompted by the mention of 'holy ones' in v. 3b and the 'myriads of Ephraim' in v. 17. The *Book of Enoch* (1.9) identifies these myriads of holiness with the angelic armies; this text is quoted in the letter of Jude (v. 14).

After the blessings of the eleven tribes (Simeon is omitted), the second part of this psalmic hymn (vv. 26-29) celebrates in four strophes the divine protection of Israel, which is called *Yešurûn*, a diminutive of *yāšār*, 'the just one' (Deut. 32.15; Isa. 44.2; Sir. 37.25: one ms.). God is beyond compare as liberator of the people (Labuschagne 1966). As 'Rider of the clouds', God protects the people and extends over them the divine arms. The final macarism, with the paronomasia *'ašrêkā Yiśrā'ēl*, 'O happy Israel', is then commented on: it is YHWH who furnishes the people with both defensive weapons (the shield) and offensive ones (the sword) which give them victory.

26 There is none like the God of Jeshurun[1]
who rides the heavens to help you,
and the clouds, in splendour.

27 The God of old provides a refuge
beneath those centuries-old arms;
God has driven the enemy before you
and gives the order: wipe them out!

28 Israel dwells in safety;
the fountain[2] of Jacob is set apart
to be a land of wheat and new wine;
even its sky drips down dew.

29 Happy are you, O Israel! Who is like you,
a people liberated by YHWH?
YHWH is your protecting shield
and the one who guides[3] your majestic sword.

---

1. The versions are followed here. MT: Without equal is God, Jeshurun.

2. This word is not translated by LXX. A text perhaps imitated by Ps. 68.27b (Tournay 1966b: 425). Corrections have been suggested (cf. Isa. 13.22).

3. *'iššer* (Isa. 3.12; 9.15; Prov. 23.19). MT is corrupt. The verb cannot mean 'to bless' (Dahood 1963: 298). 'And Shaddai' has been suggested as well.

Your enemies wish to deceive you, but you,
you shall tread on their back.[1]

The Exodus Song

The Song of Moses (Exodus 15) is an epic song of victory which expands the antiphon of his sister Miriam (15.21):

Sing for YHWH who is exalted, who is magnificent,
who has hurled horse and rider into the sea.

These two verses have a binary rhythm of 2 + 2 accents. Such a
verse of 4 accents with a medial caesura corresponds to the French
Alexandrine; this is the famous epic verse, spacious and majestic. This
song was composed probably toward the end of the period of the
monarchy and may date from King Josiah's Passover (2 Kgs 23.21;
Tournay 1958: 335; 1974: 118; 1978: 147). E. Zenger (1981: 472)
thinks it is from the 8th century, while H. Strauss (1985: 103) opts for
a post-exilic composition, but others maintain a very early date (Cross
1973; P.D. Miller 1973; Norin 1977; Johnson 1979: 30). However,
this passover song would fit well into the period when the Book of the
Covenant or of the Law, identified with the legislative sections of
Deuteronomy, was promulgated. In fact, Deuteronomic features may
be detected in the poem. It begins (v. 3) with the theme of the name
of YHWH (see pp. 100-102) and concludes with the theme of the
single sanctuary, the dwelling place of YHWH on Mount Zion (v. 17).
The theme of the outstretched arm (vv. 6, 12, 16, 17), an anthropomorphism so often found in the Deuteronomistic writings,[2] brings to
mind Deut. 33.27. In addition, it should be noted that the poet here
seems to transform the ancient Canaanite myth of the victory of Ba'al
over the sea (Kloos 1986: 139).

Verses 6-8 and 10-13 describe the marvellous intervention of
YHWH to liberate the people. What we have here is a genuine theo-
phany, and not just an epiphany as C. Westermann claims (1963: 74).
According to him, it is necessary to distinguish between an epiphany

1. TOB translates 'the heights of your land'. Cf. Hab. 3.19; Isa. 58.14; Ps. 18.34;
Amos 4.13; Mic. 1.3 (Devescovi 1961: 235; Crenshaw 1972: 39; Whitney 1979:
125).

2. Exod. 6.6; 7.19; Deut. 4.34; 5.15; 7.8, 19; 9.29; 11.2; 26.8; 1 Kgs 8.42; Isa.
9.11, 16, 20; Ezek. 20.33; Ps. 136.12. Cf. Biard 1960.

when God appears in order to save someone and a theophany when God appears as a mediator in order to speak to the people. It seems that this distinction is not necessary (Jeremias 1965: 1; Mettinger 1982: 116), especially in the case of Exodus 15, a privileged manifestation of the omnipotence and divine goodness of God towards Israel (v. 13). Sea and land obey their creator and engulf the Egyptians (vv. 10, 12; de Vaux 1978: 384). Many psalmists were inspired by this hymn (48.5-7; 68.17; 77.14ff.; 86.8; 96.10; 105.43; 106.12; Jdt. 16). Verse 2 is quoted at the end of the 'Book of Emmanuel' (Isa. 12.2) and in Ps. 118.14. We may add besides Wis. 10.20-21 and Rev. 15.3. A mythical element, the *těhôm*, the abyss (v. 8), is introduced as well (Batto 1983: 27; Kloos, 1986). However, there is no mention of a crossing of the waters by Israel (a Priestly theme).

1	I will sing of YHWH	who is exalted, who is magnificent,
	who has hurled into the sea	horse and rider.
2	YHWH is my strength and my song	I owe YHWH my salvation;
	YHWH is my God whom I admire,	God of my father whom I exalt.
3	YHWH is a warrior,	YHWH is the name.
4	The chariots of Pharaoh (and his army),[1]	God has cast them into the sea;
	the pick of their fighting men	are sunk in the Sea of Reeds.
5	The deep covers them,	they go down (like a stone),[2] into the watery depths.
6	Your right hand, YHWH	magnificent in power,
	your right hand, YHWH	shatters the enemy.
7	Boundlessly sublime,	you overthrow your opponents,
	(you let loose your fury	which consumes them like straw).[3]

1. An addition taken from the Priestly prose account, Exod. 14.4, 9, 17, 28, to which 15.9 belongs as well.

2. A possible harmonization with the priestly prayer of Neh. 9.11.

3. A colon probably moved up as a result of the resemblance between the beginnings of vv. 8 and 10; if it is transferred just before v. 10, it fills out a tristich there. Everywhere else the strophes are tristichs, including vv. 1 and 18 if considered together; these two verses form a framework for the whole poem.

8	At the blast of your nostrils	the waters pile up,
	the waves stand upright	like an embankment;
	the abyss congealed	in the heart of the sea.
9	The enemy said:	I will pursue, I will overtake them,
	I will divide the spoil,	I will gorge myself on it;
	I will draw my sword	I will pillage them.
7b	(You let loose your fury	which consumes them like straw.)
10	You blew your breath,	the sea covered them;
	they sank like lead	in the mighty waters.
11	Who is like you	among the gods, YHWH?
	Who is like you	magnificent in holiness,
	awesome in exploits,	worker of wonders?
12	You stretch out your right hand,	the earth swallows them.
13	You lead by your love	this people you have redeemed;
	you guide them in your strength	to your holy dwelling.
14	The peoples have heard,	they tremble!
	Anguish grips	the dwellers in Philistia;
15	A panic comes over	the princes of Edom.
	Terror seizes	the powerful in Moab;
	the inhabitants of Canaan	are all dismayed;
16	fear and fright	come over them.
	At the might of your arm	they stand petrified,
	until your people, YHWH,	pass over,
	until the people	you acquired pass over.
17	You lead them in and plant them	on the mountain, your inheritance,
	the place you have made,	YHWH, your dwelling,
	the sanctuary, YHWH,	that you prepared with your hands.
18	YHWH will reign	for ever and ever.

Prayer of Habakkuk

The Prayer of Habakkuk (Hab. 3), a later composition than the Canticle of Moses, refers as well to the crossing of the Red Sea, but alludes

besides to many other theophanic interventions of YHWH, such as the
victory of Joshua over the Amorites at Gibeon and the victories in the
time of the Judges. I have explained above how this prayer was
adapted for the liturgy of the feast of Pentecost. The description of the
theophany begins in v. 3. God 'comes' from the south of Palestine and
the divine glory fills the land; God is the Holy One who makes the
land and the pagan nations quake. In v. 7, Cushan brings to mind the
king of Aram Naharaim conquered by Othniel the judge (Judg. 3.8,
10). Cushan has also been compared to the name of the Kaššu tribes
mentioned in the Amarna letters; the Pharaoh sent groups of Habiru to
live in the towns of the Kaššu (Cazelles 1973: 13). Mention of Midian
takes us back to the story of Gideon (Judg. 6.1ff.). The victory over
the Amorites is referred to next, along with an indirect reference to
the crossing of the Red Sea and the Jordan. Verses 13-14 remind us of
the death of Sisera whose temple was pierced through by Jael (Judg.
5.26; cf. Num. 24.17; Pss. 68.22; 110.5-6). A storm caused the
torrent of Kishon to overflow so that the chariots of Sisera got bogged
down in the marshes of the region (still visible today). In v. 5b,
Resheph, one of the names of the god of thunder, has been translated
as 'lightning' (Yadin 1985: 259).

The versions are quite different from MT; some prefer the text preserved in the Barberini Greek manuscript (Good 1959: 11; Baars
1965: 381; Fohrer 1985: 159). This version speaks in v. 13c of death,
Hebrew _môt_, instead of MT _mibbêt_, 'of the house'. The translation in
that case is: 'You smash the head of Mot, the criminal'. This would be
an allusion to the Canaanite myth of Ba'al and his adversary Mot.
According to C.-A. Keller (1971: 172), other mythological allusions
are also perceptible here. However, the Hebrew text lends itself more
readily to the biblical allusions mentioned above. Pss. 68.14 and 83.10
take up again these historical reminiscences. Here is the translation of
Hab. 3.2-18:

> 2 'YHWH, I have heard of you;
> your work, YHWH, fills me with dread.
> In the course of the years revive it;
> in the course of the years make it known.
> When you seethe with anger,
> remember to be merciful.'
>
> 3 God comes from Teman,
> and the Holy One from Mount Paran;

divine majesty covers the heavens,
divine glory fills the earth.

4 God's brightness is like the light,
two rays flash from the hands.
There the divine power is hidden.
(6e) (To God belong the ancient routes).[1]

5 In front of YHWH marches pestilence,
and lightning follows behind.
6 YHWH stops and shakes the earth;
YHWH gazes and upsets the nations.
The age-old mountains are shattered;
the ancient hills collapse ( ).

7 I see the tents of Cushan under the flail;
in Midian, the pavilions are in turmoil.
8 Is YHWH's anger against the rivers?
Is your rage directed at the sea,
so that you mount your horses,
your victorious chariots?

9 You uncover your bow,
you riddle with arrows 'the Amorite';
you trench the earth with torrents.
10 The mountains see you and shudder;
a torrent of rain sweeps on;
the abyss roars aloud.

11 Up there the sun draws its hands away,
the moon stays in its dwelling;
they disappear at the glint of your arrows,
at the gleam of your flashing spear.
12 In fury you stride the earth,
in anger you trample the nations.
13 You have come out to save your people
and to save your anointed one.

You strike the roof of the house of the wicked;
you undermine the foundations down to the rock.[2]
14 You pierce with arrows the chief of their band
who stormed out to scatter us,
feeling sure of devouring the poor in secret.

1. A colon probably displaced in MT to the end of v. 6 through attraction of the word *'ôlām* (ancient hills/ancient routes).
2. 'Rock' correction; MT 'neck'. Same mix-up in writing in Ps. 75.6b.

15   You trampled the sea with your horses,[1]
      the swirling[2] of the mighty waters.

16   I have heard and my heart pounds;
      at that sound, my lips quiver;
      decay creeps into my bones,
      anxiety numbs my knees.
      I wait in silence the day of distress:
      it will come upon the people who attacks us.

17   No buds on the fig tree,
      in the vineyard, no vintaging;
      the olive tree bears nothing but blighted fruit,
      the fields produce nothing to eat;
      the fold is empty of sheep,
      no cattle are in the stalls.

18   As for me, I rejoice exceedingly in YHWH;
      I exult in God, my saviour [19] and my strength,[3]
      who makes me nimble as a doe
      and lets me stride upon the heights.[4]

Micah, Amos

Other theophanic texts from the period of the monarchy, though of lesser importance, should be mentioned. Here is the beginning of the book of Micah (1.3-4), a prelude to the putting of Israel and Judah on trial and to the passing of judgment on Samaria. This text must date back to before the capture of Samaria by the Assyrians in 721 BCE (Renaud 1977: 12). According to Jeremias (1965: 11), it is a good example of the primitive structure of this literary genre of theophany with its two elements: the coming of YHWH from a specific place, here from the heavenly dwelling, and the violent reaction of nature at God's approach:

1. 'His horses' (Pharaoh's!) has been suggested. MT would have been harmonized with v. 8c; final *kaph* and *wāw* can be confused.

2. Another translation is 'the mud' in the boundless space of the waters.

3. MT adds 'YHWH Adonai (is my strength)'. A liturgical addition. The text is badly divided.

4. MT 'my heights' (dittography of *yôd*? cf. LXX). This text could have been harmonized with Ps. 18.34 in the Maccabaean period, in order to insist on the right of Israel to occupy the hill country. Deut. 32.13 and Isa. 58.14: 'the heights of the land'.

3   Look, YHWH is coming from the heavenly dwelling;
     YHWH comes down and strides upon the heights of the earth.
4   The mountains melt before YHWH,
     the valleys burst open
     like wax before the fire,
     like water which cascades down a slope.

It should be noted that 4c follows on 4a, while 4d follows on 4b. The parallels to these two verses are numerous. God strides upon the heights or the high places (*bāmôt*) of the earth as in Hab. 3.19, etc. The valleys burst open as in Hab. 3.9, while the image of wax melting before the fire is repeated in Ps. 68.3. The theme of the 'descent' of God, like that of God's coming or going out, derives from the style of theophanies. The Yahwist tradition already speaks of the descent of YHWH at the Tower of Babel (Gen. 11.5) or for the punishment of Sodom and Gomorrah (Gen. 18.21). God descends as well in the Cloud of the Exodus or when the divine presence is manifested on Zion. An example of the latter would be Isa. 31.4: 'As the lion growls, as the young lion over its prey..., so YHWH Sabaoth will descend on [or: 'against'] the mountain of Zion, on its hill, there to make war'. This oracle with a double meaning (Vermeylen 1977: 421) could have been added in order to obtain a favourable sense. The same thing would be done in Isa. 63.19b–64.2 (post-exilic): 'Oh that you would tear open the heavens, that you would descend, before you the mountains would be shaken [cf. Judg. 5.5], as fire sets the brushwood alight...; before you the pagans would tremble...You would come down, the mountains would be shaken before you.' We may refer to Isa. 34.5 as well: 'My sword is drunk in the heavens; see how it descends on Edom'. Another example would be Ps. 18.10: 'YHWH inclined the heavens and came down' (Mettinger 1982: 33, 86).

The prologue of the book of Amos (1.2) uses similar imagery:

> From Zion, YHWH roars,
> and from Jerusalem shouts aloud.
> The pastures of the shepherds are desolate
> and the summit of Carmel dried up.

This anthological text (cf. Pss. 18.14; 46.7; 68.34; 64.7; Isa. 30.30; etc.; Vermeylen 1978: 521) is repeated in Jer. 25.30 with one variation: 'from on high, from God's holy dwelling'. The judgment from then on is going to be carried out against the pagan world as in Joel 4.16 where this text reappears. Probably Amos 1.2 is the work of a redactor inspired by Amos 3.4 (the lion who roars) and 9.3 (Carmel), as well as by Jer. 2.15 (where the same verbs occur), shortly before or shortly after the destruction of Jerusalem in 587 BCE. In the rest of the book of Amos, the terminology of theophany coincides with the theme of holy war (Crenshaw 1968: 203). An example would be Amos 5.17: 'I will pass through your midst' which recalls Exod. 12.12: 'That night I will go through Egypt'. The religious ideology of war was common to the whole ancient Near East. In the Hebrew Bible, it becomes a question of 'wars of YHWH', which gave rise to the ideology of the 'holy war', as may be seen in the Qumran writings (von Rad 1965; M. Weippert 1972: 460; Jones 1975: 642; van der Toorn 1987: 79).

These descriptions of theophanies, in prose as well as in poetry, are not exceptional in the hymnology and literature of the ancient Near East. Resemblances to Syro-Mesopotamian and Egyptian texts are not lacking. Prophets, psalmists and historiographers came under the influence of their environment, with its religious myths and rich symbolic iconography. While not neglecting such contacts, we should recognize the originality of biblical theophanies. God, the only God, is in control of the obscure forces of nature and of chaos: clouds in the sky, waters of the sea, monsters of the deep, etc. The earth quakes at the divine approach. God appears in order to crush the pagan nations and deliver the Israelite people. As has already been stated, it is from the time of the exile, when Israel found herself dispersed in the pagan world, that a literary symbiosis takes place. The allusions to oriental myths becomes more frequent (Stolz 1970: 60; Keel 1978; Kratz 1979; Ringgren 1981: 383). But what is involved in this case would be completely demythologized stereotyped phrases, purified of any polytheistic taint. In any case, these features borrowed from neighbouring peoples cannot be interpreted as indications for early dating. Always of interest in the eyes of historians, they have only a secondary value for the biblical theologian and the believer.

Chapter 6

THEOPHANIES OF THE DIVINE NAME

The ancient theophanic narratives and poems which recalled the interventions of YHWH on behalf of the people were reread and recited during the liturgical celebrations which actualized their past reality. In the period of the monarchy, the faithful of Jerusalem along with the pilgrims to Jerusalem celebrated in the Temple each year the three major feasts: Passover, Weeks (or Pentecost) and Tabernacles (*Sukkoth*). The ritual was meant to 'represent', or rather, 're-present' the history of salvation in order to create in Israel the consciousness of the continuing presence of YHWH in the midst of the people and the enduring power of the divine promises. Some rituals were bound to recall pagan ceremonies, but they acquired in Israel a special meaning which could not be reduced to any polytheistic ideology.

How could YHWH continue to appear in the Temple in Jerusalem? It was through the solemn proclamation of the divine name and the mysterious presence of God's glory. G. von Rad (1950: 430) and A. Weiser (1950: 523) showed how ch. 33 of Exodus laid the foundation for a whole cultic etiology, portrayed in the psalms. Even if they could not see God face to face, the permanent or occasional guests in the Temple could meet God in this divine home, bow down before God's glory and invoke the divine name, in an authentic experience of theophany. At that time the mighty deeds of YHWH, the great moments in the history of salvation, were called to mind (Schottroff 1964). It is likely that these liturgical re-enactments had an influence on the narratives of the events that they were commemorating (Beyerlin 1961; H.-P. Müller 1964: 183). The historian must take this into account. However, it is quite right to analyse these texts in their definitive configuration in order to rediscover the religious ideas that they preserved for the faithful of the Second Temple.

The existence of these cultic theophanies is accepted by many exe-

getes (Mowinckel, Weiser, Kaiser, Beyerlin, *et al.*). According to
Jeremias (1965: 121, 146), they could have as their primitive *Sitz im
Leben* the songs of victory (referred to in the preceding chapter) in
which Israel celebrated the Day of YHWH (cf. Mettinger 1982: 32;
Gonçalves 1986: 244).

Divine Names

According to the Semitic mentality, the name brings to mind the mystery of the personality; it is the surrogate for the incommunicable 'I',
as well as its voiced expression, its social manifestation.[1] This is all the
more true when it is question of the deity (Grether 1934; Tillich
1960: 55; Besnard 1962; Lévêque 1970: 148; de Vaux 1983: 48). The
worship and the celebration of the names of gods and goddesses are
attested in the hymns of the whole ancient Near East: Mesopotamia
(W. Schulz 1931: 895), Syro-Palestine, Asia Minor. In Egypt, the
name defined the qualities and power of the gods, so that each deity
possessed several names. As a result, we find such frequently used
formulas as 'in your name...', 'in your quality as...' (Barucq and
Daumas 1980: 536). There were secret names for the supreme god:
'One would drop dead of fright if one pronounced this name, intentionally or not. Not even a god knew how to call him by this name.
Hidden ['*mn*] is his name, it is so mysterious' (*Hymn to Amon*; Barucq
and Daumas 1980: 124). In magic, the evocation of the divine name
was essential; to know the name of the god was to have his power at
one's disposal, to have a hold over him. In Israel, where every kind of
magic was proscribed and where the carved image of the deity was
prohibited, the divine name acquired a special importance. It was the
equivalent of an image that was not just auditory, but visual in taking
on the role of a duplicate of the divine essence. The sacred
tetragrammaton YHWH was written, but there came a time when it
was no longer pronounced; it became a sort of hypostasis like the
Spirit or wisdom. Beginning with the exile, the name of YHWH was
the very equivalent of YHWH (Horst 1947: 19; van der Woude 1976:
956; Hayward 1981).[2] The Israelites avoided pronouncing the names

---

1. Examples of this may be seen in Exod. 31.2; Num. 1.17; Isa. 41.25; 45.3;
Luke 1.63; Jn 3.18.
2. Cf. Pss. 7.18; 9.11; 18.50; 68.5; 74.7; 86.12; 92.2; Isa. 25.1; 26.8; 56.6;

of pagan deities, which would give them the appearance of being real (Exod. 23.13); they vilified them at every opportunity; for instance, Ba'al becomes *Bōšet*, 'shame' (2 Sam. 2.8; 4.4; 11.21; etc.). But pronouncing the divine name, invoking it, proclaiming it, all these really actualize the presence of YHWH among God's own people in the context of a cultic theophany, and this becomes one of the most important acts of worship (Mettinger 1982: 125). As F. Horst writes, God allows this self-identification with this name: the name is the *Aussen-Ich* (the 'external-I') of God.

According to the Yahwist tradition, the name of YHWH was invoked for the first time by the descendants of Seth (Gen. 4.26), near relatives of the Moabites according to Num. 24.17. According to Gen. 13.4, Abram, who had erected an altar between Bethel and Ai, invoked the name of YHWH there; he did the same at Beer-sheba (Gen. 21.33). Isaac followed his example (Gen. 26.25). But according to the Elohist and Priestly traditions, it is to Moses that the name of God was revealed for the first time (Exod. 3.14; 6.3). God proclaimed this name to Moses (Exod. 33.19) in adding to it the formula often repeated in the Deuteronomic and post-exilic writings, especially in the psalms:[1] 'YHWH, a merciful and gracious God, slow to anger, full of faithfulness and loyalty...' (Exod. 34.6; Sakenfeld 1978: 122). This commentary on the sacred name is equivalent to a description of 'divine principles'; it defines the behaviour of the God of the Covenant towards Israel, YHWH's 'first-born' (Exod. 4.22).

In the Covenant Code (Exod. 23.20-21) God says to Israel: 'I am going to send an angel before you to guard you. Listen to my voice...for my name is in that angel.' The Angel in this case possesses all authority directly from God who affirms at the beginning of the code (Exod. 20.24) that the divine presence is in every place where God's name is invoked: 'In whatever place I choose for the remembrance of my name, I will come to you and bless you'. As N. Lohfink (1984b: 297) notes, this is a fundamental text, since it forms perhaps the basis for the formulas which advocate the centralization of the cult. The invocation of the name of YHWH actualizes the presence

Mal. 3.16; etc.
1. Num. 14.18; Deut. 4.31; 5.9-10; Jer. 3.12; Isa. 57.15; 63.7; Joel 2.13; Jonah 4.2; Nah. 1.3; Ezra 9.13; Neh. 9.17, 31; 2 Chron. 30.9; Pss. 78.38; 86.15; 103.8; 111.4; 116.5; 145.8.

of God who, while remaining invisible, stays close to those who are God's own (Deut. 4.7; 30.14; cf. Ps. 148.14) in the midst of the people (Deut. 6.15; 7.21; Ezek. 37.26); God's property, heritage, possession and personal portion,[1] the people who bear the divine name (Sir. 36.11).

This is what is expressed in the formula: 'My name is pronounced over Israel'.[2] Pronouncing one's own name over someone or something is to affirm an exclusive ownership as if they bore one's seal or signature (2 Sam. 12.28; Ps. 49.12; Isa. 4.1). We should mention here the priestly blessing that Aaron and his sons recited (Num. 6.24-27; Jagersma 1982: 131). They pronounced the name of YHWH three times; the formulary concludes in this way: 'May they put my name on the children of Israel, and I will bless them'. This blessing which inspired Psalm 67 (Auneau 1984: 1241) is the central theme in the Psalms of 'Ascents', according to K. Seybold (1979: 264). Its formulation could apply to the Ark (2 Sam. 6.2 = 1 Chron. 13.6; cf. Jer. 7.12), to the Temple,[3] to the city of Jerusalem.[4] In a universalist perspective, the post-exilic conclusion of Amos 9.12, repeated in Acts 15.16-17, applies this formula to Edom and other pagan nations 'on whom my name has been pronounced', that is to say, 'I am their Lord, as ruler of the universe'.

It is interesting that this theme already appears in the 14th century BCE with regard to Jerusalem in Amarna Letter 287 (lines 60-63): 'Abdu-Heba, prince of Jerusalem, writes to Pharaoh Akh-en-Aton to have him send archers quickly in order to save Jerusalem, the city where the king "has set his name for ever"' (de Vaux 1978: 104-105; *ANET*, 488).

In relation to the Deuteronomic law on centralization of cult at Jerusalem, towards the end of the monarchy, various formulas express the essential connection existing between the sacred name and the

1. Exod. 19.5; Deut. 7.6; 14.2, 21; 26.18; Ps. 135.4; Mal. 3.17.
2. Deut. 28.10; Jer. 14.9; 15.16; Isa. 43.7; 44.5; 63.19; 2 Chron. 7.14; cf. Rev. 7.3; 14.1.
3. 1 Kgs 8.43 = 2 Chron. 6.33; Jer. 7.10-11, 14, 30; 32.34; 34.15; 1 Macc. 7.37; Bar. 2.26.
4. Isa. 1.26; 60.14; 62.4, 12; Jer. 25.29; 33.16; Zech. 8.3; Dan. 9.18-19; Bar. 4.30; 5.4. On two silver amulets recently discovered in Jerusalem and dating from the 7th century BCE, G. Barkay has read the text of the priestly blessing (1986: 29-30).

sanctuary of the Temple (de Vaux 1967a: 219; H. Weippert 1980: 76; Laberge 1985: 209). The most detailed formulas would be the oldest. We may recall the beginning of the Song of Moses and Miriam: 'YHWH is a warrior; YHWH is the name' (Exod. 15.3). This text is repeated at the beginning of the Song of Judith (16.2). Some of the formulas used are: 'The place where YHWH your God will choose to make a dwelling for this name';[1] 'The place that YHWH your God will choose to put this name' (Deut. 12.5, 21; 14.24): the Temple (1 Kgs 9.3; 2 Kgs 21.7 = 2 Chron. 33.7), Jerusalem (1 Kgs 11.36; 14.21 = 2 Chron. 12.13; 2 Kgs 21.4); 'A house where my name will be' (1 Kgs 8.16; = 2 Chron. 6.5; 1 Kgs 8.29; 2 Kgs 23.27 = 2 Chron. 7.16; this refers to Jerusalem in 2 Kgs 21.4, 7; 2 Chron. 6.5; 33.4); 'A house for the name of Yhwh' (2 Sam. 7.13; 1 Kgs 3.2; 5.17, 19; 8.17-18, 20, 44, 48); 'The house that I have consecrated to my name' (1 Kgs 9.7; 2 Chron. 7.16, 20; 20.8).

Paronomasia

In the Deuteronomistic writings, the closely related formulas, *lĕšakkēn šĕmô* (*šĕmî*) *šām, lāśûm šĕmô* (*šĕmî*) *šām*, etc.,[2] make use of a mnemonic play on words already present in the Yahwist tradition. When Abraham pitched his tent between Bethel and Ai (Gen. 13.4; cf. 21.33; 26.25), he called there (*šām*) on the name (*šēm*) of YHWH. In 2 Sam. 6.2, this play on words with *šēm* and *šām* is found in some thirty Masoretic manuscripts and these are supported by the Syriac version. In the received text, they 'set out from Baalah of Judah to bring up from there [*miššām*] the Ark of God over which there was pronounced a name, the name [*šēm šēm*] of YHWH Sabaoth seated upon the Cherubim'. This is a surprising doublet which is omitted from the Septuagint; we can restore *šām*, 'there', by adopting the reading of the Hebrew manuscripts mentioned above: 'over which there was pronounced there the name...' A scribe or copyist probably tried to eliminate the allusion to a centre of a heterodox cult, named after Ba'al, where they would have venerated the holy Ark. This place, *ba'ălê yĕhûdâ* (1 Chron. 13.6), is none other, in fact, than

---

1. Deut. 14.23; 16.2, 6, 11; Jer. 7.12; Ezra 6.12 (Aramaic); Neh. 1.9.
2. Deut. 12.5-7, 11, 21; 14.23-24; 16.2, 6, 11; 26.2; 1 Kgs 8.16, 29; 9.3; 11.36; 14.21; 2 Kgs 23.27; 2 Chron. 6.5-6; 7.6; 12.13; Ezra 6.12; Neh. 1.9.

Qiryat Baʿal, Kiriath-baal, which is also called *Qiryat Yĕʿārîm*, Kiriath-jearim (Josh. 15.60; 18.14; Ps. 132.6) where the Ark remained for some time (1 Sam. 7.1).

The Deuteronomic Law on having just one sanctuary brought about the suppression of outlying sanctuaries, at least in principle, since archaeological discoveries indicate the persistence of heterodox cults denounced by the prophets. As Jer. 7.12 reminds the people of Judah, the sanctuary at Shilo (1 Sam. 1.3) where God had formerly made the divine name to dwell (*šĕmî šām*, 'my name there') was destroyed by the Philistines (Ps. 78.60) and the same thing will one day happen to the Temple of Zion ('the house which bears my name', Jer. 7.14).

The paronomasia is extended further in 1 Kgs 8.29 (= 2 Chron. 6.20) by the infinitive *lišmōaʿ*, 'to hear': 'My name will be there so as to hear the prayer...' However, it is the adverb *šām*, 'there', which acquires in these texts a quite special meaning. Such is the case in Ezek. 20.28-29. The prophet reproaches the Israelites for their idolatrous practices in the same terms as 1 Kgs 3.2 : 'The people put their trust in the high places, for they had not yet built a house for the name of YHWH at that time'. Ezekiel then spoke this oracle: '*There* they offered sacrifices, *there* they presented their annoying offerings, *there* they brought their pleasing aromas, *there* they poured out their libations. Then I said to them, "What is this high place [*bāmâ*] that you should go [*habbāʾîm*] *there*?" And so they have called its name [*šĕmāh*] Bamah [*bāmâ*] to this day.' Here Ezekiel multiplies ironical puns on the word *bāmâ* and the paronomasia *šām/šēm*. The same thing is done in Ezek. 43.7: '*There* I will dwell in the midst of the Israelites forever. The house of Israel will no longer defile my holy name' (cf. Ezek. 35.10; Exod. 29.43).

Paronomasia is further developed with the proper names *Šĕlōmōh*, Solomon, 'The Peaceful'; *Šûlammît*, 'The Peaceful' (Cant 7.1; Tournay 1988: 44-46); *Yĕrûšālēm*, 'Jerusalem', and its current etymology from *šālôm*, 'peace', *šālēm*, 'peaceful, whole, complete, flourishing'. According to Ezek. 40.1, at the beginning of that 'Torah' (cf. Ezek. 43.12), Ezekiel is taken *over there* by God to a high mountain where a magnified and idealized Jerusalem is built. At the end of this same 'Torah' (Ezek. 48.35) we read: 'From this day on, the name of the city will be *YHWH-šammâ*', that is, 'YHWH is *there*'. It is *there* that the nations will be gathered for the Judgment, we read in Joel 4.11-12.

A post-exilic text in the book of Jeremiah (3.17) echoes Ezekiel with regard to the disappearance of the Ark in 587 BCE: 'In the future they will call Jerusalem "Throne of YHWH"; all the nations will converge on her in the name of YHWH, at Jerusalem'. The last three words (name, YHWH, Jerusalem), omitted by the LXX, are sometimes thought to be an addition, but still a very significant one. Once again we have here the theme of the pagan nations going up to Jerusalem which has become the religious metropolis of humanity, as we see in Psalm 87: 'It is there [*šām*] that such a person is born' (vv. 4 and 6).

A number of psalms make use of paronomasia based on the name of Jerusalem, sometimes abbreviated to *šālēm*. One example is Ps. 76.2-4 which may be alluding to the unexpected lifting of the siege of Jerusalem in 701 BCE by the army of Sennacherib: 'In Israel great is the name [*šēm*] of God whose tent is pitched in Salem [*šālēm*]...There [*šām*] God has broken the lightning-flashes of the bow.' Psalm 122 accumulates even more puns on the name of Jerusalem: 'Jerusalem..., to there [*šām*] the tribes go up...to give thanks to the name [*šēm*] of YHWH. For there [*šām*] are set the thrones...Pray for the peace of Jerusalem [*ša'ălû šĕlôm Yĕrûšālēm*], may they rest secure [*yišlāyû*], those who love you! May there be peace [*šālôm*]...tranquility [*šalwâ*] ...I will say: Peace [*šālôm*] be within you!' The theme of Jerusalem as a city of peace (*šālôm*) appears also in Gen. 14.18; Ezek. 13.16; Tob. 13.14; Jdt. 4.4; Heb 7.2 (Durham 1983: 272).

These texts show that the adverb *šām*, 'there', indirectly came to designate Jerusalem, dwelling of YHWH. The psalmists were fond of this word to call to mind the deliverance of the holy city: 'There, trembling seizes them' (Ps. 48.7; cf. 46.9); 'There, they began to be deadly afraid' (Ps. 14.5 = 53.6); 'There, they have fallen, the evil-doers' (Ps. 36.13; Tournay 1983a: 8; 1983b: 329). Here are some more general examples: 'There, our joy is in God' (Ps. 66.16; vv. 2 and 4 celebrate the *šēm*; Crüsemann 1969: 181); 'God will save Zion... there they will dwell;...those who love God's name will inhabit it' (Ps. 69.36-37); 'There, I will make a horn grow for David' (Ps. 132.17).

In addition to the psalms, we may cite Isa. 33.20-21: 'May your eyes see Jerusalem. It is there that YHWH shows us divine power'; Isa. 65.9: 'My servants dwell there'; 'There, more new-born children...'; Joel 4.12: 'the valley of Jehoshaphat! It is there that I will sit in judgment' (cf. Zeph. 1.14). We may cite as well a text from Cave 4 (Col. IV.2-4) at Qumran, drawn from the 'Words of the Enlightened': 'Your dwelling [?]...repose [?] in Jeru[salem, the city which] you have chosen out of the whole world so that [you]r [name] may be found there forever'. There is a reference in lines 12-13 to Zion and peace (*šālôm*) (Carmignac 1963: 304; Baillet 1982: 143).

These texts inspired by the Deuteronomistic tradition are not earlier than the end of the monarchic period. T.N.D. Mettinger (1982: 61) tried to determine the context of the formulas *lĕšakkēn/lāśûm šĕmî šām* ('to settle/to put my name there'), etc. by distinguishing several redactional levels. The discussion is still open (McBride 1969; McConville 1979: 149).

The important thing to note is that a whole theological doctrine in regard to the divine name is evolving in this way. The veneration and proclamation of the ineffable name amounts to a kind of theophanic manifestation of the divinity.

This may already be seen in the royal liturgy of Psalms 20 and 21, a prayer and thanksgiving for the king on the occasion of his enthronement or on the anniversary of that event: 'May the name of Jacob's God keep you safe!' (20.2; cf. 44.5-6); 'May we unfurl our banners in the name of our God' (20.6); 'We call on the name of YHWH our God' (20.8). This liturgy is doubtless contemporaneous with the song of victory of Exodus 15 which begins with a proclamation of the name of YHWH in v. 3, as well as with Zeph. 3.12-13 where God announces that the Remnant of Israel will seek refuge in the Name of YHWH (Tournay 1959: 161).

Post-exilic Texts

Beginning with the exile, the proclamation and the invocation of the divine name occupies an eminent place in the hymns and prayers of Israel.[1] Such is the case right from the beginning of the Song of Moses (Deut. 32.3) (Carillo Alday 1970; Strauss 1985: 103): 'I will proclaim the name of YHWH'. We read in Psalm 89, which is also exilic: 'Tabor and Hermon shout with joy at your name' (v. 13), and later on, 'In your name, they [the people] rejoice all day long' (v. 17). The

---

1. Pss. 79.6; 80.19; 99.6; 105.1; 116.4, 13, 17; Isa. 41.25; 45.3; 1 Kgs 18.24-25; Joel 3.5; Zech. 13.9; etc.

same thing is found in the great supplication of Isa. 63.7-64.11: 'God gained everlasting renown' (v. 12); 'a glorious name' (v. 14); 'Our redeemer, such is your name from of old' (v. 16); 'We have for a long time been people over whom you no longer reign and who no longer bear your name' (v. 19); 'Oh, if you would only tear the heavens open and come down... to make your name known to your adversaries' (63.19; 64.1); 'There is no longer anyone to call on your name' (64.6); In the book of Ezekiel, we find the phrase 'for the sake of your name'[1] more than thirty times. It had already appeared in the prayer of Jeremiah (14.7, 21) and is found as well in Isa. 48.9; 66.5. It also becomes a leitmotif in the psalms (Dreyfus 1979: 240).[2]

In Isa. 30.27 the name of YHWH is the the focal point of a theophany whose definitive text must be from the post-exilic period (Vermeylen 1977: 417; 1978: 720): 'See, here comes the name of YHWH, with blazing anger, with terrible threats, with lips brimming with fury, with a tongue like a consuming fire, and with a breath like a torrent overflowing and rising up to the neck'. The following verses bring to mind the joyful nocturnal feast (probably Passover; cf. Gonçalves 1986: 301, 472) when they went towards the mountain of YHWH, the Rock of Israel, whose majestic voice (= the thunder) is heard in fire, rain and hail. This anthological text reminds us of Pss. 18.13-14; 105.32; 148.8; Ezek. 38.22, not to mention Isa. 26.1ff.

In Exod. 9.16, God says to Pharaoh through Moses: 'Here is why I have preserved you: to make you see my face, so that my name may be made known through the whole world'. This text, quoted in Rom 9.17, need not belong to the Yahwist tradition. It is a theological commentary on the seventh plague, the hail; a redactor wanted to emphasize the importance of that event (Noth 1959: 62). The hail had already been mentioned at the end of the oracle of Isa. 30.30, previously quoted. Making the divine name known throughout the universe is a frequent theme in the psalter.[3]

We may recall too that the second part of the book of Isaiah gives prominence to this theme of the divine name: 'I am YHWH; this is my name, and my glory; I will not give it to another' (42.8; cf. 48.11). Name and glory are associated in Isa. 43.7 and 59.19, just as in Isa.

1. Ezek. 20.9, 14, 22, 44; 36.21, 22; 39.25; etc.; Dan. 3.34, 43 (Greek).
2. Pss. 23.3; 25.11; 31.4; 79.9; 106.8; 109.21; 143.11.
3. Pss. 8.2; 22.23; 102.22; 113.3; 148.13; cf. Mal. 1.11-14.

26.13, 15; Deut. 28.58; Mal. 2.2. Isaiah 40–55 ends with these words: 'This will bring YHWH renown' (55.13). God divided the waters of the Red Sea 'to gain everlasting renown' (Isa. 63.12). It should be kept in mind that the root of the word 'renown' is *nomen*, 'name'.

The proclamation of the name of YHWH is sometimes accompanied by a blessing (Lévêque, 1970: I, 202; Faur 1984–85, 41; *ThWAT*, I: 829ff.). 'To bless the name', a recurring phrase in Jewish liturgy, is found in Job 1.21 as well as in the doxology at the end of the 3rd book of psalms (72.19), and in Pss. 103.1; 113.2; 145.1; Tob. 8.5; 11.14. There were blessings 'in the name of YHWH' as well as in the name of Elohim or in any other divine name. It was the duty of the priests to pronounce such blessings (Deut. 10.8; 21.5; 1 Chron. 23.13). In the Hellenistic period, the high priest could pronounce the sacred name, YHWH, for the feast of *Yom Kippur* (Sir. 50.20-21; *Yom.* 3.8; 6.2) before coming down from the altar (Lev. 9.22), while raising his hands over the assembled people in order to bless them (van Cangh and van Esbroeck 1980: 311; Bauer 1984: 84). This was a liturgical theophany that concluded the ceremony.

On the contrary, one could profane the holy name, according to a phrase frequently used in Leviticus and the book of Ezekiel,[1] as well as in Jer. 34.16 and Amos 2.7 (Vermeylen 1978: 536; Martin-Achard 1984: 131). As well, one could scorn and insult the name (Ps. 74.10, 18).

The psalmists have many ways of employing this theme of the name, a quasi-sacramental symbol of the ineffable God with whom the believer could converse. More than 60 psalms make mention of it: to sing praise to the name (7.18; 18.50; 92.2), to call on the name (75.2, MT corrected; 80.19; cf. Isa. 26.13; Lam 3.55; Jdt. 16.1), to praise the name (69.31; 74.21; 113.1, 3; 145.2; cf. 1 Chron. 29.13),[2] to exalt the name (34.4), to give thanks to the name (44.9; 54.8; 140.14), to announce the name (22.23; cf. 102.22; Jn 17.6), to fear the name (61.6; 86.11; 102.16; cf. Isa. 59.19, MT; Mal. 3.16-20), to know the name (9.11; 91.14), to be saved by the name (54.3; 124.8; cf. 91.14-16), to love the name (5.12; 69.37; 119.132; Isa. 56.6), not to forget the name (44.21), to seek the name (83.17). As well, one should 'sanc-

---

1. Lev. 18.21; 19.12; 20.3; 21.6; 22.2, 32; Isa. 48.11 (versions); Ezek. 20.9, 14, 22, 39; 36.20-23.
2. A phrase occurring very frequently in the Qumran texts.

tify the name', since this name is holy[1] and awesome (111.9). In Ezek. 36.23, God proclaims: 'I will manifest the holiness of my great name which has been profaned among the nations, my name which you have profaned while in their midst; then the nations shall know that I am YHWH—when I will have manifested my holiness in you before their eyes'. Keeping holy the name demonstrates how great is this name (Pss. 76.2; 99.3; Mal. 1.11; Josh. 7.9; Tob. 11.14), and eternal (Ps. 135.13); good (Pss. 52.11; 54: 8), beautiful (Ps. 135.3; cf. Pss. 27.13; 90.17; Avishur 1976, 6), awesome (Pss. 99.3; 111.9; Deut. 28.58; Mal. 1.14), and great and mighty (Jer. 10.6).

A phrase close to this is 'to glorify the name' (Ps. 86.9, 12; Isa. 24.15; cf. Jn 12.28; Rev. 15.4), from which comes the phrase 'for the glory of this name' (Dreyfus 1962: 523).[2] Name and glory, associated in hymnody, bring to mind a theophanic manifestation of the invisible God, who becomes visible and audible at the same time (Pss. 63.3-5; 102.16-17, 22; 111.2-4).

Psalm 8

Psalm 8 must be given special consideration here, since it presents a whole theology of the divine name (Tournay 1971a: 18; Loretz 1971: 104; Rudolph 1977: 388; Beyerlin 1976: 1). The refrain (vv. 2 and 10) calls the name splendid, majestic (*'addîr*), an epithet applied to God in Pss. 76.5; 93.4 and Isa. 33.21. It is the only psalm in which God is addressed throughout in the second person (Crüsemann 1969: 289, 300), just as in the prayer of David (1 Chron. 29.10-19). The frequent echoes of the post-exilic writings[3] justify the placing of Psalm 8 in the Persian period. This marvellous name replicates (*tinnâ*; MT is obscure) the divine supra-celestial majesty through the mouths of children and the very young; God has made the divine name a stronghold in the face of all foes (false gods, infidels) in order to subdue enemies and rebels. The metaphor of a fortress is applied to the divine name in Prov. 18.10 as well: 'A strong tower, the name of

---

1. Isa. 29.23; 57.15; Pss. 33.21; 99.3; 103.1; 105.3; 106.47; 111.9; 145.21; Tob. 13.11. Cf. Lk. 1.49; 11.2; Mt. 6.9.

2. Pss. 29.2 (96.8); 66.2; 72.19; 79.9; Mic. 5.3; Neh. 9.5; cf. Pss. 48.11; 102.16; 105.3; 115.1; Mal. 2.2.

3. Neh 9.5; 10.30; Joel 1.20; 2.16, 22; 4.15-17; Job 7.17; Mal. 1.11; etc.

YHWH'. From the awakening of their consciences and their first attempts to speak, the young of Israel learned to repeat the divine name, the name of their heavenly parent and their redeemer. In this way they are already initiated into the liturgy of the Temple, just as in Ps. 148.12 and Joel 2.16. Having been adopted by YHWH, created in God's image and likeness, they participate in some way in the divine glory in order to exercise sovereignty over the universe and explicitly over all living things.

Consequently, we understand better the power that there must be in a prayer such as 'Remember your name' (Bar. 3.5). Even at night, the faithful remember the divine name (Ps. 119.55, 147, 148).

We must take note of the frequency with which the name is mentioned in the psalms of Asaph (Pss. 74, 75, 76, 79, 80, 83). This is a favourite theme of those Levites who will form the first group of singers after the resumption of worship in the Second Temple in 515 BCE. In this they are dependent on the Deuteronomistic tradition which lays stress on this calling on the name, a sign and a substitute for the hidden God, really but invisibly present among the people.

Divine Names

The reading (*qĕrê*) Adonai, 'Lord', gradually replaced the direct reading of the sacred tetragrammaton YHWH (*kĕtîb*) (Howard 1977: 63; Scholem 1981). In the Elohist collection of the psalter (Pss. 42-83), *Elohim*, 'God', occurs 200 times while YHWH occurs 44 times. Other divine titles (Freedman 1976: 55; Vigano 1976) also appear in psalmic compositions along with *El, Elohim, Eloah* (Lévêque 1970: I, 163).[1] We may mention as well *Shaddai* (Pss. 68.15; 91.1), found frequently in the books of Job and Ruth; it is the name of the God of the patriarchs in the Priestly tradition; it already occurs in Gen. 49.25 with *El*, and in Num. 24.4, 16 with *Elyon* (Rouillard 1985: 416); it is found in Ezek. 1.24, Isa. 13.6 and Joel 1.15. *Elyon*, a name derived from Ugaritic, means most high, sublime; it referred to Ba'al (Lack 1962: 44). It occurs in Ps. 21.8 (end of the monarchy) and in 22 other psalms, as well as in post-exilic texts (Deut. 32.8; Lam. 3.35, 38; Isa. 14.14; Gen. 14.18; Sir. 7.9, 15; 41.4; etc.; there is a euphemistic

---

1. Deut. 32.15, 17; Hab. 3.3; Pss. 18.32; 50.22; 114.7; 139.19; Prov. 30.5; Neh. 9.17; 1 Kgs 9.8 (re-reading); Job, 41 times; etc.

rereading in 1 Kgs 9.8). It has been proposed that this divine name be restored in Deut. 33.12 (LXX translates 'God'), 1 Sam. 2.10 (Tournay 1981b: 566), Pss. 7.9 and 106.7. This title occurs again in 2 Macc. 3.31, Greek Sirach and Jewish inscriptions. Later on, out of deference to the divine transcendence, they will go so far as to use heaven (Abel and Starcky 1961: 14),[1] place (Esth. 4.14), blessed one (Mk 14.61), and the power (Mt. 26.64) as substitutes for the divine name. The divine name is incommunicable (Wis. 14.21) and should not even be pronounced (Moore 1927: 423; Larcher 1985: 824).

In the New Testament (*TDNT*, V: 270; Dupont 1960: 544), it is Jesus who receives the name which up until then had been reserved for God alone: the Lord (in Greek, *kyrios*). 'Before Abraham came to be, I am', Jesus declares (Jn 8.58; cf. 8.24, 28; 13.19). According to Phil. 2.9-11, God has bestowed on Jesus the name which is above every other name, not only in this age, Eph. 1.21 adds, but even in the age to come. The name that Jesus receives as an inheritance is incomparably above that of the angels (Heb. 1.4). He is truly Christ and Lord (Acts 2.21, 36; 3.16). It is for the sake of this name that the Apostles suffer (Acts 5.40-41 ; 21.13; 1 Pet. 4.14; 3 Jn 7) and it is this name that they announce (Acts 4.10ff.; 5.28, 40; 8.12; 9.14ff.; 11.20). Christians are those who invoke the name of Jesus (Acts 2.38; 4.12; 9.21; 22.16; 1 Cor. 1.2; 2 Tim. 2.22). Baptism is conferred in the name of Jesus and is received by invoking the name of Jesus the Lord. The power of this name manifests itself in favour of those who believe in him (Acts 19.13ff.; Mt. 8.10). It is in the name of Jesus that the miracles described in the Acts of the Apostles are performed (Acts 3.6; 4.7; 16.18; 19.13; cf. Lk. 9.49; 10.17). And it is in Jesus' name that Christians should address their prayers to God (Jn 14.13; 15.16; 16.24). It is by believing that Jesus is the Christ, the Son of God, that they will have life in his name (Jn 20.3 1; cf. Rev. 14.1; 22.4).

---

1. 1 Macc. 2.21; 3.18, 50; 4.10, 24, 40; 12.15; 16.3; Dan. 4.23; Mt. 3.2.

Chapter 7

THEOPHANIES OF THE DIVINE GLORY

The two themes of name and glory are closely connected. But while theophanies of the divine name emphasize the transcendence of the invisible God enthroned in heaven (Deut. 4.36; Isa. 66.1; Ps. 11.4; etc.), theophanies of the glory (*kābôd*) of YHWH, in other words, of the divine majesty, emphasize rather the immanence of God, present in the midst of the people as ruler, shepherd, redeemer (Stein 1939; Rentdorff 1961: 26; Mollat 1962: 412; *ThWAT*, IV: 23; Struppe 1988).

The glory of YHWH is always connected with a holy place from the time of the Exodus onward: the encampment in the desert, Sinai, Shiloh (1 Sam. 3.21), Jerusalem. During the Exodus God manifested the divine glory outside the Israelite camp. The Tent of Meeting is located in fact outside the camp instead of inside (Exod. 33.7ff.; Num. 2.2). God comes down in the cloud to speak to Moses at the entrance of the Tent, the place for oracular consultations. The theophany takes place at the entrance and ends when the cloud departs (Haran 1960a: 50; Mettinger 1982: 80).

The cloud accompanies the theophanies of the glory. In the ancient texts, it is a thick dark cloud, a storm cloud filled with water ready to be poured down on the earth to fertilize it. The imagery of the Canaanite god of the thunderstorm is here demythologized while still evoking the primitive meaning of the word *kābôd*, 'heaviness, thickness'. Such a cloud is a blessing for the country, especially in the autumn, after the scorching summer.[1] This explains why the autumn feasts, in the month of Tishri, took on such importance and why the glory of YHWH was celebrated in them. It is not without reason that Psalm 29 which describes the divine thunderstorm concludes with the

1. Deut. 11.14; 28.12; Hag. 1.10-11; Zech. 8.12; 14.17; Joel 2.23; etc.

acclamation: 'Glory!' (v. 9). Many psalms are to be connected with the celebrations of the month of Tishri (New Year, Atonement, Booths; cf. Springer 1979): the rainy season in Judah generally begins with a thunderstorm. It is no accident that the Priestly tradition closely connects the theme of glory with that of the thunderstorm.

Isaiah 6

Among the theophanies of the divine glory, the one which the prophet Isaiah describes (Isa. 6) and which took place about 740 BCE occupies a special place. Prior to this, the prophet Micaiah, son of Imlah, had seen YHWH seated on a throne and the whole host of heaven standing in the divine presence, on the right and on the left (1 Kgs 22.19). Isaiah himself sees YHWH seated on a very high throne (Greenfield 1985: 193), with the divine train filling the temple. Seraphim were stationed above YHWH and cried to one another: 'Holy, holy, holy is YHWH Sabaoth whose glory fills the whole earth'. Isaiah cries out that he is lost, for he has seen with his eyes the ruler, YHWH Sabaoth. The divine glory is here the majesty of the ruler of Israel (1 Sam. 8.7; 12.12; Exod. 15.18; etc.). The sanctuary was filled with smoke, equivalent to the cloud which filled the Tent in the desert as well as Solomon's Temple (1 Kgs 8.10-12; Ezek. 10.4; Wildberger 1972: 244; Cazelles 1984: 1411). But here it is stated that the glory fills the whole earth. This phrase however can be taken in a restricted sense here: it refers then to the land of Israel, and not to the universe. We may compare Num. 14.21-23, attributed to the combined Yahwist–Elohist tradition: 'As truly as I am living, as truly as the glory of YHWH fills the whole earth, all those who saw my glory and the signs I worked in Egypt and in the desert and who have put me to the test ten times already by not listening to me, not one of them, I swear, will see the land that I promised to their fathers'. In the same way Josh. 3.10 speaks of 'the living God' and 3.11, 13 of the 'Lord of the whole earth' (Langlamet 1969a: 113). The phrase 'the whole earth' refers solely to the whole land of Israel, the promised land. The same thing is found in Hab. 2.14: 'The land shall be filled with the knowledge of the glory of YHWH, as water covers the sea'. Isa. 11.9 repeats this text but omits 'the glory' (Vermeylen 1977: 275).

Ezekiel

In Ezekiel the concept of the glory of YHWH acquires a new dimension. The horizon is expanding. Ezekiel receives his inaugural vision in Babylon, by the River Chebar, far from the destroyed Temple. The vision was of a stormy wind, an immense cloud, a flashing fire with brightness all around it; that radiance looked like a rainbow in the clouds on a rainy day, such was the appearance of the surrounding brightness. This was the likeness of the glory of YHWH, the prophet tells us (Ezek. 1.28). Moreover, this glory was mobile; the Cherubim are no longer merely the supports for the divine throne, but propel the celestial chariot, the *merkābâ* (Sir. 49.8; Greenberg 1983). An imagery that is entirely Syro-Mesopotamian is brought to mind here, especially the motif of the storm god's chariot (Vanel 1965), which is found in Deut. 33.26, Isa. 66.15 and in the psalms (18.11; 65.12; 68.18; 104.3). Ezekiel sees the glory leaving the Temple (11.22-24). When it returns (43.2-5), again it 'will fill' the Temple (44.4). The noise of the 'animals' resembles the sound of mighty waters, the voice of Shaddai (1.24; 43.2). This glory presents a luminous, dazzling, flashing appearance, analogous to the halo (*melammu*) surrounding Babylonian divinities and kings (Cassin 1968; Keel 1977a; Marböck 1981: 109). After Ezekiel, the theme of light and fire continues throughout the whole Priestly tradition (Westermann 1974: 116; 1978: 19, 169). As for the mobility of that glory, it ensured the ubiquity of the divine presence which was to accompany the exiles. It will manifest itself among the nations. In the prophecy against Gog, God says that the divine glory will be placed among the peoples, for all the peoples will see the judgment that God will carry out and the hand that will be laid on them (Ezek. 39.21). YHWH will be glorified in the midst of Zion, the navel of the earth (38.12). Even in Sidon, the divine holiness will be manifest (28.22). Following Isaiah, Ezekiel lays stress on the divine holiness: God is holy (39.7); God's name is holy (20.39; 36.20-22; 39.7; 43.7-8); God dwells in this holy mountain (20;40; 28.14), in this holy place (42.13). Since the Ark has disappeared, the rebuilt Temple will be the site of the throne of YHWH, the place of the divine feet (Ezek. 43.7); the sanctuary will fulfil the function of the Ark, as indicated as well in Jer. 3.16-17. It is there that YHWH will manifest the divine holiness in Israel in the midst of the nations (Ezek. 39.27; cf. 2 Macc. 14.35-36).

Second Isaiah

Such a universalism centralized in Zion is the main theme of the second part of Isaiah. The prologue (Isa. 40.1-8), which takes its inspiration from the inaugural vision of Isaiah in Isaiah 6 (Tournay 1971c: 288), has two voices in dialogue, corresponding to the two Seraphim of Isaiah 6. As Isa. 40.5 says, the glory of YHWH will be revealed and all flesh will suddenly[1] 'see it, for the mouth of God has spoken'. God will add to the divine glory by bringing back the people from the exile (Elliger 1970: 20); God will be glorified (verb, *p'r*) also in the servant. R. Lack (1973) has shown that the theme of glory structures the whole final section of the book of Isaiah. In the same way, even the desert and the arid steppe will see the glory of YHWH, the splendour of the God of Israel (Isa. 35.2). However, such a theophany will no longer give rise to trembling and terror as in the time of the Exodus (Heb. 12.18-21); on the contrary, there will be exultation all through nature: mountains, hills and forests will joyfully cry out (Isa. 44.23; 49.13; 55.12), a theme repeated in the psalms (Pss. 89.13; 96.11-12; 98.7-8).

YHWH Sabaoth, creator and spouse of the new Jerusalem, is the God of the whole earth (Isa. 54.5). This latter phrase is to be understood in this case in the universal sense as in Hab. 3.3d: 'The earth is full of the (divine) glory'; Mic. 4.13: 'the Lord of all the earth' (cf. Zech. 4.14; 6.5; Jdt. 2.5; Rev. 11.4); and the doxology of the third book of the psalter: 'Blessed forever be this name of glory, the whole earth is filled with divine glory' (Ps. 72.19). The concluding section of the book of Isaiah develops these broad perspectives. The glory of YHWH has risen on Zion, the glorious city, and all the nations will walk toward this light (Isa. 60.1-3). All the kings will see this glory (Isa. 62.2). 'They will announce the glory of YHWH among the nations who have never seen it' (Isa. 66.19). These theophanic perspectives are found throughout the psalter: 'All the peoples will see this glory' (Ps. 97.6); 'All the kings of the earth will see this glory; when YHWH shall rebuild Zion, God will be seen in divine glory' (Ps. 102.16-17). The Masoretic Text has softened the verb 'they will see' (found in some manuscripts) to 'they will revere' (a *yod* is added). The same modification appears in Isa. 59.19: 'Then they will see

---

1. Literally: together, at one and the same time, at the same time. This adverb occurs frequently in Isa. 40ff.

[some manuscripts: 'they will revere'] the name of YHWH from the west, and from the east the divine glory'. The idea behind the modification is that if the Israelites cannot see God, how would this be possible for the pagans?

As Ezek. 44.4 had announced, the divine glory filled the new Temple, in 515 BCE, according to Haggai (2.7; cf. Sir. 36.13), and that glory was to surpass the old (2.9). The psalmist insists: 'The glory will dwell in our land' (85.10). God resides in this way in Zion in the midst of the people (Exod. 25.8; 29.45-46). For Jerusalem, God is an encircling wall of fire and truly its glory (Zech. 2.9; Rev. 21.11). According to a post-exilic text, Isa. 11.10, for the 'root of Jesse' from which the messianic shoot will come, 'the glory will be his dwelling'. According to the 'great apocalypse' of the book of Isaiah, God will reign in glory in the presence of the Elders (Isa. 24.23) and will give shelter from the rain, shade from the heat (25.4); God will prepare on Zion, the new Sinai, a feast for all peoples (25.6). Doubtless from the beginning of the Hellenistic period, these texts are presenting again the ideas of Exod. 24.9-11 (Wildberger 1978: 899, 960); in addition, they correspond to Isa. 4.5-6 which may allude to the feast of *Sukkoth* (Booths): God will create over all Mount Zion, over those assembled on Zion, a cloud by day and smoke with the brightness of flaming fire by night. And over all, the glory (of YHWH) will be a canopy, a leafy booth, to give shade in time of extreme heat and to serve as a refuge and shelter from the storm and rain. Like Isa. 25.4, this post-exilic addition to the book of Isaiah revives the motifs of the Exodus theophanies: smoke, cloud, fire, along with the imagery too of the nuptial canopy which evokes the concluding of the New Covenant predicted by Hos. 2.21-22 (cf. Joel 2.16; Ps. 19.5; Rev. 7.15; 15.8).

This is the context in which two passages from Exodus must be located: 16.6ff. and 24.15b-18a. According to Exod. 16.6ff., Moses and Aaron announce that the community of discontented Israelites will see in the morning the glory of YHWH, when God will give the manna to the people to satisfy their hunger. In looking back toward the desert, the community saw the glory of YHWH which appeared in the cloud (v. 10). According to Exod. 24.15ff., 'the cloud covered the mountain; the glory of YHWH remained on Mount Sinai and the cloud covered it for six days. On the seventh day [God] called to Moses from inside the cloud. The glory of YHWH became visible to the Israelites under the appearance of a devouring fire, at the top of the mountain.

Moses entered the cloud and went up the mountain.' The cloud and the glory covered the mountain just as later on they filled the Tent of Meeting and the Zion sanctuary (Avishur 1976: 15). We cannot but admire here the coherence of all these texts of the Jerusalem Priestly school. The theme of the divine glory forms a frame (Exod. 24.16-17; 29.43; 40.34-35) around the sections in which the Priestly redactor describes the regulations concerning worship in the desert (chs. 25–31) and then the carrying out of those regulations (chs. 35–40).

Leviticus 9

Originating in these same milieus, Leviticus 9 precisely describes what was meant by a 'ritual theophany' (Elliger 1966: 121; Snaith 1967; Molle 1973: 191; Porter 1976; Wenham 1978; Struppe 1988). Everything takes place, in fact, as if one were in the Jerusalem Temple. This chapter has a special vocabulary and it has been suggested that it is a continuation of Exodus 40. According to M. Noth (1965: 76), these latter chapters in Exodus together with Leviticus 9 would be the beginning of the primitive Priestly writing. Eight days after the consecration of Aaron and the first priests, sacrifices had to be offered by them: several animals together with a grain offering mixed with oil. Moses then declares: ' "For today YHWH is going to appear to you" [v. 4; the versions have a participle here]. They bring everything Moses has ordered to the front of the Tent of Meeting. Then the whole community approaches and stands before YHWH. Then Moses says: "This is what YHWH has ordered you to do, so that the glory of YHWH would appear [*wĕyērā'*] to you" ' (v. 6). There follows the description of the ritual for the sacrifices (vv. 8-22). Then Aaron raises his hands over the people and blesses them, then steps down, having completed the offering of the sacrifices. The text adds: 'Moses and Aaron then enter the Tent of Meeting, and when they come out again, they bless all the people. Then the glory of YHWH appears [*wayyērā'*] to all the people. Fire comes out from before YHWH and consumes on the altar the holocaust and the fat. All the people see [*wayyarĕ'*] this, shout with joy and fall prostrate' (vv. 22-24).

The Priestly redactor has transferred to Mosaic times the ritual of the Second Temple. He really intends to describe a liturgical theophany here, for he insists on the manifestation of the glory of YHWH before all the people (cf. Num. 14.10; 16.19; 17.7; 20.6). This theophany, with the fire, sanctions the sacrifices, and more generally the Aaronite priesthood. Corresponding to the fire on the altar (Lev. 9.10, 14, 17, 20) is the divine fire (v. 24); it was the same in the presence of Abraham (Gen. 15.17), Gideon (Judg. 6.21), Manoah (Judg. 13.20), David and Solomon (1 Kgs 8.38f.; 1 Chron. 21.26; 2 Chron. 7.1), Elijah (1 Kgs 18.38), and Amos who sees the Lord standing on the altar of sacrifices, in the fire (Amos 9.1). It is this divine fire which devours the sons of Aaron, Nadab and Abihu (Lev. 10.2), a pericope which follows Leviticus 9. It accompanies too the visions of Isaiah (the 'Seraphim' are the 'burning ones') and Ezekiel. In Exod. 24.17, the appearance (*mar'eh*) of the glory of YHWH to the Israelites was of a 'devouring fire'.

The glory is close to the people here; it no longer appears in a cloud, on a mountain, at a distance (cf. Jer. 31.3; Feuillet 1962: 122; J.A. Thompson 1980: 565). With the fire, everyone sees God; they cry out with joy. It is the same in Ps. 29.2 and 9c: they bow down, they shout with joy, they cry, 'Glory!' (cf. Zech. 4.7; Isa. 24.16; Ezek. 3.12 is unclear). These cries are followed by the blessing. They would say: 'Sing the glory of this name, proclaim God's glorious praise' (Ps. 66.2).[1] They intensify the ritual acclamations, the *těrû'â*. This ancient war cry—an extended rolling of gutturals (*rēš* + *'ayin*)—became an essential liturgical rite, as may be seen in many texts and especially in the psalms.[2] This is the way the God of Israel must be 'glorified', as Moses said to Aaron in an assonanced couplet (Lev. 10.3):

> Through those who approach me, I want to be sanctified;
> in the sight of all the people, I want to be glorified.

Kābôd

It is in the book of Psalms that the word *kābôd* occurs most often (48 times). Sirach uses it often too. It occurs 112 times at Qumran, and of these 51 are in the Hymns (*ThWAT*, IV: 39). Occasionally it is a more

---

1. Cf. Pss. 115.1; 138.5; Isa. 24.15; 42.12; Jer. 13.16; Josh. 7.19; etc.
2. Pss. 27.6; 33.3; 47.6; 89.16; 98.6; 150.5; Josh. 6.5, 20; 1 Sam. 4.4-8; Jer. 4.19; 49.2; Amos 1.14; 2.2; Zeph. 1.16; Exod. 32.17; Lev. 23.24; Num. 23.21 (Rouillard 1985: 287); 29.1; 31.6; Ezra 3.11-13; 1 Chron. 15.28; 2 Chron. 13.12; 15.14; Job 33.26 (Humbert 1946).

delicate way of writing *kābēd*, 'liver', the organ of thoughts and feelings (Gen. 49.6; Lam. 2.11; Pss. 7.6; 16.9). In Ps. 57.9 (= 108.2), *kĕbôdî*, 'my spirit' (literally, 'my glory') is in parallelism with 'my heart'. In Ugaritic, *lb*, 'heart', is used in parallelism with *kbd*, 'liver/ spirit'. In Ps. 30.13a, *kābôd* without a suffix is the subject of two verbs; the suffix *yôd*, 'my', found in the LXX, could have been dropped through haplography: ' "My" heart will sing of you without ceasing'. The term *kābôd* can be applied to humans as images of God (Ps. 8.6; Sir. 49.16), to riches (Ps. 49.17-18), to the just (Pss. 3.4; 4.3; 50.15; 62.8; 91.15; 112.9; 149.5), and to kings (Pss. 21.6; 45.14). When used of God, the word has a nuance of excellence and superiority; it is the divine majesty itself. When applied to God, the words *hôd*,[1] *hādār*,[2] *tif'eret*,[3] *nōgah*[4] also imply the idea of splendour and brilliance. Often *hôd/hādār*[5] are used together; they are found with *kābôd* in Ps. 145.5, 12. F. De Meyer (1980: 225) has suggested that *kābôd* be understood as a kind of divine name and be translated 'Glorious'. But *kābôd* is a divine attribute like *gā'ôn* (Exod. 15.7; Isa. 2.10, 19, 21; 24.14; Amos 6.8; Mic. 5.3) or *gē'ût* (Isa. 12.5; 26.10; Ps. 93.1).

If the theme of YHWH's glory has such an important place in the psalms, it is due to the fact that the Levitical singers, even after the disappearance of the Ark, insisted on the presence of the glory in the Second Temple, the place where the faithful came to invoke the divine name and see the face of God in an authentic cultic theophany. No matter how diverse the literary genres (hymns, prayers, exhortations, blessings, etc.), the psalms reflect a concrete lived experience, namely, a meeting and dialogue with God (Terrien 1978: 278; Smith 1988: 171).

Psalm 63

This is the case in Psalm 63 which begins in this way:

2   O God, you are my God, you I seek from break of day,

1. Pss. 8.2; 148.13; Hab. 3.3; Job 37.22; Sir. 10.5.
2. Pss. 29.4; 90.16; Ezek. 16.14; Mic. 2.9; Isa. 35.2.
3. Pss. 71.8; 89.18; 96.6; cf. 1 Chron. 29.11; Isa. 46.13; etc.
4. Ps. 18.13; Hab. 3.4; Ezek. 10.4.
5. Pss. 96.6; 104.1; 111.3; Job 40.10; 1 Chron. 16.27.

> my soul thirsts for you,
> after you my flesh longs,
> a land parched, thirsty, with no water.
> 3   It is then I looked to you in the sanctuary,
> contemplating your might and your glory.

This strophe is followed by two hexacola (vv. 4-6; 7-9) and two quatrains. According to the title, 'A Psalm of David. When he was in the
wilderness of Judah', it is David who is to be thought of as speaking
here. The 'parched land' brings to mind the spiritual aridity of the
believer, filled with an intense desire to meet God; it is under these
circumstances that such a one goes to the sanctuary to 'see' the glory
of YHWH. It is definitely a case of a real theophany (Mettinger 1982:
121), but of a mystical order, in a ritual and liturgical setting. The
psalmist can then state: 'Your love [*ḥesed*] is worth more than life'
(v. 4). The *ḥesed* can have a double meaning here: the love that the
Levitical singer feels for God, the deliverer and protector, and also
the love God shows in return. The two bicola at the end refer to
David, assumed to be in the wilderness of Judah (1 Sam. 25-26), the
home of jackals. It is the 'king' who finds his joy in God. The oath referred to next recalls the one in 1 Sam. 25.26: 'As YHWH lives and as
you live', Abigail declares. That concluding section of the psalm has
been compared to Isa. 65.12-16 where we find as well the themes of
the oath (by the God of truth), of being 'destined' for the sword, of
the joy of the servants of YHWH and of the death of their enemies.

Wailing and weeping, a Korahite Levite expresses in his own personal way (Ps. 42.2-3) his desire to see the face of God, the living
God of whom Deut. 5.26 speaks:

> 2   As the doe pines for the living waters,
> so my soul longs for you, my God.
> 3   My soul thirsts for God, the living God;
> when shall I be able to go to see the face of God.

The phrase 'to see the face of the king, or of the deity' is very ancient.
In Amarna Letter 147.59 we read: 'When shall I see the face of the
king, my lord?' And in Letter 169.5-10 we find: 'You give me life
and you give me death: I look towards your face'. The same thing is
found in Letters 165.7 and 166.6-8. In Akkadian, *amâru pân ili* means
'to appear before a deity'; *dagâlu panâ*, 'to watch the face', means 'to
be submissive to someone' (*THAT*, 2, 1976: 458).

Threatened by enemies, another psalmist gives evidence of a similar state of mind; this one is seeking the face of God (Ps. 143.6-8). The heading 'Psalm of David' is expanded in the LXX: 'When his son (Absalom) was pursuing him', based on v. 3 (the same modification is found in Ps. 3).

6   I stretch out my hands towards you;
        here am I before you like a parched land.
7   Quick, answer me, YHWH,
        my last breath is near;
        do not hide your face from me:
        I will be among those who fall into the pit.
8   Make me hear of your love in the morning,
        for I am counting on you.

To be sure, one cannot see God without dying and every divine image is forbidden (Deut. 5.8; Exod. 20.16; etc.). According to Deut. 4.15, the people of Israel saw no divine form or silhouette (*tĕmûnâ*) on the day when YHWH spoke at Horeb in the midst of the fire. However, the psalmists tried to express their ardent desire and intense eagerness to see the face of God or at least the reflection of the divine majesty, of the divine glory, in an experience like that of Moses (Exod. 33.23; Num. 12.8) or that of the Elders (Exod. 24.11).

Psalms 16 and 17

In line with this, the author of Psalm 17 has David, the persecuted king, speaking and pleading for the divine intervention. That prayer ends with the following wish: 'As for me, in justice [or: 'it is only just that'] I will see your face, so that when I awake I may be satisfied with your form [*tĕmûnâ*]' (17.15; Tournay 1949b: 489; van der Ploeg 1965: 273). The versions make all this clear in this way: 'When your glory will be seen' (LXX); 'I shall see the appearance [*sĕbar*] of your face, I shall be satisfied with the glory of your face, when I awaken' (Targum). In Num. 12.8 as well, *tĕmûnâ* is translated glory in the versions. The context is different in Job 4.16: Eliphaz receives a revelation and hears a voice (like Elijah); he perceives a form (*tĕmûnâ*; LXX *morphē*) which he does not recognize (Lévêque 1970: I, 260).

In Psalm 17, 'David' asks God to rise up to determine the fate of his enemies as well as his own destiny, in justice. His enemies will only be able to satisfy themselves to the full through the gains they get from life (or 'who, in life, have their share of this world'). As for the psalmist, the only satisfaction will be a new lease of life from God who will right the wrongs done him, as was already stated at the beginning of the psalm: 'From your presence my judgment will come; your eyes behold what is right' (vv. 1-2). The word *ṣedeq* (v. 15), 'justice', (Krašovec 1988) forms an *inclusio* with v. 1: 'Listen to justice, Lord!' But in v. 15 what kind of awakening is meant? Does it refer to God being called on to get up (as in Pss. 35.23; 44.24; 59.6; cf. 1 Kgs 18.27, etc.) or to the faithful psalmist, like Solomon at Gibeon (1 Kgs 3.15)? The psalmist had said in v. 3: 'You visit me at night'. A number of exegetes see an allusion here to an incubation rite in the Temple. Others see an allusion to the resurrection and place the text in Maccabean times (Dan. 12.2; 2 Macc. 7.14). This is definitely the interpretation of the Targum which understands 'when I shall awaken' as opposed to eternal sleep (Jer. 51.39, 57; Ps. 76.6; Job 14.12). But the 'awakening' can be understood in a symbolic sense of deliverance and liberation, like 'the dawn' or 'the light'. Several levels of meaning are possible and the text remains open.

Psalms 16 and 17 are very similar in style and thought, precisely in regard to the divine presence longed for by the faithful psalmist. In Psalm 16 the Levite for whom YHWH is the 'allotted portion' and the 'cup' (v. 5a), and his 'inheritance' (v. 6b), states that God, his refuge and his happiness, will not allow him to be abandoned to Sheol and the pit (v. 10b). The word 'pit' is translated by 'corruption' in the versions (cf. Acts 2.25-28; 13.35); such a meaning is attested at Qumran. The psalmist adds that God has shown him the 'path of life', a phrase borrowed by Israelite sages from their Egyptian colleagues (Couroyer 1949: 412; van Uden 1980: 386). This means for him fulness of joy (cf. Ps. 45.16) with (or, before) the face of God, and eternal delights in the right hand of God. LXX translates 'with your face', but the Targum has 'before your face', in other words, 'in your presence'. The translation 'in your right hand' is confirmed by the parallel phrase in Prov. 3.16: 'In her right hand, length of days; in her left hand, riches and honour' (cf. Isa. 44.20). The preposition *beth* rarely has the locative meaning: 'at (your right hand)' (cf. Gen. 48.13). To have this meaning here, the psalmist would have had to use either the preposition *lamed* as in Pss. 109.31 and 110.1 or the preposition *min* as in v. 8b of Ps. 16, 'at my right hand'. In Ps. 17.7, *beth* has an instrumental sense: 'by (your right hand)'. The word 'delights' in v. 11 corresponds to v. 6a, 'with delights'. What is involved here is unlimited happiness forever (the same adverb as in Pss. 13.2 ; 49.20; 74.3), complete satisfaction as in Ps. 17.15. This theme brings to mind the eschatological banquet spoken of in Ps. 22.27; Isa. 25.6; 65.13; Prov. 9.1 (cf. Mt. 8.11). Quite rightly, Kraus (1978), Weiser (1950) and Deissler (1968) speak here of a real theophany, a source of infinite happiness, whereas it is only a matter of momentary happiness in Lev. 9.24.

Psalm 16 has been reread with a setting in the life of a wandering David. It has been compared to 1 Sam. 26.19ff. which contains similar phrases: 'inheritance of YHWH', 'strange gods', 'far from the presence of YHWH', 'blood' (Tournay 1956: 502). It is through this process of Davidic re-reading that the mysterious heading *miktām* can be explained; it is found at the beginnings of Psalms 56 to 60, all of which are provided with headings which refer to a harassed David, a type of all the poor of YHWH. It would refer to 'secret' prayers, re-cited 'cryptically' (this is the meaning of *ktm*; cf. Jer. 2.22; Akkadian, Arabic), in a subdued voice, in order not to provoke the pagans and enemies of Israel (Tournay 1957: 202). This was understandable in times of persecution when the Jews had to practise their religion in secret. We may quote here Ps. 74.20-21: 'They huddle together in the hiding-places of the land, where they are forced to take shelter'. And so Psalms 16 and 17 offered an 'open' text for the faithful who could adapt them in critical situations and even see in them a stepping stone to belief in the resurrection of the just, as early as Maccabean times.

Psalm 11

The same idea of divine protection can be seen in Psalm 11 whose last verse seems to envisage a real theophany. The psalmist is the guest of YHWH; although enthroned in heaven, YHWH is a refuge for those who belong to God here below; from on high God observes what humans do, even though the wicked pretend that God sees nothing (Ps. 10.11; Ezek. 9.9; Job 22.13; etc.). This theme of divine scrutiny is found throughout the Old Testament[1] and very frequently in the

---

1. Amos 9.4; Hos. 14.9; Jer. 12.3; 24.6; Hab. 1.13; Ezek. 5.11; 7.4, 9; 8.18; 9.10; 20.17; Exod. 3.7; Deut. 11.12; 26.15; 1 Kgs 8.29; Ezra 5.5; Job 28.24; 31.4; 34.21; 2 Chron. 16.9; 24.22; Zech. 4.10; 9.8; 12.4; Isa. 57.18; 59.15.

psalms[1] (Oppenheim 1968: 173; D.L. Petersen 1984: 225). God will inflict on the wicked the punishment of Sodom and Gomorrah; God is just and loves just deeds: 'God's face shall contemplate the upright' (v. 7b). LXX translates here 'uprightness' (*yōšer*); but the Targum inverts the sentence: 'The just will see the form [*sĕbar*] of God's face', the same as in Ps. 17.15. In fact, the hapax in MT, *pānêmô* (*pnymw*) gives rise to doubt, even though the MT here is much like Ps. 17.2: 'Your eyes [LXX: 'my eyes'] gaze upon uprightness'. They could have harmonized these two texts in virtue of the principle that no one can see God; all that was necessary was to transpose the *mem* to the end of the colon, instead of reading the plural *yĕsārîm*, 'the upright' (Tournay 1946: 363; Mannati 1979: 222).

Other psalm texts speak of the vision of God as a recompense offered to the faithful. And so the end of Psalm 140 reads: 'Yes, the just shall give thanks to your name; the upright shall live before your face [= in your presence]' (v. 14). The first colon has its equivalent in Ps. 142.8. The second colon may be compared to Ps. 61.8: 'Let him [= the king] live [or: 'be enthroned']' always before God'. The Targum has softened 140.14b: 'The upright will return [verb *šûb*] to pray before you'. This is a deliberate alteration through the omission of the initial *yod*.

Psalm 27

A ritual theophany can also be detected in Psalm 27. The psalmist asserts that YHWH is his light, a theme repeated elsewhere (Pss. 18.29; 36.10; 43.3; 76.5; Isa. 10.17; Mic. 7.8). We read in an Ammonite inscription: 'Milkom is light' (Puech 1985: 24). The psalmist says that the only thing he seeks is to be always the guest of YHWH in order 'to contemplate the beauty of YHWH and visit the divine palace' (v. 4). The word *nō'am* is translated here by 'beauty', with the verb *ḥāzâ*, 'contemplate', rather than by 'gentleness' (Ps. 90.17) (Avishur 1976: 16; Levenson 1985: 61). A comparison may be made with Isa. 33.17 (a post-exilic liturgy): 'your eyes contemplate the king in his beauty'.

It is to be noted that in Ps. 26.8 LXX has read *nō'am* instead of *mĕ'ôn*, 'dwelling' (transposing consonants). Outside Israel, *nō'am* is a

1. Pss. 10.14; 11.4; 14.2; 17.2; 18.25; 25.18-19; 32.8; 33.18; 34.16; 59.5; 66.7; 74.20; 80.15; 102.20; 104.32; 113.6; 119.132; 142.5.

designation of divinity or of a hero (Knutson 1981: 495).

The Levitical singer will see the beauty of YHWH at the time of his 'visit' (verb *bqr*, 'consult, visit'; cf. Ezek. 34.11-12; Lev. 27.33) to the sanctuary in Jerusalem. There he will find a safe refuge, for God will hide him 'in the privacy of the tent', erected on the sacred rock. He then sings a psalm for YHWH: 'My heart repeats your word [literally: 'speaks for you', 'in your place', or 'about you']: "Seek my face". It is your face, YHWH, that I seek; do not hide your face from me.' God is in fact a 'hidden' God (Isa. 44.5; Ps. 89.47); there are countless texts in which it is said that God's face is hidden and the divine presence is concealed (*THAT*, 2, 1976: 180, 453; Balentine 1983). With regard to the phrase 'to seek the face of God' or simply 'to seek God', so frequent in the psalms and the books of Chronicles,[1] it is equivalent to consulting God (Hos. 5.15; Exod. 33.7; 2 Sam. 12.16; 21.1), to meeting God as one would obtain an audience with a ruler (1 Kgs 10.24; Prov. 29.26). It has been compared to an Egyptian text: 'Amon, great Lord for those who seek you, if however (?) they find you' (Barucq and Daumas 1980: 206). This is the way that pilgrims (Deut. 16.16; 31.11), as well as Levites (Pss. 24.6; 27.8; 105.4 = 1 Chron. 16.11), come to see the face of God in Jerusalem.

The author of Psalm 27 knows that God will give him a better reception than his own parents would (v. 10; Hos. 11; Jer. 31.9; Isa. 44.21; 49.15). God will rescue him from false witnesses who slander him. He concludes by saying: 'Am I not certain of seeing the goodness of YHWH in the land of the living!' (v. 13). The first word in this verse, *lûlē*, whose meaning is debated, could have been added, as is suggested by the extraordinary dots which surround it in the MT; this word, omitted by some Hebrew manuscripts and the Greek versions, could correspond to Akkadian *lû lâ*, 'that not' and be equivalent to 'surely'.[2] The word *ṭûb*, 'goodness' (cf. Pss. 25.7; 31.20; 145.7), could be translated just as well by 'beauty', like *nōʿam* in v. 4. The translation 'wealth' (Mannati 1969: 488) is not convincing. The 'land of the living' (von Rad 1958: 239) refers not only to the land of Canaan promised to Israel, but to that place where the living God

---

1. *ThWAT*, I: 313, 754; Segalla 1980: 191; Diez Merino 1982a: 129; Hunter 1982.

2. Cf. Pss. 94.17; 106.23; 119.92; 124.1. Cf. *HALAT*, 498b. Isa. 38.11 has a negative force: 'I will no longer see YHWH in the land of the living'.

dwells and where one can bless and praise God, receive God's gifts
and live in the divine presence.[1] The Targum interprets it as 'the land
of eternal life', an allusion to the immortality of the faithful. Ps. 27.13
suggests at least a ritual theophany in the sanctuary, which would connect it with Exod. 33.19: 'I will make all my beauty pass before
you...' The superscription attributes the psalm to David; LXX adds
'before being crowned [= anointed]', a reference to his life of
wandering, always in danger from Saul. God cannot abandon this
protégé who must remain strong and courageous, as the final verse
exhorts him: 'Hope in YHWH, take heart and be brave, hope in
YHWH', a text which reminds us of Deut. 3.28; 31.7; Josh. 1.6, 9
(with regard to Joshua) and Deut. 31.6 (with regard to all of Israel).

Psalm 24

The setting of a liturgical theophany can explain Psalm 24 as well, a
psalm which has given rise to so many hypotheses.[2] In its present bi-
partite form, it sets up a dialogue (vv. 3-4, 8-10) with questioning
and response. Two voices, two choirs respond to one another as in Ps.
118.19-20: it would accompany a liturgical procession taking place
with the transfer of the Ark in the time of David, who is named in the
superscription (2 Sam. 6.12ff.). But the first part of the psalm must be
post-exilic, close to Psalm 15 (Beyerlin 1985) and Isa. 33.15-16, 22.
The word *tēbēl* (v. 1) is found in post-exilic texts only. This first
panel of the diptych ends in this way in v. 6: 'Such is the race that
seeks God, that seeks your face, God of Jacob' (2 MT mss, Syriac,
LXX: 'The face of the God of Jacob'; Targum: 'his face, Jacob'). The
change of persons, frequent in poetry, has given rise to these variants.
What we have is a colon of six accents with a double caesura (2 + 2 +
2 accents). According to the received text, those who seek the face of
God would be proselytes (Zech. 8.23; Isa. 56.3-8).

In vv. 7 and 9, the gates of the Temple are challenged: they must
lift up their pediments to allow the entry of the 'Ruler of Glory'. This
phrase, which comes up again in the War Scroll at Qumran (cols. 12.8

---

1. Cf. Pss. 52.7; 116.9; 142.6; Isa. 38.11; Jer. 11.19; Ezek. 26.20; 32.23ff.
2. Vilar Huesco 1963, 7; Tournay 1968: 436; 1974: 362; Berger 1970: 335;
Wallis 1974: 145; Johnson 1979: 84; Coppens 1979: 106; Amsler 1981: 93; Cooper
1983a: 37.

and 19.1), is repeated five times and may be compared to the 'God of glory' (Ps. 29.3; cf. 93.1; 145.11-13; 1 Cor. 2.8; Eph 1.17). This majestic ruler is the God of Jacob whose face and presence and manifestation in the Temple the faithful seek. The whole thing suggests a ritual theophany. But what is the meaning of the apostrophe 'Rise up, ancient portals'? This poetic personification reminds of a passage in the *Epic of Gilgamesh* (7.1.37-49; *ANET*, 86) in which Enkidu addresses the votive gate of the temple of Enlil at Nippur. In the time of David, there was not as yet a Temple, and in the time of Solomon, the portals were new. Is this a case of high-flown style as in 'the gates of justice' (Ps. 118.19)? Must we understand that the gates are eternal, indestructible? But why are they so low? Could Lam. 2.9 provide an answer: 'The gates of Zion are sunk in the ground; God destroys and breaks her bars'? After the destruction of the Temple in 587 BCE, the rubble must have built up. Because the height of the ground had increased, entry had become difficult, even impossible. The gates were destroyed (Ps. 74.6; cf. Isa. 24.12; Jer. 51.58). We are therefore in the time of Haggai and Zechariah, and not in Davidic times.

Such a time for this psalm's composition seems confirmed in two ways: the phrase YHWH Sabaoth (v. 10) occurs frequently in Haggai and Zechariah (p. 83); the same is true of the theme of the glory of YHWH (Hag. 1.8; 2.9; Zech. 2.9, 12). The final verses of proto-Zechariah remind us of Ps. 24.6: 'Let us go to implore the face of YHWH and seek YHWH Sabaoth' (Zech. 8.21-22). The return of the glory to the Temple was announced by Ezek. 43.4-5. Psalm 24 could have been used for the renewal of ritual processions beginning in 515 BCE. Mal. 3.1 may echo these texts: 'It is the ruler that you seek, the Angel of the Covenant that you desire, who will enter into the Temple'. The perspective has become eschatological.

Psalm 29

An analogous *Sitz im Leben* can be proposed for Psalm 29, so often considered an archaic poem because of its many Ugaritic features (Craigie 1979: 135; Ravasi 1981: I, 524; Kloos 1986; Malamat 1988: 156). Recent works have shown that it is nothing of the sort: Psalm 29 is fundamentally Yahwist, no matter what its sources and prior shape might have been (Tournay 1979: 733; Loretz 1984b). It is a theophanic psalm (see p. 132) which acclaims the 'Ruler of Glory'

(vv. 3, 9-10), while the final verse ends with a divine blessing: YHWH will bless the people with peace (cf. Hag. 2.7-9; Zech. 8.12-13). This final word of the psalm sums up all the hopes of Israel (Durham 1970/1983: 272). YHWH, eternal ruler, enthroned on the celestial ocean (MT: 'the flood'), provides the beneficent rain and has concluded a covenant of peace with the people, as with Noah of old (Gen. 9.8ff.; Isa. 54.9). YHWH is the ruler of the storm which in the north affects Lebanon and Sirion (cf. Deut. 3.9; a post-exilic text) and in the south, the desert of Kadesh. The theophany of the glory causes a disturbance in nature, just like other theophanies (Nah. 1.3ff.; Pss. 18.8; 93). Psalm 29 has been compared to Jer. 10.10ff. (post-exilic): 'YHWH is the true God, the living God and the eternal ruler. When YHWH is angry, the earth quakes; the nations cannot endure the divine wrath... When God's voice sounds, there is a roaring of waters in the heavens; God brings up clouds from the end of the earth, makes lightning flash for a downpour and draws the wind from the divine storehouses. At this all stand stupefied, taken aback.' The acclamation of Ps. 29.9c, 'Glory', recalls Israel's cry in 520 BCE at the feast of Booths (Ezra 3.4, 11, 13), the ritual *tĕrû'â* with great shouts of joy (cf. Sir. 50.18).

YHWH wants to communicate the divine glory to the people; God gives the people grace and glory (Ps. 84.12) as well as divine splendour (Pss. 90.16; 149.9). Every believer can say to God: 'You are my glory' (Ps. 3.4) and exult in that glory (Ps. 149.5). All those who look towards God will become radiant (Ps. 34.6; cf. 37.6); their strength (literally: their horn) will be exalted in glory (Ps. 112.9). This is the way, it seems, that Ps. 73.24 should be interpreted: 'And then, God will take me with glory', that is, with honour, in contrast to the wicked who will be thrown into confusion and covered with shame, or to the foolish rich whose glory will not follow them to the grave (Ps. 49.18; Tournay 1985a: 198). These texts of the psalms echo Isa. 60.2 and Zech. 2.9 which describe the glory of the renewed Zion and the restored Temple: 'You shall be a crown of splendour in the hand of YHWH, a royal diadem in the palm of our God' (Isa. 62.3; cf. Zech. 9.16; Bar. 5.1ff.). Reviving the theme of the cloud and pillar of fire, Isa. 58.8 announces to the faithful that the justice of God will march ahead of them and the glory of YHWH will be their rearguard (cf. Isa. 52.12; Exod. 13.21; Deut. 1.33; Rev. 21.11; etc.).

In the Targum and the rabbinical writings, the words *kābôd* and *yĕqārā* (cf. Ezra 4.10; Esther, Daniel) are more or less synonymous.

The root *yqr* means 'to be worthy of honour' (*ThWAT*, III: 858; *TWNT*, II: 248). The theme of divine glory comes up frequently in Jewish apocryphal literature: *Book of Enoch, Apocalypse of Baruch*, etc. As for the Shekinah, it designates in the Targums, the Talmud and Midrashim the visible presence of God in paradise, in the midst of the people, in the cloud, and especially over the *kappōret* (p. 82). The Shekinah was identified in the Middle Ages with the glory of God; for the Rabbis it was the first thing created, intermediate between God and humans, omnipresent, at the same time hidden and revealed (Goldberg 1969: 468; Urbach 1975: 37; Munoz Leon 1977; Marböck 1981: 103; Chilton 1983: 69; Sievers 1984: 4). Basing themselves on Deut. 32.11, they speak of the 'wings of the Shekinah' (Basser 1984: 35). The *Memra*, that is, the word (Strack and Billerbeck 1924: 302; Hayward 1981), is the revealed presence of God, the divine message addressed to Israel and by Israel to all humanity. In this way, terms expressing the theophanic manifestations of the transcendent and ineffable God were multiplied in Judaism.

The theme of divine glory receives considerable emphasis in the New Testament, especially in the Gospel of John (*TWNT*, II: 248; Braun 1966: 195; von Balthasar 1974: 33). It was at Cana that, for the first time, Jesus manifested his glory by changing water into wine (Jn 2.11). At the time of the theophany of the Transfiguration, sometimes compared to the Jewish Autumnal festival (Ramsey 1965; van Cangh and van Esbroeck 1980: 311), the three disciples saw the glory of Jesus (Lk. 9.32), the glory that he had at the side of the Father (Jn 17.5), and the glory with which the Father should glorify him (Jn 13.31-32; 17.1; cf. 8.50). A voice coming from heaven, shortly after the messianic entry of Jesus into Jerusalem, proclaims: 'I have glorified it and I will glorify it again' (Jn 12.28). Even though no one has ever seen God (Jn 1.18; 1 Jn 4.12), except the one who comes from beside God and has seen the Father (Jn 3.11, 32; 6.46; 8.38), Jesus tells Martha before the tomb of Lazarus: 'Did I not tell you that, if you believe, you will see the glory of God?' (Jn 11.40). The vision of divine glory face to face is reserved for the blessed (Mt. 5.8 ; 1 Jn 3.2; 1 Cor. 13.12).

The prologue of the Gospel of John declares in regard to the Incarnate Word: 'We have seen his glory, glory which he receives from his Father as an only Son' (Jn 1.14). In fact, Jesus has given to his apostles the glory that his Father gave him (Jn 17.22) and they will see that glory (Jn 17.24; cf. Eph. 1.6). Such was the experience of the deacon Stephen at the moment of his death: he saw the glory of God and Jesus standing at the right hand of God (Acts 7.55). What has happened is that Jesus has been exalted into the glory (1 Tim. 3.16; cf. Acts 1.22; 2.33) and has become the Lord of glory (1 Cor. 2.8). That is why every creature cries out: 'The one seated on the throne and the Lamb that was slain are worthy to receive glory, honour and power' (cf. Rev. 4.11; 5.12-13; 7.12; 11.17-18; 12.10-12; 15.3-4; 19.1-7).

Chapter 8

OTHER POST-EXILIC THEOPHANIES

In Israel's past, theophanies had taken place at the time of the coming out of Egypt, at the revelation on Sinai, during the wandering in the wilderness and the entry into the land of Canaan as well as during the victories that followed, marking out in this way the history of Israel's origins. The salvific or punitive interventions of the Covenant God manifested themselves in violent storms, thunder and lightning, earthquakes, fire and light. By the time of the Second Temple, these theophanic features had become literary motifs, mere reminiscences.

Thus God responds to Job 'from the heart of the tempest' (Job 38.1; 40.6) and intervenes as a judge in the 'case' of Job. Job ends up by meeting his God: 'Through hearsay I knew of you, but now my eyes have seen you' (42.5). Such a direct experience was only possible for Job thanks to a special illumination by God of the eyes of his heart (Lévêque 1970: II, 509, 526). Job had hoped for this mysterious vision when he said (19.25-27):

> I know well that my vindicator lives,
> and in the end will stand up upon the dust;
> and after they have destroyed this very skin of mine,
> it is indeed outside my flesh that I will see God;
> my eyes will see one who will be no stranger to me;
> deep within me my heart pines away.

This famous text has given rise to many emendations (Lévêque 1970: II, 463, 477). The received text may be retained (Beaucamp 1977; cf. Tournay 1978: 623), provided it be compared with Job 16.18-21 where it can be seen that the witness and vindicator is none other than the cry of his spilt blood which will go up to heaven after his death:

> Earth, do not cover my blood
> and may my cry find no resting place!
> From now on I have my witness in the heavens,

> my very own vindicator is in the heights.
> My friends mock me,
> but it is to God that flow my tears.
> May it [the cry of the blood] defend the mortal against God,
> as one human pleads for another!

Job's blood which has been shed is a witness to his sufferings just as much as words carved into a rock. This cry is an unceasing appeal, like a personified prayer, which becomes for Job his ultimate witness and vindicator. In fact the earth refuses to cover the spilt blood, whether of Abel or other victims (Gen. 4.10; Lev. 17.3; Isa. 26.21; Ezek. 24.7; 2 Macc. 8.3; Heb 2.24). The cry of the blood which intervenes in this way between Job and God plays the role of *go'el*, that is, vindicator or avenger of blood. But with YHWH receiving this title too as *go'el* of Israel and of each believer (Isa. 41.14; Ps. 19.15; etc.), Job 19.25 was sure to be 're-read' in the light of the belief in the resurrection of the dead, in the Maccabaean and Hasmonaean periods, and later on in translations and commentaries on the book of Job.

Psalm 29

It is in the psalms that theophanic passages multiply (Lipiński 1979: 16). The Levitical singers loved to celebrate divine interventions, whether frightening or salvific. As I have already stated, the main text on this is Psalm 29 (Ravasi 1981: 523).

1   Ascribe to YHWH, O mighty ones,
     ascribe to YHWH glory and might;

2   ascribe to YHWH the glory due the name,
     adore Yahweh in holy attire.

3   Voice of YHWH over the waters,
     the God of glory thunders,
     YHWH over boundless waters.

4   Voice of YHWH in might,
     voice of YHWH in splendour.

5   Voice of YHWH, it breaks the cedars;
     YHWH splinters the cedars of Lebanon,

6   and makes Lebanon skip like a calf,
     and Sirion like a young buffalo.

7   Voice of YHWH, it sharpens blades of fire,

8   voice of YHWH, it shakes the desert,
     YHWH shakes the desert of Kadesh.

9   Voice of YHWH, it makes the hinds/oaks writhe
    and strips the forests bare.

    Everyone in the temple cries: Glory!
10   YHWH sits enthroned on the celestial ocean,
    and reigns, YHWH, ruler forever.
11   YHWH will give power to the people,
    YHWH will bless the people with peace.

This admirable poem multiplies anaphoras and progressive repetitions
or anadiplosis. The transfer of v. 3b before v. 9c has been suggested.
In v. 9a, two translations are possible: 'it stampedes the hinds' or 'it
makes the oaks writhe'; with the second translation, synonymous
parallelism is restored. It has been proposed that *yĕʿārôt* (9b) be
translated 'young goats' instead of 'forests' (*HALAT* 1974: 404b), and
the preceding verb by 'cause to abort' (*ibid.*: 345b); this would favour
the first translation of the parallel in v. 9a: 'makes the hinds writhe'
(cf. Job 39.1; Avishur 1984: 687). Incidentally, a double entendre
would not be impossible here as the *Midrash Tehillim* indicates.

In v. 1, *'ēlîm*, 'gods' is written *'êlîm*, 'rams' in some Hebrew
manuscripts; LXX has a conflated reading (cf. Ps. 89.7; Ezek. 32.21).
The sacred tetragrammaton, YHWH, is repeated 18 times; the thunder
or 'voice of YHWH' resounds 7 times, just as in a Ugaritic text (RS
24245) which speaks of 7 claps of thunder: in this case it is the voice
of the great Phoenician Baʿal. In Amarna Letter 147 (lines 14-15),
Abimilki writes to the pharaoh 'who thunders in the heavens like
Hadad and frightens [*rgb*] all the mountains with his thunder' (*ANET*,
484). The fourfold apostrophe to the 'sons of God', literally 'gods', in
vv. 1-2 is derived from the Canaanite theme of the *bĕnê' 'Ēl* (see
p. 22; Tournay 1949a: 48; Cunchillos 1976b). This latter theme is
developed here along with that of the flood as in Gen. 6.9ff.; moreover, the story of the flood ends with the appearance of the rainbow, a
symbol of peace, *šālôm*, the last word of Psalm 29. This peace stands
in contrast to the cosmic violence of the divine thunderstorm
described in vv. 3-9. These themes of the flood and peace are found
linked again in Isa. 54.9-13 and 26.20; 27.5. The rainbow is a feature
of the imagery of theophanies (Ezek. 1.28; Sir. 43.12; 50.7).

In v. 9c, the exclamation 'Glory!' reminds us of Lev. 9.24 and the
trisagion of Isa. 6.3 (Seybold 1980a: 208). The 'sons of God',
identified with the Levites wearing their sacred vestments (2 Chron.
20.21), glorify YHWH, the Almighty. It is hard to decide in v. 10

whether to translate *mabbûl* as 'flood' or 'celestial ocean'. With the second meaning, it would refer to the celebration of the victory of YHWH over the cosmic sea (Kloos 1986); God rules 'over the waters', regulates the rains and the storms from the 'upper chambers' (Ps. 104.3). In Mesopotamia, the god Marduk is seated on Tiamat, the salty sea. The sun god, Shamash, is represented on the stele of Nabu-apal-iddin (tablet from Sippar, 9th century BCE) seated on the ocean (*apsû*), represented by wavy lines (Mettinger 1982: 69; Keel 1977b: 153; Loretz, 1984b: 101; 1987: 415). The procession that advances towards the temple takes place at the same time on earth, for the earthly Temple is the copy or the tangible representation of the celestial Temple, a concept well attested in the Old Testament (Exod. 25.9.40; 26.30; 1 Chron. 28.19; Wis. 9.8). The Temple on Zion is like a replica of the heavenly Temple; there the Ruler of Glory is to be acclaimed.

Like the preceding Psalm 28, Psalm 29 ends with a blessing which imparts a liturgical complexion to the whole psalm. The *Midrash Tehillim* compares the 18 mentions of YHWH in Psalm 29 to the 18 rabbinic Benedictions; like the Targum, it replaces *šālôm* (11b) with *tôrâ*, 'the law'. Psalm 29 was as a matter of fact recited on the day of Pentecost which according to the tractate *Soferîm* (18.3) commemorated the giving of the law. The title of Psalm 28 (29 in MT) in the LXX, 'for the closing of the feast of Booths', indicates that it was recited for the feast of *Sukkoth* in the Autumn too (cf. Ezra 3.4) when they prayed for rain (cf. Zech. 14.16ff.), which could begin at this time of year as a blessing for the country. Psalm 29 was repeated in part in Ps. 96.7-9 and 1 Chron. 16.28-29 (Tournay 1947: 533). Instead of 'sons of gods ('*ēlîm*)' in these two texts, we find 'families of nations', which removes the allusion to the Canaanite god El. In the same way the MT text of Deut. 32.8 has changed *běnê 'Ēl*, 'sons of El', to *běnê yiśrá'ēl*, 'sons of Israel'; in Deut. 32.43 the phrase is omitted (but LXX and Qumran keep it). The phrase *hdrt qdš*, 'in holy attire' (2b) becomes 'in the sacred court' in the LXX.

As already mentioned, Psalm 29 can be dated to the beginning of the Second Temple. Haggai too speaks of the glory of YHWH, peace, blessing (2.7, 9, 19); Zechariah does the same (8.12, 13, 16, 19). This makes improbable a date close to the date of Zechariah 9, as has been proposed recently (Tournay 1956: 178) in order to connect the psalm to the campaign of Alexander the Great in Palestine. Alexander left the country of Judah and Jerusalem untouched, just like the storm described by Psalm 29, a storm which sweeps down only on Lebanon and the Negev.

Psalm 68

The imagery of the thunder god appears at the beginning and end of Psalm 68 which can be interpreted as a look back over the history of Israel beginning with the Exodus. It starts off with a repetition of Num. 10.35 and then makes use of the Ugaritic motif about the god Ba'al, the rider of the clouds (p. 23). In v. 5 we read: 'Sing to God, chant praise to God's name, clear a way for the "rider of the clouds" [MT: 'of the steppes'; see p. 83], rejoice in YHWH, dance before the divine face'. Verse 8 recalls the Exodus theophany: 'When God went forth at the head of the people and strode the desert, the earth quaked, the heavens poured down rain at the presence of the God of Israel'. Here as elsewhere, Psalm 68 draws its inspiration from the Song of Deborah (Judg. 5.4; see p. 87). The final verses of Psalm 68 repeat in an *inclusio* the theophanic motif in the universalist perspective of the post-exilic epoch: Egypt and Nubia (LXX: Ethiopia) come to adore God in the Temple.[1] God then raises the powerful divine 'voice'. Here is the final strophe.

33 Kingdoms of the earth, sing to God,
chant praise ( ) [34] for the rider of the heavens, the ancient heavens.
Listen as the divine voice sounds, a voice of power.

35 Acclaim the power of God,
whose divine splendour is over Israel, whose divine power is in the clouds!

36 You are awesome, O God, from your sanctuary.
This is the God of Israel;
who gives to this people power and strength.
Blessed be God!

We may compare here the song of Hannah, a post-exilic hymn of seven strophes (Tournay 1981b: 554). The final strophe (1 Sam. 2.10) takes up again the motif of thunder to bring to mind the divine judgment.

---

1. Cf. Isa. 19.25; 45.14; 60.6ff.; Zech. 14.18; Pss. 72.11; 87.4.

The Most High[1] will thunder in the heavens,
YHWH will judge the whole world.

Psalm 18

Psalm 18[2] contains in vv. 8-16 a theophanic description close to the
one in Psalm 29. This unit could be a later insertion. As a matter of
fact, v. 17, 'From on high God reaches out to grasp me', directly follows from v. 7: 'From the temple God hears my voice, my cry
reaches the ears of God'. On the other hand in vv. 10-11, God comes
down 'riding on a cherub' (the alliteration of *rkv* and *krv* can be
reproduced in French, *chevauchant un chérubin*, but not in English
unless we dare to say 'chartering a cherub'). Distributed in 22 cola of
5 strophes (a hexacolon and 4 quatrains), this literary unit in vv. 8-16
is distinguished by a series of *wayyiqtol* verbs, whereas the *yiqtol*
verb of v. 7 is continued by *yiqtol* verbs in vv. 17ff. In vv. 9a and
16cd, the divine anger forms a kind of *inclusio*. It is tempting to
choose in v. 16 the reading of Psalm 18: 'your voice...your anger',
instead of the parallel in 2 Sam. 22.16 which has a suffix in the third
person (the easier reading).

The theophany is preceded by 7 verses in the style of individual
complaints (Pss. 42.8; 88.9; 93.4; 116.3; Jonah 2.3). G. Castellino
(1977: 60) compared the phrase 'the cords of death' in v. 5 to the
Babylonian phrase, 'the cord tightened around a person' by the demon
etemmu (spirit of death). Here David is saved from the waters just
like Moses. The first colon, 'I love you, YHWH, my strength' is
missing in 2 Sam. 22.2. It is an addition in Psalm 18 and its
vocabulary is from a later period. The meaning 'to love' for the verb
rḥm is only found in the Hebrew of the Targums and in Aramaic; the
hapax legomenon *ḥēzeq*, 'strength', from a late period (Kutscher
1959: 361; *HALAT* 1967: 292a), is the only abstract word in this
exordium; this strength that David possesses comes from God (1 Sam.
17.37, 45; 24.16; Vesco 1987: 27). The very general 'historical'
superscription refers to David as 'servant of YHWH' just as in Ps. 36.1
(Tournay 1983a: 6); it is a messianic title consistent with vv. 50-51,

---

1. MT: 'against him' (= the adversary) instead of *'Elyôn*, restored by many commentators to conform to the parallelism.
2. Pratt 1913: 80, 159; 1914: 1, 127; Schmuttermayr 1971; Vorländer 1975: 270;
Kuntz 1983: 3; McCarter 1984: 452; Chisholm 1986: 156, 331.

the concluding verses which have a special rhythm (2 + 2 + 2; 3 + 3 + 3 accented syllables).

Here is the translation of Ps. 18.2-16:

2   I love you, YHWH, my strength!
3   YHWH, my rock, my fortress, my rescuer,
       my God, the rock who shelters me,
       my shield, my safe defence, my stronghold!
4   Praised be God! When I call on YHWH,
       I am saved from my enemies.

5   The cords of death entangled me,
       the torrents of Belial terrified me,
6   the cords of the nether world enmeshed me,
       before me were the snares of death.

7   In my distress I called on YHWH,
       to my God I sent up my cry;
       in the temple, my voice is heard,
       my cry reaches God's ears.

8   And the earth sways and quakes;
       the foundations of the mountains tremble,
       rocked by the flash of divine anger.
9   Smoke goes up from God's nostrils,
       from God's mouth a devouring fire,
       a shower of glowing coals.

10   God inclines the heavens and comes down,
       a dark cloud under the divine feet;
11   God mounts a cherub and flies,
       soaring on the wings of the wind.

12   God hides in the folds of darkness;
       God's tent, clouds upon clouds, diluvial darkness.
13   A brightness goes before, clouds pass over,
       then hail and showers of fire.

14   YHWH thunders in the heavens,
       the Most High's voice is heard,
       (hail and showers of fire).[1]
15   The divine arrows fly in all directions;
       God sends the lightning and scatters them.

16   Then the bed of the waters appears,
       the foundations of the world are laid bare
       at the rumbling of your voice, YHWH,
       at the blast with which your anger explodes.

---

1. A doublet omitted by 2 Sam. 22.14. Cf. Pss. 105.32; 148.8; Exod. 9.24; Isa. 28.2; 30.30.

The theophany begins with an earthquake and a kind of volcanic eruption, followed by a violent storm with hail and lightning. Instead of the expected flood, it is the bed of the waters (2 Sam. 22.16: of the sea) which appears, and dry land can be seen. We may note that the word *tēbēl* (derived from Babylonian *tabâlu*), 'world', occurs in 12 other psalms and in texts considered to be post-exilic. The motif of the waters being dried up recalls the crossings of the Red Sea and the Jordan (Exod. 14.21-22; 15.8; Josh. 3.14); it is found in poetry along with the theme of divine threat.[1] The perspectives here are cosmic. From the enemies of David, especially Saul (Shaul, v. 1), we move to Sheol (v. 6a) and demonic powers from which YHWH delivers the messiah in the same way as David is delivered (v. 51). The long 'historical' superscription presupposes a Davidic reading of Psalm 18, as J.-L. Vesco has clearly shown (1987: 5ff.). Verse 30 could be an allusion to the taking of the fortress of Zion; the word *gĕdûd*, 'armed band', could also be translated 'moat' (cf. Ps. 65.11). In v. 36b Vesco translates 'your humiliation [*'annôtĕkā*] has been an education for me'. Some might prefer the well-attested reading of 2 Sam. 22.36 which can be explained by Aramaic (Tournay 1956: 165): 'your help makes me great'. The verb *'ānâ* is then an Aramaism in Psalm 18 which contains other Aramaisms as well. In Arabic, *al-'māyā* means '(divine) providence'. However, the reading in Psalm 18 can be explained as a desire to give prominence to David as a model of the *'ănāwîm* (the poor of YHWH) like Moses (Num. 12.3). It involves then a 'Davidic' rereading. In any case, this complex psalm allows for several levels of readings. Finally, the fact that a certain number of elements originally mythological are here demythologized is perfectly understandable in the post-exilic period. The same thing is true of similar texts like Isa. 29.5-6; 30.27-30; and, later on, Wis. 5.21-23.

Psalm 144

The first part of Psalm 144 is modelled on Psalm 18 through the use of an 'anthological' style (Robert 1935: 348; Tournay 1984: 520). Here is the translation:

---

1. Isa. 17.13; 26.11; 50.2; 66.15; Nah. 1.4; Pss. 76.7; 80.17; 104; 7; 106.9; Mt. 8.26; Mk 4.39; Lk. 8.24.

1   Blessed be YHWH, my rock
    who trains my hands for combat
    and my fingers for battle!

2   God is my ally, my fortress,
    my stronghold and my deliverer;
    God is my shield who shelters me,
    and gives me power over my people.

3   What are people, YHWH, that you should notice them,
    human beings that you should think of them?
4   People are like a breath,
    their days are like a passing shadow.

5   YHWH, incline the heavens and come down,
    touch the mountains that they may smoke!
6   Flash forth lightning in every direction,
    shoot the arrows, scatter them.

7   From on high hold out a hand,
        [ ] and draw me from the mighty waters [ ],
11a   save me [10c] from the deadly sword,
7c=11b from the hand of foreign nations
8=11c   who speak lying words
        while their right hand is raised in perjury.

9   For you, O God, I sing a new song,
    for you, I play on a ten-stringed harp,
10 for the One who gives kings the victory,
    who saves David, God's servant.

The deadly sword can be an allusion to the sword of Goliath, as is suggested by the 'Davidic' title of the LXX: *pros ton Goliad* (concerning Goliath). The 'foreigners' are already mentioned in Ps. 18.45-46. The 'mighty waters' symbolize deadly perils (Ps. 18.17). Several doublets have disturbed the structure of the strophes. The theophanic section (vv. 5-6) preserves the double entendre of the antecedents in the suffixes of the verbs; it can be as much the dispersing of arrows or lightning as the dispersing of enemies. The conclusion of the psalm (vv. 12-15; see pp. 197-98) is a prophetic evocation of the prosperity of the messianic people of whom the new 'David' will be the king. Like the author of Psalm 96, the author of Psalm 144 expands the perspectives in comparison with Psalm 18, opening them toward the eschatological future.

Psalm 77

Once again it is to theophanic texts, Exod. 15.11-14 (Kselman 1983: 51), Hab. 3.9-11, 15 and Ps. 18.12-16, that the final section of Psalm 77 is most closely related.[1] Verses 14-21 recall the crossing of the Red Sea (cf. Ps. 74.13; 136.13-15) in the setting of the Sinai theophany: thunder, lightning, earthquakes (Exod. 19.16-18) with the drying up of the waters (Exod. 14.21). 'Has the word come to an end [the LXX omits these words] for all time?' the Asaphite psalmist asks in v. 9. Here (as in Ps. 78) he wants to make up for the silence of the great prophets and to recall the lessons of the past, the interventions of YHWH in favour of Israel, in order to discover in them the motifs for hope in the fidelity (*ḥesed*) of God, for God is *ḥāsîd*, 'faithful' (Jer. 3.12; Ps. 145.17; etc.). The Most High does not change (cf. Mal. 3.4-6; Num. 23.19; etc.): God is personally bound by oath, raising the right hand to that which is sworn (Ps. 144.8, 11). How is it possible not to remember this?

14 God, holiness is your way!
    What god is great like Elohim?
15 You, the God who works wonders!

    You make your strength known among the peoples,
16 you redeem by your arm your people,
    the children of Jacob and Joseph.

17 The waters saw you, O God,
    the waters saw you, they shuddered,
    the very depths were quaking.

18 The clouds poured down their waters,
    the skies rumbled with thunder,
    yes, your arrows flew.

19 The voice of your thunder as it rolls!
    Your lightning lit up the world,
    the earth quivered and quaked.

20 Across the sea was your way,
    your path, across the mighty waters,
    and your footprints, no one knew them.

21 You led your people like a flock,
    by the hand of Moses and Aaron.

1. Goy 1960: 56; Weiser 1961: 280; Jefferson 1963: 87; Crüsemann 1969: 195, 293.

These tricola in vv. 14-20 can be grouped in pairs. The final couplet (v. 21) repeats the phrase 'your people' from v. 16a; 'the hand of Moses and Aaron' (v. 21b) corresponds to 'your arm' (v. 16a, in the versions; MT: the arm). 'Your way' (v. 14a; Jerome: 'Your way is in the sanctuary'; cf. Ps. 68.25) forms an *inclusio* with v. 20a, 'across the sea passed your way'. We may compare Ps. 18.31: 'O God, your way is perfect' (cf. Deut. 32.4) and Hab. 3.15: 'You have trampled the sea with your horses'. The motif of 'the shepherd of Israel', at the end of the psalm, comes up frequently in the Asaphite collection (Pss. 74.1; 78.14, 52; 80.1). We should note the contacts between vv. 14-15 and Exod. 15.11; v. 16 and Exod. 15.13-14; v. 17 and Hab. 3.10. The image of the war chariot, brought to mind in v. 19a by *galgal*, 'the wheel' (Isa. 5.28; Jer. 47.3; Ezek. 23.24; 26.10), comes up as well in Ps. 65.12: 'Fatness is distilled in your tracks', not to mention Ps. 18.11, etc. The theme of the path (*šĕbîl*; Jer. 18.15) is found in Isa. 43.16; 51.10; 63.12-14 (cf. Neh. 9.11; Wis. 14.3). Part of v. 19 is found in Ps. 97.4 as well. Here then we have an example of a composition in anthological style; this in no way diminishes the poetic value of the whole.

Psalm 114

Psalm 114[1] celebrates the events of the time of the Exodus when Israel, freed from slavery, became the domain of YHWH. It is the second hymn of the Passover hallel (Pss. 113–118).

1   When Israel came out of Egypt,
     the house of Jacob from among a barbaric people,
2   Judah became for God a sanctuary,
     and Israel a domain.

3   The sea looks and flees,
     the Jordan turns back;
4   the mountains skip like rams,
     and the hills, like lambs.

5   What ails you that you flee, O Sea,
     O Jordan, that you turn back?
6   O Mountains, why skip like rams,
     and you, O Hills, like lambs?

---

1. Lubsczyk 1967: 161; Renaud 1978: 14; Auffret 1978: 103; Loretz 1979: 199; Weiss 1984: 93, 352; Watson 1984a: 189-90.

7   Tremble, O earth, in the presence of the Ruler,
      in the presence of the God of Jacob,
8   the One who changes the rock into a pool
      and the granite into a fountain.

These four quatrains form a large chiasm. The question posed in
vv. 5-6 repeats the description of vv. 3-4. The Red Sea and the
Jordan fall back, mountains and hills leap about at the sight of
YHWH's exploits on behalf of Israel which has become God's own
possession and the sanctuary where God dwells (Exod. 19.5-6; Jer.
2.3; Deut. 7.6; 26.19; Isa. 61.6). We may compare a Ugaritic passage:
'The mountains are thrilled..., the heights of the earth leap about'
(Caquot 1974: 217; *ANET*, 135), as well as Ps. 29.6 and Wis. 19.9.
Verse 7 reveals the identity of the one spoken of in v. 2a and replies
to the question posed by vv. 5-6. Verse 8 actualizes the past events of
the Exodus (Exod. 17.6; Num. 20.8; Deut. 8.15; Isa. 41.18; Ps.
107.35; 1 Cor. 10.4) with a present participle, 'the One changing' the
rock and the granite (Deut. 8.15; 32.13; Isa. 50.7; Job 28.9) into
sheets of water.

What is meant by the apostrophe 'tremble', addressed to the earth?
Does it imply joyful excitement? In the parallels it always refers to a
trembling caused by fear or surprise. Such is the case in Ps. 96.9:
'Tremble before God, all the earth!' Ps. 97.4 is the same: 'The earth
has seen God and trembles'. This is the usual distinguishing feature of
theophanies. On the other hand, it is to be noted that the title *'ādôn*
('master', here translated by the more inclusive 'ruler') is rarely
applied to YHWH, especially in the phrase 'ruler of all the earth'.
Because of this, some correct *ḥûlî*, 'tremble', to *kōl*, 'all' (the
spirantized *kaph* would have been transcribed as *heth*). Besides, this
text could have been harmonized with the parallel texts just cited (Pss.
96.9; 97.4); v. 7a would then have only three words accented, just
like the other cola. It has been suggested that *ḥûlî* is derived from *ḥîl*
and is to be understood as a participle with the meaning 'procreator,
author, creator' (Weiss 1984: 370), or even from an Aramaic verb
ḥîl, 'fortify, strengthen': 'the ruler who strengthens (the earth)'. If the
MT is retained, the word 'earth' has a broader meaning, like *tēbēl*, 'the
world', and would refer to the sea as well as the mountains. The
commotion in nature is universal in the face of the theophanic manifestations of YHWH on behalf of the people.

Psalm of Nahum

The book of Nahum begins with a theophanic hymn which brings to mind many of the preceding texts.[1]

Aleph	2	YHWH is a jealous and avenging God, YHWH is an avenger, in command of wrath, YHWH takes revenge on adversaries and is ruthless to enemies.
	3	YHWH is slow to anger, yet so strong; YHWH does not leave the guilty unpunished.
Beth		In whirlwind, in storm, YHWH advances; the cloud is the dust made by the divine feet.
Gimel	4	God threatens the sea and dries it up, and makes all the rivers run dry.
(Daleth)		Withered, Bashan and Carmel, faded, the flowers of Lebanon.
He	5	The mountains quake before God, and the hills shake;
Waw		before the divine face, the earth convulses, the world and all who dwell in it.
Zayin	6	Before God's fury, who could stand firm, who could withstand the heat of that anger?
Heth		The divine fury breaks out like a fire, the rocks are brittle before it.
Teth	7	YHWH is good; this is a shelter in the day of distress;
Yod		God knows those who seek divine refuge,
	8	when the devastating flood sweeps by.
Kaph		God reduces to nothing those who rise up in rebellion and drives back the enemies into darkness.

This alphabetic poem is incomplete like Psalms 9 and 10. The theophany is framed by two hymnic strophes. Divine anger and jealousy are let loose; the whole of nature is in turmoil, as if reduced to chaos, while Israel is protected. A whirlwind, a dark cloud, a drying up of water and vegetation (in v. 4c, the *daleth* strophe, *dālĕlû*, 'they waste away', has been suggested), an earthquake (v. 5c; versions: 'is thrown into confusion'), flooding—all these features of theophanies cannot but bring to mind Mesopotamian or Ugaritic parallels: the struggle of Marduk against Tiamat, of Baʻal against Mot and Sea (Day 1985;

---

1. Keller 1971: 109; Christensen 1975: 17; van den Wouden 1978: 79; Johnson 1979: 359; Hanson 1984: 296.

Kloos 1986); but there are many biblical parallels as well. There is a timeless perspective here, not tied in with the fall of Nineveh in 612 BCE; that event is only brought to mind in v. 8c ('God reduces to nothing her place') through a rereading with a feminine suffix which would then refer to Nineveh; but the versions (LXX, Targ., etc.) read *běqāmāyw*, 'God's opponents' or 'those who rise up against God', as in the primitive text, without any connection with the oracle against Nineveh. Although the unity of the book of Nahum is still maintained by some exegetes (Becking 1978: 107), the anthological style of the psalm and its alphabetic sequence suggest a post-exilic date for this section of the book (Hanson, *et al.*). Moreover, it is Ezekiel who is the first to connect the 'jealousy' (*qannô'*, *THAT*, 2, 1976: 647) of YHWH with the salvation of Israel for whom YHWH becomes the *gō'ēl*, 'avenger'. The perspective here is the reversal of that in the period of the monarchy when divine jealousy was the anger of love betrayed by the breaking of the covenant and by the sins of Israel. Beginning with the exile, divine 'jealousy' and divine anger are once more directed against the oppressors of Israel (Renaud 1963; Brongers 1963: 269).

We know besides that the editors of the ancient oracles, under the supervision of the Jerusalem priesthood, reread these oracles and adapted them to the needs of the community of the poor of YHWH that had to be comforted and strengthened in their faith in the one God, sole refuge and saviour of Israel.

Psalm 50

Some shorter psalm texts offer a theophanic passage by way of introduction, often preceding an oracle, as in the psalm of Nahum. Such is the case for Psalm 50, the first of the 'Asaphite' psalms, in which the theophanic prelude is followed by an oracle in the form of a long indictment, and then, to conclude, by a blessing much like that in Ps. 91.15-16. This psalm is a good example of how the Levitical singers acted as cultic prophets.

1   The God of gods, YHWH, has spoken,
     to summon the earth from the rising of the sun to its setting.
2   From Zion, perfect in beauty, God shines forth.
3   May our God come to break the divine silence!

     Going before, a devouring fire,
     all around, raging storms,

4   as God summons the heavens from on high
and the earth, for the trial of this people.

Oracle (God speaks) and theophany (God shines forth) are here closely associated (Beaucamp 1959: 10; Ridderbos 1969: 213; Gese 1976: 57). The redundant phrase in v. 1, *'Ēl 'Ělōhîm YHWH*, is an archaism as in Josh. 22.22 and other texts.[1] 'From the rising of the sun to its setting' means the whole extent of the earth. God comes to dwell in Zion which from now on takes the place of Sinai; this is the religious metropolis of humanity, restored by Nehemiah and the place whose beauty the Levitical singers never tired of celebrating, as in Ps. 48.2-3 for example (Coppens 1979: 457; Robinson 1974:118; Loretz 1979: 457). This is the city of the great Monarch (Mt. 5.35).

2   Great is YHWH, and so worthy of praise
in the city of our God,
this holy mountain, [3] beautiful in its loftiness,
joy of all the earth.

Mount Zion, heart of the North,
it is the city of the great Monarch:
4   God, in the midst of its palaces,
proves to be a true citadel.

The sequel refers to the divine intervention which foils the coalition: 'The kings see; panic-stricken, they flee'. The residents had seen that defeat right there, in Jerusalem.

In Psalm 50, the coming of God is described with the usual features of theophanies: fire and storm. The desire expressed in v. 3, 'May our God come to break the divine silence', far from being an addition, conveys the anxious expectations of the faithful of YHWH. The coming of the Reign of God, announced in Isa. 62.11, Zech. 9.9, in the psalms of the Reign of YHWH (96.13; 98.9) and by so many other texts, is ardently desired by the poor of YHWH. God knows how to be manifest and how to arise, in order to carry out the Judgment (Pss. 9.20; 10.12; 119.82, 123; etc.). It is against this background that the author of Ps. 101.2 cries out: 'When will you come to me?' In the same way the author of Isa. 63.19 exclaims: 'Oh, that you would tear open the heavens and come down!' (as of old at Sinai).

---

1. Gen. 33.20; 46.3; Num. 16.22; Deut. 10.17; Pss. 82.1; 136.2; Dan. 11.36.

Psalm 80

At the beginning of the Asaphite Psalm 80 (Eissfeldt 1966: 221; Beyerlin 1973: 9; Goldingay 1977-78: 146), God is implored, just as in Ps. 50.2, to reveal the divine splendour.

> 2   Shepherd of Israel, listen,
>   You who led Joseph like a flock,
>   You who are enthroned on the Cherubim, shine forth
> 3   before Ephraim, Benjamin and Manasseh;
>   rouse your might
>   and come to our aid.

This is how an Asaphite Levite demands a theophany of God by repeating the beginning of Deut. 33.2 where the coming of YHWH to the Promised Land is compared to the rising of the sun (cf. Hab. 3.4; Isa. 60.1ff.; 2 Sam. 23.4; *ThWAT*, III: 790). The same theophanic feature appears in the prelude of Psalm 94 (de Meyer 1981a: 22; Skehan 1964: 313).

> 1   God of vengeance, YHWH,
>   God of vengeance, shine forth,
> 2   Rise up, judge of the earth,
>   pay to the proud their reward.

The sequel begins as a complaint: 'How long. . .?'

The same thing is found in Ps. 80.5: 'How long will you be angry?' But here the situation is more concrete and a more detailed examination would be worthwhile. The northern tribes, Benjamin and the sons of Joseph, Ephraim and Manasseh, came out from Egypt at the time of the Exodus, led by the Divine Shepherd. YHWH is frequently revealed to them enthroned on the Cherubim in the Tent of Meeting. This phrase comes up again in Ps. 99.1, in another theophanic context in which there is a reference to the meetings of Moses and Aaron with God in the cloud, as well as to the intercession of Samuel. The mention of the Cherubim, like that of God Sabaoth in the refrain of Psalm 80, takes us back to Israel's past (pp. 83).

The LXX title in Ps. 80.1, 'About Assyria', does not imply a northern source for this psalm; the Asaphite psalmist could be referring to ancient Ephraimite traditions. But the allusions to the 'vine' (vv. 9-15) seem to refer to the catastrophe of 587 BCE, as is the case in Ps. 89.41-42 (cf. Ps. 74.7; Lam. 2.3; 4.11). These same three northern tribes are mentioned besides in 1 Chron. 9.3 as residents of Jerusalem in the 4th century BCE. It is possible that v. 18 ('the man at your right hand, the son of Adam to whom you have given power') refers to none other than the priest and scribe Ezra whose mission is often placed in 398 BCE. In fact, we read in the book of Ezra: 'The hand of YHWH his God was upon him' (7.6), and later on, 'I took courage, for the hand of YHWH my God was upon me' (7.28; Tournay 1961: 130). Psalm 80 would date then from that period and would be later than Psalm 50. The theme of the 'divine threat', in v. 17, is a feature of theophanies (see p. 138) which stands in contrast with 'the light of the divine face', spoken of in the refrain of vv. 4, 8 and 20.

Psalm 97

Psalm 97, a psalm of the Reign of YHWH, contains in its first part (vv. 1-6), a number of theophanic features (Feuillet 1951: 1259; Grelot 1962: 483; Coppens 1979: 168); it is another example of the 'anthological' approach.

> 1   YHWH reigns! Let the earth rejoice!
>   Joy for countless isles!
> 2   With darkness and cloud on all sides
>   and justice and judgment, the foundation of YHWH's throne.
>
> 3   Before YHWH a fire advances,
>   and consumes the foes round about;
> 4   YHWH's lightning lights up the world;
>   the earth sees and trembles.
>
> 5   The mountains melt like wax
>   before YHWH, Ruler of all the earth.
> 6   The heavens proclaim God's justice
>   and all peoples see the divine glory.

This final colon, much like Ps. 57.6, 12, reminds us of Isa. 40.5. Other contacts are discernible too (Isa. 42.10ff.; Pss. 18.9-10; 50.6; 68.3; 77.19; 89.15; etc.). Verse 3 reminds us of Zech. 12.6. The universalist perspective is directly eschatological as in other psalms of the Reign of YHWH.

Psalms 83, 84, 73

The same thing is true of Psalm 83 (Costacurta 1983: 518) in which an Asaphite Levite demands that God no longer remain silent, but begin to confound the enemies of the people: ten of them are listed (vv. 7-9). All this reminds us of the oracles against the nations. The exploits of Gideon, Deborah and Barak are called to mind. The Most High must intervene in fire, whirlwind and storm, just as in the beginning of the previous psalm, Psalm 97.

In Psalm 84 (Tournay 1947: 521; 1961: 130; L'Hour 1974: 538), the Korahite Levite describes his affection for the house of his ruler, the living God. These feelings recall those of Psalm 42-43, another Korahite psalm. In v. 11 of Psalm 84, the Levite alludes to the office of doorkeeper of the Temple, a role entrusted to the Korahites (1 Chron. 26.1). He addresses the pilgrims who have come 'to see' God on Zion. The prelude reminds us of Num. 24.5: 'How beautiful are your tents, O Jacob, and your encampments, O Israel!' The pilgrimage feasts in Jerusalem took place three times a year, with the most popular being the Feast of Tents in the Autumn. In v. 8, the MT is vocalized in such a way as to eliminate the theophanic vision of God in the Temple (the same re-reading occurs in Ps. 42.3; see p. 78). As in Ps. 50.1, we can read: *'Ēl 'Ělōhîm*, 'the God of gods', will be seen in Zion. Other corrections have been proposed, based on Lev. 9.4 or Zech. 9.14.

Verse 10 of Psalm 84 speaks of the 'anointed' of God. But does the phrase 'our shield' refer to this anointed or to God as in v. 12: 'God is sun [see p. 154] and shield' (cf. Pss. 3.4; 33.20; 59.12; 115.9, 11)? In Ps. 89.19, the metaphor of the 'shield' is applied to the king, and in Ps. 47.10, to princes. Verse 10 could then be translated: 'O God, behold our shield, look upon the face of your anointed'. The text remains ambiguous, for this 'anointed' can be the king of Israel (son of David), present or to come (cf. Ps. 132.10), the anointed high priest or the head of the post-exilic community (some think it refers to Ezra, as in Ps. 80.18), or even that community itself, a people consecrated to YHWH (cf. Ps. 28.8; Hab. 3.13).

The cultic theophanies so far examined involve the whole community; it is a collective experience for the people who have come to see the face of God in the Temple. On the contrary, it is something personal that an Asaphite Levite, the author of Psalm 73, has experienced (Irsigler 1984). Tormented by the scandal of the suffering of innocent people, of which he is one, and the apparent prosperity of the wicked, he goes to the sanctuary of the Temple (v. 17) to find the solution to his disturbing problem. A number of echoes of the account of the theophany of the prophet Elijah at Horeb (1 Kgs 19.3ff.; Tournay 1985a: 187) suggests that the Levite was aware that he was having an experience analogous to that of Elijah. Elijah was filled with an ardent 'jealousy' and asked God 'to take his life' (1 Kgs 19.4). The psalmist, too, is filled with 'jealousy' (v. 3); he meets YHWH, this time not on Mount Horeb, but on Mount Zion. He will be 'taken' with honour by God (v. 24; cf. Pss. 91.15; 149.5; Krašovec 1984: 38) after a life lived near God, 'with God'. As for the wicked, they will disappear in shame. The author of Psalm 73 acts like a cultic prophet. It is in the Temple that YHWH looks, listens, responds, comforts, gladdens and saves those who are faithful. For them God is truly Emmanuel, 'God with us', as the refrain of Psalm 46 repeats and 2 Chron 15.2; 20.17; 32.8 echo back.

Divine Fire

Having reviewed a number of theophanic psalms and sought out their sources, we can pay special attention to two main motifs, fire and light, symbols of two moods on the part of YHWH, divine anger and divine benevolence.

Fire (Heintz 1973: 63; Chisholm 1986: 165; *THAT*, 1971: 242; *ThWAT*, I: 451; Morla Asensio, 1988) accompanies the theophany at Sinai and the punitive interventions of YHWH (Deut. 9.3; Amos 7.4; Ezek. 21.3; Isa. 66.24). This fire consumes the enemies of God, their cities and their palaces (Hos. 8.14; Amos 1.4ff.), and their weapons (chariots and shields; cf. Ps. 46.10). God punishes the Korah group (Num. 16.35; Ps. 106.18), Nadab and Abihu (Lev. 10.2), and the messengers of King Ahaziah (2 Kgs 1.10; Sir. 48 .3). The Belial crowd burn like thorns (2 Sam. 23.6f.), a theme repeated in Pss. 118.12: 'The pagans are set ablaze [MT: 'die out'] like burning thorns'. They melt like wax before a fire (Mic. 1.4; Pss. 68.3; 97.5). Fire from heaven destroys Sodom and Gomorrah.[1] This theme is repeated in the psalms: in Ps. 11.6 we read: 'YHWH will rain on the wicked coals [Symmachus; MT: 'snares'] of fire and brimstone, a scorching

1. Amos 4.1; Isa. 13.19; 34.9; Ezek. 38.22; 39.6; Jer. 49.18; 50.32, 40; Zech. 9.4.

wind [or: 'indignation', Ps. 119.53; Sir. 43.17; cf. Lam. 5.10]; it is the cup they will receive as their portion'; 'May it rain on them coals of fire' (Ps. 140.11; cf. 120.4). In the most recent writings, fire becomes the supreme punishment.[1] Often compared to Iranian parallels, this motif is characteristic of apocalyptic literature (Puech 1983: 371).[2] Derived from Jeremiah (6.29; 9.6; cf. Isa. 48.10; Zech. 13.9), the theme of the fire of the crucible comes up in the psalms (17.3; 26.2; 66.10).

Divine Anger

The hagiographa often speak of the anger of YHWH (Ringgren 1963: 107; Lactance 1982; Brandscheidt 1983) whose nostrils catch fire and begin to flame. The word *'np*, 'nose', comes to designate anger; the corresponding verb is only used with YHWH as subject, as in Ps. 2.12: 'Suddenly God's anger catches fire'. The word *ḥărôn*, 'anger', designates divine anger only; other synonyms are used too: *ḥmh*, 'anger'; *z'm*, 'indignation'; *'brh*, 'exasperation'; *qṣp*, 'irritation' (see *THAT* and *TDOT, in loco*). During the time of the Exodus and the monarchy, divine anger 'rises up' against Israel which is guilty of idolatry (Ps. 78.21, 31). The prophets announce that fire will devour Jerusalem, the palace of the king, and the Temple (2 Kgs 25.9; Jer. 39.8; 52.13). The complaints in the psalms describe the anger of YHWH which is going to unleash catastrophe.[3]

From the time of the return from the exile, the divine anger is directed against the enemies of a scattered and humiliated Israel; the same thing is true of divine jealousy. Although slow to anger (Pss. 78.38; 86.15; 103.8; 145.8) and ready to pardon the repentant sinner, YHWH still executes divine vengeance on those who exploit and pillage God's people: Babylon, Edom, Egypt, Philistia, Tyre, the pagan world, the wicked, idolaters.[4]

1. Isa. 30.27, 33; 33.14; 66.24; Mal. 3.19, 21; Joel 3.3; Sir. 7.17; Jdt. 16.17; Mk 9.48.
2. Dan. 7.9-11; 10.6; *Enoch* 14.9; Rev. 1.14; 4.5; 19.20; Mt. 3.7-12; Lk. 3.7; Jn 3.36; 2 Thess. 1.8; 2 Pet. 3.7.
3. Pss. 60.3; 74.1; 77.10; 79.5-6; 80.5; 85.6; 88.17; 89.47; 90.11; 102.11. Cf. Isa. 54.8; 64.4, 8; etc. With regard to the time of the Exodus, cf. Pss. 78.21, 31, 49; 95.11; 106.29, 40.
4. Cf. Pss. 7.7; 50.3; 69.25; 76.8, 11; 79.10; 94.1; 149.7; Nah. 1.6; Isa. 31.9;

Divine anger is sometimes personified as a real attribute just like justice. This is obvious in the case of Jeremiah's image of the 'cup of Wrath' (Jer. 13.13; 25.15; 48.26; 49.12; 51.7, 39); this image reappears in the writings of the 6th century BCE: Hab. 2.16; Ezek. 23.31; Isa. 51.17, 22; Lam. 4.21. It is developed further in Pss. 60.5 and 75.9 (Tournay 1972: 46), as well as in Obad. 16; Zech. 12.2, and, in the 1st century CE, in Rev. 14.8, 10; 16.19. The cup signifies the lot, the destiny of each one (Pss. 1 1.6; 16.5; 23.5; cf. Mt. 20.22; 26.39). The divine anger generates terror; several texts speak of the 'terror of God'[1] or simply of the 'Terror' (Pss. 9.21; 14.5; 81.16 Syr; 83.16; 1 Macc. 4.32). Many other texts mention the anger of God.[2]

Pss. 58.10 and 76.11 seem to speak of personified anger too. The first of these two texts seems to be almost hopelessly difficult to translate. It is the only verse in the whole psalter that M. Dahood has given up on translating! K. Seybold (1980b: 53) in this v. 10 reads *yakkem*, 'he strikes them (with a thorn)'; but the next part remains unintelligible. It is better to assume haplography of the participle *nihar*, 'scorched', before *hārôn*, 'the anger', and translate: 'Before they sprout thorns like [*yānûbû sîrôt kĕmô*] a bramble, green or scorched, may the anger sweep them away' (Tournay 1956: 168).

Ps. 76.11 is obscure too. It has been suggested that *hmt* and *'dm* be regarded as two geographical names: Hamath and Edom. Would a double entendre be possible here? The MT can be translated: 'For the anger of men gives you glory, and the survivors of anger, you will bind around you' (Tournay and Schwab 1964: 323). There is no need to retouch the Hebrew text (cf. Tournay 1976b: 20), since it is possible to compare it to the allegory of the loincloth in Jer. 13.11. That image expresses the close union between God and those who have been saved from the anger of humans. It appears in Isa. 49.18: 'You will make of them a loincloth for yourself'. Ps. 76.5-7 may be alluding to the sudden raising of the siege of Jerusalem by Sennacherib in 701 BCE (Day 1981: 76). The anger of men would be the anger of this Assyrian king and his army: 'You shake with rage

66.16; Job 20.28; Sir. 36.6; Wis. 5.20.
1. 1 Sam. 11.7; 14.15; 2 Chron. 14.13; 17.10; 20.29; Job 13.11; 26.5, 11; Isa. 2.10, 19, 21; 17.14.
2. 2 Kgs 3.27; Isa. 26.20; Ezek. 7.3; Zeph. 1.18; Zech. 1.12; Lev. 10.6; 1 Chron. 27.24; 2 Chron. 24.18; cf. Rom. 1.18; 2.5.

against me', says God to the king of Assyria (2 Kgs 19.28 = Isa. 37.29). The following verses (a post-exilic addition; cf. Gonçalves 1986: 487) mention the Remnants (Carena 1986) of Judah and Jerusalem, who survive thanks to the divine 'jealousy'. The Asaphite psalmist in this way brings to mind this remarkable event which maintained the belief in the inviolability of Zion.

In a royal thanksgiving prayer, Ps. 21.10 mentions divine anger too in an ambiguous passage (Tournay 1959a: 177; Quintens 1978: 533): 'You will make of them a blazing fire [literally: 'a furnace of fire'] at the time of your presence [that is to say: 'when you shall appear']; YHWH in anger will consume them, a fire will devour them'. Three manuscripts omit 'YHWH'; some Greek manuscripts translate: 'Lord, in your anger, you will consume them'. The divine tetragrammaton could have been added at a later time to achieve a real theophany, whereas the original text only referred to the king, as in vv. 9 and 11-13. It would only be at the end of the psalm (v. 14) that God would be addressed: 'Rise up, YHWH, in your might!' According to this hypothesis, v. 10 could bring to mind the Egyptian motif of the *Uraeus*, the serpent emblem represented on the diadem of the Pharaoh; it was believed that it was able to burn the adversaries of anyone wearing it (Barucq and Daumas 1980: 58).

Light and Sun

If fire exterminates, light (Humbert 1966: 1; Aalen 1951; *ThWAT*, I: 166-82; Monloubou 1980: 38) brings life and salvation. These two elements predominate in the theophanies, especially in the book of Ezekiel. Having presented the negative and terrifying aspects, let us now envisage the positive and vivifying aspects of these theophanies, especially in the psalms.

The Asaphite Levite, author of Psalm 76, refers to God as 'luminous' (v. 5). God is the creator of light (Gen. 1.3; Ps. 74.16; Isa. 45.7; Job 12.22; 2 Cor. 4.6). Eternal light,[1] God is wrapped in light as in a robe (Ps. 104.2), a reflection of the splendid and majestic divine glory (Ps. 104.1, 31): Psalm 104 has been compared to Egyptian hymns to the god Ra (the sun). Light dwells near God (Dan. 2.22; cf.

---

1. Cf. Isa. 60.19; Wis. 7.26; Jn 1.5, 9; 3.19; 8.12; 12.46; Lk. 1.78; 2.32; Jas 1.17; 1 Jn 1.5.

1 Tim. 6.16). Light is a symbol of life, happiness, salvation (Ps. 27.1; Mic. 7.8), whereas darkness is the metaphor of evil, death, Sheol. From this comes the phrase 'shadow of death' (Pss. 23.4; 107.10; 112.4; Jer. 13.16; Job 10.21; Lk. 1.79; etc.). Ps. 36.10 compares life and light: 'In you is the source of life; in your light we see light'. We should note the play on words in Hebrew between *rā'â*, 'to see', and *'ôr*, 'light', as in Ps. 49.20: 'Never will they see the light' (cf. Mic. 7.9; Job 3.16; 33.28; Isa. 53.11, LXX and 4QIsa[a]). According to Ps. 132.17 as quoted in the midrashim, the 'lamp' is the messiah (cf. Rev. 21.23; Flusser 1988: 457). Rabbinic texts invoke Ps. 36.10 in order to say that one of the names of the messiah will be 'Light' (Strack and Billerbeck, 1965: I, 67, 151; 1965: II, 348; *TWNT*, II: 319). The author of this psalm is inspired by the opening chapters of Genesis (Tournay 1983a: 17). The close bond between life and light is shown as well in the phrase 'the light of the living' or 'light of life' (Ps. 56.14; cf. Job 33.28, 30), which is the light of YHWH (Isa. 2.5; cf. 10.17) in 'the land of the living' (Ps. 116.9; Isa. 38.11). God is the light of the just, illumining their eyes and reviving them;[1] God's word is a light for the just (Pss. 19.9; 119.105, 130).

The Rule of the Qumran Community speaks of contemplating the light of life (3.7). We read in a hymn from Qumran (9.26-27): 'In your glory my light appeared, because from the darkness you made a light to shine' (Carmignac 1961: 30, 244). This text reminds us of Ps. 139.12: 'Even darkness is not dark for you, and the night is as light as day; for darkness is like light to you'. The last colon, in Aramaic, is probably a gloss from v. 11b: 'And let the light around me be night!' In the main manuscript of the Psalms from Qumran (11QPs[a]), *'ēzôr*, 'loincloth', is used in this verse instead of *'ôr*, 'light'; the similar letters *waw* and *zayin* could be confused: 'I will say: let the darkness press down on me, let the night around me be a loincloth [that is, 'embrace me', 'encompass me']'. The synonymous parallelism is then restored; the whole thing becomes coherent and the origin of the gloss in MT is accounted for (Tournay, 1966c: 261; Ouellette 1969: 120; cf. Lapointe 1971: 397).

We may recall that the feast of the Dedication which celebrated the anniversary of the purification of the Temple in 165 BCE was the feast of Lights; lamps were lit as part of the celebration (1 Macc. 4.50; 2

---

1. Pss. 13.4; 18.29; 19.9; Job 29.3; Ezra 9.8; Sir. 34.17; Bar. 1.12; Rev. 22.5.

Macc. 10.3; Jn 10.22). This custom is still continued in Judaism.

Since light comes from the sun, it is natural that solar imagery (Smith 1988) occurs in theophanies: Deut. 33.2; Hab. 3.4; Isa. 60.1ff. This imagery is used in speaking of the Davidic messiah (Num. 24.17; 2 Sam. 23.4; Lk. 1.78-79; Rev. 21.23; Acts 26.13) and even of the just (Judg. 5.31; Dan. 12.3; Mt. 13.43). The title of 'sun', bestowed on the pharaohs, is used in regard to YHWH in Ps. 84.12: 'YHWH God is a sun, a shield [*māgēn*]'. We may compare Isa. 54.12 where *šemeš* designates a merlon or a battlement, but not the rampart itself. In Ps. 84.12, the roundness of the sun could have brought to mind a buckler, round like the *māgēn*; the imagery is consistent. Ps. 19.6 revives the Babylonian imagery of the god Shamash, the fiancé of the goddess Aya: each morning he came out of the nuptial tent.

The motif of the winged disk, originating in Egypt with the coming together of the solar disk and the wings of the falcon Horus, spread throughout the whole Near East in many and varying forms (Stähli 1985; *THAT*, 2, 1976: 994) down to the period of the Achemenids. We may see an allusion to it in Mal. 3.20: 'The sun of justice will shine, bringing healing in its rays [literally: 'its wings']'. In the Second Temple period the frequency of theophoric names meaning 'YHWH shines' (Zerahiah, Izrahiah: 1 Chron. 5.32; 6.36; 7.3; Ezra 7.4; 8.4; Neh. 12.42) is noticeable as well.

The Divine Face

A frequently occurring anthropomorphism in the psalms is that of the divine face. Although the phrase 'face of YHWH' can refer to YHWH personally (Johnson 1947: 155; *THAT*, 2, 1976: 446), there can be no question of any kind of representation of the divine being, since this is prohibited (Heintz 1979: 427; Dion 1981: 365). But 'the face' can bring to mind the presence and manifestation of a person, in this case God personally (Lam. 4.16; Pss. 21.10; 34.17; etc.; Smith 1988: 171). Then again, in all the Semitic languages, the light of the face is the sign of a kindly reception; it is like a smile that softens the face (Pss. 104.15; 119.58; Dan. 9.13). Two closely related phrases are made use of here: to make the face shine or lift up the face on someone (Dhorme 1923: 51; Gruber 1983: 252). They are found in the great Priestly blessing (Num. 6.26): 'May YHWH let the divine face shine on you and be gracious to you! May YHWH lift up the divine face to

you and give you peace!' At Qumran we find the phrases 'the light of
God's face' (1QH 3.3; 4.5, 27) and 'lift up the face' (1QS 2.4, 9).
These occur frequently in the psalter: 'Let your face shine on your
servant' (Pss. 31.17; 119.135), or 'on your people' (cf. Ps. 44.4; 67.2;
80.4, etc.; 89.16; Dan. 9.17). In Ps. 4.7 we have: 'Let the light of
your face rise [MT uncertain] on us!' In Ps. 90.8 we read: 'You lay out
our sins before you, our secrets under the brilliance of your face'.

There is a tradition in Exod. 34.29-35 that the skin of Moses' face
was radiant because he had spoken with God. Moses did not know it;
but Aaron and all the Israelites saw that the skin of his face was
radiant and they were afraid to come near him. Then Moses called
them and set out for them all that YHWH had said to him. After that
he put a veil over his face. The Hebrew verb 'to shine' comes from
qeren, 'horn' (from which the Vulgate has *cornuta*, 'horned'). In Hab.
3.4, this word refers to the rays of the sun. A sculpture of Michel-
angelo has made this episode famous (Terrien 1978: 160; Haran 1984:
159; cf. 2 Cor. 3.7, 18).

Morning and Awakening

The morning when the light of the sun appears is the time when
YHWH saves the chosen or punishes the guilty.[1] It is 'at daybreak' that
God delivers the people pursued by the Egyptians (Exod. 14.27) and
those besieged in Jerusalem by the Assyrians (2 Kgs 19: 35; Gonçalves
1986: 315). The theme of deliverance in the morning comes up frequently in Isaiah (8.22–9.1; 17.14; 33.2; 42.16; 49.9; 58.10; 60.1). In
the same way the psalmist cries out: 'In the evening, tears; in the
morning, cries of joy' (30.6). It is in the morning that the psalmist
sings of the love of God in greeting the dawn (Pss. 59.17; 57.9 =
108.3; 90.5; 92.3; 143.8).[2]

This is why the Levitical singers ask God, following in the steps of
the prophets (Amos 7.9; Isa. 2.19; 14.22; etc.), to get up, to wake up,
to rise up: 'Rise up, YHWH, save me, my God' (Ps. 3.8; cf. Jer. 2.27);
'Rise up, YHWH' (Pss. 7.7; 9.20; 10.12; 21.14; 68.2; 94.2; 132.8);

---

1. Cf. Pss. 17.15; 49.15; 73.14; 90.14; 101.8; 130.6; 2 Sam. 15.2; 23.4; Hos.
6.3, 5; Jer. 21.11; Zeph. 3.5; Job 7.18; 24.17; 38.15; Lam. 3.23.
2. Cf. Ziegler 1950: 281; Lipiński 1979: 733; Tournay 1982a: 51; Janowski
1989.

'Rise up in my defence' (35.2); 'Rise, YHWH, confront them' (17.13); 'Awake, why do you sleep, YHWH? Wake up' (44.24; cf. 78.65; 80.3); 'Stand up, come to our help' (44.27); 'Awake' (35.23; 59.5-6; cf. 74.22; 82.8). God should get up in the morning just like the judge who must get to court (cf. Pss. 12.6; 76.10; 101.8).

Day of YHWH

A central theme of the preaching of the ancient prophets is the day of YHWH; it is pre-eminently the time of great theophanies (Amos 5.18; Isa. 2.12ff.; Zeph. 1.14ff.; Jer. 30.7; Ezek. 7.10; 30.3; Isa. 13.9-10); in the period of the Second Temple this theme will take on an eschatological dimension (Joel 2.1ff.; Job 21.30; etc.).[1] This theme appears in the psalms: 'The Lord laughs at them [the wicked], seeing that their day is at hand' (37.13). For the wicked, this will be the day of their death. Israel has forgotten the day when God saved them from the enemy (78.42). In the messianic psalms, the day of YHWH is the day when God's 'son' (2.7) is begotten and when God 'shatters kings in the day of divine wrath' (110.5).

As the day of wrath (*dies irae, dies illa*) or day of salvation, the coming of YHWH is announced at the end of the psalms of the Reign of God (Pss. 96.11-13; 98.7-9; cf. 67.5; 82.8): all creation hails the one who will come to judge the world and peoples in justice and truth. While awaiting that day, the Levitical singers appeal to the community to listen to the voice of YHWH: 'O that today you would listen to my voice!' (Ps. 95.7; cf. Heb 3.7ff.). They exhort the faithful to draw near to the face of YHWH (v. 2). Consequently, the day of YHWH is not a distant reality, transferred to an indefinite future: each liturgical celebration before the face of God, on Zion, is 'the day which YHWH has made, for us a day of happiness and joy' (Ps. 118.24; Neh. 8.10).

This selection of theophanies from the psalms is enough to indicate the importance which the encounter with God attained, during the period of the Second Temple, for the faithful who came 'to lift the eyes toward God' and 'see the divine face'. The proper name Elioenai,

---

1. See p. 52; Bourke 1959: 191; Souza 1970: 166; Gray 1974: 5; Hoffmann 1981: 31; Lohfink 1984a: 100; Weinfeld 1986: 341.

'Towards Yah, my eyes' occurs frequently in Chronicles.[1] The Levitical singers in charge of prayer and liturgical singing wanted to actualize this presence of the hidden, invisible God, a God at work each day to save the people and manifest divine power in the eyes of the pagan nations. Inspired by the Spirit, these cultic prophets worked at comforting the poor of YHWH, in order to maintain and develop in them the hope in the coming of the Reign of God and the messiah, the son of David. This is why along with theophanic evocations they multiply divine discourses, real cultic oracles. From now on, in fact, the law comes from Zion and the word from Jerusalem.

1. 1 Chron. 3.23-24: 4.36ff.; 7.8; 8.20; 26.3; Ezra 8.4; 10.27; Neh. 12.41; Cf. Ps. 25.15 and 123.1.

Appendix

THEOPHANIC HYMN FROM QUMRAN

The Hymn (*hôdayôt*) scroll discovered at Qumran contains in column XI an apocalyptic description of the annihilation of the universe by fire. It is the only description of a theophany preserved in the Qumran writings. Here is a translation of E. Puech's French translation (1983: 370).

30　The torrents of Belial have overflown all the high banks,
　　devouring their irrigation channels with fire,
　　to destroy every tree, green [31] or dry along their canals
　　and consume with flaming whirlwinds
　　until everything which drinks there disappears.
　　It devours the clay foundations [32] and the foundations of the mainland,
　　and the foundations of the mountains become a blazing inferno,
　　and the seams of flint, torrents of tar, and it devours up to the great
　　　　[33] abyss ...

35　For God thunders with the bellowing of divine might
　　and the holy dwelling rumbles with that [36] boundless glory;
　　the army of the heavens raises its voice
　　and the eternal foundations are unsettled and shaken.
　　The war of the heavenly heroes [37] sets the world ablaze,
　　and it will not cease until the fatal final extermination
　　such as the world has never seen before.

The eschatological fire spreads like a flow of lava. A formidable thunderstorm is let loose. God thunders and the army of the heavens gives forth its voice. This world is burned and everything is exterminated. A comparison may be made with Wis. 5.21-23 and several New Testament texts (2 Thess. 1.8; 1 Cor. 3.13; 2 Pet. 3.5-7, 10; Rev. 21.8) as well as with many apocryphal texts, such as the *Book of Enoch* (102.1-3), the *Sibylline Oracles* (3.671ff.; 4.176ff.), the *Life of Adam and Eve* (49.3ff.), and also the Babylonian Talmud (*Zebahim* 116a), as well as Josephus (*Ant.* 1.70).

PART III

THE ORACLES IN THE PSALMS

'Our God comes and no longer keeps silent' (Ps. 50.3).

'It is you who spoke through the Holy Spirit and through the mouth of our father David, your servant: Why this tumult among nations. . .?' (Acts 4.25).

Chapter 9

PSALMIST'S REQUEST AND THE DIVINE RESPONSE:
AN INSPIRED DIALOGUE

In response to the Levitical singers speaking for the community, YHWH makes the divine presence known in the Temple, the dwelling place of God's name and the residence of God's glory. From Zion, the new Sinai, God's word goes out. Just as God is manifested to the people in cultic theophanies, so too God listens to them and responds in cultic oracles. It is this dialogue between God and God's 'guests' and friends that we must now examine. Thanks to the psalms, God becomes at once visible and audible in a quasi-sacramental way, in the course of the liturgical act.

The *dialogue* can begin as soon as a genuine meeting takes place. It is no longer just a matter of visiting the sanctuary to consult and question YHWH as had often been done in the past.[1] The pursuit and seeking of God should culminate in a spiritual experience like that attributed to King David in which there is renewal and transformation through the presence of God. An oracle of Amos had already proclaimed: 'Seek me and you shall live' (5.4-6, 14). The words of the prophet Hosea echo this: 'With their sheep and oxen, they go in search of YHWH, but their quest is in vain because God has withdrawn from them' (5.6). God is going to retire to the divine dwelling place until they confess their guilt and seek God's face; then they will search for God in their distress (Hos. 5.15). If Israel comes back to YHWH its God, God will listen to its prayer and care for it (Hos. 14.2, 9). Deut. 4.29 repeats Hosea here: 'From there [in the exile] you will seek YHWH your God; you will be successful in this if you search with all your heart and all your soul' (cf. Jer. 29.13; Isa. 55.6).

---

1. Cf. Gen. 25.22; Exod. 33.7ff.; 1 Sam. 9.9; 14.41; 15.16; 2 Sam. 5.23; 21.1; 1 Kgs 22.5ff.; Deut. 12.5.

In olden times the divine message was communicated by means of divination rites, such as the Urim and Thummim (de Vaux 1961: 352), and through dreams that may have been brought about through incubation. It is no longer this way in the time of the Second Temple. It is true that some have thought that they could detect allusions to incubation in the references to the bed and the couch on which the worshipper is thought to pray (Pss. 4.5; 149.5). But this could be a prayer cloth or simply a bed on which to rest (Ps. 36.5). From now on, the faithful are those who 'seek God', according to Pss. 22.27; 24.6; 42.2; 69.33; 70.5; 105.3; 119.2. The Hebrew verbs that express this 'seeking' are: *dāraš* (17 times in 11 psalms); *biqqēš* (10 times in 6 psalms); and *šāḥar* (Pss. 63.2; 78.34), a verb derived from the noun *šaḥar*, 'dawn' (cf. Ps. 130.6). The books of Chronicles have a fondness for this fundamental theme.[1] We may cite, for example, 1 Chron. 28.9: 'If you really seek God, God will let you be successful in your quest', and 2 Chron. 15.2: 'When you really seek God, God lets you have success' (cf. Mt. 6.33; 7.7).

According to the regular pattern of the prayers preserved for us in texts from the ancient Near East, the worshipper who prayed to the deity expected a response. At the end of Canaanite–Phoenician votive and dedicatory texts, the worshipper declares: 'My voice has been heard' (cf. pp. 23-24, an Ugaritic prayer). We may mention the Aramaic stele of Zakhour, king of Hamath about 800 BCE. The king describes himself at the beginning as a 'humble' man and declares later on (lines 11-13): 'I raised my hands toward the Lord of heaven [*B'lšmyn*], and the Lord of heaven listened to me. Then the Lord of heaven spoke to me through seers [*ḥzyn*] and omens [*'ddn*] and said to me: "Do not fear..."' (Donner and Röllig 1968: 20).

The repetition of these same formulas is explained by an oral stage prior to their being put in writing (Culley 1967: 35). We must, however, note that the psalmists could vary their prayer formulas (Berlin 1985: 127). But beyond the diverse literary genres, the essential theme is the appeal directed to YHWH in order to receive a response (cf. Isa. 58.9; Jer. 33.3). As YHWH says to Solomon: 'My name will be there to hear the prayers' (1 Kgs 8.29; 2 Chron. 6.20; 30.27). If, as we have seen, the dialogue between God and the prophets has come to an end,

---

1. 1 Chron. 22.19; 2 Chron. 12.14; 14.3, 6; 15.12-13; 16.12; 17.3-4; 19.3; 20.3; 22.9; 24.22; 26.5; 31.21; 34.3.

the dialogue between God and the faithful continues. It is quite right to say that prayer goes from the people to God and oracles go from God to the people.

Before dealing with the oracular psalms, we must mention here the countless texts in the psalms in which God is asked to reply and does so. The list that follows is not an exhaustive one.

'I cry aloud to YHWH; God answers me from the holy mountain' (3.5); 'When I call, answer me...; listen to my prayer...; YHWH listens when I cry out' (4.2, 4); 'YHWH, listen to my words...; at dawn you hear my voice' (5.2-4); 'YHWH hears my weeping, YHWH hears my pleading, YHWH accepts my prayer' (6.9-10); 'The prayer of the poor you answer, YHWH..., you do pay heed' (10.17); 'Look, answer me, YHWH' (13.4); 'Listen, YHWH,...pay heed to my prayer ...I have called to you; you will answer me' (17.1, 6); 'I cried out to God who heard my voice' (18.7); 'May the words of my mouth be favourably received' (19.15); 'May YHWH answer you in the day of distress...From the heavenly sanctuary God answers...Answer us the day we call' (20.2, 7, 10); 'God listened to their cry for help' (22.35); 'Listen YHWH to my cry for help...; answer me' (27.7); 'YHWH, I call to you...; do not turn a deaf ear to me...Hear the sound of my pleading when I cry to you...Blessed be YHWH who hears the sound of my pleading' (28.1-2, 6); 'YHWH, it is you I called ...Listen, YHWH...' (30.9, 11); 'Incline your ear to me...You listened to my prayer when I cried to you' (31.3, 23); 'I turned to YHWH and was answered...The poor cry out; YHWH listens... YHWH listens to those who cry for help' (34.5, 7, 18); 'It is you, my God, who will answer me' (38.16); 'Listen to my prayer, YHWH; turn an ear to my cries; do not be deaf to my weeping' (39.13); 'God heard my cry' (40.2); 'O God, hear my prayer; listen to the words of my mouth' (54.4); 'O God, listen to my prayer...; pay heed to me; I beg you, answer me...As for me, I call to God...God has heard my cry ...May God hear!' (55.2-3, 17-18, 20); 'My enemies turn back when I call; from this I know that God is with me' (56.10); 'I cry out to God, the Most High' (57.3); 'Answer us' (60.7); 'O God, hear my cry, answer my prayer...From the end of the earth I call to you...It is you who have accepted my vows' (61.2-3, 6); 'Listen to my voice, O God, as I lament' (64.2); 'You listen to prayer...You answer us... with wonders' (65.3, 6); 'When I directed my cry to God..., God listened; God hears the sound of my prayer' (66.17, 19); 'I grow weary crying out...Answer me...YHWH listens to the poor' (69.4, 14, 17, 18, 34); 'Incline your ear to me' (71.2); 'I cry out to God for help that I may be heard' (77.2); 'Then YHWH heard' (78.21, 59); 'Shepherd of Israel, hear us' (80.2); 'In distress you called...; I answered you...' (81.8); 'YHWH, God of hosts, listen to my prayer; pay heed, God of Jacob' (84.9); 'YHWH, listen to me, answer me...Listen to my prayer...Be attentive to my voice...I call to you; you answer me' (86.1, 6-7); 'Let my prayer come up to you; open your ear to my cry!...I call to you all day long, YHWH...I cry out to you, YHWH' (88.3, 10, 14); 'Whoever calls on me, I will answer them' (91.15); 'Moses, Aaron...called upon YHWH...You answered them' (99.6, 8); 'YHWH, hear my prayer; let my cry come up to you...The day I call to you, quickly answer me' (102.2-3); 'God hears their cries' (106.44); 'They cried out...; God rescued them' (refrain of 107.6, etc.); 'Answer us' (108.7); 'YHWH hears my voice in supplication...; I will call to God...I call upon the name of YHWH' (116.1-2, 4; cf. v. 13); 'In my anguish I cried to YHWH who answered me' (118.5); 'You answer me...I call out with all my heart, answer me...Listen to my voice' (119.26, 145, 149); 'In my distress I cried to YHWH who answered me' (120.1); 'Out of the depths I cry to you, YHWH; God, hear my voice. May your ear be attentive to the sound of my pleading' (130.1-2); 'You have heard the words of my mouth...The day I called, you answered me' (138.1, 3); 'Hear, YHWH, my voice in supplication' (140.7); 'YHWH, I call to you...; listen to my voice when I call to you' (141.1); 'I cry out to YHWH...Pay attention to my cries' (142.2, 7); 'YHWH, hear my prayer; give ear to my appeals...Answer me, YHWH...At dawn make me hear of your love' (143.1, 7-8); 'God listens to their cry and saves them' (145.19).

Most often these appeals to God come from psalms of supplication and individual and national laments. It would appear that God is silent (35.22; 50.3; 83.2; 109.1; cf. Tournay 1982a: 52), or sleeps (44.24) or is deaf (39.13) or hides from view and stands far off,[1] or forgets.[2] The supplicant agonizes in the face of this apparent silence of God: 'My God, I cry out by day, and you do not answer; by night and receive back nothing but silence' (22.3) (Puech 1984: 94). But in v. 22c

---

1. Pss. 10.1; 22.12; 27.9; 30.8; 44.25; 88.15; 89.47.
2. Pss. 10.12; 13.1; 42.10; 44.25; 74.19, 23; 77.10; 94.7.

it is stated that God did respond.[1] In fact, most of the time the psalmist speaks of the divine response (cf. Jonah 2.3). As we shall see, that response can be expressed in a genuine cultic oracle.

All these prayers would be the kind of prayers we would associate with the poor of YHWH, those Judaeans living under the occupation of the Achemenids and the Greeks, surrounded by pagan peoples and exposed to the mockery of the renegades and the wicked (the *rĕša'îm*), enemies of YHWH and YHWH's people (Ittmann 1981: 103). As already stated, these 'poor' had an obvious model in King David, a poet and musician, persecuted and humiliated (cf. 2 Sam. 16.12; 1 Kgs 2.26; Pss. 89.23; 132.1). A new Moses, just as humble as the first, David was considered a prophet, responsible for psalmic prayer. Moreover, he had repented of his sin and had been pardoned (2 Sam. 12; Ps. 51.1). For all these reasons David could become the spiritual father of the official psalter. The Levitical singers would consider themselves to be speaking for David and would be aware that they were taking on in this way the role of cultic prophets.

---

1. In Ps. 65.2, the MT reading, 'For you, silence is praise', is a rereading inspired by Ps. 62.2 and is worth consideration. But the original reading, confirmed by the versions, *domiyyâ*, 'is fitting, due, proper', should be accepted because of the context and the parallels (Pss. 33.1; 147.1).

Chapter 10

THE ORACULAR PSALMS

Like the theophanic passages in the psalter, the oracles contained in the psalms help give to this collection a perceptible prophetic dimension. These oracles are sometimes explicit, at other times implicit. They all exhibit a two-sided message: salvation and liberation, threat and judgment (Harris 1971; Hanson 1975: 303; Blenkinsopp 1984: 252). The salvation oracle may be summarized in this way: 'Do not fear; do not be afraid!' The second part of the book of Isaiah is a good example of this kind of comforting discourse in which God reiterates divine fidelity to the covenant and to the promises (Begrich 1964: 217; Dion 1967: 198; van der Toorn 1987: 63). As the antithesis of this, the divine lawsuit (*rîb*), frequently occurring in oracles from the period of the monarchy (Vermeylen 1977: 43) and in the exilic period in the 'Song of Moses' (Deuteronomy 32) is found in Psalms 50, 81 and 95. It is necessary as well to put in a special class by themselves the 'messianic' oracles found in Psalms 89 and 132, 110 and 2; there will be a special study devoted to them in Chapter 12.

Right from the beginning of the psalter, the word of God recorded in the Torah and the messianic adoption of the son of David are presented as the two essential components of the Jewish faith: law and messiah, past and future. Psalms 1 and 2 form in this way a literary block made more cohesive by close links in vocabulary and by being framed by a twofold 'macarism': 'Happy are those. . .! Blessed are they who put their trust in God!'

Psalm 12.6

The psalm begins with an appeal: 'Help!' The hapax *passû* in v. 2, translated on the basis of the context '(loyalty) has vanished', is read *sapû* by the Targum (cf. Ps. 73.19), but with the same meaning. A euphemistic retouching could have brought about the metathesis of the verb's consonants: all the loyal people have not 'vanished'! The sequence denounces lying and duplicity. Verse 4 is close to Prov. 10.31-32 and the Wisdom of Ahikar (Greenfield 1971a: 48). God then arises and begins to speak in v. 6, which may be compared to Isa. 33.10; 56.1; Zeph. 3.8. The psalmist then comments on the oracle by contrasting human disloyalty with the loyalty of YHWH who pledges to save the unfortunate. Here is the oracle of v. 6.

> 'For the poor who are oppressed, the needy who groan, now I
>   will arise'—says YHWH;
> 'I will bring salvation'—YHWH personally affirms it.

The last two words, *yāpîaḥ lô*, are difficult to translate (P.D. Miller 1979: 495; Loewenstamm 1980: 137). The following translations have been suggested: 'to them on whom one breathes / on whom one spits / that one despises', or 'to them who aspire to it' (cf. Hab. 2.3), or based on the parallelism: '(God) testifies / bears witness / declares for (the unfortunate)' (cf. Pss. 10.5; 27.12). This last interpretation, confirmed by Ugaritic, is found in the Targum: *šehad*, 'witness'. For God, an oracular declaration is not enough; there must be a pledge in favour of the poor to whom help and liberation are promised, as if by an oath.

This is why, in the following verses, the Levitical singer declares that the divine words are reliable, sincere, like silver smelted in the crucible of the earth and refined sevenfold (cf. Mal. 3.3; 1 Chron. 29.4). God will carry out what has been promised and will protect the unfortunate forever from the progeny of liars and hypocrites. On all sides the wicked are on the move as debauchery increases (March 1971: 610). The picture is grim, but there is still hope for YHWH's intervention and final liberation.

Psalm 12, like Ps. 33.4 and Isa. 45.19, insists on the reliability of the word. This word is without alloy (Ps. 18.31; Prov. 30.5), truthful and clear (Ps. 19.8-9). When YHWH sends this word like a messenger (Pss. 107.20; 147.15, 18), it does not return without having an effect (Isa. 55.11).

Is the attribution of the psalm to David due to the contact between v. 2b and 2 Sam. 20.18-19? The latter text is obscure and poorly transmitted: 'Let them ask. . .whether what the faithful of Israel have established is finished'. In any case, it is certain that the psalmist is here comparing David to a prophet and has him give an oracle, as in 2 Sam. 23.2.

Psalm 32.8-9

8   I will instruct you and show you the way to follow;
     I will counsel you, keeping my eye on you.

9   Do not be like a horse or mule;
     it understands neither bit nor bridle;
     rounded up to be broken in, it refuses to come near you.

This exhortation in a didactic tone[1] has sometimes been considered to be, not a divine oracle, but the words of a teacher of wisdom to a disciple. According to Crüsemann (1969: 236), the three last words of v. 9 (it refuses...) would be a gloss recalling the end of v. 6: 'They shall not reach him'. Verse 9 has been compared to a Babylonian text: 'I am a donkey to be saddled; I am teamed with a mule; I pull a chariot; I put up with a bit' (Lambert 1960: 242). But with Kraus, Mannati, *et al.*, it is better to assume that we have an oracle here, because of the phrase 'keeping my eyes on you' which can bring to mind the idea of the divine gaze (Pss. 31.8; 33.13-14, 18; 34.16; 35.17, 22). Keeping an eye on people is to look after them (Jer. 24.6). This gaze can be stern (Amos 9.4; Ezek. 5.11; Deut. 7.16).

The divine oracle seems to be a response to the prayer of vv. 6-7: 'Each of your faithful prays to you...; you surround me'. The dialogue continues between the supplicant and God who has been addressed in the second person from the end of v. 5: 'And you forgive the wrong I did'. Psalm 32 begins and ends with thanksgiving; it develops in vv. 6-7 the theme of God as a shelter for the just, a theme connected to that of being a guest of YHWH. The love of God 'surrounds' the just who trust in God (v. 10). All this is the setting for the oracle studied here, while the concluding 'rejoice' links up with the beginning of Psalm 33: the same verb *rānan*, 'to rejoice', is a *mot crochet* between the two psalms.

The superscription of Psalm 32, *maśkîl*, occurring just this one time in the first book of the psalter (Pss. 1–41), should be connected up with the beginning of the oracle: 'I will instruct you' (same root *śkl*;

---

1. Castellino 1952: 27; 1955: 388; Macintosh 1974: 454; Perdue 1977: 338, n. 133.

cf. Ps. 101.2). The superscription 'of David' suggests comparisons
with the books of Samuel. One example would be the words of David
after the census of the people (2 Sam. 24.10, 17): 'I have committed a
grave sin. And now, YHWH, please forgive your servant for this sin,
for I have really acted like a fool [verb *skl*, a homonym of *śkl*!].'
Another is the response of Nathan to David (2 Sam. 12.13): 'YHWH
too has forgiven your sin'.

In this Davidic context, the psalm exhibits a certain unity if it is
reread in the way the Levite responsible for the definitive text read it,
in the light of the eventful life of David, the repentant sinner, the fool
now wise and become a prudent man (1 Sam 18.14-15), protected by
God.

Psalm 35.3

This is the complaint of a just individual who is persecuted; this individual has been seen as David, pursued by his enemies and considered
a 'servant of God' (v. 27). This explains the superscription 'of
David'. The Levitical singer begs God to rise to his defence; he asks
straight away for an oracle: 'Say to my soul: It is I, your salvation'
(v. 3b). This brief oracle is a verse of 2 + 2 accents, a rhythm that
differs from that of the previous verses (3 + 2 accents). But v. 4a has
the same rhythm as v. 3b. On the other hand, the psalmist too has
something personal to say: 'All my bones will say: Who is like
you. . .?' (v. 10). The assailants are made to speak twice: 'Ha! Ha!'
(vv. 21, 25). Finally, the faithful are given a chance to speak: 'Great
is YHWH. . .' (v. 25). It should be noted that the psalmist likes to be
involved personally, as indicated by the repetition of 'his/my soul'
(vv. 3, 7, 9, 12, 13, 17; cf. v. 25). The phrase 'my salvation' appears
in v. 9. In this way, this short oracle in v. 3b is from a literary point
of view incorporated into the psalm as a whole. It could be inspired
by Ps. 3.3: 'How many are saying of my soul: There is no salvation
for it in God!' Here the psalmist asks God to intervene: 'Do not be silent any longer' (v. 22). God will see (v. 22), will rise up (v. 23),
and will end the silence with a cultic oracle like that of v. 3b or like
those toward the latter part of the book of Isaiah: 'All flesh will know
that I, YHWH, I am your deliverer' (Isa. 49.26); 'You will know that
it is I, YHWH, who saves you' (Isa. 60.16).

Psalm 46.11

At the end of the third and final strophe of Psalm 46[1] YHWH pronounces the following oracle.

> 11 Wait a moment; know that I, I am God;
> I rule over the nations, I rule over the earth.

'Wait a moment' has the sense here of 'stop, give up' (cf. 1 Sam. 15.16). What follows reminds us of the formula current in Ezekiel (more than 20 times): 'And you will know that I am YHWH' (Ezek. 6.7; etc.). The second colon ends, just like vv. 3a, 7b, 9b and 10a, with the word 'earth', which is here the universe, the dwelling of the pagans (*gôyim*), in parallelism with 'kingdoms' (v. 7a) . The perspective here is the same as in the final part of the book of Isaiah and in the psalms of the Reign of YHWH. The repetition 'exalted, exalted' or 'I rule, I rule' expresses emphatically a frequent theme in the psalter.[2] The phrase 'I, I am God' (Pss. 50.7; 81.11) occurs again in Isa. 43.11-12. The central theme of Psalm 46 is the permanent presence of YHWH in YHWH's own city of Zion: YHWH is for the people Emmanuel (cf. Isa. 7.14; 8.8, 10) and saves them at daybreak (see p. 155). The river (v. 5) reminds us of the tunnel of Hezekiah (2 Kgs 18.17; 20.20), a figure of the symbolic river (Ezek. 47.1ff.) which waters the new Eden. This theme is repeated in Isa. 33.21; Zech. 14.8 and Joel 4.18. The links with Joel are very close: 'God's voice resounds' (v. 7b; Joel 2.11; 4.16); 'And you will know that I am in the midst of Israel, that I am your God and no one is my equal' (v. 6a; Joel 2.27); 'You will know then that I am YHWH your God who dwells in Zion, my holy mountain. Jerusalem will be a holy place' (v. 5; Joel 4.17). The prophetic theme of the end of wars[3] is found in Ps. 46.10: 'God breaks the bow, snaps the spear, burns the chariots [LXX and Targ.: 'the shields']', and in Ps. 76.4 as well: 'There (in Jerusalem!), God has put an end to the flashings of the bow, the shield, the sword and war'.

1. Krinetzki 1961: 52; Wanke 1966: 10, 74; Lutz 1968: 157; Weins 1984: 314.
2. Pss. 18.47; 21.14; 57.6; 89.14; 99.2; 113.4; 138.6; Isa. 33.10; 57.15; Ezek. 10.4.
3. Hos. 2.20; Mic. 4.3; Isa. 2.4; 9.4; Ezek. 39.9-10; Joel 4.19; Zech. 9.10.

Psalm 50

The oracles contained in Pss. 50.5-23;[1] 81.7-17 and 95.8-11 are modelled on the ancient prophetic lawsuits or indictments (*rîb*; Vermeylen, 1977: 42, 65; Murray 1987: 95) directed against Israel. Psalms 50 and 81 belong to the Asaphite collection. Psalm 50, as we have seen (p. 144), begins with a theophanic prelude. S. Mowinckel describes Psalm 50 as *nachprophetisch* (close to prophecy). Many commentators place it in the post-exilic period (*dōpî*, v. 20a, is an Aramaic word; *'Ĕlôah*, v. 22a, occurs 46 times in Job). Here is the admonition of Ps. 50.5-23:

5　'Gather before me my faithful ones,
　　who sealed a covenant with me over a sacrifice.
6　The heavens proclaim divine justice:
　　it is God who is the judge.　　　　　　　　　　　(Pause)

7　'Listen, my people, I am speaking;
　　Israel, I want to warn you:
　　it is I, God, your God;
21c　(I denounce you and draw up my case against you):

8　'It is not your sacrifices that I denounce;
　　your holocausts are always before me.
9　I will not take a bull from your house,
　　nor goats from your pens.

10　'For every animal of the forest is mine;
　　the animals on the mountains by the thousands;
11　I know all the birds of the heavens;[2]
　　the animals of the fields are mine.

12　'If I am hungry, I will not tell you,
　　for the world and all it holds is mine.
13　Am I going to eat the flesh of bulls,
　　and drink the blood of goats?

14　'Offer a thanksgiving sacrifice to God,
　　fulfill your vows to the Most High;
15　then call upon me in the day of trouble;
　　I will set you free and you shall glorify me.'

16　But to the wicked God declares.
　　'What are you doing reciting my laws,

1.　Mannati 1973: 27; 1975: 659; Gese 1976: 57; Schwartz 1978: 77; Nielsen 1978: 104; 1979: 309.
2.　'Heavens', versions; 'mountains', MT.

and paying lip service to my covenant,
17 you who detest discipline
and cast my words to the winds?

18 'If you see a thief, you hang out with him,
you feel at home with adulterers;
19 you loosen your lips for evil
and your tongue devises deception.

20 'You sit there slandering your own kinsfolk,
you dishonour your own mother's child.
21 This is what you do, and I am to keep silent?
Do you think I am like yourself?
(I denounce you and draw up my case against you.)

22 'Be very careful, you who forget God,
or I will corner you and tear you to pieces!
23 Those who offer thanksgiving sacrifices,
such people glorify me;
on the path they will have picked,
I will show them the salvation of God.'

Verse 5 brings to mind the covenant meal ('my covenant', v. 16c) which concluded the Sinai Covenant (Exod. 24.9-11). Israel must fulfil the requirements of that covenant. According to v. 16a (Reindl 1981: 344), the indictment involves the wicked and not the people in general. In addition, v. 21c, 'I denounce you and draw up my case against you', seems to be superfluous after the bicolon of v. 21. It would be a rereading intended to unburden Israel by dealing gently with the *Ḥăsîdîm* ('my faithful ones', v. 5). In this case, v. 21c would have originally completed the tricolon of v. 7. All the other strophes of the psalm consist of quatrains (v. 23 has an extra colon which lengthens the final strophe).

As a matter of fact, a real trial is not intended here. God merely wants 'to dispense justice' to this people and put them on guard against a formalistic worship that is merely external, without any real devotion. Four quatrains (vv. 8-9, 10-11, 12-13, 14-15) condemn this ritualism. It is as if one were reading Malachi and other oracles filled with reproaches (Amos 4.5; 5.25; Hos. 6.6 ; Isa. 1.11; Jer. 7.22; Mt. 9.13). The *tôdâ* or thanksgiving sacrifice should supersede (vv. 14a, 23a) immolation rites (Lipiński 1979: 64). This spiritualizing of worship was characteristic of the religious life of Judaeans during the period of the Second Temple. After 587 BCE they had to resign themselves to the cessation of sacrifices. Psalm prayers (hymns and complaints) developed under the influence of the Levitical singers, the cultic prophets. The only valid response to the salvation bestowed by God ('the salvation of God', v. 23b) is therefore the *tôdâ* in which the community confesses in the form of thanksgivings the mighty divine acts in favour of Israel; this is what we find in Psalms 100, 105, 106, 107 and many other psalm texts.[1] This *tôdâ*, developed by Lev. 7.12; 22.29, was accompanied by music (Pss. 33.2; 92.2-4). It occupies a predominant place in the ritual of the Second Temple.

Ps. 50.23b could be translated: 'And they will take the way (in which) I will show them the salvation of God'. Some Masoretic manuscripts and some versions (LXX, Syr) read *šām*, 'there (is the way. . .)', instead of *śām* (3rd person singular of *śîm*, 'place, take'). Symmachus and Jerome read *tam*, 'the upright person (in the way)' (cf. Prov. 10.29; 13.6; Job 4.6; Ps. 119.1). The consonant *taw* pronounced as a spirant can be mistaken for *sin* or *shin*. As a result, we find these textual variants.

This verse has been compared to Ps. 85.14: 'Justice shall go on before [as a herald, before YHWH], and will prepare [= trace] the way with its footsteps'. This verse concludes an implicit oracle introduced in v. 9 this way: 'I want to listen to what YHWH God says: "Peace for my people and my faithful ones"'. The final verses of Psalm 91, verses 14-16 (cf. Psalm 23.6), are presented too as a divine oracle and seem to depend on Psalm 50. Someone faithful to God is in some danger and appeals to God who replies (Hugger 1971; Malamat 1982).

14   Because you cling to me I rescue you;
       I protect you, for you know my name.
15   You call me and I answer you.
       'I am with you in distress;
       I want to deliver you and glorify you;
16   with a long life I want to favour you
       and show you my saving power.'

We should note that the oracles in Psalms 50 and 91 both open with the announcement of a cultic theophany (Kraus 1978: 530). The believer 'will see' salvation. They may be compared to Isa. 52.10: 'All the nations of the earth will see the salvation [= the victory] of our

---

1. Pss. 26.7; 40.7, 10; 51.18; 56.13; 69.31-32; 95.2; 107.22; 116.17-18; 147.7. Cf. Isa. 51.3; Jer. 17.26; 30.19; 33.11; Jonah 2.10; Neh. 12.27; 2 Chron. 29.31; 33.16.

God', a text repeated in Ps. 98.3. We read in the Damascus Document from Qumran (20.34): 'God will pardon them and they will see salvation, for they will be sheltered by God's holy name' (Carmignac 1961: 182). The aged Simeon proclaims: 'My eyes have seen your salvation' (Lk. 2.30).

The same sequence, oracle–theophany, is found in Psalm 90 (Auffret 1980: 262; H.P. Muller 1984: 265; Howell 1984). The heading 'Of Moses, man of God' brings to mind the idea that Moses, just like David, was a prophet (cf. Josh. 14.6, etc.). The psalmist in v. 1 follows Deut. 33.27, a verse near the end of the blessings of Moses, 'man of God' (Deut. 33.1). Verse 2 can bring to mind the creation of the world ('before the mountains were born') and the revelation of the burning bush ('From everlasting to everlasting, you are God'; cf. Sir. 42.21). Verse 3 repeats in the form of an oracle the death sentence of Gen. 3.19:

> You turn us back to dust,
> saying, 'Go back, children of the earth'.[1]

The meditation in these three verses of Psalm 90 takes its inspiration then from the beginning and end of the 'Mosaic' Torah: Genesis and Deuteronomy. The motif of divine anger is found in vv. 7, 9, 11. This meditation on humanity in general is limited in the final verses to Israel and the servants of YHWH: they wish for the 'return' of YHWH and seek an oracle from God in v. 13. In vv. 16 -17 there is a prayer for some demonstration of the divine presence:

> Show forth your work to your servants
> and your splendour to your children!
> May the gentleness of YHWH our God be with us!

In this way the psalmist foresees here again the realization of a cultic theophany.

Psalm 81

The hymnic prelude of this Asaphite psalm is followed by a long oracle (Ps. 81.6c-17: Mowinckel 1962: 72; Booij 1975: 465; 1978: 165), much like those in Psalms 50 and 95. Here is the translation of Psalm 81:

---

1. Cf. Num. 16.29; 2 Sam. 14.14; Job 10.9; 34.14; Pss. 89.49; 103.14; 104.29; 146.4; Sir. 14.17; 40.11; Qoh. 3.20; 12.7; 1 Macc. 2.63.

2   Cry out for joy to honour God our strength;
     acclaim the God of Jacob;
3   start the music; sound the drum,
     the melodious zither and the harp;
4   blow the horn at the new moon,
     at the full moon, for our feast day.

5   For such is the law for Israel,
     an order from the God of Jacob,
6   who made it a rule for Joseph
     when marching against the land of Egypt.

     I hear a new language:
7   'I relieved their shoulder of the burden;
     their hands were freed from the basket.
8   In your oppression you called and I rescued you;
     hidden in the storm, I answered you;
     I tested you near the waters of Meribah.

9   'Listen, my people, I am warning you;
     if you could only listen to me, Israel!
10   Let there be no other god among you,
     no worship of a strange god.
11   I, YHWH, am your God,
     who led you up from the land of Egypt;
     open wide your mouth and I will fill it.

12   'My people did not listen to my voice;
     Israel did not want to obey me.
13   I left them in the hardness of their heart,
     so that they would keep on with their own schemes.

14   If only my people would listen to me,
     if Israel would follow my ways,
15   at once, I would humble their enemies;
     against their oppressors I would turn my hand.

16   The opponents of YHWH would come cringing;
     they would be terror-stricken forever.
17   I would feed Israel with finest wheat;
     with honey from the rock I would fill you.'

The solemn appeal, 'Listen, Israel' (v. 9; cf. Deut. 6.4) is developed
here as in Pss. 50.7 and 95.7, but in a very insistent way; the verb
'listen' appears five times. The two tricola in vv. 8 and 11 should be
noted. Verse 6c really belongs with v. 7 to introduce the following
oracle: 'I hear a new language. . .' The Asaphite Levite, spokesperson
for the community, is alert to hear the divine message or precept or
instruction (*'ēdût*; Couroyer 1975: 216; van der Toorn 1985: 181) just

like the Korahite of Ps. 85.9: 'I listen to what God says. . .' In the past it was not this way: at the time of the Exodus, during the wandering in the wilderness, in Canaan, Israel did not listen as it should have to the voice of the Lord. Along with Ps. 95.8, Ps. 81.8 alludes to the revolts at Meribah, meaning 'discord' or 'quarrelling', and Massah, meaning 'testing' or 'temptation'.[1]

Psalm 81 was used for the feast of Tabernacles, at the autumn full moon, on the day of 'our feast' (v. 4): *kēseh*, derived from Babylonian *kusī'u*, refers to the full moon (Lemaire 1973: 171; Lev. 23.25; Num. 29.12; Deut. 16.13; Ezek. 45.25). God freed Israel from forced labour (Exod. 1.14; 6.6; Deut. 5.6) and answered it in the obscurity of the storm (Exod. 19.16ff.; Pss. 18.12, 14; 77.19; etc.). The unknown and new language refers to the covenant and its stipulations, too often forgotten (v. 9a repeats Ps. 50.7; v. 9b corresponds to Ps. 95.7). The strange gods have often been denounced by the prophets, especially Jeremiah (2.25; 3.13; 5.19; cf. Ps. 44.21). The first commandment forbids the adoration of other gods (Exod. 20.3; 34.14; Deut. 4.28; 6.14; Langlamet 1969b: 490). Verse 11b which repeats Deut. 20.1 and recalls v. 6b may be an addition, which produces the present tricolon. Verse 11c serves as a transition and prepares for v. 17.

The second part of the oracle (vv. 12-17) is an exhortation in prophetic style. Israel should no longer be hard-hearted (Jer. 3.17; Isa. 6.10; etc.; Hesse 1955; Räisänen 1972; Couroyer 1981: 216; Schenker 1986: 563). They should listen to God who liberated them by spreading terror (*ḥittām* correction, auditory confusion of *ḥeth* and *'ayin*; MT: *'ittām*, 'their time/their fate?'; Syr., Targ.: 'terror') among their enemies and by nourishing them with the best products of the land 'flowing with milk and honey'.[2] This final verse of the psalm draws its inspiration from Deut. 32.13-14.

Psalm 95

A processional hymn like Psalms 24 and 68, this psalm is connected to Ps. 94.22 by the motif of the 'Rock', the refuge of Israel (Deut. 32.4,

1. Exod. 17.7; Num. 20.24; 27.14; Deut. 6.16; 9.22; 32.51; 33.8; Ps. 106.32.
2. Cf. Pss. 36.9; 78.24; 105.40; Exod. 16.4; Num. 11.7; Deut. 8.3; Wis. 16.20; 1 Cor. 10.3; Jn 6.49.

etc.; Isa. 30.29; Pss. 18.3, 32, 47; 19.15). This hymn introduces the group of psalms of the Reign of YHWH with Psalm 100 presenting the final doxology; these psalms prophetically announce (like Pss. 22.28-32; 47.9; etc.) the coming of the universal Reign of YHWH. Verse 3 recalls Pss. 47.3 and 96.4. Verse 6 describes the sequence of acts of adoration (cf. Neh. 8.6; 9.3; 2 Chron. 29.29-30). Verse 7 is close to Pss. 79.13 and 100.3; its final colon, 'Today, will you listen to God's voice?', introduces the oracle which follows (Ps. 95.7d-11: Schmid 1972: 91; Henton Davies 1973: 183) and is joined to vv. 8 and 9 to form a strophe of five cola just like the final strophe (vv. 10-11).

1   Come, let us cry out with joy for YHWH;
      let us acclaim the Rock who saves us;
2   let us go before God giving thanks;
      to the sound of music let us hail our God.

3   Yes, for YHWH is a great God,
      a great Ruler above all gods;
4   in the hands of God are the depths of the earth,
      and the summits of the mountains too;
5   the sea as well belongs to the one who created it,
      and the dry land which divine hands have fashioned.

6   Come, let us bow down, let us prostrate ourselves;
      let us adore YHWH who made us.
7   For YHWH is our God, and we,
      the people divinely shepherded,
      the flock led by God's hand.

      Today, will you listen to God's voice?
8   'Do not close your heart as in the desert,
      as in the days of temptation and dissension,
9   when your ancestors tested and provoked me,
      although they had seen my work.

10   'Forty years I was disgusted by their generation,
      and I said: this horde have hearts gone astray;
      these people have not known my ways.
11   Then, I swore in my anger.
      never shall they enter my resting-place.'

The Hebrews of the time of the Exodus had seen the work (a hapax; cf. Hab. 3.2; Pss. 90.16; 92.5; 111.3; 143.5) of YHWH, their liberator. Israel has no excuse, for YHWH continues to speak to it in the Temple as Ruler and Creator of the universe. The charge is a serious one. Just as in Psalm 50, the primitive text has been toned down so as not to shock the *Ḥăsîdîm*. In v. 10, the MT simply speaks of 'the generation (of the desert)', whereas the versions read it with a demonstrative, 'that (generation)'. Moreover, instead of the *textus receptus*, 'the people', some Hebrew manuscripts have 'always' (*'ad* instead of *'am*), the reading of the Septuagint and probably the original reading. The translation would then be: 'Always with hearts gone astray [cf. Ps. 119.176; Isa. 21.4; 29.24], they did not know my ways'. It is easier to understand then the severity of the final verse and the divine oath with which the oracle concludes: 'Never shall they enter my resting-place'.

The allusion to Massah and Meribah often occurs elsewhere (Meinertz 1957: 283; Guillet 1948: 275). But the *Ḥăsîdîm* who cele-brated the feast of Tabernacles knew how 'to listen' to the voice of the Lord, in God's 'resting place' (Deut. 12.9; Ps. 132.8, 14; etc.). The author of the Epistle to the Hebrews will comment on this text, show-ing how faith in Jesus Christ introduces the believer into the rest of God (Heb 3.7–4.11; Vanhoye 1968: 9).

Psalms 57, 60, 108

As T. Booij has clearly shown (1978: 130), Psalm 60[1] is an example, like Psalms 85 and 132, of a secondary kind of prophecy. The oracle of vv. 8-14 is repeated in Ps. 108.8-14, just as Ps. 57.8-12 is repro-duced in Ps. 108.2-6 where it serves as a hymnic prelude. Psalms 57 and 60 form part of the extensive Elohist collection (Pss. 42-72) and are both preceded by historical superscriptions which refer to David. Their re-use in Psalm 108 is evidence of their importance in the li-turgy of the Second Temple. Some manuscripts even attribute Psalm 108 to Asaphite Levites, responsible for so many oracles and theo-phanies in the psalms. Here is the translation of Psalm 60:

3   O God, you have rejected us, broken us;
      you were angry: restore us!
4   You have rocked the earth, torn it open;
      repair its rifts, for it is collapsing.

5   You let your people see hardship;
      you have given us wine that makes us stagger;
6   to your faithful you have given the signal
      that they may flee from the arrows of the archers.   (Pause)

---

1. Lipiński 1969: 60; Aharoni 1971: 13; Kellermann 1978: 56; Bellinger 1984: 73; Ogden 1985: 83.

7   May those who love you be rescued;
      save them by your right hand and answer us!

8   In the sanctuary God has spoken.
      'In triumph I parcel out Shechem;
      I measure off the valley of Succoth.

9   'Mine is Gilead, and mine Manasseh;
      Ephraim is the helmet for my head;
      Judah, my commander's staff.

10   'Moab serves as my washbowl;
      on Edom I cast my sandal.
      Shout victory over me, Philistia!'

11   Who will bring me into the fortified city,
      who will lead me as far as Edom?

12   Is it not you, O God, who rejects us
      and goes forth no more with our armies?

13   Give us aid against the oppressor;
      human help is useless!

14   With God we will perform deeds of valour;
      it is God who will trample our oppressors.

The national disaster referred to at the beginning of Psalm 60 presupposes the invasion of Israelite territory. God has to rally the people that they may escape the arrows of the enemy (Jer. 4.6; 6.1; Couroyer 1984: 5). It is interesting that the psalmist multiplies plays on words and paronomasia (see below). Most exegetes, for example U. Kellermann, think that Psalm 60 refers to the catastrophe of 587 BCE, much like Psalms 44, 74, 77, 80, 89. The resentment shown in regard to Edom (vv. 10-11) is understandable after the pillaging of Jerusalem by the Edomites. An extensive anti-Edomite documentation comes from this period.[1]

The Levitical singer acts as a cultic prophet in introducing the oracle, in v. 7, by 'answer us' (cf. Ps. 20.2, 10). This oracle is in the middle of the psalm just as in Psalms 2, 12, 75, 85, 89, etc. In three tricola (vv. 8-10), God pledges to bring back the golden age of the beginnings of the monarchy: the union of the North and Judah, the fullest extension of the kingdom on both sides of the Jordan, as in the time of Joshua (Josh. 13–21). The oracle is not introduced by the

---

1. Ps. 137.7; Lam. 4.22; Isa. 34 and 63.1; Amos 9.12; Isa. 11.14; Mal. 1.3-5; Jer. 49.15-16; Ezek. 25.12; 35.5, 12; Obad.; Num. 24.18 (Rouillard 1985: 436-46, 471).

phrase: 'Thus says YHWH', but by 'God has spoken in the sanctuary (the Temple)', or 'by my holiness', that is, by what is most personal (cf. Pss. 89.36; 105.42; Amos 4.2; Jer. 23.9). This oath would sanctify the eschatological oracle. There is no need to correct the beginning of the oracle: 'I triumph, I parcel out...', translated here as 'In triumph, I parcel out' ('I will go up' in Ps. 108.8, in one ms. and LXX; cf. C.R. North 1967: 242).

The valley of Succoth is the region of Deir 'Alla near the beginning of Wadi Jabbok (east bank of the Jordan). What Joshua did, God will do too: God will measure off (*mdd*, cf. 2 Sam. 8.2; Hab. 3.12) this valley. Shechem and Succoth are mentioned together in Gen. 33.17-18 (Otto 1979).

Seven regions are mentioned then as in the post-exilic addition of Isa. 11.10-16, which has links with Psalm 60. Gilead and Manasseh, Ephraim and Judah depict the two sides of the Jordan. God is presented as a warrior leader wearing a helmet (literally: a shelter), Ephraim. The commander's staff belongs to Judah (Gen. 49.10; Num. 21.18): it is the tribe of David from which the messiah will come. The washbowl of Moab is the Dead Sea whose water is undrinkable. The scornful irony continues. Casting the sandal on Edom denotes the appropriation of that territory in the same way as putting the foot on a field gave possession (Ruth 4.7; Josh. 1.3; 10.24). The final colon of v. 10 has a double meaning: 'Utter cries against me, Philistia', or 'shatter yourself against me' (cf. Isa. 24.19; Jer. 50.15; Pss. 2.9; 65.14). Some Masoretic manuscripts and the Syriac version have the same reading as in Ps. 108.10: 'Against Philistia I utter a war cry'; this eliminates the ambiguity.

The psalmist draws this lesson from the oracle: God is the only one able to restore Israel as far as Idumaea; nothing should be expected through human help. The community of the faithful has lost its national independence, but has no doubts about the future realization of this oracle (cf. Pss. 14.7; 55.7). A double meaning seems possible for v. 11a: 'Who will bring me (in tribute) the fortified city?' (cf. Pss. 45.15-16; 68.30; 76.12) or 'Who will bring me into the fortified city?' There is a play on words with *māṣôr*, 'fortified', and Bosra, capital of Idumaea. It is YHWH who leads the armies of Israel (cf. Pss. 44.10b; 68.8; Num. 14.14). For the moment God has apparently rejected the people of Israel (v. 12a, *inclusio* with v. 3a; cf. Ps. 44.10a). Aside from this, Edom seems to be going into decline (cf. Ps. 120.5; Isa.

42.11; Ezek. 35; Isa. 63.4); its ruin is described in Isa. 34; Obad., v. 19; Amos 9.12 and Mal. 1.4, texts which can be dated to about 450 BCE. Psalm 60 has been compared to Isa. 21.15, a text dated to the first years of the return from exile (Gosse 1986: 70): 'They flee from the swords, from the naked sword, from the taut bow, from the heat of the battle'. Psalm 60 would therefore be some decades earlier than 450 BCE.

The phrase 'for teaching' in the superscription of Psalm 60 does not occur elsewhere in the psalter and is found again only in 2 Sam. 1.17 at the beginning of David's elegy for Saul and Jonathan. A song as nationalistic as Psalm 60 must have become a classic in Israel. Its memorization was facilitated by an abundance of paronomasia: *qāšâ/hišqîtānû* (v. 5); *nēs/hitnôsēs* (v. 6); *māṣôr/miṣṣar* (vv. 11, 13); *'Edôm/'ādām* (vv. 11, 13). The 'historical' superscription refers to 2 Sam. 8.13 (1 Chron. 18.13) which speaks of 18,000 Edomites instead of the 12,000 in the heading of Psalm 60 (*šmwnh/šnym*). The 'valley of salt' designates the Arabah south of the Dead Sea, as in 2 Kgs 14.7 (Amaziah defeated 10,000 Edomites there). It was not Joab, but Abishai (1 Sam. 26.6-9), the brother of Joab, who defeated the Edomites, while Joab fought the Arameans (2 Sam. 10.9-10). 2 Sam. 8.13 speaks of David only. Dom Calmet had already observed that the title of Psalm 60 did not correspond to the contents of the psalm. The beginning of the superscription: 'According to "a lily [is] the decree"', could be given a different interpretation here as well as in Ps. 80.1 (Ps. 45.1 has been abbreviated) by merely changing the vocalization: 'Against those who tamper with [Lam. 4.1; Prov. 24.21] the testimony', that is, the instruction, the law (Pss. 78.5; 81.6). We should note that the LXX already translates it 'those who are changed (transformed)'. It would be a question here of Hellenized and apostate Jews in Maccabean times. The following word, *miktām* (p. 123) would indicate a 'secret' prayer, said in a subdued voice, during the night or recited secretly (as by David in the cave!). We may note finally that the mention of the bow (v. 6b) could lead one to make a comparison with 2 Sam. 1.17, 22 where it is a question again of the bow. What we have here is midrashic exegesis which was already evident in the books of Chronicles where David occupies an increasingly greater role as prophet and initiator of the psalms and a model of piety for the 'poor of YHWH' (Tournay 1957: 202; Childs 1971: 137; Slomovic 1979: 350; Pietersma 1980: 213; Cooper 1983b: 117;

Wilson 1985).

Psalm 57 (Auffret 1977a: 65; Kellenberger 1982: 145), whose two final strophes (vv. 8-12) serve in Psalm 108 as an introduction to the oracle from Psalm 60, is also preceded by a 'historical' title which brings to mind the persecution of David by Saul: 'When he escaped from Saul in the cave' (cf. 1 Sam. 24.4ff.). We meet again the heading *miktām*, followed by 'Do not destroy!' as in the titles of Psalms 58, 59 and 75. This is no doubt an allusion to David who agrees to spare Saul: 'Do not kill him! Who can lift a hand against the anointed of YHWH?' (1 Sam. 26.9, 15; cf. Deut. 9.26; Ps. 78.38).

The beginning of v. 5 should be translated: 'I may then lie down. . .' This verb in the cohortative has most of the time been badly translated. The versions supply a verb, 'and he saved', before 'my soul' ('stretch out my soul/myself').

> I may then lie down in the midst of lions
> which devour like fire human prey;
> their teeth, a spear and arrows,
> their tongue, a sharp-edged sword.

The psalmist ('David') is aware of being protected by God who sends love and truth (vv. 4, 11: a classic word-pair) to the rescue. The 'lions' who devour like fire (Madros 1984: 722) symbolize the slanderers who set snares for the just (David, Daniel); but they themselves will fall into these very snares (v. 7).

> They stretched out a net for my feet;
> I was about to fall into the snare;
> they dug a pit for me;
> they fell into it themselves.

This is why the psalmist sings the praises of the love and truth of YHWH whose glory rules the whole world. This allusion to a theophany is a fitting way to complete the strophe. God has done everything for this friend (v. 3b; cf. Ps. 138.2, 8). With this interpretation Psalm 57 is seen to have a certain unity.

Composed by the union of Pss. 57.8-12 and 60.7-14, Psalm 108 must be interpreted in the context of holy war which is given a sacred character as is the case in Chronicles. The perspectives have been universalized. Edom becomes the symbol of all the enemies of God and God's people, as will be the case in Rabbinic literature where Edom will designate Rome. Here is the first part of Psalm 108:

2   My heart is ready, O God;
        I want to sing and chant praise,
        O my glory!

3   Awake, harp and zither,
        that I may awake the dawn!

4   I will give thanks to you among the peoples, YHWH;
        I will chant your praise in every nation.

5   Your love towers above the heavens;
        to the very clouds, your truth!

6   O God, be exalted above the heavens,
        so that your glory may rule the whole earth!

7   That your loved ones may be rescued,
        save them by your right hand and answer us!

8   In the sanctuary, God has spoken.
        ('I triumph. . .').

The end of v. 2, 'O my glory', is ambiguous. Another translation is: 'Such is my glory!' This may refer to the psalmist (cf. Ps. 7.6c), or to YHWH (Pss. 3.4b; 62.8) whose glory is celebrated in v. 6b, or even to the divine glory bestowed on the believer (Pss. 8.6b; 73.24b) (McKay 1978: 167; König 1927: 536). Ps. 57.8 repeats 'my heart is ready/ firm' and has the verb 'awake' before 'my glory' (*kĕbôdî*) in 57.9 (cf. Cant. 5.2). One manuscript of the MT and Syriac have 'my zither' (*kinnôrî*); this would be a doublet.

At the end of v. 4 of Psalm 108, the MT divides *bal-'ummîm*, 'not the peoples' (cf. Ps. 117.1; Num. 25.15), as in Pss. 44.15; 57.10 and 149.7. The usual form is *le'ummîm*, 'the peoples' (Pss. 2.1; 47.4; 65.8; etc.). The negative *bal* is poetic and this way of writing it could be intended to be disparaging.

Psalm 75

This Asaphite psalm (Tournay 1972: 43) is a prophetic exhortation filled with reminiscences. God casts blame on the insolent wicked and announces that there is going to be a universal judgment. Here is the translation:

2   We give you thanks, O God, we give you thanks;
        near is your name, that they may proclaim your wondrous deeds!

3   'Yes, at the time that I will have set,
     I myself will dispense strict justice.
4   That the earth and its inhabitants may not collapse,
     I am the one who set in place the pillars.   (Pause)

5   'I say to the arrogant: enough arrogance!
     and to the wicked: do not raise your horn!
6   Do not raise your horn so high;
     do not dare to speak so insolently!'

7   Neither from the east, nor from the west,
     neither from the desert does relief come.
8   No, it is God who judges,
     who humbles one, and raises up the other.

9   In YHWH's hand there is a cup
     in which a heady wine ferments;
     when it is poured, they lick up its dregs;
     they drink it, all the wicked of the earth.

10   But as for me, I will declare this forever,
     as I sing praise for the God of Jacob:
11   'I will break the horns of the wicked,
     but the horns of the just shall be lifted up.'

It all sounds as if Psalm 75 was the response to the anguished appeals of the preceding Psalm 74, a lament over the destruction of the Temple in 587 BCE. The psalmist in v. 9 makes use of the image from Jeremiah of the cup of wrath (see p. 151). The symbol of the 'horn' is used to designate an arrogant demeanour (vv. 5-6, 11; Rouillard 1985: 295). We may compare this to the second vision of Zechariah (2.1-4): the prophet sees four horns, symbols of the enemies who have dispersed Judah to the four cardinal points. 'The people did not dare raise their heads any more' (Zech. 2.4). Attempts have been made to find the four directions in v. 7 of Psalm 75; however, the north is missing. In v. 7 too, instead of MT 'the desert of mountains' which would indicate the region of Edom, it is preferable to read *midbār* as in some Hebrew manuscripts. The last word in v. 7 refers to 'raising up' or 'restoration', here translated as 'relief' (the verb *rûm*, 'lift up' is found in vv. 5-6), a theme taken up again at the end of v. 8.

The links with the Song of Hannah (1 Sam. 2.1-10; Tournay 1981b: 567) are especially close: 'My face ['my horn'] is exalted' (v. 1b); 'Do not keep repeating such haughty words, so that arrogance may not come from your mouth' (v. 3ab); 'YHWH humbles, but also exalts' (v. 7b); 'The pillars of the earth belong to YHWH' (end of v. 8);

'YHWH exalts the power ['the horn'] of the anointed one' (end of v. 10). This final colon corresponds to the final colon of Psalm 75. It should be noted, however, that the motif of 'thunder' (1 Sam. 2.10b) is not present in Psalm 75. Nevertheless, it may be supposed that these two poems come from the same literary circle of Levitical singers. In the final quatrain of Ps. 75.10-11 the psalmist becomes the spokesperson for the God of Jacob and proclaims the closing oracle in God's name.

Psalm 82

Like Psalm 75, Psalm 82 (Jungling 1969; Hoffken 1983; Stendebach 1986: 425) envisages the eschatological judgment. YHWH presides over the heavenly court, made up of the gods, the progeny of *'Elyôn* (v. 6b). The Asaphite Levite makes use here of the ancient mythology of Canaan, bringing to mind the assembly of gods presided over by the god El (Mullen 1980). These celestial powers are responsible for the injustices in the world. They amount to nothing and must fall and disappear, while YHWH will arise to rule the universe.

1   God presides in the divine council,
       judging in the midst of the gods.

2   'How long will you judge unjustly,
       favouring the cause of the wicked?
3   Provide justice for the weak and the orphan;
       defend the afflicted and the needy.
4   Rescue the weak and the poor;
       deliver them from the clutches of the wicked.'

5   Ignorant and obtuse, they grope in the dark;
       and all the foundations of the earth are shaken.
6   I said to them: 'You are gods,
       descendants of the Most High, all of you!
7   Yet you shall die like mortals;
       every one of you, O Rulers, you will fall.'

8   Rise, O God; judge the earth,
       for all the nations are yours.

Analysis of the psalm reveals its anthological make-up, intensified by reminiscences from Ugaritic sources, so frequent in post-exilic poetry (cf. Pss. 7.8; 29; 89.6-8; etc.). Verse 1 reminds us of Isa. 3.13. The indictment (vv. 2-4) brings to mind Isa. 3.14-15 and other oracles or texts of Deuteronomic origin (Deut. 10.18; 24.17; 27.19; etc.). As an extra-biblical parallel we may cite, for example, a passage from the Keret epic from Ugarit (Caquot 1974: 573; Gibson 1978: 102): 'You do not defend the cause of the widow, you do not provide justice for the unfortunate, you do not drive out those who rob the poor, you do not give food to the orphan before your face nor to the widow behind your back' (Gordon 1978: 129).

In the second hexacolon, v. 5a brings to mind Isa. 44.9, 18; v. 5b recalls Isa. 50.10b, while v. 5c reminds us of Isa. 24.18-20; Ps. 18.8; Mic. 6.2. O. Loretz (1971: 113) omits v. 5 as a gloss; but this 'tricolon' can be a bicolon of 4 + 3 accents like v. 8, with v. 5 having two proclitic negatives. Verse 6 recalls Isa. 41.23; and v. 7a, Isa. 41.29; 44.11. Verse 8 reminds us of Pss. 9.20; 10.12; 76.10; Zech. 2.16. 'God as judge' forms an *inclusio* (vv. 1 and 8).

The versions and commentators hesitate about the translation of v. 7b: 'together', or 'like any ruler', or 'that you may be the first of the rulers', or 'every one of you' (the preferred translation here; cf. Qoh. 11.6; Akkadian *kima išten*). Who are these gods, descendants of the Most High? Are they pagan deities (as at Ugarit), angels, earthly rulers (Ackerman 1966: 186; Emerton 1980: 329; Manns 1985: 525)? The same question comes up with regard to other texts: Exod. 4.16; 7.1; 21.6; Pss. 58.2; 138.1. The context here immediately brings to mind, it seems, the 'death' of the pagan gods when confronted by the absolute sovereignty of YHWH, so often asserted in the OT, especially in Isaiah and the Psalms. But the indictment asks us to see in these beings who will be reduced to nothingness the motivators of tyrants and oppressors. This links it up then with the great apocalypse of Isa. 24.19ff.: the earth will sway and fall; YHWH will come to punish at one and the same time the armies of heaven and the rulers of earth. All will be 'shut up in prison', when YHWH reigns on Zion and in Jerusalem. The wicked rulers and judges, blind and senseless, put in jeopardy the very foundations of all society (Ps. 11.2-3; 1 Sam. 2.7-8; Jer. 4.22; Mic. 4.12; Isa. 56.11). Only monotheism and its morality can bring to humanity justice and respect for the rights of everyone.

Psalms 68.23 and 105.11, 15

Psalm 68 (see p. 135), a processional hymn, presents by way of allusion and in an epic style (verses of 4 accents) a retrospective tableau of the history of Israel, beginning with the time of the Exodus (Tournay 1959b: 358). After a reminder of a past theophany in vv. 8-9 and an implicit oracle in v. 12, there is an oracle containing a threat in v. 23:

> 23   The Lord said: 'I am bringing them back from Bashan;
>   I am fetching them from the depths of the sea,
> 24   so that you may plunge your feet in blood
>   and the tongues of your dogs may have their share of your ene-
>   mies'.

This passage takes us back to the predictions of the prophet Elijah about the death of King Ahab (1 Kgs 21.19; 22.38), as well as of his son Joram who was wounded at Ramoth-gilead and brought to Jezreel (2 Kgs 8.29; 9.15) and finally of the queen, Jezebel (2 Kgs 9.36; cf. Hos. 13.8). Criminals may seek asylum in pagan lands as much as they want: God will know how to find them there. The depths of the ocean, in so far as they are the domain of Rahab and Leviathan (Fensham 1960: 292; Booij 1978: 77) can symbolize the infernal powers of paganism (Exod. 15.5, 8; Mic. 7.19).

Although quite different from Psalm 68, Psalm 105 (Fensham 1981: 35) recalls in a different way the marvellous history of Israel beginning with Abraham and leading up to the taking possession of the land promised to the ancestors. Verses 8-11 correspond to vv. 44-45. In v. 11, God adds an oath to the promise: 'I am giving you the land of Canaan as your portion of the inheritance'. This recalls the sacred promise to Abraham, God's servant (v. 33).

God pronounces another oracle in v. 15: 'Do not touch those consecrated to me, and to my prophets do no harm' (cf. 1 Chron. 16.22). The parallelism tempts us to see here an allusion to priests and inspired Levites. This would be a rereading of the history of the monarchy; anointing was conferred on kings; after the exile, it was conferred on the Aaronide priests (Exod. 30.30), and first of all on the high priest (Exod. 29.7), now the head of the community.

Psalm 87

A short oracle has sometimes been noted in v. 4 (Beaucamp 1962-63: 53):

> 4   'I mention Rahab and Babylon
>   among those who know me.

> Look at Tyre, Philistia, Nubia;
> it is there that such a one is born.'
> 5   But of Zion they say.
> 'In her, everyone is born.'
> And the one who supports Zion is the Most High.

We may compare v. 4 to Ps. 36.11 and Job 24.1 where 'those who know me' are those who know YHWH. The Septuagint presupposes an oracle: 'I mention Rahab and Babylon to those who know me'. But the Korahite psalmist addresses Zion in v. 3: 'They speak of you because of your glory, O city of God'. It is only natural for Zion to respond to such an apostrophe by mentioning the peoples who know Jerusalem. After that, Zion is spoken of in the third person, except in v. 7 where the second person is used, according to the MT: 'In you are all our water-sources' (cf. Isa. 12.3; Ps. 68.27). But the Septuagint reading, 'all those who dwell (in you)', presupposes *kullām 'ônê* in Hebrew. This meaning fits in perfectly with the context and this reading could represent the primitive text. The same variation between the Septuagint 'habitation' (*mā'ôn*) and the MT 'water-source' (*ma'yān*) is found in Ps. 84.7.

Psalm 55.23

If the author of Psalm 55 (with the heading 'of David') is speaking like Jeremiah in denouncing the evil hidden in Jerusalem, while being accused in turn of wrongdoing, it is not certain that the author in that case would have inserted in v. 23 this oracle of salvation, as some claim (Kraus 1978: 564).

> Cast your care upon YHWH;
> the virtuous will never be allowed to stumble.

This advice (repeated in 1 Pet. 5.7) would be a response then to the demands in vv. 2-3 and 17-18. But it is possible that such words are merely an ironical example of remarks by a false friend (v. 22). Furthermore, the text seems to be in disorder; it is difficult to choose between the two interpretations (Mannati 1967: II, 182).

Chapter 11

IMPLICIT ORACLES IN THE PSALMS

The survey of oracular psalms has shown the importance of the prophetic dimension of the psalms of Israel. The oracles already studied contain promises of salvation and blessing or, on the contrary, threats of punishment and annihilation. The same thing will be true for the oracles contained in the so-called 'messianic' psalms (Chapter 12). There remains the task of inquiring into the possible existence of implicit oracles in the psalter.

According to M. Mannati (1966: 65) ten psalms should be classified as liturgies developed around an oracle: four psalms with I (Pss. 3, 54, 46, 57); three with we (Pss. 20, 60, 85); one psalm with a change from I to we (Ps. 108); to these should be added Psalm 61 (a psalm of one who wants to dwell with YHWH) and Psalm 28 (a psalm directed against the wicked). Psalms 60 and 108 have already been studied (pp. 177-79).

Psalm 20

Psalm 20 (Tournay 1959a: 161) must be examined separately; this prayer for the king is followed by a thanksgiving for the help granted by God to the king. This royal liturgy can quite probably be dated to the 7th century BCE; it shows signs of literary and thematic links with writings from the end of the monarchy (Zephaniah, Jeremiah, Exodus 15, etc.). Ps. 20.2-6 precedes a holocaust (cf. v. 4b). In v. 7 the officiating high priest (perhaps Hilkiah; cf. 2 Kgs 22.4) pronounces a favourable cultic oracle: 'Yes, now I know: YHWH grants victory to the anointed and from the sanctuary of the heavens answers with victorious deeds by God's own right hand'. The cultic oracle was in current use in Egypt and for the Pharaoh was a means of governing. Here in Psalm 20, the oracle does not go beyond promising victory to the king. Since the heading of the psalm is 'of David', it is the 'prophet' David, the ancestor of the messiah, who promises divine assistance to his descendant, as in Psalm 21.

Psalm 20 has recently been compared to an Aramaic hymn in demotic script in Papyrus Amherst 63 (Steiner 1983: 261). This pagan hymn is dated by Smelik (1985: 78) to the first half of the first millennium BCE. The psalmist could have adapted this hymn, eliminating the pagan gods, by replacing Zaphon with Zion. The psalmist also added the cultic oracle to v. 7 and introduced the Deuteronomic doctrine of the name of YHWH (Weinfeld 1985: 130).

Psalm 61.6-9

Much like the diptych, Psalms 20–21, Ps. 61.6-9 is a prayer for the king: 'Days upon days add to the king's life; to his years, generation upon generation! May he be enthroned forever before the face of God! Assign love and truth to guard him!' (vv. 7-8). The Targum, followed by many commentators, applies this text to the Davidic messiah. The heading 'of David' would support this interpretation. Immediately one would think of David, on the one hand when he was a fugitive (2 Sam. 17.24): 'From the end of the earth I call to you' (v. 3), or on the other hand 'enthroned before God' (v. 8; 1 Chron. 17.16). In v. 6, 'David' declares that YHWH has already answered him; he is assumed then to be speaking as a prophet and to be announcing the destiny reserved by God for this messianic descendant. But originally, it could have been the prayer of a Levite exiled far from the Temple, after the deportation of 598 BCE, and praying for King Zedekiah. It can be seen from this example how many levels of interpretation are possible for a psalm.

Psalm 62.12-13

Ps. 62.12-13 (De Meyer 1981b: 350) ends with a divine message in the form of a numerical proverb. This is a classical device in wisdom literature[1] (Roth 1965; Honeyman 1961: 348).

12   Once God said one thing;
         two things I heard.

---

1. Amos 1–2; Prov. 6.16; 30.15; Job 5.19; 33.14; 40.5.

> first this: that power belongs to God,
> 13   and to you, YHWH, loving kindness!
>
> and then this: you repay people
> as their deeds deserve.

This is the traditional doctrine on retribution. God repays people according to their works and treats people according to the conduct of each one (Job 34.11). This retribution is carried out with might as much as mercy. Although God saves those who are faithful, the liars and hypocrites and those who are violent and greedy are less than a breath before God. We should mention that M. Mannati (1967: II, 230) has compared Psalm 62 with Isaiah 30: 'the double record' (30.8), the wall which collapses (30.13), tranquillity and trust (30.15), grace (30.18). We would have here a new example of 'prophetic' style; the psalmist would be inspired by this oracle of Isaiah.

Psalm 85

The first half of Psalm 85 (Booij 1978: 139; Auffret 1982a: 285) is a collective prayer of the Judaeans repatriated at the end of the 6th century BCE. Divine anger had been unleashed against Israel; but the successive returns of the exiles were as many signs of divine pardon. Nevertheless, the situation of the Judaeans remained difficult as national laments like Psalms 79, 80, etc. indicate. God should be devoted to restoring life to this people and should intervene in their favour: 'Show us, YHWH, your loving kindness (*hesed*), so that your salvation may be given to us!' (v. 8). The Korahite Levite is going to listen, for God is going to speak to him (LXX: 'what is said to me').

> 9   I am listening to what God YHWH says;
> yes, what is said means peace,
> for God's people and for those who are faithful;
> may they no longer return to their folly!
>
> 10   Salvation is very near for those who fear God,
> and glory will dwell in our land.

The final part of v. 9 is unclear (Kselman 1984: 23). The word *kislâ* has a double meaning: folly, trust (Job 4.6; Pss. 49.14 ; 78.7). Some give this translation: 'That they may not sit down without confidence'. The LXX translation is: 'And for those who turn their heart to God'. (cf. 1 Kgs 12.27). The Vulgate translates: 'And those who seriously reflect about themselves [literally: 'about their heart']'. Since the verb *šûb* is found five times in Psalm 85 with varying shades of meaning (return, restore, turn round, be converted), it is possible that the present text of v. 9 results from a harmonization and that the primitive text of v. 9d would have been 'and for the upright hearts'—Pause (cf. 3b): *yišrê-lēb*, *Selâ*. *Beth*, *kaph* and *resh* would have been confused (Bradley 1920: 243).

Verses 11-14 develop the implicit oracle of peace and salvation.

> 11   Love and truth are meeting;
>   justice and peace are embracing;
> 12   truth will spring out of the earth,
>   and from heaven justice will stoop down.
>
> 13   The Lord will bestow happiness too
>   and our land will yield its fruit;
> 14   justice will go before
>   and step by step will trace the way.

We should take note of the repetition of certain words: peace, salvation, justice, truth. These personified divine attributes go before God to lay out the way (cf. Pss. 43.3; 89.15; 97.2-3). These are the heralds and attendants of YHWH, as in the book of Isaiah (58.8; 59.14; 62.11; 32.16-17). They form a retinue, a kind of mystical ballet as God comes near to bring benefits that procure peace: abundance, happiness, joy, salvation. The glory of YHWH will come to inhabit and fill the new Temple, on 'our land', the 'land promised' to Abraham and restored to the repatriated Judaeans.

The Gnostic treatise *Pistis Sophia* comments in five places on these verses of Psalm 85. Piety, truth, justice, peace are presented as the four hypostases of the one God who brings salvation (Trautmann 1979: 551). Similar reflections are found in Jewish apocryphal and rabbinical traditions on the subject of angels (*Testaments of the Twelve Patriarchs, 1 Enoch*, the *Midrash Bereshith Rabbah*, etc.).

Psalm 3

Should we speak of an implicit oracle in Psalm 3? M. Mannati (1966: 96) raises this question. She suggests that the verbs, 'lie down, sleep, wake' (v. 6) should be seen as alluding to an incubation rite, like the one Solomon participated in at Gibeon (1 Kgs 3.4-6). The worshipper would pass the night in the Temple, on the holy mountain and there would receive a response from God.

> 5   I cry aloud to YHWH
>   who answers me from the holy mountain.
>
> 6   Now I lie down and sleep,
>   and then wake up: YHWH sustains me.

L. Jacquet (1975: I, 247) holds the opposite opinion and refuses to see any such allusion; he writes that Mannati 'lets herself be trapped into playing with fables of her own invention'. To clear up this matter, we must refer to an essential element unduly neglected by commentators, namely, the heading and the 'historical' superscription: 'Of David. When he was fleeing from his son Absalom' (a similar title is found in the version of Ps. 142, LXX). It refers to 2 Sam. 15.12f. As is the case for other psalms provided with a 'historical' superscription, we are in the presence of a 'Davidic' rereading. The beginning of Psalm 3 mentions many adversaries, which fits in with 2 Sam. 15.12 which speaks of a great number (*rab*) of Absalom's supporters. They wanted besides to make sure from the beginning of the psalter that David, father of the psalms, is supposed to be expressing himself here as a prophet to whom God speaks and as a model of the poor and persecuted that God saves from all perils, no matter what they may be.

Psalm 4

According to M. Mannati, the author of Psalm 4 expresses the hope of being favoured with a prophetic dream (1966: 104). But vv. 5 ('your bed') and 9 ('I lie down') do not suggest such an interpretation. On the other hand, a divine oracle could be seen in v. 3, according to the received text.

> You people, how long (will) my glory (be) insulted,
> how long will you love nothingness and seek after lies?

However, the context indicates that this text referred exclusively to the believer whose honour is ridiculed and slandered. LXX translates 'How long will you have a heavy heart? Why do you love nothingness...?' This altered division (*kibdê lēb lāmmâ* instead of *kĕbôdî liklimmâ*) with a double question seems to be primitive. Hardening of the heart is a basic theme in Jeremiah. The re-reading of the MT would be explained as a tendency to make God speak more. Jacquet emphasizes the solemnity of this phrase which sounds like a prophetic oracle (1975: I, 257).

Psalm 57

M. Mannati (1967: II, 194) thinks she can detect in Psalm 57, which is close to Psalm 3 in substance and style, a nocturnal revelation received during sleep, because of v. 5: 'I lie down among the lions', and because of v. 9 as well: 'I will wake the dawn'. She also points to the phrase 'in the shadow of God's wings'. But the cohortative of v. 5 must be translated correctly: 'I may then lay myself down in the midst of lions which devour...' The psalmist is sure that God will come to the rescue even when there are wild beasts all around; this idea is repeated in Psalm 53. According to this interpretation, David, prophet and poet, is considered to be speaking the whole psalm in which a prayer is followed by a hymn, not a rare occurrence in the psalter.

Psalm 28

In Psalm 28, the hypothesis that an oracle is part of the psalm (Mannati 1966: 272) would be consistent with the request for a divine response in v. 1, and with the mention of the *děbîr*, the 'holy of holies' where YHWH delivers oracles. This oracle would be similar to the one in Ps. 12.6, while the final blessing, much like the blessing in Ps. 29.11, reminds us of the one in Ps. 3.9. The worshipper is certain of being answered. Such a hypothesis is not improbable. But would it not be simpler to ascribe such confidence to the prophet David for whom YHWH is strength and shield (v. 7). This 'Davidic' theme is a classic one. It is the king who blesses YHWH and wants to give thanks to God in song (v. 7). The style of Psalm 28 is modelled on that of the ancient oracles, especially Isa. 5.12 and several passages in Jeremiah (1.10; 24.6; 31.28; 42.10; 45.4; 50.29).

Psalm 54

According to M. Mannati (1967: II, 174), we have in Ps. 54.3-4 a request for an oracle, and in vv. 6-9 ('See how God comes to my aid...') the reaction to that oracle, similar to the usual 'I know...' (Pss. 20.7; 56.10; 140.13). But we do not know the content of the oracle or the ritual used by the supplicant, just as we do not know the danger that was threatening. The 'historical' note has no apparent connection with the content of the psalm: 'When the Ziphites came and said to Saul, "Is not David hiding among us?"' However, it should be noted that, in 1 Sam. 23.15, Saul is looking for David in order to kill him; this corresponds to v. 5b: 'Violent men seek my life'. We may compare as well 1 Sam. 26.24 where David says to Saul: 'YHWH will deliver me from all distress' to v. 9a: 'God has delivered me from all distress'. It is definitely David who is supposed to be speaking here in his role as prophet just as Jeremiah did when he too faced personal enemies who are described as 'violent' (Jer. 15.21).

Psalm 140

In Ps. 140.13, 'I know' does not imply the occurrence of an oracle which would have brought to the supplicant the certitude of being saved (Mannati 1968: 235). If the judgment of condemnation of the wicked and of salvation for Israel implies a real revelation, it would be the revelation already received by the 'ancient prophets'. The Levitical singer has David speak as one inspired. This explains the heading 'Of David'. The same thing is true of Psalm 141 which prolongs Psalm 140. In Ps. 140.11b, the word *mhmrt*, 'abyss', is now attested at Ugarit (Loewenstamm 1980: 528). In v. 12b, *mdhph* means 'corral' (Greenberg 1978: 125; Meshel 1974: 129).

Psalm 56

As was the case in Ps. 140.13, 'I know' in Ps. 56.10 is not a reaction to an oracle as M. Mannati thinks (1967: II, 187). It is true that the refrain in three cola of vv. 5 and 11-12 (11b is a doublet) accentuate the word of YHWH, object of the supplicant's praise. But the end of v. 3, 'from above [*mārôm*]. . .' cannot be invoked in order to speak of a theophany or a special divine intervention. As a matter of fact, v. 3b can be translated: 'Many are those who attack me from high up'. Perhaps we have an allusion here to the siege of Jerusalem in 701 BCE or to other sieges of the city: the besieging army has taken up positions on the hills which tower above the city (cf. Ps. 125.2). Some exegetes translate *mārôm* as 'haughtily, insolently'. According to Ibn Ezra, it is a reference to angels. Various conjectures have been proposed.

The title of Psalm 56 is enigmatic: 'According to "The Dove of the Distant Gods". Of David. In a whisper. When the Philistines seized him at Gath.' This incident is recounted in 1 Sam. 21.11-16. Like this latter text, the psalm speaks of 'fear' (v. 4) and a life of wandering (v. 9). Furthermore, the verb *hālal*, 'to praise' (vv. 5 and 11) can also mean 'to be insane' (1 Sam. 21.14). After his life as a vagabond in the desert of Judah, David is assumed to be desirous of fulfilling the offering of the *tôdâ* sacrifice and from then on to walk in the presence of God in the light of the living (or: of life). The obscure heading in the title could date from the Hellenistic period and be translated: 'Against the oppression [cf. Zeph. 3.1] of distant deities', namely, Zeus and the gods introduced into Israel by the Greeks. As a result, this prayer could only be recited in a whisper or secretly so as not to provoke the pagans.

Psalm 83

The author of Psalm 83 (Costacurta 1983: 518), an Asaphite Levite, pictures an immense coalition of some ten pagan nations leagued together against YHWH and YHWH's people (cf. Pss. 2.2; 48.5; 74.23; Isa. 17.12; 1 Macc. 3.42; 12.53). The Levite implores the intervention of the divine judge. As M. Mannati (1967: III, 112) has pointed out so well, what stirs up this 'prophet' is not a desire for revenge, but the glorification of the divine name by a theophanic manifestation. To God is left the task of personally meting out justice. Shame and fear are meant to bring about the conversion of the pagans who will end up by recognizing the one true God. The psalmist in this way echoes the numerous oracles of the 'ancient prophets' against the nations.

Psalm 76

This same kind of reference to foreign nations was found in Psalm 60. The same thing is true of the Asaphite Psalm 76.9-10: 'From the heavens you pronounced the sentence; the earth fears and is speechless when God rises in judgment, to save all the humble of the earth'. A solemn silence here precedes the divine verdict on the day of YHWH as is found in so many other texts (cf. Zeph. 1.7; Hab. 2.20; Isa. 41.1; Zech. 2.17; Wis. 18.14; Rev. 8.1).

Prophetic Motifs

The search for implicit oracles in the psalter brings out the remarkable frequency of prophetic motifs. P.E. Bonnard (1960) had called attention to the links between thirty-three psalms and the book of Jeremiah. Mannati for her part characterizes sixteen psalms as prophetic admonishments or indictments of the wicked: Pss. 9–10, 11, 12, 14 (= 53), 28, 52, 59, 62, 64, 75, 99, 106, 109, 119, 135, 139. Four psalms (Pss. 59, 64, 83, 94) would be on the periphery of such a genre on account of the greater emphasis on supplication. Psalms 140 and 141 could be connected with this latter group. Psalm 9–10 is close to the great apocalypse of Isaiah (25.1-5); the psalmist confidently contemplates the eschatological judgment condemning the oppressors of the poor of YHWH. It is really David (Ps. 9.1), the prophet, who is considered to be lending his voice to the whole community of Israel. The same thing is true of Psalm 11 (Mannati 1979: 122) which recalls the punishment of Sodom and Gomorrah and revives Jeremiah's metaphor of the 'cup'. The phrase 'eat up my people' in Ps. 14.4 is derived from the prophets.[1] The compendium of morality drawn up in Psalm 15 for those who would enter the Temple, reminds us of several oracles.[2]

Mannati (1967: II, 166) compares the portrait of the wicked as sketched in Psalm 52 to the oracles of Isa. 22.17-18 and Jer. 4.22; 9.4; 18.18. She compares too (1967: II, 202) Deut. 32.32-33 and the vengeful oracle of Ps. 58.7-12. As a prophet the author of Psalm 59 calls down terrible imprecations (Mannati 1967: II, 210); the punishment of the wicked will involve an actual theophany: 'That they may know that this is God who rules in Jacob and to the ends of the earth' (v. 14). Psalm 64 reminds us of Jer. 17.9-10; these 'prophetic words' (Mannati 1967: II, 243) bring to mind the great eschatological combat and final judgment. We should add that all these psalms have the heading 'Of David'. It is the king-prophet who is considered to be speaking these words.

Psalm 143, a prayer in anthological style, has as its heading, 'Of David'. The psalmist, as a matter of fact, takes as a personal title, 'servant' of YHWH (vv. 2 and 12), a title given to David (Pss. 18.1; 36.1; 86.16; 144.10). LXX adds in the title: 'When his son pursued him', like Psalm 3, very probably because of v. 3: 'The enemy is in pursuit of my life'. The Levitical singer awaits a response from God: 'Quick,

1. Isa. 9.11; Jer. 10.25; 30.16; Hab. 1.13; 3.14; Mic. 3.3.
2. Isa. 1.16-17; 26.2-3; 33.15; Mic. 6.6-8; Zech. 8.16-17; Ezek. 18.7-9.

answer me' (v. 7a); 'Let me hear at dawn of your love' (v. 8a). An important element is added here to the prayer of petition. The psalmist demands of God to be led by God's 'good spirit' to a level place free of obstacles. This faithful follower had earlier complained of being exhausted in spirit (vv. 4a, 7b; cf. Pss. 77.4; 142.4). This intervention of the divine spirit is a feature of prophecy and would concern David precisely as a prophet. It is he who declares in 2 Sam. 23.2: 'The Spirit [the breath] of YHWH has spoken through me, and God's word is on my tongue...'

Again it is David as prophet who cries out in Ps. 51.12-13: 'Renew a steadfast spirit within me...Do not deprive me of your holy spirit'. This passage has often been compared to oracles from a time fairly close to the resumption of worship in 515 BCE (Ezek. 36.27; Hag. 2.5; Isa. 63.11ff.; cf. Neh. 9.20; Jn 16.13). We may place in such a prophetic context v. 17: 'Lord, open my lips and my mouth will proclaim your praise'. The Levitical singers were keenly aware of being cultic prophets, inspired by God: 'From you comes my praise in the Great Assembly', we read in Ps. 22.26. Ps. 40.4 is the same: 'In my mouth God put a new song, praise to our God'. The phrase 'in my mouth' or 'by my mouth' refers to the prophetic word.[1] Here are some examples: Ps. 71.15: 'My mouth shall declare your justice, every day your salvation'; Ps. 89.2: 'Age after age I will proclaim by my mouth your fidelity'; Ps. 109.30 : 'I will give thanks to YHWH by my mouth'; Ps. 145.21: 'May my mouth speak the praise of YHWH!'

Psalm 144.12-15

In Psalm 144, an anthological poem attributed to David and inspired by Psalm 18 (Tournay 1984: 520), the king-musician sings for God a new song and plays on a ten-stringed harp. His song celebrates the victory God gave to 'David' over his enemies, as well as the fruits of prosperity and peace which resulted for the people of Israel. Verses 12-15 represent then a prophetic anticipation on which YHWH one day will put the definitive seal. David is here assumed to be speaking as a prophet: God is with him just as God is with this people.

---

1. Exod. 4.12; Deut. 18.18; Num. 22.28; 23.12; Isa. 6.7; Jer. 1.9: Ezek. 3.3; Isa. 59.21.

12   Therefore, here are our sons like saplings
       growing strong from their earliest years;
       our daughters, graceful as columns
       sculpted to adorn a palace.

13   Our storehouses, filled to overflowing,
       are packed with produce of every kind;
       our sheep are in the thousands, even in the tens of thousands;
       in our fields, [14] our cattle are prolific.

       No more breach in the wall nor flight,
       nor cries of alarm in our streets!
15   Happy the people endowed in this way;
       happy the people who have YHWH for their God.

This prophetic tone is met again in the messianic psalms as we will see in the following chapter. It is David who makes himself the spokesperson of YHWH. For example, here is Ps. 2.7: 'I proclaim the decree of YHWH, who said to me...' Psalm 110 begins like Psalm 36 with the word 'oracle'; it is David who speaks as a prophet.

We may add that wisdom and prophecy are intermingled in the psalms just as in the other writings. Deuteronomy 32 presents in didactic form the teaching of the ancient prophets. The solemn exordiums of Pss. 49.2-5 and 78.1-2 exhibit a close relationship to the exordium of Deut. 32.1-3. The terms *māšāl* (Rouillard 1985: 246) and *ḥîdâ* (Pss. 49.4; 78.2), 'proverb' and 'riddle', belong to the vocabulary of the sages, but the prophets also use them to proclaim their oracles. In this case it is not a matter of personal reflections of an expert in wisdom, but of a message of YHWH addressed to the whole people. The command 'hear' fits in perfectly with this form of prelude. We may give as an example Ps. 45.11: 'Hear, O daughter; see and turn your ear'. In all such cases, the psalmist speaks with the authority of a prophet, an authority greater than that of an expert in wisdom, an authority like that of Jeremiah (Jer. 7) or Ezekiel (Ezek. 20). It is addressed in the first person to 'my' people (Isa. 3.12). This 'my' (see p. 67) represents not only the poet-psalmist's own person, but the entire community, itself inspired like the prophet by the same divine Spirit.

Chapter 12

MESSIANIC PSALMS AND THE
EXPECTATION OF THE MESSIAH

In the period of the monarchy, royal anointing conferred on the king
of Israel a special charism, the gift of the Spirit (1 Sam. 10.5ff.; Acts
10.38) and of wisdom (1 Kgs 3.4ff.); it made the king an anointed
person, a 'messiah'. This anointing was a contractual rite involving the
king and his people, the king and his God, YHWH. As a consequence
of this, the Davidic filiation included in some way the divine 'filiation'
by a kind of adoption on the part of YHWH (Schlisske 1973: 105;
Mettinger 1976). This Davidic covenant, however, is not given the
name *běrît* before the period of the exile. According to the primitive
tenor of the prophet Nathan's oracle (2 Sam. 7; 1 Chron. 17; Ravasi
1983: 826), before the retouches of the Deuteronomistic school, the
main point revolves around a double entendre: 'YHWH promises to
make you a house [the Davidic dynasty], you whose son [Solomon]
will build me a house [the Temple]. Your house will exist before me
forever.' Therefore, the foundation of the house of God by the son of
David leads to the house of David being founded forever (Caquot
1981: 69; Coppens 1982: 91). In fact, for the chronicler, the Davidic
dynasty is definitely established forever (Williamson 1977: 154; 1983:
305). Such was the starting point for royal messianism.

After the disappearance of the monarchy in Judah and beginning
with the building of the Second Temple in 515 BCE, the rite of
anointing is transferred back to the high priest 'Aaron' (by extrapola-
tion) and, in actual fact, is then bestowed on his descendants by right
of inheritance. It is true that Zerubbabel embodied the messianic hope
for a while (Hag. 2.23). But after him, it was necessary to defer the
messianic coming to an indefinite future. The high priest, the head of
the community of believers, became the priestly 'anointed'. This
anointing limited to the high priest was later extended to all the priests

(Exod. 40.15) so that a 'perpetual priesthood' was conferred on them.

The passive participle *māšîaḥ*, 'anointed', occurs ten times in the psalms, as well as in 1 Chron. 16.22 (= Ps. 105.15) and 2 Chron. 6.42 (= Ps. 132.10). It is found 18 times in the books of Samuel (for example, 1 Sam. 2.10) and only four times in the Pentateuch.[1]

It is well known that exegetes are divided on the question of the origin and meaning of the word 'messianism'. The royal ideology of the ancient Near East, including Egypt, has provided numerous parallels, and it is tempting to see in Israelite messianism merely a variation of the commonly accepted idea about the religious character of all Near-Eastern kingship. Should the messianic psalms be explained then against the background of court style in the ancient Near East, with its hyperboles and its imagery, which would allow for it being situated in the period of the monarchy? Or is it necessary to see it rather as the expression of a post-exilic messianic hope, based on the promises made to David? For H. Cazelles (1978), as well as A. Gelin (1957) and R. de Vaux (1967), biblical messianism is ancient and developed in the setting of the successive dramas of the Israelite monarchy, with its infidelities, its humiliations, its defeats and its exiles. It is only after the exile that the eschatological and apocalyptic currents in messianism developed. Each ruler of Israel is already a messiah, God's vassal and chosen one. For J. Becker (1977; 1980), on the contrary, there is no real messianism in the period of the monarchy; true messianism in the religious sense did not appear before the 2nd century BCE.

The problem remains insoluble as long as the various texts which speak of the messiah cannot be dated even approximately. It is a completely different matter if a relative chronology at least can be suggested, while at the same time a vicious circle is avoided. However, all that need be done is to consult manuals and commentaries to see that a particular messianic psalm can be assigned to any period of biblical history from early times to Maccabean times (Lagrange 1905: 39, 188; Coppens 1968; 1974; Wagner 1984: 865). What is needed then are reliable and converging criteria, starting from the clearest texts.

A preliminary observation must be made. When we turn to the books of Chronicles, we discover that at the time they were written the throne of David and his successors is considered to be nothing else

---

1. Cf. also Isa. 45.1 (Cyrus); Lam. 4.21; Hab. 3.13; Dan. 9.25-26. See *ThWAT*, V: 46.

but the very throne of God which stands forever (1 Chron. 17.14; 28.5; 29.20-23; 2 Chron. 9.8). Now this crucial theme is found in several psalms. We read in Ps. 89.19: 'Yes, to YHWH belongs our shield, to the Holy One of Israel our ruler'. In Ps. 132.10, 17, the psalmist, addressing YHWH, speaks of 'your messiah', and in Ps. 2.6, YHWH speaks of 'my ruler' (YHWH's 'anointed', v. 2). In Ps. 18.51, David is referred to as 'your (God's) ruler', 'your anointed'. The beginning of Ps. 45.7 can be translated: 'Your throne is from God. . .' What is more, it is only in the time of Chronicles that the covenant of YHWH with David is linked to the covenant concluded with Abraham by the 'God of our ancestors' (1 Chron. 16.16; 29.18; 2 Chron. 20.7; Neh. 9.7-8). It is that same perspective of looking back to ancestors that is met again at the end of Pss. 45.17 and 72.17 (see pp. 222-27).

Again, in this quest we must go from the better known to the lesser known. Psalm 89 alone seems to contain enough features to allow us to place it in a particular period, namely, between the fall of the Judaean monarchy in 587 BCE and the rebuilding of the Temple near the end of the 6th century BCE (Veijola 1982). The study of the messianic psalms must begin then with Psalm 89.

Psalm 89

This is a complex psalm (Coppens 1979: 150). A hymn by an individual (vv. 6-19) extols YHWH as the creator and the controller of cosmic chaos as well as liberator of God's people (Crüsemann 1969: 285, 306). The oracle which follows (vv. 20-38) takes up again the theme begun in the prelude (vv. 2-5): God will remain faithful to the promises made to the house of David. The supplication which concludes the psalm looks to the messianic past (vv. 39-46) and the messianic future (vv. 47-52: Tournay 1976a: 380). The beginning and end of the psalm correspond (cola of 4 accents); the section vv. 20-46 is composed of pairs of bicola in ternary rhythm. The frequent repetition of words and phrases is striking (Ravanelli 1980: 7). This gives rise to a unique unity in the psalm. The same controlling principle presides over its definitive redaction, beyond the diversity of genres that it contains (Jacquet 1977: 690). There is some consensus on this among exegetes.[1]

1.   Ward 1961: 320; Becker 1968: 279; Dumortier 1972: 176; Vosberg 1975;

The attempt of E. Lipiński (1967a) to restore a royal poem (vv. 1-5, 20-38) should be given up, since it is based on a Qumran fragment (4Q236) which has been described by experts as a poor text, doubtless written from memory and inferior to the Masoretic text (Skehan 1982: 439; van der Ploeg 1982: 471). The mythical-cultic interpretation advocated by G.W. Ahlström (1959) must be rejected too; according to him, Psalm 89 is perhaps earlier than the prophecy of Nathan and would have been part of the Canaanite ritual singing the praises of the ruler who has suffered but has been rescued (cf. 1 Kgs 5.11; Mosca 1986: 496).

Once the unity of Psalm 89 is accepted, it is then possible to attempt to situate it, as for example T. Veijola has done, among such writings from the time of the exile as the great national laments (Isa. 63.7ff.; Pss. 44, 74, 79, etc.). According to Veijola, Psalm 89 would have been composed at Bethel, in Benjaminite territory. Mizpah, also in the territory of Benjamin, could be considered as well; it was there that some of the people of Judah had gathered around Gedaliah, grandson of the royal scribe Shaphan who had supported the reform of King Josiah (Jer. 40). Mizpah became for a while the religious centre (cf. 1 Macc. 3.46) from where they could see the ruins of Jerusalem. There the scribes of the Deuteronomistic school doubtless worked; we may suppose that these scribes were no strangers to the composition of the so-called Lamentations of Jeremiah and this great Psalm 89 (Tournay 1982b: 255). The 'anointed' referred to in Ps. 89.52 would be none other than King Jehoiachin, prisoner of the Babylonians until 562 BCE, the 37th year of the Babylonian captivity (2 Kgs 25.27; Jer. 52.31), when the king was released by Evil-merodach, son of Nebuchadnezzar. Psalm 89 would then belong a little before this release.

Here is the exordium of Psalm 89:

> 2   YHWH's love I will sing forever;
>   my mouth shall proclaim your fidelity age after age.
> 3   I have said: 'This is a love established forever;
>   your fidelity is as firm as the heavens'.

The psalmist wants to celebrate the *hesed* of YHWH just as in Isa. 63.7: 'I am going to sing the praises of YHWH's favours [*hasdê*]' (cf. Isa. 55.3; Lam. 3.22; Ps. 107.43). In v. 2b, 'my mouth' serves to

Clifford 1980: 35.

emphasize the prophetic activity that is being exercised. What is involved here is the Davidic covenant, the choice of David, the servant of YHWH, and the unending continuation of the Davidic dynasty (v. 3b: read *tikkôn*, as in v. 22a).

> 4   'With my chosen one I have made a covenant;
>   I have sworn to David, my servant:
> 5   I have established your dynasty forever;
>   I have built you a throne for ages without end.'
>
> 6   And may the heavens give you thanks for this wonder, YHWH,
>   and the assembly of holy ones for your fidelity!

The divine oracle (vv. 4-5) is joined to the following hymn by a *waw* consecutive, 'so that...' The motif of the divine oath (v. 4) reappears in vv. 36 and 50, and that of the throne (v. 5) in vv. 37 and 45. In v. 15, the throne is 'the throne of God'. The connection is therefore unmistakable between the theme of God as Creator of the universe and that of God in charge of the history of Israel, just as in Pss. 74.12-17 and 102.26-28.

The oracle in vv. 20-38 occupies the central position and imparts a genuinely prophetic dimension to the whole psalm. Verse 19, at the end of the hymn, serves as a transition.

> 19 Yes, our shield belongs to YHWH;
>   our ruler, to the Holy One of Israel.
>
> 20 Of old in a vision, you spoke
>   and (you) said to your friends:
>   'I have helped a man from the elite;
>   I have exalted a youth from the people.
>
> 21 'I have found David my servant;
>   I have anointed him with my sacred oil.
> 22 I will support him too with a firm hand,
>   and my arm will make him strong.
>
> 23 'The enemy shall not be able to surprise him;
>   the rebel shall not be able to humble him;
> 24 I will crush his foes before him,
>   and I will smite those who hate him.
>
> 25 'My love and my fidelity shall be with him;
>   because of my name he will hold his head high.
> 26 I will stretch out his hand over the sea
>   and his power over the rivers.

27   'He shall say to me: you are my father,
      my God, the Rock who saves me.
28   And as for me, I will make him the first-born,
      highest of the rulers of the earth.

29   'Forever I will keep my love for him;
      my covenant with him shall endure.
30   I will establish his dynasty forever
      and his throne as long as the heavens last.

31   'If his descendants forsake my law
      and do not follow my precepts,
32   if they violate my decrees,
      and fail to keep my commands,

33   'I will punish their rebellion by striking them
      and their iniquity with blows;
34   but my love I will not take back from him,
      nor be false to my fidelity.

35   'Never will I violate my covenant,
      nor change what my lips have uttered;
36   once by my holiness I have sworn;
      I will never lie to David.

37   'His dynasty will last forever
      and his throne like the sun before me;
38   like the moon in its constancy,
      a faithful witness in the sky.'

This oracle is made up of ten quatrains with ternary rhythm. A concentric structure can be seen in the second part, vv. 29-38: v. 29 corresponds to vv. 35-36, while v. 30 corresponds to vv. 37-38. The central affirmation is the continuance of the Davidic throne, even if David's descendants break the covenant; what this amounts to is that God cannot break the covenant (v. 34: *'āsîr*, 'take back' in 13 manuscripts, Syr., Jerome; MT: *'āpîr*, 'break'). We may note the verbal link between v. 25b, 'lift up the horn [the head]' (translated here 'hold his head high') and the preceding hymn (v. 10a: 'our horn will be lifted up'). The cosmic victory of God over the powers of chaos is continued by the victory of 'David' over all his enemies as in Psalm 18. The ideology of 'Holy War' (Weinfeld 1983: 121) in which God fights and brings victory to Israel is combined here, just as in the whole ancient Near East, with the traditional royal ideology which makes the ruler the elect of God as well as offspring of the divinity. The twin terms 'love' and 'fidelity', leitmotifs of all of Psalm 89, provide the secure foundation for both the divine throne (v. 15) and the throne of David (vv. 34-37). Adopted by YHWH, the ruler-messiah becomes the most high (*'Elyôn*) over all the rulers of the earth (vv. 27-28), with an arm as strong as the divine arm (vv. 11, 14, 22). Verse 38 brings to mind Ps. 72.5, 7 (Avishur 1976: 16). A comparison may also be made with a Phoenician inscription from Karatepe: 'May the name of Azitawadda endure forever like the name of the sun and the moon' (Lipiński 1967a: 78; Mullen 1983: 207; *ANET*, 653-54).

The four quatrains which follow the oracle recall the fall of the dynasty.

39   And yet you have rejected and despised,
        you have become enraged at your anointed.
40   You have repudiated the covenant with your servant,
        defiled in the dust his crown.

41   You have broken through all his walls;
        you have reduced his fortresses to ruins.
42   All the passers-by have plundered him;
        there he is, scorned by his neighbours.

43   You have built up the power of his foes;
        you have filled with joy all his enemies;
44   you have even turned back the blade of his sword;
        you have not sustained him in battle.

45   You have put an end to his splendour
        and cast his throne to the ground;
46   you have shortened the days of his youth
        and covered him with shame.

God's 'anointed' and 'servant' has been rejected by God and his crown (v. 40b) and his throne (v. 45b) have been thrown to the ground. The blade of his sword has even been turned back on him (cf. Ps. 37.15; Veijola 1982: 45), the ultimate rejection! Therefore, the psalmist is going to conclude his poem with a supplication: the hidden God must appear in a theophany:

47   How long, YHWH, will you remain hidden?
        How long will you let the fire of your anger blaze?
48   Remember how short is my life;
        for what oblivion you have created all mortals!
49   Who then can live and not see death?
        Who can escape the clutches of Sheol?

50 Lord, where are those first fruits of your love
    when you swore fidelity to David?
51 Remember, Lord, how your servant has been insulted;
    I bear deep in my heart the enmities of the nations,
52 the insults with which your enemies taunted me, YHWH,
    with which they taunted your anointed at every step.

As official spokesperson for King Jehoiachin still imprisoned in Babylon, the psalmist recalls to what an extent the last ruler of Judah is humiliated and insulted by the pagans (Tournay 1976a: 382). According to the Targum, the steps of the anointed of YHWH (v. 52) evoke the slowness of the pace and the delay in the coming of the messiah expected by Israel. In the obvious sense, these steps (literally 'the heels') evoke the situation of the poor king of Judah, fallen and handed over to Babylonian jailers. The pagans ridicule him and maliciously 'follow on his heels' (cf. Pss. 49.6; 56.7) instead of kissing his feet as royal protocol demanded.

He must resign himself to enduring this disgrace like the 'Servant of YHWH', described in Isaiah 53 (fourth Servant Song); but he awaits with confidence the day when God will carry out what has been sworn. We may add that the last ruler of Judah represents and recapitulates in some way all his people: they share the same sorrowful fate. The MT reading 'your servants' in v. 51a demonstrates the passage from the individual to the collective (cf v. 20b as well). The theme of the 'Servant' in the book of Isaiah allows for the same fluidity (Tournay 1984b: 309). These writings could be more or less contemporary.

Psalm 132

The contacts between Psalms 89 and 132 are very close. T. Veijola (1982: 161) has noted 28 such contacts; 16 identical words or phrases are found in 18 verses. The two psalms are influenced by Deuteronomistic theology; this is especially true in the case of Psalm 132 (Fretheim 1967: 289; Loretz 1974: 237; Bee 1978a: 49; Huwiler 1987: 199) which emphasizes God's choice of Zion for a dwelling: God's resting-place is *there*; it is *there* that power (literally: 'a horn') will sprout for David and a lamp will be prepared for God's anointed. This last reference leaves room for the assumption that this lamp is at present extinguished (cf. 1 Kgs 11.36; 15.4; 2 Kgs 8.19). There are other indications that permit the placing of Psalm 132 like the other Psalms of Ascents in the post-exilic period. This is the opinion of many commentators: Hermann 1965: 110; Loretz 1979: 211; Seybold 1979: 256; Coppens 1979: 207; Veijola 1982: 71; Kruse 1983: 279.

Questions have sometimes been raised in regard to the unity of Psalm 132; but the many repetitions in the vocabulary make this psalm a veritable literary interlacing, a kind of tapestry (Brekelmans 1983: 262). It should be noted that King David is mentioned at the beginning (v. 1), the middle (v. 10) and at the end (v. 17).

1	Remember David, YHWH, all his hardships.
2	He is the one who swore to YHWH, who made this vow to the Mighty One of Jacob.
3	'I will not enter the tent, my house; I will not mount my bed to lie down;
4	I will give no sleep to my eyes nor rest to my eyelids,
5	until I find a place for YHWH, a dwelling for the Mighty One of Jacob.'
6	Look, it is the talk of Ephrathah; we found it at Fields-of-the-Forest;
7	let us go to God's dwelling place; let us worship at God's footstool.
8	Arise, YHWH, to your resting place, you and the ark of your might;
9	your priests shall be clothed in justice and your devoted ones shall cry out with joy.
10	For the sake of your servant David, do not turn away the face of your anointed.
11	YHWH swore to David and will not go back on this word.
	'It is the fruit of your body that I will set on the throne made for you.
12	If your descendants keep my covenant, my testimony that I make known to them, their descendants too for evermore shall sit on the throne made for you.'
13	For YHWH has chosen Zion, and desires it for a dwelling:
14	'This is my resting place for evermore; here I will sit enthroned, for I have desired it.

15   'Its provisions I will bless with abundance;
      its poor I will satisfy with bread;
16   its priests I will clothe with salvation
      and its devoted ones shall sing out for joy.

17   There I will make the power of David spring up;
      I will prepare a lamp for my anointed;
18   his enemies I will clothe with shame,
      while on him his diadem will prosper.'

Psalm 132 is made up of two symmetrical parts. Verses 1-9 look to
the past (the transfer of the Ark), while verses 10-18 look to the messianic future and the destiny of Zion. The division must be made before v. 10: 'For the sake of your servant David' (cf. 2 Sam 7.21; 1
Chron. 17.19). Pronouns in the 2nd and 3rd person referring to God
alternate in vv. 10-11, just as in vv. 1-2. The midrashic aspect of the
psalm is undeniable (Bloch 1957: 1274). The 'hardship' or 'toil' of
David (v. 1b; LXX translates 'sweetness') included bringing back the
Ark, installing it in Zion as well as combating all his enemies while
suffering humiliations and betrayals. David's oath (v. 2a), mentioned
nowhere else, corresponds to YHWH's oath (v. 11a). According to 1
Chron. 28.2, David had merely declared: 'I had set my heart on building a house where the ark of the covenant of YHWH and the footstool
of the feet of our God might repose'. The psalmist then has the companions and servants of David speaking and recalling the place where
they went looking for the Ark: near Bethlehem (cf. Mic. 5.1; Ruth
4.11), and in Ephrathah, a name which evokes *pĕrî*, 'fruit' and means
'fertile' or 'fruitful' (Renaud 1977: 225). The following verses
resemble an anthem at the beginning of a procession in the Temple
(Ps. 68.2; Num. 10.33; Isa. 33.3).

   In response to the psalmist's prayer, 'Remember David' (v. 1), God
replies with a twofold oracle. The first one repeats Nathan's prophecy,
like Psalm 89, by stating a condition: the descendants of David must
obey the decrees of YHWH if they wish to preserve the throne of
David 'for evermore' (a post-exilic phrase: Isa. 26.4; 65.18; Pss.
83.18; 92.8). The oracle on the choice of Zion is longer. The verb
bāḥar, 'choose, elect', refers here, not to David (2 Sam. 6.21; Ps.
78.70), but to Zion, in conformity with Deuteronomistic teaching (cf.
2 Chron. 6.6). The word 'provisions' in v. 15a came into use after
the exile (Ps. 78.25; Josh. 9.5, 14; Job 38.41; Neh. 13.15). The final
strophe resembles the messianic texts on the 'shoot' (Zech. 3.8; 6.12;

Isa. 11.1; Jer. 33.15; 2 Sam. 23.5). This same term occurs in the dynastic vocabulary found at Ugarit and in Neo-Punic royal inscriptions (Dambrinne 1971; Amsler 1981: 84) Instead of 'his diadem' (v. 18b; Ps. 89.40), LXX and Syriac have 'my diadem' which corresponds to 'my anointed' (v. 17b), as is the case in 1 Sam. 2.10 and Ps. 18.51. This final strophe is close to the final strophe of the Song of Hannah (1 Sam. 2.10; Tournay 1981b: 567) which has several links in other ways with Psalm 132: YHWH gives the poor their fill and protects those who are faithful while humbling those who are enemies of God.

The 'Mighty One of Jacob' (v. 2b; Isa. 49.26; 60.16) will always be enthroned on Zion, but without the Ark of God's might (cf. Ps. 78.61); it had disappeared (Jer. 3.16). Just as in Psalm 24, the Levitical singer calls to mind a distant past, a pledge of the future. The situation is like that described in Neh. 12.36-43 when the walls of Jerusalem were dedicated by Nehemiah at the end of the 5th century BCE. Priests and Levites purified themselves and the people were filled with joy. The same kind of enthusiasm is expressed in vv. 9 and 16 of Psalm 132, a kind of refrain reminding one of Isa. 61.10. Since the Ark has disappeared, Zion has become the footstool of YHWH (Lam. 2.1; Ezek. 43.7; Ps. 99.5). It is true that Isa. 66.1 has relativized this idea by affirming that the earth is God's footstool.

As in Ps. 122.5, the psalmist in vv. 11d and 12d speaks of the 'thrones of the house of David'. Psalm 132 fits naturally into the Psalms of Ascents and forms part of the liturgy of pilgrims to Jerusalem during the Second Temple period. It bears witness to the intense messianic hope in Israel in the Persian period, expressed so precisely in Pss. 130.7 and 131.3. We may point out that, according to B.G. Ockinga (1980: 38), the theme of the diligence of the king in building a temple for his god is found in several Egyptian royal inscriptions.

Verses 8-10 of Psalm 132 have been incorporated freely by the chronicler in an anthological composition (2 Chron. 6.41-42), serving as a conclusion to the prayer of Solomon and repeating Ps. 130.2 and Isa. 55.3 as well (Williamson 1977: 143).

Psalm 110

The oracles (vv. 1-4) are followed by a sort of commentary (vv. 5-7). This oracular and messianic psalm has as a heading, 'Of David'. The Targum retains this attribution, but paraphrases only a part of the

MT (Grelot 1985: 86). Commentators disagree a great deal in regard to the structure (Auffret 1982b: 83) and interpretation of Psalm 110. Here is its translation:

1   YHWH's oracle to my Lord: 'Sit at my right hand
        until I make your enemies your footstool'.

2   YHWH will extend the power of your sceptre.
        'From Zion, rule in the very midst of your enemies.'

3   The day your power appeared, you are a ruler,
        with the holy insignia from the very beginning [ ] the dawn of
                your youth.

4   YHWH has sworn an oath that shall not be revoked.
        'You are a priest forever according to the order of Melchizedek.'

5   At your right hand, Lord,
        he strikes the kings on the day of his anger;

6   he will be the judge of the nations; corpses pile up;
        he strikes the leaders everywhere on the earth;

7   at the torrent he quenches his thirst on the way;
        this is why he lifts up his head.

This poem is composed of cola of 2 + 2 accents, except in the bicolon of v. 7 which has a ternary rhythm of 3 beats (3 + 3 accents); the *maqqeph* after 'the day' in v. 5 of MT must be suppressed as in v. 3a. The poet lays stress on the messiah's enemies (vv. 1- 2) who are first of all the rulers (v. 5). These will be struck by the new David, judge of the nations, on the day of his anger, the day of YHWH. As in the other messianic psalms (Pss. 2, 45, 72), what develops is a holy war against the enemies of YHWH. We should note that nowhere else is a ruler seated at the right of YHWH; there are references to the ruler sitting on the throne of YHWH (1 Chron. 29.23; Ps. 45.7). The theme of the footstool is a standard one in the ancient Near East with enemies being depicted trampled under the feet of the victorious ruler. We may draw attention by way of reminiscence to the 'sceptre of power' in Ezek. 19.11; Jer. 48.17. This can be compared to Joel 4.12-13: 'I am going to sit in judgment there on all the nations round. Use the sickle. . ., come, take over.' Other parallels will be noted later on.

The mention of Melchizedek (v. 4) in the middle of the poem should be a clue to the proper interpretation of the poem. This personage is mentioned elsewhere only in Gen. 14.18-20. As J.W.

Bowker states (1967: 31), the understanding of Psalm 110 depends to a great extent on the meaning given to Gen. 14.18-20. In fact, the passing allusion in Psalm 110 would have been beyond comprehension in the Second Temple period, if it did not bring to mind the narrative of the meeting of Abraham and Melchizedek, a priest of *'Ēl-'Elyôn* (*ThWAT*, VI: 146), ruler of Salem, a name used of Jerusalem in Ps. 76.3 (cf. Ezek. 13.16; Ps. 122.6; Tob. 13.16; Jdt. 4.4); however, Salem is sometimes identified with a village near Shechem.

> 18   Melchizedek, ruler of Salem, brought out bread and wine.
> he was a priest of God, the Most High.
>
> 19   He blessed (Abram) with these words.
> 'Blessed be Abram by the Most High God who creates the heavens and the earth!
>
> 20   And blessed be the Most High God
> who has delivered your adversaries into your hands!'
> He [Abram] gave him a tithe of everything.

It should be noted that this literary unit separates vv. 17 and 21 which speak of the king of Sodom. But does this mean that vv. 18-20 are an insertion? J. Doré (1981: 90) has shown that this unit has a central place in Genesis 14 and could even have been the starting point in the redaction of this disconcerting chapter. Despite its 'historical' appearance, this narrative is more and more being considered a learned composition, intended to focus attention on Abraham as a warrior leader like one of the Judges. Some exegetes speak here of a midrashic account with archaic features, but originating in the post-exilic period. R. de Vaux (1978: 216, 258) speaks of a late, scholarly composition. This was the opinion of J. Wellhausen too (1899: 312); it is an opinion shared by many exegetes.[1] If such is the case, we would have here a *terminus a quo* for the composition of Psalm 110. It could be objected that oral traditions could have existed independently of Genesis 14. But there is no trace of them before the Qumran texts and the Jewish apocrypha.

On the other hand, the author of Gen. 14.20 makes Abraham a perfect model for observance of tithing, paid to the high priest of Jerusalem (de Pury 1975: II, 444; Caquot 1982: 257). For the book of

---

1.   Meyer 1966: 236; Zimmerli 1967: 255; Bartlett 1968: 1; Schatz 1973: 296; T.L. Thompson 1974: 320; Schreiner 1977: 216; Loretz 1979: 166; Leineweber 1980: 60; Andreasen 1980: 59; Gianotto 1984: 30.

Jubilees (13.25) Melchizedek is a kind of personification, or else an ideal ancestor of the Levitical priests (Auneau 1984: cols. 1284, 1325). This is the way all the descendants of Abraham should imitate their ancestor. No matter what its antecedents (Deut. 14.22; 26.12; Amos 4.4; Gen. 28.22; 1 Sam. 8.15), the institution of the tithe, so vital for the Jerusalem priesthood had to be brought forcefully to the minds of the faithful. Mal. 3.10 gives this command: 'Bring the whole tithe to the storehouse. That there may be food in my house!' Neh. 10.38-40 reminds the people that they are to bring the tithe of the land to the Levites. Supervisors were appointed for the storerooms set aside for the levy of first fruits and tithes (Neh. 12.44). Then all Judah brought the tithe of grain, new wine and oil to be put away in the storerooms (Neh. 13.5, 12). The Priestly laws (Num. 18.21-32; Lev. 27.30-32) imposed the obligation of tithing on all Israelites. According to Tob. 1.6-8 even the practice of the three tithes was in general use. It is easily understandable why the priesthood of Jerusalem had wanted to give a 'historical' foundation to this observance. This is why they would bring on the scene, in the time of Abraham, the high priest Melchizedek, whose name has a Phoenician or Canaanite sound, of the same type as Adonizedek, Amorite king of Jerusalem mentioned in the time of Joshua (Josh. 10.3). If Genesis 14 is not earlier than the 5th century BCE, Psalm 110 should be later than this. Converging indications allow for its composition being placed with some probability around the 4th or 3rd centuries BCE (Tournay 1960a: 5; Meyer 1966: 236; Deissler 1968: 170; Schreiner 1977: 222; Loretz 1979: 166).

When inserted into the fifth book of the psalter, Psalm 110 was placed after Psalm 109, apparently because of the *mot crochet* 'at the right hand' (109.31). Among the literary contacts between Psalm 110 and other writings, the oracles of Balaam must be cited. In fact, Psalm 110 begins like the 3rd and 4th oracles (Num. 24.3, 15), to which is added the beginning of the 'last words of David' (2 Sam. 23.1). Another comparison may be made between 'he strikes the rulers. . . ; he strikes the leader(s). . .' (vv. 5-6) and Num. 24.17: 'The sceptre [*šebeṭ*] of Israel strikes the brows of Moab and the skulls of the sons of Sheth' (a text repeated in Jer. 48.45). In the same way, Ps. 110.2a, 'From Zion [cf. Ps. 20.3b], rule [verb *rdh*] in the very midst of your enemies' reminds us of Num. 24.18-19: 'his enemies, and Israel deploys its power [*ḥayîl*, a word repeated in Ps. 110.3a] and rules from Jacob'. The final strophe of Psalm 110 is similar in some ways to Num. 23.24: 'The people...drink [*yišteh*] the blood of their victims'. According to H. Rouillard (1985), the two final oracles of Balaam would be from the post-exilic period (like Ps. 110 and 2 Sam. 23.1ff.).

Instead of *šēbeṭ*, 'sceptre (of Israel)', Psalm 110 has the word *maṭṭēh* (v. 2a) which designates elsewhere the staff of Aaron (Num. 17.18, 25) and would be appropriate for a priest according to the order of Melchizedek. Now, right after the pericope on Balaam (Num. 23-24), Numbers 25 recounts the intervention of the priest Phinehas, son of Eleazar, son of Aaron, who stops the plague striking the Israelites. YHWH concludes a covenant with him which assured him the priesthood in perpetuity, *kĕhunnat 'ôlām* (Num. 25.13). The divine oath in Ps. 110.4 speaks besides of a perpetual priesthood (cf. Exod. 29.9; 40.15; Ps. 106.31; Sir. 45.24; 1 Macc. 14.41; de Vaux 1961: 114, 310, 374). But it is a priesthood of a unique type, which cannot be transmitted through inheritance and is not communicable. As everyone is aware, Melchizedek is mentioned extensively in the Jewish apocryphal writings and at Qumran (Lipiński 1970: 56; Fitzmyer 1974: 223; Gianotto 1984). At that time he was identified with the Archangel Michael; he became a sort of divine hypostasis, which would permit this translation of v. 4c: 'according to my order, Melchizedek' (Milik 1972: 125, 138).

Verse 3 of Psalm 110 has been transmitted to us in several forms. The Septuagint seems to reflect the most primitive Hebrew text (*'immĕkā nĕdîbūt*, 'with you is dominion'). The MT 'your people is willing' (*nĕdābōt*) may be a re-reading based on the parallels (Ps. 113.8; Judg. 5.2; Num. 21.18; 1 Macc. 2.42) and on the chronicler who is fond of the theme of voluntary engagement (*ndb*: van der Ploeg 1950: 53; Tournay 1988b: 108, fn. 16). 'Yours the dew [of your youth]' is missing in the Septuagint. The text could have been harmonized with Ps. 2.7: 'Today I have begotten you'. The Septuagint already had 'I have begotten you', but translated 'before the dawn', which would correspond to *miššîaḥar*, instead of the hapax *mišḥār*, 'dawn'. We might ask whether this is an attempt at paronomasia with *māšîḥ*, 'anointed', just as there is between *reḥem* (v. 3b) and *yinnāḥēm* (v. 4a). It is important to note the links in vocabulary with Qoh. 11.10: *yaldût*, 'youth', *šaḥarût*, 'dawn', which are abstract forms like *nĕdîbūt* and belong to the language of a later period; the same thing is true in the case of *'al dibrātî,* 'according to the order' (v. 4b; cf. Qoh. 3.18; 7.14; 8.2; Zuckerman 1983: 125).

Many Hebrew manuscripts as well as Symmachus and Jerome have the rereading 'on the holy mountains' in v. 3, once again a harmonization with Ps. 2.6. The theme of 'sacred garments' in v. 3 (MT) is linked to that of priesthood and in this is similar to Ps. 29.2; it corresponds to 1 Chron. 16.29 and 2 Chron. 20.21. It is possible that *ḥlyk* (v. 3a) was interpreted as if it was from the root *ḥîl,* 'suffer the pains of childbirth', from which would come 'give birth', given the mention of womb which follows. This theme of the birth of the messiah could have given rise to an Aramaic Talmudic gloss, later than the Septuagint translation: 'you, child' (*lk ṭl[y]*); this was interpreted subsequently according to the Hebrew *ṭal,* 'the dew', under the influence of contacts with the story of the activity of Gideon (Judg. 6.37-40; see below). 'Yours, the dew [of your youth]' has become the present MT. There is no basis for conjectures such as 'like the dew' (*kĕṭal*), 'the dew shall come' (*yēlēk ṭal*).

Whatever we make of these variants, the sacred character of the messiah is presented here as existing from birth, which is precisely the case for the high priest of Jerusalem, Melchizedek. What we have now is a very elaborate messianic ideology. After the premature disappearance of Zerubbabel, it is the high priest who sits on the throne (Zech. 6.13): hierocracy is born in Israel. Jer. 33.14-26 (a post-exilic text) announces that royal and priestly powers will be associated. In the meantime, the high priest receives the anointing formerly reserved for rulers and is prayed for as one anointed (Ps. 84.10; cf. p. 148). But the sovereign priesthood of the messianic ruler could not be inferior to the Aaronic priesthood.

In the second part of Psalm 110 (vv. 5-7), the psalmist speaks to YHWH and comments on the oracles which precede. The verbs in vv. 5-7 should have the same subject attributed to them, namely, the ruler-messiah. No change in the consonants is necessary (Möller 1980: 287; Gilbert and Pisano 1980: 343). This second part is placed in a context of holy war, visited upon the pagan world by a lieutenant of YHWH. We find here the vehement tone of the oracles of Ezekiel against Gog and Magog. The anger of God is the anger of God's lieutenant also (cf. Pss. 2.5; 21.10). To the 'ruler of justice' (Melchizedek) stand opposed 'the rulers' whose heads will be broken (cf. Ps. 68.22; Hab. 3.14; Sir. 36.9), while the head of the messianic ruler will be lifted up (cf. 1 Sam. 2.10; Pss. 3.4; 27.6). The psalmist mentions in v. 2a the powerful sceptre, which originally was only a war-club, a bludgeon. Verse 6 must have proved shocking, for a number of versions (Aquila, Symmachus, Jerome) substituted *gē'āyyôt*, 'valleys' for *gᵉwiyyôt*, 'corpses', words very similar in appearance. The Hebrew word *gewiyyā,* 'corpse', is a hapax in the book of Psalms. It is possible that it was chosen because of its resemblance to *gôyim*, 'pagans'. The theme of 'valleys' reminds us of Ezek. 32.5; 35.8; 39.11, more especially since Ezek. 39.18-19 announces that the wild beasts and birds 'will drink the blood of the princes of the land' (cf. Isa. 34.7; Zech. 9.15). Some commentators (*Midrash Tehillim* and Kimhi) have even thought of a torrent of blood in v. 7, which reminds us of Num. 23.24 (cf. Isa. 15.9 ; 34.3; Jer. 46.10; Ezek. 32.6; Deut. 32.42; Rev. 16.6; 17.6; Becker 1986: 17). The text is obscure, for it could also refer to a torrent of water (Jer. 31.9; Ezek. 47), which could then be compared to Ps. 36.9: 'From your delightful stream, you give them to drink'. In such an interpretation, the messianic ruler would emerge victorious in the holy war after having drunk at the fountain of divine graces. The messianic dignity and power are gifts from YHWH. Some have even considered here 1 Sam. 30.9 where David passes by the Wadi Besor, as well as 1 Kgs 17.4 and 18.40 where the prophet Elijah drank from the stream and slaughtered the prophets of Baal at the Kishon brook.

But we cannot help thinking here of the pre-monarchical period when Joshua put to death the five Amorite rulers (Josh. 10.26), when Jael pierced the head of Sisera (Judg. 5.26), and when a woman fractured the skull of Abimelech (Judg. 9.53). It is especially the feats of Gideon which seem to be in the background, along with the oracles of Balaam. In fact, the angel of YHWH says to Gideon (Judg. 6.12): 'YHWH is with you [*'immᵉkā*] mighty warrior [*gibbôr heḥāyîl*]'. Gideon receives the severed heads of Oreb and Zeeb (7.25); he killed Zebah and Zalmunna (8.21). He led his own people to drink from the brook and massacred the Midianites (7.5ff.); this episode was well remembered (Isa. 9.3; Hab. 3.7; Ps. 83.12). Gideon's enemies no longer lifted up their heads (Judg. 8.28; Olivier 1981: 143). Finally, there is the well-known episode of the dew (Judg. 6.37-40; Humbert 1957: 487). Dew is a symbol of life and fecundity: 'I will be like the dew for Israel' (Hos. 14.6); 'The remnant of Jacob will be like dew coming from YHWH' (Mic. 5.6). In Ps. 72.6, instead of the MT: 'He

will come down like rain on the aftercrop', the versions translate 'on
the fleece'. This theme appears in Isa. 45.8: 'Heavens, drop down victory like a dew from on high'. It is not surprising that the Aramaic
gloss in v. 3 was later interpreted in this messianic context, with the
Gideon incident as background. This makes clear that the psalmist
would have been thinking of the pre-monarchical period. As B.
Renaud has shown (1977: 273, 412) in regard to Deutero-Micah
(chs. 4–5), if there is a bond between the time of the Judges and the
time of David (cf. 2 Sam. 7.7, 11), the same is true of the period of
the Second Temple, with the anxious expectation of eschatological
times, of the coming of the New David, of the universal reign of God
after the victory of God's lieutenant over his enemies, already described in Psalms 108 and 109.

An anthological psalm with midrashic tendencies, Psalm 110 seems
to take delight in multiplying allusions and baffles translators. For example, in v. 6b *rō'š* remains ambiguous: does it mean 'head' or
'chief'? Or is it a collective word? We face the same problem in the
following phrase: 'over the wide earth' (cf. Ps. 78.15). Does it refer
to the territory of the enemies or to the universe (Ps. 72.8)? In spite
of its obscurity and its vehement tone, Psalm 110 is cited in the New
Testament (Mt. 22.44 and parallels; Acts 2.34) and especially in the
Epistle to the Hebrews. Verse 1 brings up the symbolism of sitting at
the right hand. This imagery is used to express the paschal faith, the
sitting of Jesus at the right hand of God (Gourgues 1978; Longenecker
1978: 161). The priest and ruler, Melchizedek, superior to Abraham
and the Aaronic priests, has become as a consequence a prophetic
figure of Christ, perfect and eternal priest of the New Covenant.

Psalm 2

This psalm (Tournay 1966: 46; Zenger 1986: 495) is cited 17 times in
the New Testament, and of these 9 involve v. 7; in Acts 4.25 the
psalm is attributed to the 'prophet' David. After the apostles Peter and
John are freed from prison, the community of believers address this
prayer to God.

> Our sovereign, it is you who created the heaven, the earth, the sea and all
> that is in them, you who through the Holy Spirit put these words in the
> mouth of our father David your servant.

'Why are these nations in an uproar, why this useless snarling of peoples?
The rulers of the earth rise up; the leaders confront YHWH and the
Messiah.'

Such was the first liturgical prayer of the Christian community
(Rimaud 1957: 99). They considered Psalm 2 to be given to David
through the inspiration of God. In Acts 13.33, Paul refers to Ps. 2.7
in these words: 'As it is written in the first psalm. . .' Psalms 1 and 2
at that time were counted as a single psalm; such is the case too in the
Babylonian Talmud (*b. Ber.* 9b). These two psalms, so close in vocabulary, celebrate in fact the two foundations of Judaism: the Mosaic
law and the messianic promise.

The first strophe of Psalm 2 describes the pagan coalition directed
against YHWH and the messiah. It involves a religious and not a political revolt. The pagan world and its leaders refuse to submit to God
and God's terrestrial lieutenant.

> Come, let us break their fetters;
> come let us throw off their bonds.

The one enthroned in the heavens (cf. Pss. 11.4; 123.1; Isa. 40.22;
66.1) responds ironically and gives free rein to anger.

4   The One who sits enthroned in the heavens laughs;
    YHWH scoffs at them;
5   then, in anger God speaks to them,
    and in a rage strikes them with terror.

6   'It is I who have anointed my ruler
    on Zion, my holy mountain.'

The messianic ruler then personally proclaims the divine decree (cf.
Ps. 105.10; Job 14.5; Isa. 24.5) of investiture and consecration:

7   I proclaim the decree of YHWH.
    God said to me: 'You are mine;
    today I have begotten you.

8   Ask me and I will give you the nations as your inheritance;
    I will submit to you the ends of the earth.

9   You shall crush them with an iron sceptre;
    you shall shatter them like a potter's jar.'

The final strophe of Psalm 2 draws the lesson of the oracle and ends
like Ps. 1.6: 'The way of the wicked is going to lead to doom'.

10   Now, you rulers, understand;
         examine yourselves, judges of the earth.

11   Serve YHWH with fear;
         with trembling pay your homage.

12   Or God will be angered and your way doomed;
         in a flash God's anger will be kindled.

         Happy are those who find in God their refuge.

As can be seen, Psalm 2 presents a concentric pattern with the oracle at the centre. Without dealing here with this literary aspect (Auffret 1977b; 1982a: 143; Ringgren 1983: 91), we must lay stress on the content in order to situate Psalm 2 in relation to other messianic psalms. The opinions of exegetes are sharply divergent. No conclusions can be drawn from the presence of three Aramaic words (*rgš, r'', br*); but an examination of parallels and of some of the terms used indicates that a more recent date is preferable (Deissler 1981: 283).

As a matter of fact, the religious rebellion directed against the Ruler on Zion reminds us of several texts that are forerunners of apocalyptic texts; such pre-apocalyptic texts would be Ezek. 38-39 (compared to Psalm 2 by the *Midrash Tehillim*; Isa. 17.12; 25.3-5; 33.3-5, 11-14; Joel 4.9; Zechariah 12–14, as well as Psalms 46, 83, 149. We should note the close links with Pss. 31.14 and 55.6, 15, 20; the post-exilic usage of the word-pair 'nations/peoples'; and the verb *bhl* in the *piel* (v. 5b; VanderKam 1977: 245), the same as in Ps. 83.16. The anthological approach involved in reusing the word-pair 'fetters-bonds' (Hos. 11.4; Jer. 2.20) must be stressed too. The oracle especially directs us to the period of Chronicles. Mount Zion and the ruler-messiah belong to YHWH, the celestial ruler: the mountain, the throne, the ruler, the messiah all belong to God. Psalm 2 may be associated with the parallel places in Pss. 18.51; 45.7; 89.19; 1 Sam. 2.10. It is true that there is some discussion about the meaning of *nsk*, v. 6a: translated as 'crown' (Targum), or 'anoint', 'install' (*ThWAT*, V: 492). A derivation from *skk*, 'weave', should be ruled out (Gilbert 1979: 209). Instead, it should be compared to *nāsîk*, 'one who is invested', namely, the sheik (Akkadian: *nasîku*; cf. Mic. 5.4).

The terseness of v. 7b: 'God said to me: you are mine; today I have begotten you' implies that the nature of this messianic filiation was well known in Israel. We may refer to Ps. 89.27: 'He [the son of

David] will call me: my Father, my God, the Rock who saves me'. This text refers to the oracle of Nathan who makes use of an adoption formula: 'I will be to him a father, and he will be for me an offspring' (2 Sam. 7.14; 1 Chron. 17.13). Through the Mosaic covenant, the people of Israel had become 'children of God' (Exod. 4.22; Hos. 11.1). Through the Davidic covenant, the ruler-messiah had become this in a unique way.[1]

The 'today' in v. 7c reminds us of 1 Kgs 1.48: 'YHWH has today picked someone to sit on my throne'. But the perspective is new and is similar to that found in 1 Chron. 28.5-7: 'I [God] have prepared for him [for Solomon] an eternal royal dignity, if he unswervingly keeps my commandments and my laws as he keeps them today'. This promise can only be realized in a perspective which infinitely surpasses the duration of the reign of Solomon and includes the Davidic messiah who will reign for ever and ever (Pss. 45.7; 72.7), from now to eternity (Heb. 1.5; 5.5). It is not a question of a feast day (Tabernacles) as in Pss. 95.7 and 118.24, but of the day of the anger of God, when God will come to judge the world, as announced in the psalms of the 'Reign of YHWH'.

Verse 8 resembles 1 Kgs 3.5. Solomon, anointed ruler of Israel, sees YHWH in a dream at Gibeon. God says to him: 'Ask whatever you want me to give you'. Every filial relationship gives a right to an inheritance! In Psalm 2, the messiah is supposed to inherit all the nations of the world (cf. Mic. 5.3; Jn 3.35). We should note that the word 'ăḥuzzâ, parallel to naḥălâ, 'inheritance', is a word occurring very frequently in post-exilic writings. Rulers and leaders rise up in rebellion against this divine decision, because they do not understand the divine plan (cf Mic. 4.12). God gives all power to the messiah who will crush all opposition and conquer the pagan world, a theme repeated in Psalm 110 (cf. Jn 16.33).

Instead of 'you will crush them' (v. 9a, MT, *r''*, an Aramaic verb), LXX translates 'you will shepherd them' (*tir'ēm*), eliminating in this way the parallelism with the second colon, 'you will shatter them' (Emerton 1979: 495). This reading turns up again in the 17th psalm of Solomon, v. 24, and in Revelation (2.27; 12.5; 19.15); this weakens the sentence. A double entendre seems possible in the unvocalized

---

1. Georges 1965: 206; *ThWAT*, VIII: 347; Schlisske 1973; Larcher 1981: 260; del Agua Perez 1984: 391; Hengel 1984.

Hebrew (in the verbs *r''*, 'crush' and *r'h*, 'shepherd'). Is this what is being suggested by 'understand' (v. 10 a)? We may note the plays on words: *nsk/nšq*; *'bd/'bd* (as in Isa. 60.12), not to mention the alliterations (Emerton 1979: 495). The act of breaking clay pots reminds us of Egyptian execration rites; they wrote the names of enemies on pottery or ceramic figurines and then broke them. In other respects, the theme of ruler-shepherd is traditional (Wilhelm 1977: 196).

The psalmist issues an ultimatum to the kings at the end of Psalm 2. As a teacher of wisdom would do, the psalmist invites them to meditate on the divine oracle (cf. Ps. 64.10) in order to avoid punishment and ruin. They must serve God as Israel does: 'It is God whom you should fear and whom you should serve' (Deut. 6.13). In vv. 11b-12a, the MT could be translated: 'And tremble [cf. Hos. 10.5] in fear [cf. Isa. 33.14]; embrace the son [*bar*, an Aramaic word]', or instead 'that which is pure', namely, the Torah (Ps. 19.9). Many conjectures have been proposed (Holladay 1978: 110). Following Bertholet (1908), some have suggested transposing v. 12a before v. 11b and reading *běraglāyw*, 'at the feet'. From this comes 'trembling, kiss the feet', and in a paraphrase, 'trembling, pay homage'. As is known, the ritual of proskynesis was practised before pagan kings and idols; besides, it was shocking to speak of the 'feet' of God. They consequently tried to eliminate the anthropomorphism, while at the same time they could evoke the Torah, thanks to the ambivalence of the word *bar*, the Aramaic equivalent of *bēn*, 'the son' (spoken of in v. 7b). This possible allusion to the law was perhaps taking into account the unexpected translation in the LXX, followed by the Vulgate and the Targum: 'Receive instruction'. On the other hand, we would have here the oldest mention of the ritual of kissing the sacred scroll.

The last colon of v. 12 is similar to Pss. 55.24 and 84.13. The final strophe has inspired Wis. 6.1ff. in which Solomon is considered to be inviting the kings to reflect, since they dictate the laws for the whole world. An allusion to the power of Rome might possibly be present in this text of Wisdom (Larcher 1984: 402).

A universal sovereign with absolute power, the ruler-messiah is presented in Psalm 2 as a sacred personage begotten of God. According to the New Testament, it is at the moment of the resurrection that Jesus was enthroned as Son of God (Mt. 3.17; Mk 1.11; Lk. 3.22) and took possession of his inheritance and royal dignity (Jn

18.37). All power was given to him in heaven and on earth (Mt. 28.18) and everything was put into his hands (Jn 3.35; Col. 1.16). First-born of the dead (Col. 1.18), Jesus is ruler of the kings of the earth (Rev. 1.5) and supreme ruler of nations (Rev. 15.3) whom he will judge on the last day.

Psalm 45

Unparalleled in the whole psalter, Psalm 45 is a royal poem in which a Korahite cultic prophet celebrates the enthronement of a young ruler and his marriage to a princess.

2   My heart is astir with eloquent words.
    I will recite my poem in honour of a ruler;
    my tongue is the pen of a skilful scribe.

3   'You are handsome, the most handsome of all,
    grace is poured upon your lips;
    therefore you are blessed by YHWH forever.

4   Strap your sword at your side, O gallant one;
    in splendour and brilliance, [5] [ ]¹ ride on and triumph
    for the cause of truth, justice and the poor.

    Your right hand will lead you to awesome deeds;
6   your arrows are sharp; here are the people at your mercy;
    they lose heart, these enemies of the king.

7   Your throne is from God, to last forever;
    a sceptre of right, your royal sceptre;
8   you love justice, you hate wickedness.

    Therefore, YHWH, your God, has anointed you
    with an oil of gladness over all your peers.
9   All your robes are myrrh, aloes and cassia.

    From ivory palaces, orchestras entertain you.
10 Royal princesses are there among your honoured guests;
    at your right hand, the consort in gold of Ophir.

11 'Hear, O daughter, consider and give ear;
    forget your own people and the house of your parents.
12 Then the ruler will desire your beauty.
    Share in the honour given this lord!
13 The people of Tyre, with their presents, delight your eyes;
    the wealthiest, [14] with so many jewels [ ] set in gold.'

---

1. The doublet is omitted.

Attired [15] in embroidered finery the princess is taken
inside to the ruler, with maidens in her retinue;
16   they lead in (15) the companions chosen for her;
with great rejoicing, they enter the royal palace.

17   'Children will be yours in place of your forebears;
you will make them rulers over the whole earth.
18   I will make your name live through all generations
and people will give you thanks for ever and ever.

According to the superscription, this is a 'love song', namely, an epi-thalamium. The heading 'according to the lilies' (Tournay 1968: 437) reminds us of the Song of Songs with which Psalm 45 has so many affinities (Tournay 1963: 168). The many Egyptian elements con-tained in these two compositions fit in perfectly with the marriage of Solomon and an Egyptian princess (1 Kgs 3.1). No other ruler can be considered here, especially not Ahab despite the mention of 'ivory palaces' (1 Kgs 22.39) and the 'daughter of Tyre'. In v. 13a, all the textual witnesses have a *waw*, 'and', before 'the daughter of Tyre', except for one Hebrew ms.; a vocative is impossible then. Therefore, it is an example of a collective noun (cf. Ps. 9.15; 137.8) referring to the population of Tyre, well known for its wealth in the time of Hiram. But is it a question of the historical Solomon or of the new Solomon, the ruler-messiah (Mulder 1972; Tournay 1973b: 603)?

The vocabulary of Psalm 45 includes several Aramaisms: the words *rḥš* (the first word in the psalm!), *'ōmēr 'ānî* (v. 2), *ypyp* (v. 3), *qěsî'â* (v. 9), and the use of *lamed* before *rěqāmôt* (v. 15). The word *šēgal* (v. 10), borrowed from Babylonian, is found elsewhere only in Neh. 2.7. The word *malkût* (v. 7) is typical of the language of Chronicles. Several words (*penîmâ, šěběṣôt, riqmâ, yāṣaq*) belong to the vocabulary of the Priestly tradition. The perfumes named in v. 9 are part of the ingredients in the oil of anointing, the priestly chrism (Exod. 30.22ff.). Links with such post-exilic texts as Isaiah 61 and Zech. 9.9 have been pointed out as well. If we follow the Septuagint translation in v. 7a, 'your throne, O God...', it would be possible to consider the Ptolemaic period (Couroyer 1971: 211). But we may suggest another interpretation: 'Your throne [the one from] God' (cf. Num. 25.12: 'my covenant of peace', etc.); this would be in confor-mity with the ideology of Chronicles: David, Solomon, and their suc-cessors, including the future messiah, sit on the 'throne of YHWH' (1 Chron. 17.14; 28.5; 29.20, 23; etc.).

No matter what the prehistory of Psalm 45 might be, we get nowhere by regarding it as a poem of the royal court from the period of the monarchy. Does not *šēgal*, 'consort' (v. 10), bring to mind the ancestor of the chosen people, the beautiful Sarah, come from Mesopotamia, and through her, the daughter of Zion, the spouse of the new Solomon, the ruler-messiah? This prophetic-messianic theme shows through in the two discourses, one addressed to the king (vv. 3-10) and the other, the shorter one, to the queen (vv. 11-14) (Mannati, 1967: II, 106). This approach would then agree with the interpretation in the Targum which paraphrases v. 3 this way: 'Your beauty, O ruler-messiah, surpasses that of everyone; the spirit of prophecy has been given to your lips...' The title of Psalm 45 in the Targum already spoke of a prophecy (see p. 31).

In this prophetic-messianic perspective we may speculate that under the longer form, *yēhôdukā* (v. 18), '[the peoples] will praise you', there is hidden the name *yēhûdâ*, Judah, the tribe from which the messiah will issue (Gen. 49.10; Mic. 5.1; Zech. 10.3) and of whom it is said: 'Judah, your brothers will praise you' (cf. Gen. 29.35; 49.8). Similarly, v. 17 could refer to predictions concerning the descendants of Abraham and Jacob from whom there issue 'leaders' (*śārîm*), as Gen. 17.6 and 35.11 state. It is from Sarah, the 'princess', that 'princes' will be born. With Abraham, Sarah was asked 'to leave her people and the house of her parents' (Gen. 12.1; Ruth 2.11). We must emphasize as well the links between Psalm 45 and 1 Chron. 29.22ff. which describes the accession of King Solomon, taking his seat on the 'throne of YHWH'.

The Levite-prophet celebrates the beauty of the king as well as that of his spouse. Would he not be thinking of the beauty of David, the magnificence of Solomon and the beautiful Sarah? These texts prefigure the beauty of the daughter of Zion and that of the ruler-messiah (cf. Isa. 33.17). The young ruler must successfully defend justice (Olivier 1979: 45) and the poor. The divine blessing and anointing make him the lieutenant of YHWH, installed forever on this divine throne (cf. Ps. 72.5). Perfumes and music embellish the nuptial procession (in v. 15 the two words translated 'the princess' and 'inside' are found earlier in the MT, v. 14). There are connections with Cant. 3.6-11 where the retinue and the escort of King 'Solomon' on 'his wedding day' are described. In addition, myrrh, incense, silver, gold, heroes armed with swords, not to mention aloes (Cant. 4.14; Rouillard

1985: 360) are all features which can be compared to those in Psalm 45 (Tournay 1988a: 44, 60, 106).

In the oracles of Hosea, Jeremiah, Ezekiel, and of the book of Isaiah, the nuptial allegory is used to throw light on the loving relationships between YHWH and the people of Israel. In the Song of Songs, according to the text that has come down to us, it is a question as well of the privileged relationship between the new 'Solomon', son of David, and the daughter of Zion, the Shulammite. According to the interpretation proposed here, the same perspective is present in Psalm 45, under a psalmic and liturgical form.

This messianic 'espousal' attained its complete fulfilment in the setting of the New Covenant, with the union of Jesus and the Church, his spouse. The last chapters of the book of Revelation (Rev. 19.7; 21.2) describe the heavenly Jerusalem, the immolated Lamb's spouse, coming down from heaven after having been made as beautiful as a young bride prepared to meet her husband. Heb. 1.8-9 applies to Christ vv. 7-8 of Psalm 45 according to the translation of the LXX: 'Your throne, O God, stands forever and ever. . .'

Psalm 72

The superscription of the Psalm mentions Solomon; 8 Hebrew mss. omit this mention and 3 mss. join Psalm 72 to Psalm 71. That this royal psalm is at the same time a prayer and an oracle becomes obvious, if we take into account the tenses of the verbs (jussives and imperfects; the LXX has future tenses in vv. 4-16). We therefore cannot dissociate the petition from the oracle. The psalmist asks of YHWH a just and peaceful reign for the 'offspring of the ruler', a happy and prosperous reign without limits in time or space. The doxology (vv. 18-19) closes the 2nd collection of the psalter and is followed by the colophon: 'End of the prayers of David, son of Jesse'.

1   O God, endow the ruler with your judgments;
    the royal offspring, with your justice.
2   that your people may be governed equitably
    and that the poor may receive justice!

3   Mountains, bring peace to the people,
    and you hills, justice.
4   May the poor of the people receive their rights;
    may the needy be saved; may the oppressor be crushed.

5   May this rule endure as long as the sun and moon
    through all generations!
6   May all this descend like rain on the aftercrop,
    like showers watering the earth!

7   In those days justice will flourish
    and profound peace till the moon is no more.
8   May this rule be from sea to sea
    and from the River to the ends of the earth.

9   The desert tribes will come bowing down
    and enemies will bite the dust.
10 The rulers of Tarshish and the islands
    will bring their tribute.

    The rulers of Sheba and Seba will make their offering;
11 all the rulers will pledge their allegiance;
    all the countries will give their service.

12 There will be liberation for the poor when they cry out
    and for the afflicted who have no help;
13 the weak and needy will be cared for
    and the lives of the poor will be saved.

14 They will be rescued from violence and oppression;
    their blood is precious in the eyes of this ruler.
15 Long may such a one live! And be lavished with gold from
        Sheba.
    They will pray for this one constantly;
    all day long will they bestow their blessings

16 May there be an abundance of grain on the earth;
    may it sway on the mountain summits,
    like Lebanon which makes fruits and flowers flourish
    just like grass in the fields!

17 May this ruler have an eternal name;
    as long as the sun may this name endure!
    In this one will people bless themselves;
    all countries will call such a one blessed.

In this psalm which has a very regular structure (except for v. 15), the quatrains may be grouped in pairs to bring out the meaning: 1-4, 5-8, 9-11, 12-15, 16-17. The poet multiplies repetitions and is inspired by episodes from the life of Solomon (1 Kgs 3.12, 28; 4.20; 5.14; 10.1, 8, 22; 11.42). Verse 6 reminds us of Gen. 13.10; v. 8 envisages the realization of Gen. 15.18; and v. 17, the realization of Gen. 12.2-3 and 22.18 (cf. Sir. 44.21). The whole psalm has close links with Isa. 60 (Steck 1986: 291) and Zech. 9.9ff.; comparisons with many other texts have been made as well.[1] It is therefore an anthological psalm and related to the post-exilic writings as is indicated also by the Aramaisms (*zarzîp* in v. 6, *pissat* in v. 16, etc.). The Targum and the Judaeo-Christian tradition gave the psalm a messianic interpretation. The MT had already offered some messianic rereadings: in v. 7a: 'the just' (cf. Jer. 23.5; Zech. 9.9) instead of 'justice' (3 mss. and the versions); in v. 17b, *yinnôn* (MT *qěrê*; *kětîb*: *yānîn*), 'will have offspring' or 'will be prolific' (from *nîn*, 'descendant'; Ps. 74.8), a verb which becomes one of the names of the messiah in the rabbinic tradition; but the reading presumed to be the primitive text, *yikkôn*, 'it will endure', is attested by the versions and one Hebrew ms. (cf. Ps. 89.38). The pre-existence of the messiah would already be indicated by translating in v. 5, 'before the moon', and in v. 17, 'before the sun', as the LXX and rabbinic commentaries understood it. The Targum has this paraphrase: 'Before the sun was, his name was prepared'. We should note that in v. 17b LXX adds 'all the tribes of the earth' (Gen. 12.3; 28.14), words doubtless omitted in the MT by homoeoteleuton and translated here by 'people'. A defective vocalization in v. 5a, 'they will fear you' (cf. Isa. 59.19) must be corrected according to the versions 'may it endure'. The references to peace (vv. 3, 7) and to the name (v. 17) bring to mind the name of Solomon (cf. Sir. 47.16), son of David. Psalms 2 and 72 form a frame around the collection (books 1 and 2 of the psalter).

However, modern commentators are struck here by the use of 'court style', so much in vogue in royal inscriptions from the ancient Near East. In this court language they wish the ruler a long life, absolute supremacy, a reign of peace and justice, a paradisiacal prosperity. Verse 16 speaks of abundant harvesting and vintaging (the MT has been damaged: it should be read *wěṣîṣô*, 'and its flowers'; Tournay 1964: 97). There is no denying the resemblance to Babylonian, Syrian, Phoenician and Egyptian texts.[2] But these links alone are not enough to give a full account of the text. According to E. Podechard (1949: 314), vv. 4c, 10, 15a, and perhaps vv. 5, 6, 14, 16 as well, should be omitted as additions. Such a solution is not acceptable. Is not

---

1. Job 29.12; Isa. 45.8; 49.23; Mic. 5.3-4; 7.17; Ezek. 27.15; Ps. 116.15; etc. On Tarshish, see Alvar 1982: 211; C.H. Wagner 1986: 201.

2. Pautrel 1961: 157; Grelot 1957: 319; Veugelers 1965: 317; Greenfield 1971b: 267; Paul 1972: 351; Malamat 1982: 215.

the simplest interpretation a messianic exegesis? The expected messiah will be a new Solomon (Peterca 1981: 87). We should note, nevertheless, that Psalm 72 is never cited in the New Testament, except implicitly in the story of the Magi (Bonnard 1981: 259). St Justin quotes the entire psalm in the *Dialogue with Tryphon.*

Psalm 101

Psalm 101 (Kaiser 1962: 195; Kenik 1976: 391) is a royal psalm of a unique type. Like the second part of Psalm 2, it contains a 'speech from the throne' which is stern toward the wicked as well as opponents. According to the title it is David who is supposed to be speaking.

1   I want to sing of justice and kindness;
     for you, YHWH, I sing a psalm.
2   I want to advance in the way of integrity;
     when will you come to me?

     I will lead a blameless life
     within my house.
3   I will not even give a thought
     to anything wicked.

     I detest the deeds of apostates;
     I will have nothing to do with them;
4   far from me the perverse heart;
     the scoundrel I ignore.

5   Whoever slanders a neighbour in secret
     will be reduced to silence;
     the haughty look, the ambitious heart
     I cannot tolerate.

6   I will know how to pick out the upright in the land;
     they shall be seated at my side;
     only those who behave blamelessly
     shall enter my service.

7   There is no place in my household
     for those who practise deceit;
     whoever speaks falsehood
     shall not stand before my gaze.

8   Each morning I will reduce to silence
     all the wicked in the land,

uprooting from the city of YHWH
all those who are evildoers.

In the hymnic prelude (vv. 1-2ab; in the MT the strophic division is poorly done) which reminds us of the prelude to Ps. 89.2, David is supposedly intoning a psalmic song, in conformity with the tradition about him (2 Sam. 23.1); it is set to music (*zmr*; cf. Greenfield 1987: 11), in conformity with tradition too (1 Sam. 16-18). But he speaks here more as a sage and even as a prophet. A kind of ideal ruler, like the ruler of Psalms 18, 45, and 72, he pledges the establishment of the justice and *ḥesed* which flow from the covenant concluded between YHWH and the 'house' (vv. 2, 7; 2 Sam. 7.11; 23.5) of David. He will be upright and faithful in the city of YHWH (v. 8c), namely, Jerusalem, like the David of Ps. 18.21-25. He will reject those who are at heart hypocrites (cf. Ps. 18.27). The poet is inspired by the stories of David and Solomon. Right from the exordium, the king promises to make progress, to succeed like David, the *maśkîl* (1 Sam. 18.5, 14-15), and like Solomon the sage as long as he kept the divine laws (1 Kgs 2.3). The title of *maśkîl* is attributed elsewhere to the Servant of YHWH (Isa. 52.13), to the Levitical singers (2 Chron. 30.22), to the sages spoken of in Dan. 11.33, 35, and to the Teacher of Righteousness at Qumran (Carmignac 1963: 35). In Ps. 2.10, the king warns the rebels to show themselves wise and intelligent by submitting to YHWH. The psalmist speaks as a teacher of wisdom in Psalm 101 as well; that discourse reminds us of many passages in Proverbs. M. Weinfeld (1982: 224) has compared this psalm to the protestations of innocence in Egyptian texts, especially in the instructions for visitors to the temples. Kselman (1985: 45) has proposed the idea that there is a divine oracle in vv. 7-8. As a matter of fact, the comportment of the ruler here corresponds to that of God (Mannati 1967: III, 251). The verb 'serve' (v. 6d) already has a strong cultic tone. YHWH too keeps an eye on the faithful (see p. 167) and reduces the wicked to silence on the day of Judgment (Pss. 54.7; 73.27; 94.23; 143.12). Only the good are admitted into intimacy with God (Pss. 5.5-6; 15.1ff.; 24.3ff.; etc.).

What is more, the ideal ruler should extirpate all the deeds of Belial (v. 3; translated 'anything wicked'; cf. Ps. 41.9), calumnies, lies and wickedness, as is stated at the end of the 'last words of David' (2 Sam. 23.6). The ruler should cause evil to disappear, a Deuteronomistic theme which was already present in Babylonian texts, such as the Epic of Gilgamesh and the Code of Hammurabi (Dion 1980: 338). This motif is found specifically in the story of David (2 Sam. 4.11). He orders the death of the two Benjaminite assassins of Ishbaal, son of Saul; David exclaims: 'Am I not bound to wipe you from the earth?' This judgment should take place each morning, a symbolic time for settlement of disputes, for discharging of debts, for salvation, or as the Targum states, for the future world.

This portrait of the ideal ruler is combined with the desires expressed in Psalm 72 and describes in advance what 'my servant David', the expected messiah will be like. This is why the enquiry made of God by the psalmist at the beginning of the psalm ('When will you come to me?') expresses strongly the anxious waiting of the Levitical singers. What is taken up here again under a different form is the query of 'David': 'Will God not bring to fruition all the salvation I desire?' (2 Sam. 23.5). The coming of the messiah, offspring of David, this alone will be able to realize this reign of justice and holiness. It is not without reason then that the Judaeo-Christian tradition has seen the messiah in the ideal ruler of Psalm 101.

At the end of this account of the 'royal' psalms, placed back into their prophetic and oracular setting, it can be seen how this group of psalms cannot be interpreted separately from the rest of the psalter. As a matter of fact, they express in a very coherent way, starting from the ancient messianic oracles, the hope of the Levitical singers, spokespersons for the whole community in the period of the Second Temple. Of course, like the other psalms, they had their more or less remote antecedents in Israel and the whole ancient Near East. But we lack definite criteria in attempting to re-establish their earlier stages. To understand them well in their definitive terms, it is necessary to interpret them in the setting of the Davidic covenant as it is presented in the writings of the Persian and Hellenistic periods (Feuillet 1985: 5). This epoch must be considered the golden age of biblical literature. The inspired sacred writers at that time tried to compensate for the disappearance of the great prophets and to re-animate the faith of believers in the divine promises, in spite of the silence of God. It is in this historical context that it is possible to situate the composition of the psalms which outline in advance the features of the messianic ruler, descendant of David.

CONCLUSION

At the end of this study, it is apparent that there is a prophetic dimension within Israelite psalmody. All through the psalter, and more generally in all Israelite hymnology, theophanic evocations and cultic oracles continually appear. The God of Israel is a living God, present among the people, although in an invisible way. This God can be seen and heard by those who have faith and are doing their utmost in seeking God through the prayers of the psalms, for then they will be given the opportunity to find God.

In addition to the classical approaches, such as the examination of genres and literary structures, or comparisons with extra-biblical parallels, it is this essential aspect which permits the discovery of all the spiritual richness of this psalmody. As we have seen, the Levitical singers of the Second Temple were fully aware of this. They deeply desired to comfort the community of believers gathered around the newly rebuilt sanctuary on Zion. Bearers of divine promises, guardians of the traditions and the writings of the past, they wanted to compensate for the disappearance of the great prophets and the apparent silence of the God of the covenant.

Thanks to the liturgical celebrations, they were given the opportunity to be able to call to mind the reasons for hoping in the coming of the reign of God and of God's chosen one, the messiah, a new David and a new Solomon. Faced with increasing loss of faith, godlessness, apostasy and religious persecution, the Jewish people learned in this way to meet God with the eyes of faith, to enter into dialogue with God, to remain in the divine presence (Terrien 1978) with the one who is Emmanuel, God with us, in the midst of us (Exod. 17.7). Right from their birth, YHWH had seen, yes, definitely had seen the misery of the people (Exod. 3.7), and had freed them from their oppressors. God remained through the course of centuries their unique redeemer: nothing escaped the divine gaze, the divine hearing. Every believer could in this way go to see the face of God and present their requests.

God would reply through the cultic oracles inserted in the canticles and psalms.

We have already seen that these psalmic prayers were not something isolated, but formed part of a group of texts from the same epoch: Malachi, Jonah, Job, Obadiah, Joel, and the post-exilic additions to the prophetic collections of Isaiah, Jeremiah, Ezekiel and Zechariah. These were joined together with the writings of Deuteronomistic inspiration and with the Priestly tradition.

It was consequently quite obvious that they should be interpreted in this same *Sitz im Leben*, in an epoch in which the anxiety of a people awaiting the day of YHWH asserted itself. These incessant appeals for a divine intervention were born from a profound conviction: the hidden God could not abandon them because they were God's special possession; God is faithful to the divine promises and will call forth in God's good time a new world, flowing from the new and eternal covenant (Jer. 31.31; Ezek. 37.26; Isa. 55.3; 59.21; 61.8): 'When will you come to me?' (Ps. 101.2); 'Oh, that you would tear the heavens open and come down!' (Isa. 63.19).

This eternal covenant was the one YHWH had concluded with the prophet David (2 Sam. 23.5) and the one which has to be realized by the coming of his messianic descendant. Not without reason then, the Aramaic Targum of the psalms, followed by the Judaeo-Christian tradition, attributes a messianic understanding to the psalms. The same is true of the Song of Songs in which the dialogue between the partners opens into the mysterious dialogue between the Davidic–Solomonic messiah and the daughter of Zion: 'Come, my beloved!' (Cant. 7.12; Tournay 1988a: 167-68).

For that reason the disciples of Jesus immediately adopted the book of Psalms, cited so often (126 times)[1] in the New Testament. In Jerusalem, the first Christians, coming in part from Judaism, were well acquainted with the psalms; moreover, from the psalms came the inspiration for the *Benedictus* and *Magnificat*. Jesus too must have used them from an early age; according to the Gospels, he applied them to himself. From the cross he intoned Psalm 22. The evangelists multiplied the citations of the psalms in the narratives of the Passion.[2]

---

1. Saint-Arnaud 1979: col. 207.

2. Mt. 26.23; 27.43, 46, 48; Mk 14.18; 15.55; Lk. 22.69; 23.34-35; Jn 19.24, 28, 36.

After his resurrection, Jesus reminded the apostles that he had said before his death: 'Everything written about me in the law of Moses and the prophets and psalms has to be fulfilled' (Lk. 24.44; Ravasi 1981: 25). 'The Old Testament was his book; his God, the Father, is the God of the First Covenant; in fact, Jesus asserts that Scripture speaks of him, announces him' (Larcher 1962: 45).

From the beginning of the Christian community, the psalms have inspired the preaching, the liturgy of the word, private prayers, apologetics. At the beginning of one of the oldest baptismal liturgies presently known (Salles 1958: 39), those who were to be baptized were examined to find out 'whether their preparation for baptism has taken place, whether they have read the Scriptures, and whether they have learned the psalms'. The Syriac *Didascalia*, from the 3rd century CE, says that they passed the Easter Vigil in 'reading the Scriptures and the Psalms' (Vööbus 1979: 199). The *Canons* of Hippolytus (Dix 1968: 57) and the *Canons of the Apostles* (Canon 19) prescribe the recitation of the psalms (Trublet 1986: col. 2518). St Hilary of Poitiers writes: 'No matter who the person may be in whom the Spirit of prophecy has spoken, the whole message is still intended as an instruction on the coming of our Lord Jesus Christ, his incarnation, his passion and his reign, and to refer to the glory as well as the power of our resurrection' (*Instructio Psalmorum* 5; *PL* IX, 235).

Singing of the psalms is mentioned at the turn of the 2nd–3rd centuries in the apocryphal work called the *Acts of Paul*. What is described is a Eucharist connected with the agape or love feast and accompanied by singing: 'Everyone shared in the bread and restored themselves, as was the custom during the time of fasting, with the singing of the psalms of David and canticles' (Gelineau 1978: 101). In a letter to Marcelin (*Patrologia Graeca*, XII) St Athanasius writes: 'The book of psalms brings together all the treasures of the other books, like a garden, and joins to them an additional charm specific to it, namely, singing'. We may quote as well St Basil (Letter 207; *Patrologia Graeca*, XXXII, 764): 'The singing of psalms is organized in the same way in all the churches of God; it pleasantly re-echoes there. People get up at night and go to the house of prayer, and. . . , when they have prayed, they sing psalms. . . After having spent the night in singing psalms, they sing the penitential psalm [Ps. 51].' St Basil concludes by asking himself '. . . why such preference is shown the psalms?. . . Because hymns are human formularies, while the psalms are the songs of the Spirit' (Trublet 1986: col. 2518).

In a Greek commentary on Psalm 146, from the 8th or 9th century and preserved in a palimpsest edited by J. Noret (1987: 462-63), there is an allusion to ch. 3 of 2 Kings, a passage which has hardly attracted the attention of Christian writers at all, but which shows how singing of psalms inspires prophecy: 'Praise the Lord, for a psalm is a good thing... How could a psalm not be good, when Elisha, from whom Jehoshaphat and Jehoram had demanded a prophecy, sought someone who would sing psalms, for the psalm was needed to inspire him to prophesy. And if, when someone else sings psalms, we are enraptured [*energoumetha*], how can it not be more so when we ourselves sing the psalms?'

A New Temple

After the Ascension of Christ, the Christian world found itself in a situation that resembled to some extent that of Jews living in the period of the Second Temple. Since revelation ended with the death of the last apostle, it was invisibly that Jesus, the living God, remained close to his own until the consummation of ages (Mt. 28.20; cf. Jn 14.19). It is only through faith that the Christian Church can come into contact with the divine spouse (Jn 20.29), while awaiting the day of our Lord Jesus Christ, his Second Coming, the Parousia (Jn 8.56; Mt. 24.3; Lk. 17.30; 1 Cor. 1.8; 15.23).

The Second Temple disappeared in 70 CE. But the body of the risen Christ became the new Temple, a spiritual Temple not made by hands (Jn 2.19-22; cf. Congar 1958: 275). The true temple is the Christian (Jn 14.23; Rev. 3.20) in whom God dwells; this is what the Epistle of Barnabas explains in commenting on the psalter (Vesco 1986: 18). Instead of figures and symbols of the Old Covenant, there are the realities of the sacramental order, awaiting the celestial consummation in the realities of the Kingdom. The great paschal theophany is actualized in the midst of the Christian community by the celebration of the Eucharist which is, as the name indicates, the act of thanksgiving *par excellence*. There the Lord continues speaking to the faithful, to each one of them, through the representatives of God. When two or three disciples gather together to pray to Christ and invoke his name, he is there, in the midst of them (Mt. 18.20). While giving thanks to God, we can make ourselves spokespersons for other women and men, especially for those whose voice is stifled by intolerance, persecution, or atheism.

So many voices are raised today throughout the world to proclaim that 'God is dead', echoing here those who asked the Jews, 'Where is your God?' The response to that practical atheism is the affirmation of the presence of the Spirit in the midst of the Church of Christ. The desire of Moses: 'Oh! Would that all the people were prophets!' (Num. 11.29) is in fact realized beginning with the day of Pentecost (Acts 2.16-18; cf. Joel 3.1ff.). From that time the Spirit animates the Church. 'The Paraclete, the Holy Spirit, whom the Father will send in my name, will instruct you in everything and remind you of all that I told you' (Jn 14.26).

The community at Qumran was conscious of participating in the heavenly liturgy while praising God and celebrating the Sabbath offering (Newsome 1985). We read in column 11 of the *Manual of Discipline*: 'To those whom God has chosen an eternal possession has been given; their inheritance has been placed with the portion of the Saints; God has associated their assembly with the children of the heavens, according to the ideals of the Community' (lines 7-8; Carmignac and Guilbert 1961: 77).

The praise given by the Christian community through the psalms corresponds too in a mysterious way to the praise of the heavenly beings.[1] From here below, this prayer of the psalms continued through the centuries makes us participate in the worship of the heavenly temple, while experiencing a kind of communion with the angels and the blessed: 'I sing to you in the presence of angels' (Ps. 138.1). The book of Revelation multiplies hymns of praise and thanksgiving sung by the angels and the elect in heaven.[2]

> Speak to one another in psalms, hymns and inspired songs; sing and praise the Lord with all your heart! (Eph. 5.19).
>
> Maranatha! (1 Cor. 16.22).
>
> Come, Lord Jesus! (Rev. 22.20).

---

1. Rev. 4.8-11; 5.9-14; 11.17-18; 12.10-12; 15.3-4; 19.1-7.
2. On the 'celestial liturgy', cf. E. Petersen 1935; Grondijs 1962; Philonenko 1985.

BIBLIOGRAPHY

This bibliography includes only the books and articles mentioned in the course of the investigation. For a more complete bibliography on the Psalms and the liturgy of the Jerusalem Temple, consult the *Catalogue de la Bibliothèque de l'École Biblique et Archéologique Française de Jérusalem* (12 volumes in 4° with supplements); the annual *Elenchus* of *Biblica*; and the commentary of G. Ravasi, *Il libro dei Salmi. Commento et Attualizzatione*, Vol. 1 (1–50), vol. 2 (51–100), vol. 3 (101–150) (Bologna: Dehoniane, 1981–84).

Abel, F.-M. and J. Starcky
    1961   *Les livres des Maccabées* (*BdJ*; Paris: Cerf, 3rd edn).
Ackerman, J.S.
    1966   'The Rabbinic Interpretation of Psalm 82 and the Gospel of John', *HTR* 59: 186-91.
Agua Perez, A. del
    1984   'Procedimientos derásicos del Sal 2, 7b en el Nuevo Testamento. "Tu eres mi hijo, yo te he engendrado hoy" ', *EstBíb* 42: 391-414.
Aharoni, Y.
    1971   'The Conquest of David according to Psalm 60 and 108', in *Bible and Jewish History... Dedicated to the Memory of J. Liver* (Tel-Aviv: Tel Aviv University, Faculty of Humanities), 13-17 (in Hebrew).
Ahlström, G.W.
    1959   *Psalm 89. Eine Liturgie aus dem Ritual des leidenden Königs* (Lund: Gleerup).
Aletti, J.-N. and J. Trublet
    1983   *Approche poétique et théologique des Psaumes. Analyse et méthodes: initiations* (Paris: Cerf).
Allen, L.C.
    1986   'David as Exemplar of Spirituality: The Redactional Function of Psalm 19', *Bib* 67: 544-46.
Allman, J.E.
    1984   *A Biblical Theology of the Hymns in the Book of Psalms* (Ann Arbor: University Microfilms), 142-99.
Alonso Schökel, L.
    1988   *A Manual of Hebrew Poetics* (Subsidia Biblica, 11; Rome: Editrice Pontificio Istituto Biblico).
Alvar, J.
    1982   'Aportaciones al estudio del Tarshish biblico', *Rivista di Studi Fenici* 10: 211-30.

Amit, Y.
1983 'The Role of Prophecy and Prophets in the Book of Chronicles', *Beit Mikra* 93: 113-33.
Amsler, S., *et al.*
1981 *Aggée, Zacharie, Malachie* (Commentaire de l'A.T., XIc; Neuchâtel: Dela-chaux and Niestlé).
Andersen, F.I. and D.N. Freedman
1980 *Hosea* (AB, 24; Garden City, NY: Doubleday).
Andreasen, N.-E.A.
1980 'Genesis 14 in its Near Eastern Context', in *Scripture in Context*, 59-77.
Arens, A.
1961 *Die Psalmen im Gottesdienst des alten Bundes. Eine Untersuchung zur Vorgeschichte des christlichen Psalmengesanges* (Trier: Paulinus).
Attridge, H.W. and R.A. Oden
1981 *Philo of Byblos. The Phoenician History* (CBQMS, 9; Washington, DC: Catholic Biblical Association of America).
Auffret, P.
1977a 'Note sur la structure littéraire du Psaume LVII', *Sem* 27: 59-73.
1977b *The Literary Structure of Psalm 2* (JSOTSup, 3; Sheffield: JSOT Press).
1978 'Notes conjointes sur la structure littéraire des Psaumes 114 et 29', *EstBíb* 37: 103-13.
1980 'Essai sur la structure littéraire du Psaume 90', *Bib* 61: 262-76.
1981 *Hymnes d'Égypte et d'Israël. Etudes de structures littéraires* (OBO, 34; Fribourg, Switzerland: Editions Universitaires).
1982a *La sagesse a bâti sa maison* (OBO, 49; Fribourg, Switzerland: Editions Universitaires).
1982b 'Note sur la structure littéraire du Psaume CX', *Sem* 32: 83-88.
Auneau, J.
1985 'Sacerdoce', *DBS* X: cols. 1170-1254.
Avishur, Y.
1976 'Studies of Stylistic Features Common to the Phoenician Inscriptions and the Bible', *UF* 8: 1-22.
1984 *Stylistic Studies on Word-Pairs in Biblical and Ancient Semitic Literatures* (AOAT, 210; Neukirchen–Vluyn: Neukirchener Verlag).
Baars, W.
1965 'A New Witness to the Text of the Barberini Greek Version of Habakkuk III', *VT* 15: 381-82.
Baillet, M.
1982 *Qumrân, Grotte 4, III (4Q482–4Q520)* (Discoveries in the Judaean Desert, VII; Oxford: Clarendon Press).
Balentine, S.E.
1983 *The Hidden God: The Hiding of the Face of God in the Old Testament* (Oxford Theological Monographs; Oxford: Oxford University Press).
Balthasar, H. Urs von
1974 *La gloire et la croix. Les aspects esthétiques de la Révélation. III. Théologie. L'ancienne Alliance* (Théologie, 82; Paris: Aubier), 33-183.

Baltzer, K.
1968   'Considerations regarding the Office and Calling of the Prophet', *HTR* 61: 567-81.
Barkay, G.
1986   *Ketef Hinnom. A Treasure Facing Jerusalem's Walls* (Jerusalem: The Israel Museum).
Barré, M.L.
1986   'The Formulaic Pair *ṭôb (we)ḥesed* in the Psalter', *ZAW* 98: 100-105.
Bartlett, J.R.
1968   'Zadok and his Successor at Jerusalem', *JTS* ns 19: 1-18.
Barucq, A.
1962   *L'expression de la louange divine et de la prière dans la Bible et en Égypte* (Cairo: Institut français d'archéologie orientale).
1979   *Cahiers d'Évangile* (Supplément au cahier, 27; Paris: Cerf).
Barucq, A. and F. Daumas
1980   *Hymnes et prières de l'Égypte ancienne* (LAPO, 10; Paris: Cerf).
Basser, H.W.
1984   *Midrashic Interpretations of the Song of Moses* (Frankfurt: Peter Lang).
Batto, B.F.
1983   'The Reed Sea: *Requiescat in Pace*', *JBL* 102: 27-35.
Beaucamp, É.
1959   'La théophanie du Ps 50 (49)', *NRT* 81: 897-915.
1962–63   'Le problème du Ps 87', *SBFLA* 13: 53-75.
1977   'Le goel de Jb 19,25', *LavTP* 33: 309-10.
1979   'Psaumes', *DBS* IX: cols. 125-206.
Becker, J.
1966   *Israel deutet seine Psalmen* (SBS, 18; Stuttgart: Katholisches Bibelwerk).
1968   Review of E. Lipiński, *Le poème royal du Psaume LXXXIX 1-5. 20-38*, *Bib* 49: 275-80.
1977   *Messiaserwartung im Alten Testament* (SBS, 83; Stuttgart: Katholisches Bibelwerk).
1980   *Messianic Expectation in the Old Testament* (Philadelphia: Fortress Press).
1986   'Zur Deutung von Ps 110,7', in *Freude an der Weisung des Herrn. Festgabe H. Gross* (Stuttgart: Katholisches Bibelwerk), 17-31.
Becking, B.
1978   'Is hat boeck Nahum een literaire eenheid?', *NedTTs* 32: 107-24.
Bee, R.E.
1978a   'The Textual Analysis of Psalm 132: A Response to Cornelius B. Houk', *JSOT* 6: 49-53.
1978b   'The Use of Syllable Counts in Textual Analysis', *JSOT* 10: 68-70.
Begrich, J.
1934   'Das priesterliche Heilsorakel', *ZAW* 54: 81-92.
1964   *Gesammelte Studien zum A.T.* (TBü, 21; Munich: Kaiser Verlag), 217-31.
Bellinger, W.H., Jr
1984   *Psalmody and Prophecy* (JSOTSup, 27; Sheffield: JSOT Press).
Berg, W.
1974   *Die sogenannten Hymnenfragmente im Amosbuch* (Bern: M. Lang).

Berger, P.R.
    1970   'Zu Ps 24, 7 und 9', *UF* 2: 335-36.
Bergler, S.
    1979   'Der längste Psalm, Anthologie oder Liturgie?', *VT* 29: 257-88.
Berlin, A.
    1985   *The Dynamics of Biblical Parallelism* (Bloomington, IN: Indiana University Press).
Bernhardt, K.H.
    1961   *Das Problem der altorientalischen Königsideologie im A.T.* (VTSup, 8; Leiden: Brill), 183-261.
Besnard, A.-M.
    1962   *Le mystère du nom* (LD, 35; Paris: Cerf).
Beyerlin, W.
    1961   *Herkunft und Geschichte der ältesten Sinaitraditionen* (Tübingen: Mohr).
    1973   'Schichten im 80. Psalm', in *Das Wort und die Wörter. Festschrift G. Friedrich* (Stuttgart: Kohlhammer), 9-24.
    1976   'Ps 8, Chancen der Überlieferungskritik', *ZTK* 73: 1-22.
    1985   *Weisheitlich-kultische Heilsordnung. Studien zum 15. Psalm* (BTS, 8; Neukirchen–Vluyn: Neukirchener Verlag).
Beyse, K.-M.
    1972   *Serubbabel und die Königserwartungen der Propheten Haggai und Sacharja* (Stuttgart: Calwer Verlag).
Biard, P.
    1960   *La puissance de Dieu* (Travaux de l'Institut Catholique de Paris, 7; Paris: Bloud & Gay).
Blenkinsopp, J.
    1984   *A History of Prophecy in Israel* (London: SPCK).
Bloch, R.
    1957   'Midrash', *DBS* V: cols. 1263-81.
Boismard, M.-E.
    1988   *Moïse ou Jésus. Essai de christologie johannique* (ETL, 84; Leuven: University Press/Vitgeverij Peeters).
Bonnard, P.E.
    1960   *Le psautier selon Jérémie* (LD, 26; Paris: Cerf).
    1981   'Le psaume 72. Ses relectures, ses traces dans l'oeuvre de Luc?', *RSR* 69: 259-78.
Booij, Th.
    1978   *Godswoorden in de Psalmen. Hun Funktie en Achtergronden* (Amsterdam: Rodopi).
    1984a   'Mountain and Theophany in the Sinai Narrative', *Bib* 65: 1-26.
    1984b   'The Background of the Oracle in Psalm 81', *Bib* 65: 465-75.
Boston, J. R.
    1968   'The Wisdom Influence upon the Song of Moses', *JBL* 87: 198-202.
Bourke, J.
    1959   'Le jour de Yahvé dans Joël', *RB* 66: 191-212.
Bowker, J.W.
    1967   'Psalm CX', *VT* 17: 31-41.

Bradley, H.
1920   'Psalm LXXXV, 9', *JTS* 21: 243-44.
Brandscheidt, R.
1983   *Gotteszorn und Menschenleid. Die Gerichtsklage des leidenden Gerechten in Klgl 3* (Trierer Theologische Studien, 41; Trier: Paulinus).
Braude, W.G.
1959   *The Midrash on Psalms. Midrash Tĕhillîm* (Yale Judaica Series, XIII, 1 and 2; New Haven: Yale University Press).
Braun, F.-M.
1966   *Jean le Théologien. III. Sa théologie. I. Le Mystère de Jésus-Christ* (EBib; Paris: Gabalda), 195-209.
Brekelmans, C.
1983   'Psalm 132: Unity and Structure', *Bijdragen* 44: 262-65.
Broadribb, D.
1972   'A Historical Review of Studies of Hebrew Poetry', *AbrN* 13: 66-87.
Brongers, H.A.
1963   'Der Eifer des Herrn Zebaoth', *VT* 13: 268-84.
Brown, R.E.
1966   *The Gospel according to John (I–XII)* (AB, 29; Garden City, NY: Doubleday).
Brueggemann, W.
1982   'Vengeance: Human and Divine', in *Praying the Psalms* (Winona, MN: St Mary's Press), 67-80.
Buss, M.J.
1978   'The Idea of *Sitz im Leben*. History and Critique', *ZAW* 90: 157-70.
Camponovo, O.
1984   *Königtum, Königsherrschaft und Reich Gottes in den frühjüdischen Schriften* (OBO, 58; Göttingen: Vandenhoeck & Ruprecht).
Caquot, A.
1981   'Brève explication de la prophétie de Natan (2 Sam 7, 1-17)', in *Mélanges H. Cazelles* (AOAT, 212; Neukirchen–Vluyn: Neukirchener Verlag), 51-70.
1982   'Le livre des Jubilés. Melkisedeq et les dîmes', *JJS* 33: 257-64.
Caquot, A., M. Sznycer and A. Herdner
1974   *Textes ougaritiques. I. Mythes et Légendes* (LAPO, 7; Paris: Cerf).
Caquot, A., J.M. de Tarragon and J.L. Cunchillos
1988   *Textes ougaritiques. II. Les Rituels* (LAPO. 14; Paris: Cerf).
Carena, O.
1985   *Il Resto di Israele. Studio storico-comparativo delle iscrizioni reali assire e dei testi profetici sul tema del resto* (Bologna: Editione Dehoniane).
Carlson, R.A.
1969   'Élie à l'Horeb', *VT* 19: 416-39.
Carmignac, J. and P. Guilbert
1961   *Les textes de Qumran traduits et annotés*, I (Paris: Letouzey & Ané).
Carmignac, J., E. Cothenet and H. Lignée
1963   *Les textes de Qumran traduit et annotés*, II (Paris: Letouzey & Ané).

Carniti, C.
1985   *Il salmo 68. Studio letterario* (Biblioteca de Scienze, 68; Rome: LAS).
Carrillo Alday, S.
1970   *El Cantico de Moises (Dt 32)* (Madrid: C.S.I.C., Instituto Fr. Suárez).
Carroll, R.P.
1979   *When Prophecy Failed. Reactions and Responses to Failure in the Old Testament Prophetic Traditions* (London: SCM Press).
Cassin, E.
1968   *La splendeur divine. Introduction à l' étude de la mentalité Mésopotamienne* (Paris: Mouton).
Castellino, G.
1940   *Le lamentazioni individuali e gli inni in Babilonia e in Israele* (Turin: Società Editrice Internationazale).
1952   'Psalm XXXII, 9', *VT* 2: 37-42.
1955   *Libro dei Salmi* (La Sacra Bibbia; Turin/Rome: Marietti).
1977   'Mesopotamian Parallels to some Passages of the Psalms', in *Beiträge zur alttestamentlischen Theologie. Festschrift W. Zimmerli* (Göttingen: Vandenhoeck & Ruprecht), 60-68.
Cazelles, H.
1960   'Nouvel An (Fête du)', *DBS* VI: cols. 620-45.
1961   *Les livres des Chroniques* (*BdJ*; Paris: Cerf, 2nd edn).
1973   'The Hebrews', in *Peoples of Old Testament Times* (ed. D.J. Wiseman; Oxford: Clarendon Press).
1978   *Le Messie de la Bible* (Paris: Desclée).
Chary, T.
1955   *Les prophètes et le culte à partir de l'exil* (Paris: Desclée).
Childs, B.S.
1962   *Memory and Tradition in Israel* (London: SCM Press).
1971   'Psalm Titles and Midrashic Exegesis', *JSS* 16: 137-50.
1976   'Reflections on the Modern Study of the Psalms', in *Magnalia Dei. The Mighty Acts of God...In Memory of G.E. Wright* (Garden City, NY: Doubleday), 377-88.
Chilton, B.D.
1983   *The Glory of Israel. The Theology and Provenience of the Isaiah Targum* (JSOTSup, 23; Sheffield: JSOT Press), 48-56, 69-77.
Chisholm, R.B.
1986   *An Exegetical and Theological Study of Psalm 18 (2 Samuel 22)* (Ann Arbor: University Microfilms).
Christensen, D.L.
1975   'The Acrostic of Nahum Reconsidered', *ZAW* 87: 17-30.
1984b   'Two Stanzas of a Hymn in Deuteronomy 33', *Bib* 65: 382-89.
1984b   'Zephaniah 2:14-15: A Theological Basis for Josiah's Program of Political Expansion', *CBQ* 46: 669-82.
1985   'Prose and Poetry in the Bible. The Narrative Poetics of Deuteronomy 1.9-18', *ZAW* 97: 179-89.

Clifford, R.J.
1972   *The Cosmic Mountain in Canaan and the Old Testament* (HSM, 4; Cambridge, MA: Harvard University Press).
1980   'Psalm 89. A Lament over the Davidic Ruler's Continued Failure', *HTR* 73: 35-47.
Cody, A.
1969   *A History of Old Testament Priesthood* (AnBib, 35; Rome: Biblical Institute Press).
Collins, T.
1987   'Decoding the Psalms. A Structural Approach to the Psalter', *JSOT* 37: 41-60.
Congar, M.-J.
1958   *Le mystère du Temple* (LD, 22; Paris: Cerf), 275-93.
Conroy, A.M.
1985   Review of R.K. Gnuse, *The Dream Theophany of Samuel*, *Bib* 56: 429-33.
Cooper, A.
1983a   'Psalm 27:7-10. Mythology and Exegesis', *JBL* 102: 37-60.
1983b   'The Life and Times of King David according to the Book of Psalms', in *The Poet and the Historian. Essays in Literary and Historical Biblical Criticism* (HSS, 26; Chico, CA: Scholars Press), 117-31.
Coppens, J.
1961   'Les psaumes 6 et 41 dependent-ils du livre de Jérémie?', *HUCA* 32: 217-26.
1968   *Le messianisme royal. Les origines, son développement et son accomplissement* (LD, 54; Paris: Cerf).
1974   *Le messianisme et sa relève prophétique. Les anticipations vétérotestamentaires. Leur accomplissement dans le Christ* (BETL, 38; Leuven: Peeters).
1979   *La relève apocalyptique du messianisme royal. I. La royauté. Le règne. Le royaume de Dieu, cadre de la relève apocalyptique* (BETL, 50; Leuven: Peeters).
1982   'La prophétie de Nathan. Sa portée dynastique', in *Von Kanaan bis Kerala. Festschrift...van der Ploeg* (AOAT, 211; Neukirchen–Vluyn: Neukirchener Verlag), 91-100.
Costacurta, B.
1983   'L'agressione contro Dio. Studio del Salmo 83', *Bib* 64: 518-41.
Costecalde, C.B.
1985   'Sacré', *DBS* X: cols. 1346-1415.
Couroyer, B.
1949   'Le chemin de vie en Egypte et en Israël', *RB* 56: 412-32.
1971   'Dieu ou Roi? Le vocatif dans le psaume XLV (vv. 1-9)', *RB* 78: 233-41.
1975   'Un egyptianisme dans Ben Sira 4, 11', *RB* 82: 206-17.
1981   ' "Avoir la nuque raide": ne pas incliner l'oreille', *RB* 88: 216-25.
1988   ' *'EDUT*: Stipulation de traité ou enseignement', *RB* 95: 321-31.
Crenshaw, J.L.
1968   'Amos and the Theophanic Tradition', *ZAW* 80: 203-15.
1972   'Wĕdōrēk 'al-bāmôtê 'āreṣ', *CBQ* 34: 39-53.

Cross, F.M.
1973   *Canaanite Myth and Hebrew Epic* (Cambridge, MA: Harvard University Press).
1981   'The Priestly Tabernacle in the Light of Recent Research', in *Temples and High Places in Biblical Times* (ed. A. Biran; Jerusalem: Jewish Institute of Religion), 169-78.
Cross, F.M. and D.N. Freedman
1975   *Studies in Ancient Yahwistic Poetry* (SBLDS, 21; Missoula, MT: Scholars Press).
Crüsemann, F.
1969   *Studien zur Formgeschichte von Hymnus und Danklied in Israel* (WMANT, 32; Neukirchen–Vluyn: Neukirchener Verlag).
Culley, R.
1967   *Oral Formulaic Language in the Biblical Psalms* (Toronto: University of Toronto Press).
Cunchillos, J.L.
1976a   *Cuando los Angeles eran Dioses* (Bibl. Salmant. XIV; Estudios 12; Salamanca: Universídad Pontificia).
1976b   *Estudio del Salmo 29* (Valencia: Institutión S. Jerónimo).
Curtis, A.H.W.
1979   Review of Eaton, *Kingship and the Psalms*, *JSS* 24: 276-77.
Dahood, M.
1966   *Psalms I, 1-50* (AB, 16; Garden City, NY: Doubleday).
1968   *Psalms II, 51-100* (AB, 17; Garden City, NY: Doubleday).
1970   *Psalms III, 101-150* (AB, 17A; Garden City, NY: Doubleday).
Dambrinne, L.
1971   *L'image de la croissance dans la foi d'Israël. Études sur la racine ṣmh et ses dérivés* (Mémoire dactylographié; Lausanne: Université de Lausanne).
Davies, G. Henton
1973   'Psalm 95', *ZAW* 85: 183-95.
Day, J.
1981   'Shear-Jashub (Isaiah VII 3) and the "Remnant of Wrath" (Psalm LXXVI 11)', *VT* 31: 76-78.
1985   *God's Conflict with the Dragon and the Sea. Echoes of a Canaanite Myth in the Old Testament* (Oriental Publications, 35; Cambridge: Cambridge University Press).
Deissler, A.
1955   *Psalm 119 (118) und seine Theologie. Ein Beitrag zur Erforschung der anthologischen Stillgattung im Alten Testament* (Munich: Karl Zink Verlag).
1968   *Le livre des Psaumes 76–150* (Verbum Salutis; Paris: Beauchesne).
1981   'Zum Problem des messianischen Charakter von Psalm 2', in *De la Tôrah au Messie. Mélanges H. Cazelles* (Paris: Desclée), 283-92.
Del Olmo Lete, G.
1984   'David's Farewell Oracle (2 Samuel XXIII 1-7). A Literary Analysis', *VT* 34: 414-37.

Delekat, L.
1964   'Zum hebräischen Wörterbuch', *VT* 14: 35-49.
Delitzsch, F.
1983   *Die Psalmen* (BKAT; 4th edn; Neukirchen–Vluyn: Neukirchener Verlag).
De Meyer, F.
1980   '*kbd* comme nom divin en éblaïte, ougaritique et hébreu', *RTL* 11: 225-28, 272.
1981a   'La sagesse psalmique et le Psaume 94', *Bijdragen* 42: 22-45.
1981b   'La dimension sapientiale du Psaume 62', *Bijdragen* 42: 350-65.
Descamps, A.
1962   'Les genres littéraires du Psautier. Un état de la question', in *Le Psautier* (ed. R. de Langhe; Louvain: Publications Universitaires/Institut Orientaliste), 73-88.
Devescovi, U.
1961   'Camminare sulle alture', *RivB* 9: 235-42.
De Waard, J.
1971   'The Quotation from Deuteronomy in Acts 3, 22-23 and the Palestinian Text, Additional Arguments', *Bib* 52: 537- 40.
Dexinger, F.
1985   'Der "Prophet wie Mose" in Qumran und bei den Samaritanern', in *Mélanges M. Delcor* (AOAT, 215; Neukirchen–Vluyn: Neukirchener Verlag), 97-111.
Dhorme, P.
1923   *L'emploi métaphorique des noms de parties du corps en hébreu et en akkadien* (Extrait de la *RB* 1920–1923; Paris: Gabalda), 51-60.
Diez Merino, L.
1982a   'Il vocabolario relativo alla "Ricerca di Dio" nell'Antico Testamento. Il termino *biqqeš*', *BeO* 24: 129-45.
1982b   *Targum de Salmos* (Bibliotheca Hispanica Biblica, 6; Madrid: Instituto F. Suárez).
Dion, P.-E.
1967   'The Patriarchal Tradition and the Literary Form of the "Oracle of Salvation" ', *CBQ* 29: 198-206.
1975   *Dieu universel et peuple élu* (LD, 83; Paris: Cerf), 102-107.
1980   'Tu feras disparaître le mal du milieu de toi', *RB* 87: 321-49.
1981   'Ressemblance et image de Dieu', *DBS* X: cols. 366-403.
Dix, G.
1968   *The Apostolic Tradition of St Hippolytus* (London: SPCK).
Donner, H.
1967   'Ugaritismen in der Psalmenforschung', *ZAW* 79: 322-50.
Donner, H. and W. Röllig
1968   *Kanaanäische und aramäische Inschriften*, II (2nd edn; Wiesbaden: Otto Harrassowitz).
Doré, J.
1981   'La rencontre Abraham–Melchisédech et le problème de l'unité littéraire de Genèse 14', in *De la Tôrah au Messie. Mélanges H. Cazelles* (Paris: Desclée), 75-95.

Dreyfus, F.
    1962   'Sauve-nous pour la gloire de ton nom', *VSpir* 106, May: 523-31.
    1979   'Pour la louange de sa gloire (Ep 1, 12.14). L'origine vétérotestamentaire
                de la formule', in *Paul de Tarse, apôtre de notre temps* (Rome: S. Paolo),
                233-48.
Drijvers, P.
    1965   *The Psalms. Their Structure and Meaning* (New York: Herder & Herder).
Duchesene-Guillemin, M.
    1984   *A Hurrian Score from Ugarit: The Discovery of Mesopotamian Music*
                (Sources Ancient Near East, 2/2; Malibu: Undena Publications).
Dumortier, J.-B.
    1972   'Un rituel d'intronisation: le Ps 89, 2-38', *VT* 22: 176-96.
Dupont, J.
    1960   'Nom de Jésus', *DBS* VI: cols. 514-41.
    1969   *Les Béatitudes*. II. *La Bonne Nouvelle* (EBib; Paris: Gabalda), 11-142.
Durham, J.I.
    1970/1983   '*šlwm* and the Presence of God', in *Proclamation and Presence. Old Testa-
                ment Essays in Honour of G.H. Davies* (London: SCM Press), 272-93.
Eaton, J.H.
    1976 [1986] *Kingship and the Psalms* (London: SCM Press [2nd edn: Sheffield: JSOT
                Press]).
    1983   'Music's Place in Worship: A Contribution from the Psalms', *OTS* 23: 85-
                107.
Ehrlich, E.
    1953   *Der Traum im Alten Testament* (BZAW, 73; Berlin: Töpelmann).
Eissfeldt, O.
    1955   'Zwei verkannte militär-technische Termini im Alten Testament', *VT* 5:
                232-38.
    1958   *Das Lied Moses Deuteronomium 32, 1-43 und das Lehrgedicht Asaphs
                Psalm 78 samt einer Analyse der Umgebung des Mose-Liedes* (Berlin:
                Akademie Verlag).
    1963   'Zur Frage nach Alter der Phönizischen Geschichte des Sanchuniaton', in
                Kleine Schriften, II (Tübingen: Mohr), 127-29.
    1966   'Psalm 80', in *Kleine Schriften*, III (Tübingen: Mohr), 221-32.
Ellermeier, F.
    1968   *Prophetie in Mari und Israel* (Herzberg: Erwin Jungler).
Elliger, K.
    1966   *Leviticus* (HAT, 4; Neukirchen–Vluyn: Neukirchener Verlag), 121-31.
    1970   *Jesaja II* (BKAT, XI, Neukirchen–Vluyn: Neukirchener Verlag).
Emerton, J.A.
    1960   'The Interpretation of Psalm LXXXII in John X, 34', *JTS* ns 11: 329-32.
    1978   'The Translation of the Verbs in the Imperfect in Psalm II, 9', *JTS* ns 29:
                499-503.
Faur, J.
    1984–85   'Delocutive Expressions in the Hebrew Liturgy', *JANES* 16-17: 41-54.

Fensham, F.C.
   1960   'Ps 68:23 in the Light of the Recently Discovered Ugaritic Tablets', *JNES*
               19: 292-93.
   1965   'A Covenant-Song?' *ZAW* 77: 193-202.
   1981   'Neh. 9 and Pss. 105, 106, 135 and 136. Post-exilic Historical Traditions
               in Poetic Form', *Journal of Northwest Semitic Languages* 9: 35-51.
Feuillet, A.
   1951   'Les psaumes eschatologiques du Règne de Yahweh', *NRT* 73: 244-60,
               352-63.
   1962   'Note sur la traduction de Jér XXXI 3c', *VT* 12: 122-24.
   1985   'Les problèmes posés par l'exégèse des Psaumes. Quatre Psaumes royaux
               (II, XLV, LXXII, CX)', *RTh* 85: 5-37.
Fitzmyer, J.A.
   1971   'Now This Melchizedek...', in *Essays on the Semitic Background of the
               New Testament* (Missoula, MT: Scholars Press), 223-27.
   1972   'David "Being therefore a Prophet..." (Acts 2:30)', *CBQ* 34: 332-39.
Flusser, D.
   1988   *Judaism and the Origins of Christianity* (Jerusalem: Magnes Press), 457-
               58.
Fohrer, G.
   1985   'Das "Gebet der Prophet Habakuk" (Hab 3, 1-16)', in *Mélanges M. Delcor*
               (AOAT, 215; Neukirchen–Vluyn: Neukirchener Verlag), 159-67.
Foresti, F.
   1981   'Funzione semantica dei brani participiali di Amos: 4,13; 5,8s.; 9,5s.', *Bib*
               62: 169-84.
Freedman, D.N.
   1976   'Divine Names and Titles in Early Hebrew Poetry', in *Magnalia
               Dei... G.E. Wright* (ed. B.S. Childs; Garden City, NY: Doubleday), 55-
               107.
   1980   *Pottery, Poetry and Prophecy. Studies in Early Hebrew Poetry* (Winona
               Lake, IN: Eisenbrauns).
Fretheim, T.E.
   1967   'Psalm 132: A Form-Critical Study', *JBL* 86: 289-300.
Fritsch, C.T.
   1982   'A Study of the Greek Translation of the Hebrew Verbs "to see" with Deity
               as Subject or Object', in *Harry M. Orlinsky Volume. Eretz Israel* 16: 51*-
               56* (in Hebrew).
Frost, S.B.
   1952   *Old Testament Apocalyptic. Its Origins and Growth* (London: Epworth
               Press).
Garcia López, F.
   1984   'Un profeta como Moisés. Estudio crítico de Dt 18, 9-22', in *Simposio
               Bíblico Español* (Madrid: Universidad Complutense), 289-308.
Garr, W.R.
   1983   'The Qinah: A Study of Poetic Meter, Syntax and Style', *ZAW* 95: 54-75.

Gelin, A.
1957   'Messianisme', *DBS* V: cols. 1165-1212.
1964   *The Poor of Yahweh* (Collegeville: Liturgical Press).
Gelineau, J.
1978   'Les Psaumes à l'époque patristique', *Maison-Dieu* 135: 99-116.
Geller, S.A.
1979   *Parallelism in Early Biblical Poetry* (HSM, 20; Missoula, MT: Scholars Press).
Georges, A.
1965   'Jésus, Fils de Dieu dans l'évangile selon S. Luc', *RB* 72: 185-209.
Gerleman, G.
1962   *Zephanja. Textkritisch und literarisch untersucht* (Lund: Gleerup).
Gerson-Kiwi, E.
1956   'Musique de la Bible', *DBS* V: cols. 1411-68
Gese, H.
1973 [1974] 'Zur Geschichte der Kultsänger am zweiten Tempel', in *Abraham unser Vater. O. Michel Festschrift* (Leiden: Brill), 222-34.
1976   'Psalm 50 und das alttestamentliche Gesetzverständnis', in *Rechtfertigung. Festschrift E. Kasemann* (Tübingen: Mohr), 57-77.
Gianotto, C.
1984   *Melchisedek e la sua tipologia. Tradizioni giudaiche, cristiane e gnostiche (sec. II a.C.-sec. III d.C.)* (RivBSup, 12; Brescia: Paideia Editrice).
Gibson, J.C.L.
1977   *Canaanite Myths and Legends* (2nd edn; Edinburgh: T. & T. Clark).
Gilbert, M. (ed.)
1979   *La Sagesse de l'Ancien Testament* (BETL, 51; Leuven: Peeters), 209-11.
Gilbert, M. and S. Pisano
1980   'Psalm 110 (109), 5-7', *Bib* 61: 343-56.
Girard, M.
1984   *Les Psaumes, analyse structurelle et interprétation. Psaumes 1–50* (Recherches Nouvelle Série, 2; Paris: Cerf).
Globe, A.
1974   'The Text and Literary Structure of Judges 5, 4-5', *Bib* 55: 168-78.
Gnuse, R.K.
1984   *The Dream Theophany of Samuel. Its Structure in Relation to Ancient Near Eastern Dreams and its Theological Significance* (Lanham, MD: University Press of America).
Goldberg, A.
1969   *Untersuchungen über die Vorstellung von der Schekhinah in der frühen rabbinischen Literatur* (Studia Judaica, 5; Berlin: de Gruyter).
Goldingay, J.
1977-78 'Repetition and Variation in the Psalms', *JQR* 68: 146-51.
Gonçalves, F.
1986   *L'expédition de Sennachérib en Palestine dans la littérature hébraïque ancienne* (EBib, ns 7; Paris: Gabalda).
Good, E.M.
1959   'The Barberini Greek Version of Habakkuk III', *VT* 9: 11-30.

Goodwin, D.W.
1969   *Text-Restoration Methods in Contemporary U.S.A. Biblical Scholarship* (Naples: Istituto Orientale di Napoli).
Gordon, C.
1978   'History of Religion in Psalm 82', in *Biblical and Near Eastern Studies. Essay in Honor of W.S. LaSor* (Grand Rapids: Eerdmans), 129-31.
Görg, M.
1967   *Das Zelt der Begegnung* (BBB, 27; Bonn: Peter Hanstein).
1977   'Eine neue Deutung für *kǎpporaet*', *ZAW* 89: 115-18.
Gosse, B.
1986   'Le "moi" prophétique de l'oracle contre Babylone d'Isaïe XXI, 1-10', *RB* 93: 70-84.
Goulder, M.D.
1982   *The Psalms of the Sons of Korah* (JSOTSup, 20; Sheffield: JSOT Press).
Gourgues, M.
1978   *À la droite de Dieu. Résurrection de Jésus et actualisation du Psaume 110:1 dans le Nouveau Testament* (EBib; Paris: Gabalda).
Goy, W.-A.
1960   'Dieu a-t-il changé? Psaume 77', in *Hommage à W. Vischer*, 56-62.
Gradwohl, R.
1963   *Die Farben im Alten Testament* (BZAW, 83; Berlin: Töpelmann).
Graf Baudissin, W.W.
1915   ' "Gott schauen" in der alttestamentlichen Religion', *ARW* 18: 173-239.
Gray, J.
1974   'The Day of Yahweh in Cultic Experience and Eschatological Prospect', *SEÅ* 39: 5-37.
Greenberg, M.
1978   'Psalm 140', *Eretz Israel* 14: 125*-26* (88-99 in Hebrew).
1983   *Ezekiel 1–20* (AB, 22; Garden City, NY: Doubleday).
Greenfield, J.C.
1971a   'The Background and Parallel to a Proverb of Ahiqar', in *Hommages à Dupont-Sommer* (Paris: Adrien-Maisonneuve), 48-49.
1971b   'Scripture and Inscription: The Literary and Rhetorical Element in Some Early Phoenician Inscriptions', in *Near Eastern Studies in Honor of W.F. Albright* (ed. H. Goedicke; Baltimore: Johns Hopkins University Press), 253-68.
1979   'Early Aramaic Poetry', *JANES* 11: 45-50.
1985   'Ba'al's Throne and Isa. 6:1', in *Festschrift M. Delcor* (AOAT, 215; Neukirchen–Vluyn: Neukirchener Verlag), 193-98.
1987   'To Praise the Might of Haddad', in *La Vie de la Parole. Mélanges P. Grelot* (Paris: Desclée), 3-12.
Grelot, P.
1957   'Un parallèle babylonien d'Isaïe LX et du Psaume LXXII', *VT* 7: 319-21.
1962   *Sens chrétien de l'Ancien Testament* (Paris: Desclée).
1985   *Les Targums. Textes choisis* (Cahiers Évangiles, Sup 54), 86-87.
Grether, O.
1934   *Name und Wort Gottes im Alten Testament* (BZAW, 64; Berlin: Töpel-

mann).

Grondijs, M.L.-H.
1962   'Croyances, doctrines et iconographie de la liturgie céleste (le trône de grâce et le Christ-prêtre officiant)', *Mélanges d' Archéologie et d' Histoire* 74: 665-703.

Gross, M.
1967   *Le prétendu 'ministère prophétique' en Israel* (RechBib, 8; Bruges/Paris: Desclée de Brouwer), 93-105.

Gruber, M.I.
1983   'The Many Faces of Hebrew *nāśā' pānîm*, "lift up the face" ', *ZAW* 95: 252-60.

Guggisberg, F.
1979   *Die Gestalt des Mal' ak Jahwe im Alten Testament* (Dissertation, Neuchâtel).

Guillet, J.
1948   'Cette génération infidèle et dévoyée', *RSR* 35: 275-81.

Gunkel, H.
1925   *Die Psalmen* (Göttingen: Vandenhoeck & Ruprecht).

Gunkel, H. and J. Begrich
1928-33   'Das prophetische in den Psalmen', in *Einleitung in die Psalmen*
[1966]   (Göttingen: Vandenhoeck & Ruprecht), 329-81.

Haglund, E.
1984   *Historical Motifs in the Psalms* (ConBOT, 23; Malmö: Gleerup).

Halperin, D.J.
1980   *The Merkabah in Rabbinic Literature* (AOS, 62; New Haven: American Oriental Society).

Hanson, P.D.
1971   'Jewish Apocalyptic against its Near Eastern Environment', *RB* 78: 31-58.
1975   *The Dawn of Apocalyptic* (Philadelphia: Fortress Press).
1984   *Alphabetic Acrostics. A Form-Critical Study* (Ann Arbor: University Microfilms), 296-314.

Haran, M.
1960a   'The Nature of the '*ohel mo'edh* in Pentateuchal Sources', *JSS* 5: 50-65.
1960b   'The Uses of Incense in the Ancient Israelite Ritual', *VT* 10: 113-29.
1979   *Temples and Temple Service in Ancient Israel: An Inquiry into the Character of Cult Phenomena and the Historical Setting of the Priestly School* (Oxford: Clarendon Press).
1984   'The Shining of Moses' Face: A Case Study in Biblical and Ancient Near Eastern Iconography', in *In the Shelter of Elyon...G.W. Ahlström* (JSOTSup, 31; Sheffield: JSOT Press), 159-73.

Harris, J.S.
1971   *Prophetic Oracles in the Psalter* (Ann Arbor: University Microfilms).

Haupt, P.
1914   'Die Psalmverse in I Chr 25, 4', *ZAW* 34: 142-45.

Hauret, C.
1959–1960 'L'interprétation des Psaumes dans l'École "Myth and Ritual"', *RevScRel* 33: 321-46; 34: 1-34.
1961 'Un problème insoluble? La chronologie des Psaumes', *RevScRel* 35: 225-56.

Hayward, R.
1981 *Divine Name and Presence: The Memra* (Totoura, NJ: Alanheld).

Heintz, J.-G.
1969 *Oracles prophétiques et 'guerre sainte' selon les archives royales de Mari et l'AT* (VTSup, 17; Leiden: Brill), 112-38.
1973 'Le "feu devorant", un symbole du triomphe divin dans l'A.T. et le milieu sémitique ambiant', in *Le feu dans le Proche-Orient antique* (Actes du Colloque de Strasbourg, 1972; Leiden: Brill), 63-78.
1979 'De l'absence de la statue divine au "Dieu qui se cache" (Esaïe 45/15): aux origines d'un thème biblique', in *Prophètes, Poètes et Sages d'Israël. Hommages à E. Jacob = RHPR* 59: 427-37.

Hemmerdinger, B.
1971 'Selah', *JTS* ns 22: 152-53.

Hengel, M.
1984 *Il figlio di Dio; l'origine della christologia et la storia della religione giudeo-ellenistica* (Studi Biblici, 67; Brescia: Paideia Editrice).

Herrmann, A.
1964 *Die prophetischen Heilserwartung im A.T., Ursprung und Gestaltwandel* (WMANT, 5/5; Neukirchen–Vluyn: Neukirchener Verlag).

Hertzberg, H.W.
1950 'Die prophetische Kritik am Kult', *TLZ* 75: 219-26.

Hesse, F.
1955 *Das Verstockungsproblem im Alten Testament. Eine Frommigkeits-geschichtliche Untersuchung* (BZAW, 74; Berlin: Töpelmann).

Hiebert, T.
1986 *God of my Victory. The Ancient Hymn in Habakkuk 3* (HSM, 38; Atlanta: Scholars Press).

Hill, A.E.
1983 'Patchwork Poetry or Reasoned Verse? Connective Structure in 1 Chronicles XVI', *VT* 33: 97-101.

Höffken, P.
1983 'Werden und Vergehen der Götter. Ein Beitrag zur Auslegung von Ps 82', *TZ* 39: 129-37.

Hoffman, Y.
1981 'The Day of the Lord as a Concept and a Term in the Prophetic Literature', *ZAW* 93: 37-50.

Holmberg, Bo
1983 'The Lord and the Cloud in the Old Testament', *SEÅ* 48: 31-47 (in Swedish).

Honeyman, A.M.
1961 ' 'ID, DŪ and Psalm LXII 12', *VT* 11: 348-50.

Horst, F.
    1947   'Segen und Segenhandlungen in der Bibel', *EvT* 7: 19.
Houk, C.B.
    1978   'Psalm 132, Literary Integrity, and Syllable-Word Structures', *JSOT* 6:
                41-48, 54-57.
Howard, G.
    1977   'The Tetragram and the New Testament', *JBL* 96: 63-83.
Howell, J.C.
    1984   *A Hermeneutical Approach to Psalm 90* (Ann Arbor: University Mi-
                crofilms).
Hugger, P.
    1971   *Jahwe meine Zuflucht. Gestalt und Theologie des 91. Psalms* (Munich:
                Vier-Türme Verlag).
Hultgård, A.
    1985   'Théophanie et présence divine dans le judaïsme antique', in *La litteraturé
                intertestamentaire* (Paris: PUF), 43-55.
Humbert, P.
    1932   'Le problème du livre de Nahum', *RHPR* 12: 1-15.
    1946   *La terou'a. Analyse d'un rite biblique* (Neuchâtel: Secrétariat de
                l'Université).
    1957   'La rosée tombe en Israël. A propos d'Esaïe 26, 19', *TZ* 13: 487-93.
Hunter, A.V.
    1982   *Seek the Lord! A Study of the Meaning and Function of the Exhortations in
                Amos, Hosea, Isaiah, Micah and Zephaniah* (Baltimore: St Mary's Semi-
                nary and University).
Hurvitz, A.
    1968   'The Chronological Significance of "Aramaisms" in Biblical Hebrew', *IEJ*
                18: 234-40.
    1972   *The Transition Period in Biblical Hebrew. A Study in Post-Exilic Hebrew
                and its Implications for the Dating of the Psalms* (Jerusalem: Môsâd Bialik)
                (in Hebrew).
    1985   'Originals and Imitations in Biblical Poetry. A Comparative Examination of
                1 Sam 2:1-10 and Ps 113:5-9', in *Biblical and Related Studies. Presented
                to S. Iwry* (Winona Lake, IN: Eisenbrauns), 115-21.
Huwiler, E.F.
    1987   'Patterns and Problems in Psalm 132', in *The Listening
                Heart*... (JSOTSup, 58; Sheffield: JSOT Press), 199-215.
Irsigler, H.
    1984   *Psalm 73. Monolog eines Weisen* (St Ottilien: EOS).
Ittman, H.
    1981   *Die Konfessionen Jeremias* (WMANT, 54; Neukirchen–Vluyn: Neukirch-
                ener Verlag).
Jacob, E. and H. Cazelles
    1979   'Ras Shamra', *DBS* IX: cols. 1425-39.
Jacquet, L.
    1975–79   *Les Psaumes et le coeur de l'homme* (3 vols.; Gembloux: Duculot).

Jagersma, H.
1982   'Some Remarks on the Jussive in Numbers 6, 24-26', in *Von Kanaan bis Kerala. Festschrift van der Ploeg* (AOAT, 211; Neukirchen–Vluyn: Neukirchener Verlag), 131-36.

Janowski, B.
1986   *Rettungsgewischeit und Epiphanie des Heils... I. Alter Orient* (WMANT, 59; Neukirchen–Vluyn: Neukirchener Verlag).
1989   'Das Königtum Gottes in den Psalmen', *ZTK* 86: 389-454.

Japhet, S.
1968   'The Supposed Common Authorship of Chronicles and Ezra–Nehemia Investigated Anew', *VT* 18: 330-71.
1977   *The Ideology of the Book of Chronicles and its Place in Biblical Thought* (Jerusalem: Môsād Bialik) (in Hebrew).
1985   'The Historical Reliability of Chronicles', *JSOT* 33: 83-107.

Jefferson, H.G.
1963   'Psalm LXXVII', *VT* 13: 87-91.

Jenni, E.
1980   'Aus des Literatur zur chronistischen Geschichtsschreibung', *TRu* 45: 97-108.

Jeremias, Jörg
1965   *Theophanie. Die Geschichte einer alttestamentlichen Gattung* (WMANT, 10; Neukirchen–Vluyn: Neukirchener Verlag).
1970   *Kultprophetie und Gerichtsverkündigung in der späten Königszeit Israels* (WMANT, 35; Neukirchen–Vluyn: Neukirchener Verlag).
1987   *Das Königtum Gottes in den Psalmen. Israels Begegnung mit dem kanaanäischen Mythos in den Jahwe-König-Psalmen* (FRLANT, 141; Göttingen: Vandenhoeck & Ruprecht).

Jocken, P.
1977   'War Habakuk ein Kultprophet?', in *Bausteine biblischer Theologie...Festschrift G. Botterweck* (BBB, 50; Köln/Bonn: Hanstein), 319-32.

Johnson, A.R.
1944 [1962]   *The Cultic Prophet in Ancient Israel* (Cardiff: University of Wales Press).
1947   'Aspects of the Use of the Term *pānîm* in the Old Testament', in *Festschrift O. Eissfeldt* (Halle: M. Niemeyer), 155-59.
1955 [1967]   *Sacral Kingship in Ancient Israel* (Cardiff: University of Wales Press).
1979   *The Cultic Prophet and Israel's Psalmody* (Cardiff: University of Wales Press).

Jones, G.H.
1975   ' "Holy War" or "Yahweh War" ', *VT* 25: 642-58.

Jüngling, H.-W.
1969   *Der Tod der Götter. Eine Untersuchung zu Ps 82* (SBS, 38; Stuttgart: Katholisches Bibelwerk).

Kaiser, O.
1962   'Erwägungen zu Psalm 101', *ZAW* 74: 195-205.

Kapelrud, A.S.
1975a   'Some Aspects of the Relationships between the Texts of Ras Shamra and

the Old Testament', *SEÅ* 40: 5-17 (in Swedish).

1975b   *The Message of the Prophet Zephaniah. Morphology and Ideas* (Oslo: Universitetsforlaget).

Kaufmann, Y.

1977   *History of the Religion of Israel.* IV. *From the Babylonian Captivity to the End of Prophecy* (New York: Ktav), 449-84.

Keel, O.

1977a   *Jahwe-Visionen und Siegelkunst* (SBS, 84-85; Stuttgart: Katholisches Bibelwerk).

1977b   *Die Welt der orientalischen Bildsymbolik und das A.T. Am Beispiel der Psalmen* (2nd edition).

1978   *The Symbolism of the Biblical World. Ancient Near Eastern Iconography and the Book of Psalms* (New York: Seabury Press).

Kellenberger, E.

1984   *ḥäsäd wä'ämät als Ausdruck einer Glaubenserfahrung* (ATANT, 69; Zurich: Theologischer Verlag).

Keller, C.-A. and R. Vuilleumier

1971   *Michée–Nahoum–Habacuc–Sophonie* (Commentaire de l'A.T., XI b; Neuchâtel: Delachaux and Niestlé).

Kellermann, U.

1978   'Erwägungen zum historischen Ort von Psalm 60', *VT* 28: 56-65.

Kenik, H.A.

1976   'Code of Conduct for a King: Psalm 101', *JBL* 95: 391-403.

Kim, E.K.

1986   *The Rapid Change of Mood in the Lament Psalms, with a Special Inquiry into the Impetus for its Expression* (Ann Arbor: University Microfilms).

Kittel, R.

1959   *Theologisches Wörterbuch zum Neuen Testament. 6. Prósôpon* (Stuttgart: Kohlhammer), 769-81.

Kloos, C.

1986   *Yhwh's Combat with the Sea. A Canaanite Tradition in the Religion of Ancient Israel* (Leiden: Brill).

Knibb, M.A.

1982   'Prophecy and the Emergence of the Jewish Apocalypses', in *Israel's Prophetic Tradition. Essays in Honour of P.R. Ackroyd* (ed. R.J. Coggins, A. Phillips and M.A. Knibb; Cambridge: Cambridge University Press), 155-80.

Knutson, F. Brent

1981   *Divine Names and Epithets in the Akkadian Texts. Ras Shamra Parallels* 3 (AnOr, 51; Rome: Biblical Institute Press), 471-618.

Koenig, J.

1966   'Aux origines des theophanies iahvistes', *RHR* 169: 1-36.

1973   'Les indices volcaniques de l'ancienne littérature israélite: bilan et problèmes majeurs', in *Le feu dans le Proche-Orient Antique* (Colloque de Strasbourg, 1972; Leiden: Brill), 79-92.

König, E.

1927   *Die Psalmen* (Gütersloh: Bertelsmann).

Krašovec, J.
1977   *Der Merismus im Biblisch-Hebräischen und Nordwestsemitischen* (Rome: Biblical Institute Press).
1983   'Merism, Polar Expression in Biblical Hebrew', *Bib* 64: 231-39.
1984   *Antithetic Structure in Biblical Hebrew Poetry* (VTSup, 35; Leiden: Brill).
1988   *La justice (SDQ) de Dieu dans le Bible hébraïque et l'interprétation juive et chrétienne* (OBO, 76: Göttingen: Vandenhoeck & Ruprecht).
Kratz, R.
1979   *Rettungswunder: Motiv-, traditions- und formkritische Aufarbeitung einer biblischen Gattung* (Frankfurt: Peter Lang).
Kraus, H.-J.
1978   *Psalmen 1-59; 60-150* (BKAT XV, 1, 2; 5th edn; Neukirchen–Vluyn: Neukirchener Verlag).
Kreuzer, S.
1983   *Der lebendige Gott* (BWANT, 116; Stuttgart: Kohlhammer).
Krinetzki, L.
1961   'Der anthologische Stil des 46. Psalms und seine Bedeutung für die Datierungsfrage', *MTZ* 12: 52-71.
Kruze, H.
1983   'Psalm CXXXII and the Royal Zion Festival', *VT* 33: 279-97.
Kselman, J. S.
1976   'A Note on Numbers 12:6-8', *VT* 26: 500-505.
1983   'Psalm 77 and the Book of Exodus', *JANES* 15: 51-58.
1984   'A Note on Psalm 85:9-10', *CBQ* 46: 23-27.
1985   'Psalm 101: Royal Confession and Divine Oracle', *JSOT* 33: 45-62.
Kuchler, F.
1918   'Das priesterliche Orakel in Israel und Juda', in *Festschrift Baudissin* (BZAW, 33; Berlin: Töpelmann), 285-301.
Kugel, J.L.
1981   *The Idea of Biblical Poetry. Parallelism and its History* (New Haven: Yale University Press).
1984   'Some Thoughts on Future Research into Biblical Style: Addenda to *The Idea of Biblical Poetry*', *JSOT* 28: 107-17.
Kuntz, J.K.
1974   'The Canonical Wisdom Psalms of Ancient Israel. Their Rhetorical, Thematic and Formal Dimensions', in *Rhetorical Criticism. Essays in Honor of J. Muilenburg* (Pittsburgh: Pickwick Press), 186-222.
1983   'Psalm 18. A Rhetorical-Criticism Analysis', *JSOT* 26: 3-31.
Kutsch, E.
1963   *Salbung als Rechtsakt im Alten Testament und im Alten Orient* (BZAW, 87; Berlin: Töpelmann).
Kutscher, E.Y.
1959   *The Language and Linguistic Background of the Isaiah Scroll* (Jerusalem: Magnes Press) (Hebrew; English summary).
Laberge, L.
1985   'Le lieu que YHWH a choisi pour y mettre son Nom', *EstBíb* 43: 209-36.

Labuschagne, C.J.
    1966   *The Incomparability of Yahweh in the Old Testament* (Leiden: Brill).
    1971   'The Song of Moses: Its Framework and Structure', in *De Fructu Oris Sui,
            Essays in Honor of ...van Selms* (Leiden: Brill), 85-98.
    1974   'The Tribes in the Blessings of Moses', *OTS* 19: 97-112.
Lack, R.
    1962   'Les origines d'Elyôn, le Très-Haut, dans la tradition cultuelle d'Israël',
            CBQ 24: 44-64.
    1973   *La symbolique du livre d'Isaïe. Essai sur l'image littéraire comme élément
            de structuration* (AnBib, 59; Rome: Biblical Institute Press).
Lactance (Lactantius)
    1982   *La colère de Dieu* (Sources chrétiennes, 289; trans. C. Ingremeau; Paris:
            Cerf).
Lagrange, M.-J.
    1905   'Notes sur le messianisme dans les Psaumes', *RB* 14: 39-57, 188-202.
Lambert, W.G.
    1960 [1975]   *Babylonian Wisdom Literature* (Oxford: Clarendon Press).
Landy, F.
    1984   'Poetics and Parallelism: Some Comments on James Kugel's *The Idea of
            Biblical Poetry*', *JSOT* 28: 61-87.
Langlamet, F.
    1969a   *Gilgal et les récits de la traversée du Jourdain* (Cahiers de la *RB*, 11; Paris:
            Gabalda).
    1969b   'Israël et "l'inhabitant du pays"', *RB* 76: 481-507.
    1970   'Les récits de l'institution de la royauté (I Sam VII–XII)', *RB* 77: 161-200.
    1972   Review of W. Richter, *RB* 79: 275-88.
Lapointe, R.
    1971   'La nuit est ma lumière', *CBQ* 33: 397-402.
Larcher, C.
    1962   *L'actualité chrétienne de l'A.T. d'après le N.T.* (LD, 34; Paris: Cerf).
    1969   *Études sur le livre de la Sagesse* (EBib; Paris: Gabalda).
    1983–85   *Le livre de la Sagesse ou la Sagesse de Salomon* (EBib; Paris: Gabalda, I,
            1983; II, 1984; III, 1985).
Le Déaut, R.
    1963   *La nuit pascale. Essai sur la signification de la Pâque juive à partir du Tar-
            gum d'Exode XII 42* (AnBib, 22; Rome: Biblical Institute Press).
    1966   *Introduction à la littérature targumique*, Part I (Rome: Biblical Institute
            Press).
Le Déaut, R. and J. Robert
    1971   *Targum des Chroniques, I-II* (AnBib, 51; Rome: Biblical Institute Press).
Leineweber, W.
    1980   *Die Patriarchen im Licht der archäologischen Entdeckungen* (Bern: H.
            Lang).
Lemaire, A.
    1973   'Le sabbat à l'époque royale israélite', *RB* 80: 161-85.
    1976   'Prières en temps de crise: les inscriptions de Khirbet Beit Lei', *RB* 83:
            558-68.

Levenson, J.D.
1985   'A Technical Meaning for *n'm* in the Hebrew Bible', *VT* 35: 61-67.
Lévêque, J.
1970   *Job et son Dieu, I-II* (EBib; Paris: Gabalda).
Levine, B.A.
1976   'More on the Inverted Nuns of Num. 10:35-36', *JBL* 95: 122-24.
L'Hour, J.
1974   'Yahweh Elohim', *RB* 81: 524-56.
Lindblom, J.
1961   'Theophanies in Holy Places in Hebrew Religion', *HUCA* 32: 91-106.
1987   *The Identity of the Individual in the Psalms(JSOTSup, 44; Sheffield: JSOT Press).*
Lipiński, E.
1965   *La royauté de Yahvé dans la poésie et le culte de l'ancien Israël* (Brussels: Koninklijkle Academie).
1967a   *Le poème royal du Psaume LXXXIX 1-5, 20-38* (Cahiers de la *RB*, 6; Paris: Gabalda).
1967b   'Judges 5, 4-5 and Psalm 68, 6-11', *Bib* 48: 185-206.
1969   *La liturgie pénitentielle dans la Bible* (LD, 52; Paris: Cerf).
1970   'Études sur des textes "messianiques" de l'A.T. II. L'investiture du pretre Sadoq: Psaume 110, 4-5', *Sem* 20: 41-57.
1979   'Psaumes', *DBS* IX: cols. 1-125.
Loewenstamm, S.E.
1980   *Comparative Studies in Biblical and Ancient Oriental Literatures* (AOAT, 24; Neukirchen–Vluyn: Neukirchener Verlag), 137-45, 173-89, 528.
Lohfink, N.
1984a   'Zefanya und das Israel der Armen', *BK* 39: 100-108.
1984b   'Zur deuteronomischen Zentralisationsformel', *Bib* 65: 297-329.
1986   'Von der "Anawim-Partei" zur "Kirche der Armen"', *Bib* 67: 153-76.
Long, Burke O.
1972   'Prophetic Call Traditions and Reports of Visions', *ZAW* 84: 494-500.
1973   'The Effect of Divination upon Israelite Literature', *JBL* 92: 489-97.
Longenecker, R.
1978   'The Melchizedek Argument of Hebrews: A Study in the Development and Circumstantial Expression of New Testament Thought', in *Unity and Diversity in New Testament Theology. Essays in Honour of G.E. Ladd* (Grand Rapids: Eerdmans), 161-85.
Longman, T.
1982   'A Critique of Two Recent Metrical Systems', *Bib* 63: 230-54.
Loretz, O.
1971   'Poetischer Aufbau von Psalm 8', *UF* 3: 104-15.
1974   'Stichometrische und textologische Probleme...Anhang III. Ps 132', *UF* 6: 237-40.
1979   *Die Psalmen*, II (AOAT, 207/2; Neukirchen–Vluyn: Neukirchener Verlag).
1984a   *Der Prolog des Jesaja-Buches (1,1–2,5). Ugaritologische und kolometrische Studien zum Jesaja-Buch*, I (Altenberge: Akademische Bibliothek).
1984b   *Psalm 29. Kanaanäische El- und Baaltraditionen in jüdischer Sicht*

(Ugaritisch-Biblische Literatur, 2; Soest: CIS).

1987   'KTU 1.101: 1-3a und 1.2 IV 10 als Parallelen zu Ps 29, 10', *ZAW* 99: 415-21.

Lubsczyk, N.

1967   'Einheit und heilsgeschichtliche Bedeutung von Ps 114/115 (113)', *BZ* 11: 161-73.

Lutz, H.-M.

1968   *Jahwe, Jerusalem und die Völker* (WMANT, 27; Neukirchen–Vluyn: Neukirchener Verlag).

Luzarraga, J.

1973   *Las tradiciones de la nube en la Biblia y en judaísmo primitivo* (AnBib, 54; Rome: Biblical Institute Press).

Macholz, C.

1980   'Psalm 29 und 1 Könige 19, Jahwes und Baals Theophanie', in *Werden und Wirken des Alten Testaments. Festschrift Westermann* (Neukirchen–Vluyn: Neukirchener Verlag), 325-33.

Macintosh, A.A.

1974   'A Third Root *'dh* in Biblical Hebrew', *VT* 24: 454-73.

Madros, P.

1984   *Six Arabic Translations of the Psalms. Problems of Exegesis and Philology* (thesis, Jerusalem).

Maiberger, P.

1984   *Topographische und historische Untersuchungen zum Sinaiproblem* (OBO, 54; Göttingen: Vandenhoeck & Ruprecht).

Maier, J.

1965   *Das altisraelitische Ladeheiligtum* (BZAW, 13; Berlin: Töpelmann).

Malamat, A.

1980   *Mari and the Bible. A Collection of Studies Enlarged* (2nd edn; Jerusalem: Hebrew University Press).

1982   'Longevity: Biblical Concepts and Some Ancient Near Eastern Parallels', in *Der Begriff des 'Lebens' [BLT] in den Vorstellungen des Alten Orients* (AfO Beiheft, 19; Horn: Berger), 215-24.

1988   'The Amorite Background of Psalm 29', *ZAW* 100, Suppl.: 156-60.

Mann, T.W.

1977   *Divine Presence and Guidance in Israelite Traditions: The Typology of Exaltation* (Baltimore: Johns Hopkins University Press).

Manns, F.

1985   'Exégèse rabbinique et exégèse johannique', *RB* 92: 525-38.

Mannati, M.

1966–68   *Les Psaumes*, 1, 2, 3, 4 (Paris: Desclée de Brouwer, 1, 1966; 2, 3, 1967; 4, 1968).

1969   'ṬÛB-Y. en Ps XXVII 13: La bonté de Y., ou les biens de Y.?', *VT* 19: 488-93.

1973   'Le psaume 50 est-il un *rîb*?', *Sem* 23: 27-50.

1975   'Les accusations du Psaume L 18-20', *VT* 25: 659-69.

1979   'Le psaume XI', *VT* 29: 222-28.

Marbock, J.
1981   'Henoch–Adam–der Thronwagen', *BZ* 25: 103-11.

March, W.E.
1971   'A Note on the Text of Psalm XII 9', *VT* 21: 610-12.

Margalit, B.
1980   *A Matter of 'Life' and 'Death'. A Study of the Baal–Mot Epic* (CTA 4-5-6) (AOAT, 206; Neukirchen–Vluyn: Neukirchener Verlag), 219-28.

Martin-Achard, R.
1984   *Amos. L'homme, le message, l'influence* (Geneva: Labor et Fides).

Mays, J.L.
1986   'The David of the Psalms', *Int* 40: 143-55.

McBride, S.D.
1969   *The Deuteronomic Name Theology* (Cambridge, MA: Harvard University Press).

McCarter, Jr, P.K.
1984   *II Samuel* (AB, 9; Garden City, NY : Doubleday).

McConville, J.G.
1979   'God's "Name" and God's "Glory" ', *TynBul* 30: 149-63.

McKane, W.
1974   'Observations on the *tikkûnê sôpĕrîm*', in *On Language, Culture, and Religion. In Honor of E.A. Nida* (The Hague: Mouton), 53-68.
1980   '*ms*' in Jeremiah 23, 33-40', in *Prophecy. Essays Presented to G. Fohrer* (BZAW, 150; Berlin: de Gruyter), 35-54.

McKay, J.W.
1978   'My Glory, A Mantle of Praise', *SJT* 31: 167-72.

Meinertz, M.
1957   ' "Dieses Geschlecht" im N.T.', *BZ* ns 1: 283-89.

Menasce, J.P. de, *et al.*
1970   'Pour ou contre les psaumes d'imprécation', *VSpir* 122: 291-336.

Merrill, A.L. and J.R. Spencer
1984   'The "Uppsala School" of Biblical Studies', in *In the Shelter of Elyon. Essays in Honor of G.W. Ahlström* (JSOTSup, 31; Sheffield: JSOT Press), 13-26.

Meshel, Z.
1974   'New Data about the Desert Kites', *Tel Aviv* 1. 129-43.

Mettinger, T.N.D.
1976   *King and Messiah. The Civil and Sacral Legitimation of the Israelite Kings* (Lund: Gleerup).
1982   *The Dethronement of Sabaoth. Studies in the Shem and Kabod Theologies* (Lund: Gleerup).
1982–83   *A Farewell to the Servant Songs. A Critical Examination of an Exegetical Axiom* (Scripta Minora, 3; Lund: Gleerup).

Metzger, B.M.
1983   *The Old Testament Pseudepigrapha*, I (ed. J.H. Charlesworth; Garden City, NY: Doubleday).

Metzger, M.
1970   'Himmlische und irdische Wohnstadt Jahwes', *UF* 2: 139-58.

Meyer, R.
1966 'Melchisedek von Jerusalem und Moresedek von Qumran', in *Volume de Congrès Genève 1965* (VTSup, 15; Leiden: Brill), 228-39.

Michaeli, F.
1967 *Les livres des Chroniques, d'Esdras et de Néhémie* (CAT, 16; Neuchâtel: Delachaux and Niestlé).

Milik, J.T.
1972 '*Milkî-ṣedeq* et *Milkî-reša'* dans les anciens écrits juifs et chrétiens', *JJS* 23: 95-144.

Miller, J.M.
1970 'The Korahites of Southern Judah', *CBQ* 32: 58-68.

Miller, P.D.
1973 *The Divine Warrior in Early Israel* (HSM, 5; Cambridge, MA: Harvard University Press).
1979 'YĀPÎAH in Psalm XII 6', *VT* 29: 495-500.
1984 'Meter, Parallelism, and Tropes: The Search for Poetic Style', *JSOT* 28: 99-106.

Moberly, R.W.L.
1983 *At the Mountain of God: Story and Theology in Exodus 32–34* (JSOTSup, 22; Sheffield: JSOT Press).

Mollat, D.
1962 'Gloire', in *Vocabulaire de théologie biblique* (Paris: Cerf), cols. 412-20.

Mölle, H.
1973 *Das 'Erscheinen' Gottes im Pentateuch. Ein literaturwissenschaftlicher Beitrag zur alttestamentlichen Exegese* (Europäische Hochschulschriften, XXIII/18; Frankfurt: Peter Lang).

Möller, H.
1980 'Der Textzusammenhang in Ps 110', *ZAW* 92: 287-89.

Monloubou L.
1980 *L'imaginaire des psalmistes. Psaumes et symboles* (LD, 101; Paris: Cerf).

Moor, J.C. de and P. van der Lugt
1974 'The Spectre of Pan-Ugaritism', *BibOr* 31: 3-26.

Moore, G.F.
1927 [1958] *Judaism in the First Centuries of the Christian Era. The Age of the Tannaim*, I (Cambridge, MA: Harvard University Press).

Moran, W.L.
1969 'New Evidence from Mari on the History of Prophecy', *Bib* 50: 15-56.

Morla Asensio, V.
1988 *El fuego en al antiguo testamento. Estudio de semántica lingüística* (Bilbao: Institución San Jerónimo).

Mosca, P.G.
1986 'Ugarit and Daniel 7: A Missing Link', *Bib* 67: 496-517.

Mowinckel, S.
1921-24 [1961] *Psalmenstudien. II-III. Kultprophetie und prophetischen Psalmen* (reprint, Amsterdam: Verlag P. Schippers).
1963 *The Psalms in Israel's Worship* (2 vols.; Oxford: Basil Blackwell).

Mulder, J.S.M.
1972 *Studies on Psalm 45* (dissertation, Nijmegen).
Mullen, Jr, E.T.
1980 *The Divine Council in Canaanite and Early Hebrew Literature* (HSM, 24; Missoula, MT: Scholars Press).
1983 'The Divine Witness and the Davidic Royal Grant: Ps 89: 37-38', *JBL* 102: 207-18.
Müller, H.-P.
1964 'Die kultische Darstellung der Theophanie', *VT* 14: 183-91.
1984 'Der 90. Psalm. Ein Paradigma exegetischer Aufgaben', *ZTK* 81: 265-85.
Muller, K.
1982 ' "Die Propheten sind schlafen gegangen". SyrBAR 85.3', *BZ* 26: 179-207.
Muñoz Léon, D.
1977 *Gloria de la Shekiná en los Targumím del Pentateuco* (Madrid: CSIC: Instituto Francisco Suárez).
Murphy, R.
1959 'A New Classification of Literary Forms in the Psalter', *CBQ* 21: 83-87.
Murray, D.F.
1987 'The Rhetoric of Disputation: Re-examination of a Prophetic Genre', *JSOT* 38: 95-121.
Murray, R.
1982 'Prophecy and the Cult', in *Israel's Prophetic Tradition. Essays in Honour of Peter Ackroyd* (ed. R.J. Coggins, A. Phillips and M.A. Knibb; Cambridge: Cambridge University Press), 200-16.
Myers, J.M.
1965a *I Chronicles. II Chronicles* (AB, 12-13; Garden City, NY: Doubleday).
1965b *Ezra, Nehemiah* (AB, 14; Garden City, NY: Doubleday).
Nasuti, H.P.
1988 *Tradition, History and the Psalms of Asaph* (Atlanta: Scholars Press).
Newsom, C.
1985 *Songs of the Sabbath Sacrifice: A Critical Edition* (HSS, 27; Atlanta: Scholars Press).
Newsome, J.D.
1975 'Toward a New Understanding of the Chronicler and his Purposes', *JBL* 94: 201-17.
Niditch, S.
1983 *The Symbolic Vision in Biblical Tradition* (HSM, 30; Missoula, MT: Scholars Press).
Nielsen, K.
1978 *Yahweh as Prosecutor and Judge. An Investigation of the Prophetic Lawsuit (Rîb Pattern)* (JSOTSup, 9; Sheffield: JSOT Press).
1979 'Das Bild des Gerichts (rîb-Pattern) in Jes. I–XII. Eine Analyse der Beziehungen zwischen Bildsprache und dem Anliegen der Verkündigung', *VT* 29: 309-24.
1986 *Incense in Ancient Israel* (VTSup, 38; Leiden: Brill).

Nilssen, L.H.
1985/86   *Hjälpmedel för Unga Psalmforskare. Literatur i marknaden* (B. I, Luleå, 1985; B. II, Bibliografi, 1986).
Noret, J.
1987   'Fragments palimpsestes d'un commentaire inconnu du psaume 146', in *Texte und Textkritik. Eine Aufsatzsammlung* (Text und Untersuchungen zur Geschichte der altchristlichen Literatur, 133; Berlin: Akademie Verlag), 457-68.
Norin, S.I.L.
1977   *Er spaltete das Meer. Die Auszugsüberlieferung in Psalmen und Kult des alten Israel* (Lund: Gleerup).
North, C.R.
1967   'Psa. LX 8; Psa. CVIII 8', *VT* 17: 242-43.
North, R.
1972   'Prophecy to Apocalyptic via Zechariah', in *Congress Volume Uppsala 1971* (VTSup, 22; Leiden: Brill), 47-71.
Noth, M.
1959   *Das zweite Buch Mose. Exodus* (ATD, 5; Göttingen: Vandenhoeck & Ruprecht).
1962a   *Exodus* (OTL; Philadelphia: Westminster Press).
1962b   *Das dritte Buch Mose. Leviticus* (ATD, 6; Göttingen: Vandenhoeck & Ruprecht).
1966   *Das vierte Buch Mose. Numeri* (ATD, 7; Göttingen: Vandenhoeck & Ruprecht).
1977   *Leviticus* (OTL; Philadelphia: Westminster Press).
1980   *Numbers* (OTL; Philadelphia: Westminster Press).
Nötscher, F.
1924 [1969]   *'Das Angesicht Gottes schauen' nach biblischer und babylonischer Auffassung* (Darmstadt: Wissenschaftliche Buchgesellschaft).
Ockinga, B.G.
1980   'An Example of Egyptian Royal Phraseology in Psalm 132', *BN* 11: 38-42.
O'Connor, M.
1980   *Hebrew Verse Structure* (Winona Lake, IN: Eisenbrauns).
1983   'Ugarit and the Bible', in *The Bible and its Traditions, Michigan Quarterly Review* 22: 205-18.
Ogden, G.S.
1985   'Ps 60: Its Rhetoric, Form and Function', *JSOT* 31: 83-94.
Olivier, J.P.J.
1979   'The Sceptre of Justice and Ps 45:7b', *Journal of Northwest Semitic Languages* 7: 45-54.
1981   'The Day of Midian and Isaiah 9:3b', *Journal of Northwest Semitic Languages* 9: 143-49.
Oppenheim, A.L.
1956   'The Interpretation of Dreams in the Ancient Near East, with a Translation of an Assyrian Dream-Book', in *Transactions of the American Philosophical Society* (ns 46, part 3; Philadelphia).

1968 'The Eyes of the Lord', *JAOS* 88: 173-80.

O'Rourke, W.J.
1963 'Moses and the Prophetic Vocation', *Scripture* 15: 44-55.

Otto, E.
1979 *Jakob in Sichem* (BWANT, 110; Stuttgart: Kohlhammer).

Ouellette, J.
1969 'Variantes qumraniennes du Livre des Psaumes', *RQ* 7: 105-23.

Paul, S.
1972 'Ps 72,5. A Traditional Blessing for the Long Life of the King', *JNES* 31: 351-55.

Pautrel, R.
1961 'Le style de cour et le Psaume LXXII', in *A la rencontre de Dieu. Mémorial A. Gelin* (Le Puy: X. Mappus), 157-63.

Perdue, L.G.
1977 *Wisdom and Cult* (SBLDS, 30; Missoula, MT: Scholars Press).

Peterca, V.
1981 *L'immagine di Salomone nella Bibbia ebraica et greca. Contributo allo studio del 'Midrash'* (Rome: Biblical Institute Press).

Petersen, D.L.
1977 *Late Israaelite Prophecy. Studies in Deutero-Prophetic Literature and in Chronicles* (SBLMS, 23; Missoula, MT: Scholars Press).
1981 *The Roles of Israel's Prophets* (JSOTSup, 17; Sheffield: JSOT Press), 41-50.
1984 *Haggai and Zechoriah 1–8. A Commentary* (OTL; Philadelphia: Westminster Press).

Petersen, E.
1935 *Das Buch von den Engeln. Stellung und Bedeutung der heiligen Engel im Kultus* (Leipzig: Jakob Hegner).

Philonenko, M.
1985 'Prière du soleil et liturgie angélique', in *Colloque de Strasbourg (19 Oct. 1983)* (Paris: Presses Universitaires de France), 221-28.

Pietersma, A.
1980 'David in the Greek Psalms', *VT* 30: 213-26.

Plöger, O.
1954 'Prophetische Erbe in den Sekten des frühen Judentums', *TLZ* 79: 291-96.

Podechard, E.
1949/54 *Le psautier* (Lyon: Facultés Catholiques).

Polk, T.
1984 *The Prophetic Persona: Jeremiah and the Language of the Self* (JSOTSup, 32; Sheffield: JSOT Press).

Porter, J. R.
1976 *Leviticus* (Cambridge Bible Commentary; Cambridge: Cambridge University Press).

Potin, J.
1968   *La théophanie du Sinaï et le don de la loi dans le cadre de la liturgie juive de la fête de la Pentecôte*. 1. *Étude des textes liturgiques*. 2. *Textes, les Targums d'Exode 19–20* (2 vols.; Paris: Cerf).
1971   *La fête juive de la Pentecôte. Étude des textes liturgiques.* 1. *Commentaire.* 2. *Textes* (LD, 65; Paris: Cerf).

Pratt, S.
1913-14   'Studies in the Diction of the Psalter', *JBL* 32: 80-106, 159-83; 33: 1-24; 127-51.

Puech, E.
1971   'Sur la racine *ṣlḥ* en hébreu et en araméen', *Sem* 21: 5-19.
1983   'La racine *śyt-śʾt* en araméen et en hébreu', *RevQ* 11: 367-78.
1984   'Un emploi méconnu de *WL*' en araméen et en hébreu', *RB* 91: 88-101.
1985   'L'inscription de la statue d'Amman et la paléographie ammonite', *RB* 92: 5-24.
(in press) 'Palestinian Funerary Inscriptions', in *Anchor Bible Dictionary* (Ann Arbor: University of Michigan Press).

Pury, A. de
1975   *Promesse divine et légende cultuelle dans le cycle de Jacob* (EBib, 1-2; Paris: Gabalda).

Quintens, W.
1978   'La vie du roi dans le Psaume 21', *Bib* 58: 516-41.

Rad, G. von
1930   *Das Geschichtsbild des chronistischen Werkes* (BWANT, 4/3; Stuttgart: Kohlhammer).
1950   ' "Gerechtigkeit" und "Leben" in der Kultsprache der Psalmen', in *Festschrift Bertholet*, 418-37.
1958   *Gesämmelte Studien zum A. T.* (München: Kaiser Verlag), 225-47.
1964   *Das fünfte Buch Mose* (ATD, 8; Göttingen: Vandenhoeck & Ruprecht).
1965   *Der heilige Krieg im alten Israel* (Zurich, 1951; Göttingen: Vandenhoeck & Ruprecht, 4th edn).
1966a   *Deuteronomy* (OTL; Philadelphia: Westminster Press).
1966b   'The Levitical Sermon in I and II Chronicles', in *The Problem of the Hexateuch and Other Essays* (ed. E.W.T. Dicken; Edinburgh: Oliver & Boyd), 267-80.

Räisänen, H.
1972   *The Idea of Divine Hardening* (Publication of the Finnish Exegetical Society, 25; Helsinki).

Ramlot, L.
1972   'Le prophétisme', *DBS* VIII: cols. 811-1222.

Ramsey, A.-M.
1965   *La gloire de Dieu et la transfiguration du Christ* (LD, 40; Paris: Cerf).

Ravanelli, V.
1980   'Aspetti letterari del Salmo 89', *Liber Annuus* 30: 7-46.

Ravasi, G.
1981-84   *Il libro dei Salmi. Commento e attualizzazione* (3 vols.; Bologna: Dehoniane).

Reindl, J.
1970   *Das Angesicht Gottes in Sprachgebrauch des A.T.* (Leipzig: St Benno Verlag).
1981   'Weisheitliche Bearbeitung von Psalmen. Ein Beitrag zum Verständnis der Sammlung des Psalters', in *Congress Volume Vienna* 1980 (VTSup, 32; Leiden: Brill), 333-56.
Renaud, B.
1963   *Je suis un Dieu jaloux. Étude d'un thème biblique* (LD, 36; Paris: Cerf).
1977   *La formation du livre de Michée* (EBib; Paris: Gabalda).
1978   'Les deux lectures du Ps 114', *RevScRel* 52: 14-28.
1986   'La figure prophétique de Moïse en Ex 3,1–4,17', *RB* 93: 510-34.
Rendsburg, G.
1980   'Hebrew '*šdt* and Ugaritic *išdym*', *Journal of Northwest Semitic Languages* 8: 81-84.
Rendtorff, R.
1961   'Die Offenbarungsvorstellungen im A.T.' in *Offenbarung als Geschichte* (Göttingen: Vandenhoeck & Ruprecht), 26-32.
1966   'El, Ba'al und Jahwe', *ZAW* 78: 277-92.
Richter, W.
1971   *Exegese als Literaturwissenschaft. Entwurf einer alttestamentlichen Literaturtheorie und Methodologie* (Göttingen: Vandenhoeck & Ruprecht).
Ridderbos, N.H.
1969   'Die Theophanie in Ps L, 1-6', *OTS* 15: 213-26.
Rimaud, D.
1957   'La première prière liturgique dans le livre des Actes', *La Maison-Dieu* 51: 99-115.
Ringgren, H.
1963   'Einige Schilderungen des göttlichen Zorns', in *Tradition und Situation. Studien zur alttestametliche Prophetie. A. Weiser...* (Göttingen: Vandenhoeck & Ruprecht), 107-13.
1981   'Jahvé et Rahab-Léviatan', in *Mélanges H. Cazelles* (AOAT, 212; Neukirchen–Vluyn: Neukirchener Verlag), 387-93.
1983   'Psalm 2 and Bêlit's Oracle for Ashurbanipal', in *The Word of the Lord Shall Go Forth. Essays in Honor of David Noel Freedman...* (Winona Lake, IN; Eisenbrauns), 91-95.
Robert, A.
1935   'Les attaches littéraires bibliques de Prov. I–IX,' *RB* 44: 344-65.
1937   'La sens du mot Loi dans le Ps CXIX', *RB* 46: 182-206.
1939   'Le psaume 119 et les sapientiaux', *RB* 48: 5-20.
1949   'Historique (Genres)', *DBS* IV: cols. 19-23.
1953   'L'exégèse des Psaumes selon les methodes de la "Formgeschichteschule"', in *Miscellanea Biblica B. Ubach* (Montserrat), 211-25.
Robertson, D.A.
1972   *Linguistic Evidence in Dating Early Hebrew Poetry* (SBLDS, 3; Cambridge, MA).
Robinson, A.
1974   'Zion and Saphon in Psalm XLVIII 3', *VT* 24: 118-23.

Rosenthal, F.
1969   'Canaanite and Aramaic Ins. cj̣iⱥions. Azitawadda of Adana', in *ANET*;
         (3rd edn; ed. J.B. Pritchard; Princeton, NJ: Princeton University Press),
         653-54.
Roth, W.M.W.
1965   *Numerical Sayings in the Old Testament. A Form-Critical Study* (VTSup,
         13; Leiden: Brill).
Rouillard, H.
1985   *La péricope de Balaam (Nombres 22–24). La prose et les 'oracles'* (EBib,
         ns 4; Paris: Gabalda).
Rowley, H.H.
1956   'Ritual and the Hebrew Prophets', *JSS* 1: 338-60.
Rudolph, W.
1977   ' "Aus dem Munde der jungen Kinder und Säuglinge... " (Psalm 8, 3)',
         in *Festschrift W. Zimmerli* (Göttingen: Vandenhoeck & Ruprecht), 388-
         96.
Ruppert, L.
1983   'Klagelieder in Israel und Babylonien. Verschiedene Deutungen der Ge-
         walt', in *Gewalt und Gewaltlosigkeit im A.T.* (ed. E. Haag *et al.*; Freiburg:
         Herder), 111-58.
Sabourin, L.
1964   'Un classement littéraire des Psaumes', *Sciences Ecclésiastiques*, 1: 23-58.
1969   *The Psalms. Their Origin and Meaning* (Staten Island, NY: Alba House).
Saebø, M.
1978   'Vom Grossreich zum Weltreich. Erwägungen zu Ps 72,8; 89,26; Sach
         9,10b', *VT* 28: 83-91.
Saint-Arnaud, I.
1979   'Psaumes', *DBS* IX: col. 207.
Sakenfeld, K.H.
1978   *The Meaning of Ḥesed in the Hebrew Bible* (HSM, 17; Missoula, MT:
         Scholars Press).
Salles, A.
1958   *Trois antiques rituels du baptême* (Sources chrétiennes, 59; Paris: Cerf).
Sanders, J.A.
1967   *The Dead Sea Psalms Scroll* (Ithaca, NY: Cornell University Press).
Sanders, J.T.
1983   *Ben Sira and Demotic Wisdom* (SBLMS, 28; Chico, CA: Scholars Press).
Sauer, B.G.
1974   'Die Ugaritik und die Psalmenforschung', *UF* 6: 401-406.
Sawyer, J.F.A.
1972   'Joshua 10, 12-14 and the Solar Eclipse of 30 September 1131 B.C.',
         PEFQS, 104: 139-46.
Schäfer, P.
1972   *Die Vorstellungen von Heiligen Geist in der rabbinischen Literatur*
         (Munich: Kösel).
Schatz, W.
1972   *Genesis 14. Eine Untersuchung* (Bern: H. Lang).

Schenker, A.
1986 'Gerichtsverkündigung und Verblendung bei den vorexilischen Propheten', *RB* 93: 563-80.

Schlisske, W.
1973 *Gottessohne und Gottessohn im A.T.* (BWANT, 97; Stuttgart: Kohlhammer).

Schmid, R.
1972 'Heute, wenn ihr auf seine Stimme Hort (Ps 95, 7)', in *Wort, Lied und Gottesspruch. Festschrift J. Ziegler*, II (Stuttgart: Katholisches Bibelwerk), 91-96.

Schmidt-Colinet, C.
1981 *Die Musikinstrumente in der Kunst des Alten Orients. Archäologisch-philogische Studien* (Bonn: Bouvier-Grundmann).

Schmitt, R.
1972 *Zelt und Lade als thema alttestamentlicher Wissenschaft* (Gütersloh: Gütersloher Verlagshaus).

Schmuttermayr, G.
1971 *Psalm 18 und 2 Sam 22. Studien zu einem Doppeltext* (Munich: Kösel).

Schnutenhaus, F.
1964 'Das Kommen und Erscheinen Gottes im A.T.', *ZAW* 76: 1-22.

Scholem, G.
1983 *Le nom et les symboles de Dieu dans la mystique juive* (Paris: Cerf).

Schottroff, W.
1964 *'Gedenken' im alten Orient und im Alten Testament. Die Wurzel Zãkar in semitischen Sprachkreis* (WMANT, 15; Neukirchen–Vluyn: Neukirchener Verlag).

Schreiner, S.
1977 'Psalm CX und die Investitur des Hohenpriesters', *VT* 27: 216-22.

Schulz, H.
1973 *Das Buch Nahum. Eine redaktionskritische Untersuchung* (BZAW, 129; Berlin: de Gruyter).

Schulz, W.
1931 'Der Namenglaube bei den Babyloniern', *Anthropos* 26: 895-928.

Schwartz, B.
1978 'Psalm 50. Its Subject, Form and Place', *Shnaton* 3: 77-106.

Seeligmann, I.L.
1953 'Voraussetzungen der Midraschexegese', in *Congress Volume Copenhagen 1952* (VTSup, 1; Leiden: Brill), 150-81.
1964 'A Psalm from Pre-Regal Times', *VT* 14: 75-92.

Segalla, G.
1981 ' "Quaerere Deum" nei Salmi', *Quaerere Deum. Atti della XXV Settimana Biblica* (Brescia: Paideia Editrice), 191-212.

Seidel, H.
1986 *Musik im Altisrael. Untersuchungen zur Musikgeschichte und Musikpraxis Altisraels anhang biblischer und ausserbiblischer Texte* (Bern: Peter Lang).

Sendrey, A.
1969 *Music in Ancient Israel* (London: Vision Press).

Seybold, K.
1979   'Die Redaktion der Wallfahrtspsalmen', *ZAW* 91: 247-68.
1980a   'Die Geschichte des 29. Psalms und ihre theologische Bedeutung', *THZ*
            36: 208-19.
1980b   'Psalm LVIII. Ein Lösungsversuch', *VT* 30: 53-60.
1981   'Beitrage zur Psalmenforschung', *TRu* 46: 1-18.
Sievers J.
1984   'Là où deux ou trois... Le concept rabbinique de Shekina et Matthieu 18,
            20', *SIDIC* 16: 4-11.
Skehan, P.W.
1979   'Qumran', *DBS* IX: cols. 805-22.
1982   'Gleanings from Psalm Texts from Qumran. I. 4Q236 (= 4QPs 89): A
            Practice Page Written from Memory?', in *Mélanges H. Cazelles* (AOAT,
            212; Neukirchen–Vluyn: Neukirchener Verlag), 439-45.
Slomovic, E.
1979   'Toward an Understanding of the Formation of Historical Titles in the
            Book of Psalms', *ZAW* 91: 350-80.
Smelik, K.A.D.
1985   'The Origin of Psalm 20', *JSOT* 31: 75-81.
Smith, M.S.
1988   ' "Seeing God" in the Psalms: The Background to the Beatific Vision in
            the Hebrew Bible', *CBQ* 50: 171-83.
Snaith, N.H.
1967   *Leviticus and Numbers* (New Century Bible; London).
Sorg, R.
1968   *Habaqquq III and Selah* (Fifield, WI: King of Martyrs Priory).
1969   *Ecumenic Psalm 87. Original Form and Two Rereadings. With an Appen-
            dix on Psalm 110, 3* (Fifield, WI: King of Martyrs Priory).
Souza, B. de
1970   'The Coming of the Lord', *SBFLA* 20: 53-66.
Springer, S.
1979   *Neuinterpretation im A.T. Untersucht an der Themenkreisen des Herbst-
            festes und der Königspsalmen in Israel* (Stuttgart: Katholisches Bibel-
            werk).
Stähli, H.P.
1985   *Solare Elemente im Jahweglauben des Alten Testaments* (OBO, 66; Göttin-
            gen: Vandenhoeck & Ruprecht).
Steck, O.H.
1968   'Das Problem theologischer Strömungen in nachexilischer Zeit', *EvT* 28:
            445-58.
1986   'Der Grundtext in Jesaja 60 und sein Aufbau', *ZTK* 83: 261-96.
Stehly, R.
1979   'David dans la tradition islamique à la lumière des manuscrits de Qumrân',
            RHPR 59: 357-67.
Stein, B.
1939   *Der Begriff Kěbod Jahweh und seine Bedeutung für die alttestamentliche
            Gotteserkenntnis* (Emsdetten: H.v.J. Lechte).

Steiner, R.O.
1983 'A Paganized Version of Psalm 20:2-6 from the Aramaic Text in Demotic Script', *JAOS* 103: 261-74.

Stendebach, F.J.
1986 'Glaube und Ethos. Uberlegungen zu Ps 82', in *Freude an der Weisung des Herrn. Beiträge zur Theologie der Psalmen. Festgabe zum 70. Geburtstag von H. Gross* (SBB, 13; Stuttgart: Katholisches Bibelwerk), 425-40.

Stolz, F.
1970 *Strukturen und Figuren im Kult von Jerusalem* (BZAW, 118; Berlin: de Gruyter).
1983 *Psalmen in nachkultischen Raum* (Theologische Studien 129; Zurich: Theologischer Verlag).

Strack, H.L. and P. Billerbeck
1956–65 *Kommentar zum N.T. aus Talmud und Midrasch* (ed. J. Jeremias with K. Adolph; Munich, I-IV, 1965; V, 1956; VI, 1961).

Strauss, H.
1985 'Das Meerlied des Mose, Ein "Siegeslied" Israels?', *ZAW* 97: 103-09.

Struppe, U.
1988 *Die Herrlichkeit Jahwes in der Priesterschrift. Eine semantische Studie zu kĕbôd YHWH* (Klosterneuburg: Verlag Oesterreichisches Bibelwerk).

Stuart, D.K
1976 *Studies in Early Hebrew Meter* (HSM, 13; Missoula, MT: Scholars Press).

Talmon, S.
1986 'Emendation of Biblical Texts on the Basis of Ugaritic Parallels', *Scripta Hierosolymitana* 31: 279-300.

Tarragon, J.-M. de
1979 'David et l'arche: II Samuel VI', *RB* 86: 514-23.
1981 'La Kapporet est-elle une fiction ou un élément du culte tardif?', *RB* 88: 5-12.

Teeple, H.M.
1957 *The Mosaic Eschatological Prophet* (SBLMS, 10; Philadelphia: Society of Biblical Literature).

Terrien, S.
1978 *The Elusive Presence. Toward a New Biblical Theology* (New York: Harper & Row).

Thompson, J.A.
1980 *The Book of Jeremiah* (NICOT; Grand Rapids: Eerdmans).

Thompson, T.L.
1974 *The Historicity of the Patriarchal Narratives* (BZAW, 133; Berlin: de Gruyter).

Thureau-Dangin, F.
1912 *Une relation de la 8ᵉ campagne de Sargon (714 av. J.-C.)* (Paris: Geuthner).

Tillich, P.
1960–61 'The Divine Name', *Christianity and Crisis* 20: 55-119.

Torczyner, H.
1949   'A Psalm by the Sons of Heman', *JBL* 88: 247-49.
Tournay, R.J.
1946   'Poésie biblique et traduction française', *RB* 53: 349-64.
1947   'Les psaumes complexes', *RB* 54: 521-42.
1949a   'Les psaumes complexes', *RB* 56: 37-60.
1949b   'L'eschatologie individuelle dans les Psaumes', *RB* 56: 481-506.
1956   'En marge d'une traduction des Psaumes', *RB* 63: 161-181, 496-512.
1957a   'Sur quelques rubriques des Psaumes', in *Mélanges Bibliques A. Robert* (Paris: Bloud & Gay), 197-204.
1958a   'Le psaume et les bénédictions de Moïse', *RB* 65: 181-213.
1958b   'Recherches sur la chronologie des Psaumes', *RB* 65: 321-57.
1959a   'Recherches sur la chronologie des Psaumes', *RB* 66: 161-90.
1959b   'Le Psaume LXVIII et le livre des Juges', *RB* 66: 358-68.
1960a   'Le Psaume CX', *RB* 67: 5-41.
1960b   Review of O. Eissfeldt, *Das Lied Moses. . . . ,RB* 67: 121-23.
1960c   Review of G.W. Ahlström, *Psalm 89, RB* 67: 10-21.
1961   Review of H.-J. Kraus, *Psalmen, RB* 68: 127-34.
1963a   'Les affinités du Ps XLV avec le Cantique des Cantiques et leur interprétation messianique', in *Congress Volume Bonn 1962* (VTSup, 9; Leiden: Brill), 168-212.
1963b   Review of R. de Langhe, *Le Psautier, RB* 70: 591-94.
1964   'Le Psaume 72, 16 et le réveil de Melqart', in *Mémorial du cinquantenaire de l'École des Langues Orientales de l'Institut Catholique* (Paris: Bloud & Gay), 97-104.
1966a   'Le Psaume II (Ps 2). Le Roi-Messie', in *Assemblées du Seigneur, Fête du Christ-Roi*, 88 (Bruges: Abbaye Saint-André), 46-63.
1966b   Review of E. Lipiński, *La Royauté de Yahvé . . . , RB* 73: 420-25.
1966c   Review of J.A. Sanders, *The Psalms Scroll of Qumran Cave II, RB* 73: 258-65.
1968   Review of M. Mannati, *Les Psaumes, RB* 75: 433-39.
1969   Review of H.J. Van Dyck, *Ezekiel's Prophecy on Tyre, RB* 76: 449-50.
1970   Review of A.C.M. Blommerde, *Northwest Semitic Grammar and Job, RB* 77: 619-20.
1971a   'Le Psaume 8 et la doctrine biblique du nom', *RB* 78: 18-30.
1971b   Review of Jörg Jeremias, *Kultprophetie . . . , RB* 78: 264-66.
1971c   Review of K. Elliger, *Jesaja II, RB* 78: 288-89.
1971d   Review of N.J. Tromp, *Primitive Conceptions of Death. . . , RB* 78: 292-94.
1972   'Notes sur les Psaumes (Ps XLII, 9; LXXV, 7-9; XC, 5 et LXXVI, 2ss)', *RB* 79: 39-58.
1973a   Review of S. Carrillo Alday, *El Cantico de Moises (Dt 32), RB* 80: 440-41.
1973b   Review of J. Mulder, *Studies on Psalm 45*, RB 80: 603-605.
1974a   'Zacharie XII–XIV et l'histoire d'Israël', *RB* 81: 355-74.
1974b   Review of D.A. Robertson, *Linguistic Evidence in Dating Early Hebrew Poetry, RB* 81: 463-64.

1975   Review of P.D. Miller, *The Divine Warrior in Early Israel*, *RB* 82: 281-82.
1976a   'Note sur le Psaume LXXXIX, 51-52', *RB* 83: 380-89.
1976b   'Psaume LXXVI, 11: Nouvel essai d'interprétation', in *Studia Hierosolymitana*. II. *Studi esegetici* (Jerusalem: Franciscan Printing Press), 20-26.
1976c   Review of P.D. Hanson, *The Dawn of Apocalyptic*, *RB* 83: 150-53.
1976d   Review of F.M. Cross and D.N. Freedman, *Studies in Ancient Yahwistic Poetry*, *RB* 83: 625-26.
1978   Review of L.L. Grabbe, *Comparative Philology and the Text of Job*, *RB* 85: 622-23.
1979   'El Salmo 29: estructure e interpretation', *Ciencia Tomista* 106: 733-53.
1981a   'Les "dernières paroles de David". II Samuel XXIII 1-7', *RB* 88: 481-504.
1981b   'Le Cantique d'Anne. I Samuel II, 1-10', in *Mélanges D. Barthelemy* (OBO, 38; Göttingen: Vandenhoeck & Ruprecht), 553-76.
1981c   Review of F.I. Andersen and D.N. Freedman, *Hosea*, *RB* 88: 612.
1982a   *Quand Dieu parle aux hommes le langage de l'amour. Études sur le Cantique des Cantiques* (Cahiers de la *RB*, 21; Paris: Gabalda).
1982b   Review of T. Veijola, *Verheissung in der Krise...89. Psalms*, *RB* 89: 254-56.
1983a   'Le Psaume XXXVI: structure et doctrine', *RB* 90: 5-22.
1983b   'Le Psaume CXLI: nouvelle interprétation', *RB* 90: 321-33.
1983c   Review of M.D. Goulder, *The Psalms of the Sons of Korah*, *RB* 90: 603-605.
1984a   'Le Psaume CXLIV. Structure et interprétation', *RB* 91: 520-30.
1984b   Review of T.N.D. Mettinger, *A Farewell to the Servant Songs*, *RB* 91: 308-209.
1985a   'Le Psaume LXXIII: relectures et interprétation', *RB* 92: 187-99.
1985b   'Le Psaume LI et les murs de Jérusalem', in *Festschrift M. Delcor* (AOAT, 215; Neukirchen–Vluyn: Neukirchener Verlag), 417-24.
1985c   'Le Psaume 149 et la "vengeance" des Pauvres de YHWH', *RB* 92: 349-58.
1986   Review of W.G.E. Watson, *Classical Hebrew Poetry*, *RB* 93:306.
1988a [1990] *Word of God, Song of Love* (translation of *Quand Dieu parle aux hommes le langage de l'amour*) (Mahwah, NJ: Paulist Press).
1988b [1990] *Le Psautier de Jérusalem* (Paris: Cerf).
1989   'Psaumes 57, 60 et 108: Analyse et interprétation', *RB* 96: 5-26.

Tournay, R.J. and R. Schwab, *et al.*
1964   *Les Psaumes* (La Sainte Bible) (3rd edn; Paris: Cerf).

Trautmann, C.
1979   'La citation du psaume 85 (84), 11-12 et ses commentaires dans le Pistis Sophia', *RHPR* 59: 551-57.

Trublet, J.
1986   'Psaumes', *Dictionnaire de Spiritualite* XII: cols. 2504-62.

Tsevat, M.
1955   *A Study of the Language of the Biblical Psalms* (JBLMS, 9; Philadelphia: Society of Biblical Literature).

Urbach, E.E.
1975   *The Sages. Their Concepts and Beliefs* (Jerusalem: Magnes Press), 37-65.

Utzschneider, H.
1980   *Hosea. Prophet vor dem Ende. Zum Verhältnis von Geschichte und Institution in der alttestamentlichen Prophetie* (OBO, 31; Göttingen: Vandenhoeck & Ruprecht).

van Cangh, J.-M. and M. van Esbroeck
1980   'La primauté de Pierre (Mt 16, 16-19) et son contexte judaïque', *RTL* 11: 310-24 (English summary: 404).

van der Berghe, P.
1962   ' *'Ani* et *'Anaw* dans les Psaumes', in *Le Psautier. Ses origines. Ses problèmes littéraires. Son influence* (ed. R. de Langhe; Louvain: Publications Universitaires/Institut Orientaliste), 273-96.

VanderKam, J.
1977   '*BHL* in Ps 2:5 and its Etymology', *CBQ* 39: 245-50.

van der Lugt, O.
1980   *Strofische Structuren in de Bijbels-Hebreeuwse Poëzie* (Kampen: J.H. Kok).

van der Ploeg, J.
1950   'Les chefs du peuple d'Israël et leurs titres', *RB* 57: 40-61.
1965   'Le Psaume XVII et ses problèmes', *OTS* 14: 273-95.
1966   'Réflexions sur les genres littéraires des Psaumes', in *Studia Biblica et Semitica T. Ch. Vriezen...dedicata* (Wageningen: H. Veenman), 265-77.
1969   'L'étude du Psautier, 1960–1967', in *De Mari à Qumran...Hommage à Mgr. J. Coppens* (Gembloux/Paris: Duculat/Lethielleux), 174-91.
1982   'Le sens et un probleme textuel du Ps LXXXIX', in *Mélanges H. Cazelles* (AOAT, 212; Neukirchen–Vluyn: Neukirchener Verlag), 471-81.

van der Toorn, K.
1985   *Sin and Sanction in Israel and Mesopotamia: A Comparative Study* (Studia Semitica Neerlandica, 22; Assen–Maastricht: van Gorcum).
1987   'L'oracle de victoire comme expression prophétique au Proche-Orient ancien', *RB* 94: 63-97.

van der Woude, A. S.
1976   'Shem', *THAT* 2: 953-63.
1978   *Jona–Nahum–Habakuk–Zefanja* (De prediking van het Oude Testament; Nijkerk, The Netherlands: Callenbach).

Vanel, A.
1965   *L'iconographie du dieu de l'orage dans le Proche-Orient ancien jusqu'au VIIe siècle avant J.-C.* (Cahiers de la RB, 3; Paris: Gabalda).
1986   'Sagesse (Courant de)', *DBS* XI: cols. 4-58.

Vanhoye, A.
1968   'Longue marche ou accès tout proche?', *Bib* 49: 9-26.

van Imschoot, P.
1938   'Sagesse et Esprit dans l'Ancien Testament', *RB* 47: 23-49.

van Selms, A.
1982   'The Expression "The Holy One of Israel"', in *Von Kanaan bis Kerala. Festschrift van der Ploeg* (AOAT, 211; Neukirchen–Vluyn: Neukirchener

Verlag), 257-69.

van Uden, D. J.
1980   ' "Als je leven zoekt". De interpretative van het woord "leven" in Ps 16, 11 in de rabbijnse Literatuur', *Bijdragen* 41: 386-400.

Vaux, R. de
1961   *Ancient Israel* (London: Darton, Longman & Todd).
1966   Review of various editions of Ugaritic texts, *RB* 73: 463-68.
1967a   'Le lieu que Yahvé a choisi pour y établir son nom', in *Das Ferne und Nahe Wort. Festschrift F. Rost* (BZAW, 105; Berlin: Töpelmann), 219-28.
1967b   'Les chérubins et l'arche d'alliance, les sphinx gardiens et les trônes divins dans l'Ancien Orient', in *Bible et Orient* (Paris: Cerf), 231-59.
1971   'The King of Israel, Vassal of Yahweh', in *The Bible and the Ancient Near East* (Garden City, NY: Doubleday), 152-66.
1978   *The Early History of Israel* (Philadelphia: Westminster).
1983   'The Revelation of the Divine Name YHWH', in *Proclamation and Presence. Old Testament Essays...E.H. Davies* (Richmond: John Knox Press), 48-75.

Veijola, T.
1982   *Verheissung in der Krise. Studien zur Literatur und Theologie der Exilszeit anhand des 89. Psalms* (Helsinki: Suomalainen Tiedeakatemia).

Vermeylen, J.
1971   Review of Jörg Jeremias, *Kultprophetie. . . .RB* 78: 264-66.
1977-78   *Du prophete Isaïe à l' apocalyptique* (EBib 1, 1977; 2, 1978; Paris: Gabalda).

Vesco, J.-L.
1986   'La lecture du Psautier selon l'épître de Barnabé', *RB* 93: 5-37.
1987   'Le Psaume XVIII: relecture davidique', *RB* 94: 5-62.
1990   *L'Ancien Testament. Cent ans d'exégèse à l'Ecole Biblique* (Cahiers de la *RB*, 28; Paris: Gabalda), 159-81.

Veugelers, P.
1965   'Le Psaume LXXII, poeme messianique?', *ETL* 41: 317-43.

Vigano, L.
1976   *Nomi e titoli di YHWH alla luce del semitico del Nord-Ovest* (Rome: Biblical Institute Press).

Vilar Huesco V.
1963   'El Salmo 24. Unidad literaria y ambiente historico', *Anales del Seminario del Valencia* 3: 5-16.

Vogt, E.
1965   ' "Die Himmel troffen" (Ps 68, 9)?', *Bib* 46: 207-209.

Vööbus, A.
1979   *Didascalia Apostolorum in Syriac* (CSCO, 408; Scriptores Syri 180, II, Chs. XI-XXVI; Louvain: Secrétariat du Corpus Scriptorum Christianorum Orientalium).

Vorlander, H.
1975   *Mein Gott. Die Vorstellungen vom persönlichen Gott im Alten Orient und im AT* (AOAT, 33: Neukirchen–Vluyn: Neukirchener Verlag).

Vosberg, L.

1975   *Studien zum Reden vom Schöpfer in den Psalmen* (Munich: Kaiser Verlag).

Vuilleumier, R.

1960   *La tradition cultuelle d'Israël dans la prophétie d'Amos et d'Osée* (Cahiers Théologiques, 45; Neuchâtel: Delachaux).

Wagner, C.H.

1986   'Tartessos y las tradiciones literarias', *Rivista di Studi Fenici* 14: 201-28.

Wagner, M.

1966   *Die lexikalischen und grammatikalischen Aramaismen im alttestamentlichen Hebräisch* (BZAW, 96; Berlin: Töpelmann).

Wagner, S.

1984   'Das Reich des Messias. Zur Theologie der alttestamentlichen Königspsalmen', *TLZ* 109: col. 865-74.

Wanke, G.

1966   *Die Zionstheologie der Korachiten* (BZAW, 97; Berlin: Töpelmann).

1984   'Prophecy and Psalms in the Persian Period', in *The Cambridge History of Judaism. I. Introduction. The Persian Period*, ch. 8 (ed. W.D. Davies and L. Finkelstein; Cambridge: Cambridge University Press), 162-88.

Ward, J.M.

1961   'The Literary Form and Liturgical Background of Psalm LXXXIX', *VT* 11: 321-339.

Watson, W.G.E.

1982   'Trends in the Development of Classical Hebrew Poetry. A Comparative Study', *UF* 14: 265-77.

1984a   *Classical Hebrew Poetry* (JSOTSup, 26; Sheffield: JSOT Press).

1984b   Review of Kugel's *The Idea of Biblical Poetry*, *JSOT* 28: 89-98.

Watts, J.D.W.

1965   'Yahweh Malak Psalms', *TZ* 21: 341-48.

Weinfeld, M.

1973   ' "Rider of the Clouds" and "Gatherer of the Clouds" ', *JANESCU* 5: 421-66.

1981   'Sabbath, Temple and the Enthronement of the Lord, Problem of the *Sitz im Leben* of Genesis 1:1–2:3', in *Festschrift H. Cazelles* (AOAT, 212; Neukirchen–Vluyn: Neukirchener Verlag), 501-12.

1982   'Instructions for Temple Visitors in the Bible and in Ancient Egypt', *Scripta Hierosolymitana* 28: 224-50.

1983   'Divine Intervention in War in Ancient Israel and in the Ancient Near East', *History, Historiography and Interpretation. Studies in Biblical and Cuneiform Literatures* (ed. H. Tadmor and M. Weinfeld; Jerusalem: Magnes Press), 121-47.

1985   'The Pagan Version of Psalm 20:3-6. Vicissitudes of a Psalmodic Creation in Israel and in its Neighbours', *Eretz Israel* 18: 130-40 (English summary: 70*).

1986   'The Day of the Lord. Aspirations for the Kingdom of God in the Bible and Jewish Liturgy', *Scripta Hierosolymitana* 31: 361-72.

Weippert, H.

1980 'Der Ort, den Jahwe erwählen wird, um dort seinem Namen wohnen zu lassen. Die Geschichte einer alttestamentlichen Formel', *BZ* ns 24: 76-94.

Weippert, M.

1972 ' "Heiliger Krieg" in Israel und Assyrien; Kritische Anmerkungen zu Gerhard von Rads Konzept des "Heiligen Krieges im alten Israel" ', *ZAW* 84: 460-93.

1984 ' "Ecce non dormitabit neque dormiet, qui custodit Israel". Zur Klärung von Psalm 121, 4', in *Lese-Zeichen für A. Findeiss zum 65 Geburtstag am 15 Marz 1984* (Heidelberg: DBAT), 75-87.

Weiser, A.

1950 'Zur Frage nach den Beziehungen der Psalmen zum Kult. Die Darstellung der Theophanie in den Psalmen und im Festkult', in *Festschrift Bertholet* (Tübingen: Mohr), 513-31.

1961 *Glaube und Geschichte im Alten Testament und andere ausgewählte Schriften* (Göttingen: Vandenhoeck & Ruprecht).

Weiss, M.

1984 *The Bible from Within* (Jerusalem: Hebrew University Press), 93-100, 352-78.

Welch, J.W. (ed.)

1981 *Chiasmus in Antiquity, Structures, Analyses, Exegesis* (Hildesheim: Gerstenberg).

Wellhausen, J.

1899 *Die Composition des Hexateuchs...* (Berlin: George Reimer).

Wenham, G.J.

1979 *The Book of Leviticus* (NICOT; Grand Rapids: Eerdmans).

Wernberg-Møller, P.

1957 *The Manual of Discipline Translated and Annotated with an Introduction* (Leiden: Brill).

Werner, E.

1984 *The Sacred Bridge*, II (New York: Ktav).

Westermann, C.

1954 *Das Loben Gottes in den Psalmen* (Göttingen: Vandenhoeck & Ruprecht).

1965 *The Praise of God in the Psalms* (Richmond: John Knox Press).

1974 'Die Herrlichkeit Gottes in der Priesterschrift', in *Forschung am A.T. Gesammelte Studien*, 2 (Theologische Bücherei, A.T. 55; Munich: Kaiser Verlag), 115-37.

1978 *Theologie des A.T. in Grundzügen. Grundrisse zum A.T.* (Göttingen: Vandenhoeck & Ruprecht).

Whitney, J.T.

1979 ' "Bamoth" in the Old Testament', *TynBul* 30: 125-47.

Wildberger, H.

1965-82 *Jesaja* (BKAT, X; Neukirchen–Vluyn: Neukirchener Verlag).

Wilhelm, G.

1977 'Der Hirt mit dem eisernen Szepter. Überlegungen zu Psalm II 9', *VT* 27: 196-204.

Willi, T.

1972a   *Die Chronik als Auslegung. Untersuchungen zur literarische Gestaltung der historischen Überlieferung Israels* (FRLANT, 106; Göttingen: Vandenhoeck & Ruprecht).

1972b   'Das Erlöschen des Geistes', *Judaica* 28: 110-16.

Williamson, H.G.M.

1977   'Eschatology in Chronicles', *TynBul* 28: 115-54.

1979   'The Origins of Twenty-Four Priestly Courses. A Study of Chronicles XXIII–XXVII', in *Studies in the Historical Books of the Old Testament* (VTSup, 30; Leiden: Brill), 251-68.

1983   'The Dynastic Oracle in the Book of Chronicles', in *Festschrift I.L. Seeligmann*, III (Jerusalem: Rubinstein), 305-18.

Willis, J.T.

1974   'Ethics in a Cultic Setting', in *Essays in Old Testament Ethics. J.P. Hyatt In Memoriam*, 145-69.

Wilson, G.H.

1983   'The Qumran Psalms Manuscripts and the Consecutive Arrangement of Psalms in the Hebrew Psalter', *CBQ* 45: 377- 88.

1985   *The Editing of the Hebrew Psalter* (SBLDS, 76; Chico, CA: Scholars Press).

Wilson, R.R.

1980   *Prophecy and Society in Ancient Israel* (Philadelphia: Fortress Press).

Wolff, H.W.

1986   *Dodekapropheton VI. Haggai* (BKAT, XIV, 6; Neukirchen–Vluyn: Neukirchener Verlag).

Woudstra, M.H.

1981   *The Book of Joshua* (NICOT; Grand Rapids: Eerdmans).

Yadin, Y.

1985   'New Gleanings on Resheph from Ugarit', in *Biblical and Related Studies Presented to S. Iwry* (Winona Lake, IN: Eisenbrauns, 259-78.

Zenger, E.

1972   'Psalm 87, 6, und die Tafeln vom Sinai', in *Wort, Lied und Gottesspruch. Festschrift J. Ziegler*, II (Stuttgart: Katholische Bibelwerk), 97-103.

1981   'Tradition and Interpretation in Exodus XV 1-21', in *Congress Volume Vienna 1980* (VTSup, 32; Leiden: Brill), 452-83.

1986   ' "Wozu tosen die Völker...?" Beobachtungen zur Entstehung und Theologie des 2. Psalms', in *Freude an der Weisung des Herrn. Beiträge zur Theologie der Psalmen. Festgabe zum 70. Geburtstag von H. Gross* (SBB, 13; Stuttgart: Katholisches Bibelwerk), 495-511.

Ziegler, J.

1950   'Die Hilfe Gottes am Morgen', in *Festschrift F. Nötscher* (BBB, 1; Bonn: P. Hanstein), 281-88.

Zimmerli, W.

1967   'Abraham und Melchisedek', in *Das Ferne und Nahe Wort. Festschrift Rost* (BZAW, 105; Berlin: Töpelmann), 255-64.

1979   *Ezekiel. 1. A Commentary on the Book of the Prophet Ezekiel, Chapters 1–24* (trans. R.E. Clements; Philadelphia: Fortress Press).

1983   *Ezekiel. 2. Chapters 25–48* (trans. J.D. Martin; Philadelphia: Fortress
            Press).

Zuckerman B.
    1983   ' "For your sake … ": A Case Study in Aramaic Semantics', *JANESCU*
            15: 119-29.

INDEXES

INDEX OF REFERENCES

OLD TESTAMENT

INDEX OF AUTHORS